Close to Home

Close to Home:
Human Services and the Small Community

Emilia E. Martinez-Brawley

With the research collaboration of Paz M.-B. Zorita

NASW PRESS

National Association of Social Workers
Washington, DC

Ruth Mayden, MSS, LSW, ACSW, *President*
Josephine Nieves, MSW, PhD, *Executive Director*

Cheryl Y. Mayberry, Director, Member Services and Publications
Paula L. Delo, Executive Editor
Steph Selice, Senior Editor
William F. Schroeder, Staff Editor
Anne Grant, Hyde Park Publishing, Copy Editor
Rebecca Maksel, Proofreader
Deborah E. Patton, Indexer

Cover by Metadog Design Group, Washington, DC
Typeset by Cynthia N. Stock, Electronic Quill Publishing Services,
   Silver Spring, MD
Printed and bound by Batson Printing, Benton Harbor, MI

© 2000 by NASW Press

Library of Congress Cataloging-in-Publication Data

Martinez-Brawley, Emilia E., 1939–
    Close to home : human services and the small community / Emilia E. Martinez-Brawley
        p.   cm.
    With the research collaboration of Paz Méndez-Bonito Zorita.
    Includes bibliographical references and index.
    ISBN 0-87101-312-6 (alk. paper)
    1. Social service, Rural. 2. Community. 3. Community life. 4. City and town life. 5. City and town life in literature. I. Title.

HV67.M37 2000
361–dc21   99-088670

Printed in the United States of America

To my family back home, who exemplified
attachment to a small town and to
Allan, Stephen, Ewan, Evelyn, and Alice

Contents

List of Exhibits
(Illustrations and Figures)

Illustrations

Figures

Foreword

I live in a small community, Waterville, Maine, population 17,000. It is one of hundreds of what Down Easters call "towns," many much smaller, spread across this vast state. It is now 10 years since I moved here after having lived in many large cities all over the United States, yet in some ways Waterville remains an enigma. On one hand, its small size lends the town a sense of transparency and openness. On reading the daily eight-page newspaper, it is easy to connect with people, organizations, and events that are already quite familiar. One refrains from gossip since the subject of the idle talk is likely to be a friend or relative of your audience. But I remain puzzled: I am always mystified by an elusive kind of interiority of spirit, culture, or a way of doing things. It is not something that is intentionally hidden from those who local folks call "people from away," because all you have to do is ask and their eager stories will flow. But it is something that is deeply rooted in the many generations of families' lives, in the harmony with and adaptation to the rivers, mountains, and forests that shape their environment here.

It turned out that my best source of learning about this town and its people are the obituaries I read every day. Here I find the heritage and connections of families, the sources of identities in occupations in industries long gone, the organizations, lodges, and service groups that provided purpose and membership, the churches that offered spiritual respite, their favorite pets, and even the simple leisure activities that gave meaning to individual lives. The obituaries, written by grieving relatives, are just some of the stories that make up chapters of the past. And they lead to curiosity about the narratives of the present, for it is in these accounts that we begin to grasp the colloquial understanding of the small community.

Three things a small town is not. First, although this town (like many others) has many of the physical elements of any city—industry, public housing, a main street, public and administrative services, a Wal-mart, even a latte café and other up-to-date amenities—it is not a miniaturized version of the ordinary city that can be studied, defined, and dealt with in scaled-down ways. Modes of inquiry that apply to urban areas may well be irrelevant for the small town. Neither is this type of community a Rockwellian image of homey, nostalgic, small-town life where old-timers lounge at the barber shop and all the houses have wraparound front porches. And finally, small size cannot be equated with homogeneity. Ethnic, racial, religious, and socioeconomic diversities are as common but not as evident in my town as in cities where geographical divisions carve up these groups into discrete areas. Yet the sense of belonging and identity are no less powerful, as Dr. Martinez-Brawley illustrates in the portraits she renders in the pages that follow.

But my intention is neither to offer a homily on the virtues or deficits of small-town life nor to sociologize on the mores and patterns of the small community. Rather, I want to reaffirm Dr. Martinez-Brawley's observation that to understand the small community we need to understand "the meanings that small communities have for those who live in them."

Just one of the many merits of this book is how her version of "starting where the client is" becomes a unifying principle that humanizes practice in any setting with all people. To be sure, the pursuit of understanding of lives and communities calls for many forms of inquiry—from computational to historical, from descriptive to ethnographic—if we wish to capture the many facets and poignancies of community life. But to truly understand the deeper meanings residents give to their small-town lives, we need to get hold of their personal and shared metaphors and idioms, the language that enlivens and allows them to share their world of experience. Without reference to the ironies and absurdities that regularly intrude into their dearest hopes and best-laid plans, any account of their seemingly ordinary lives would merely be the same shade of gray. We need to gain some awareness of what counts for them in the moral choices that are made or those that are rejected. And we also need to have some sense not just of their religious identities but also of the spiritual beliefs that give them comfort and release from adversity.

In Dr. Martinez-Brawley's creative authorship I discover a kindred spirit with whom I share this conviction: that literature in its many forms and styles offers a special richness of understanding of the often curious and unexpected meanings people construct to give purpose and reason to their lives. In this book, the journalistic, fictional, and historic illustrations, the essays and recollections, transport us vicariously into many lives in the small community, into experiences and meanings we could not otherwise recognize nor comprehend as a basis for effective human services.

Howard Goldstein, DSW
Professor Emeritus, Case Western Reserve University
Editor, *Families in Society*

Acknowledgments

I am indebted to the hard work of my colleague, Professor Paz Zorita, who participated in the research for this book, spending many hours helping me search the literature and make selections of appropriate text illustrations. She also provided solid advice drawing on her many years of practice, particularly with Puerto Rican families from small towns and rural areas who have recently settled in the mainland United States.

I also want to acknowledge the cooperation of many other individuals who were instrumental in helping me bring this book to fruition. Elmer Duntz of KBDZ-FM in Prairieville/St. Genevieve, Missouri, offered comments on the current situation faced by small-town radio stations. Jack Sherman, reference librarian at the Rutland, Vermont, Free Library, provided much-needed assistance in identifying illustrations that addressed issues discussed in New England town meetings. Many reference librarians at Arizona State University helped me, particularly Charlotte Cohen, who went out of her way to see to it my searches were effective. Bill Welsh, mayor of State College, Pennsylvania, generously offered material related to current political issues in small-town government. Joseph Rose, reporter, and Bob Crider, editor at the *Yakima Herald-Republic* in Washington State, gave me positive and prompt responses to my questions. *American City and County* magazine (published by Morgan Grampian Publishing Co. of Atlanta) provided needed reprints.

Special mention must be made of the many editors and reporters of small-town and city newspapers who generously permitted me to use their illustrations as a courtesy. Their papers include the *Arizona Daily Sun*, Flagstaff; the *Arizona Republic*, Phoenix; the *Centre Daily Times*, State College, Pennsylvania; the *Christian Science Monitor*; the *Columbus Dispatch*, Columbus, Ohio; the *Dallas Morning News*; the *Detroit News*; the *Omaha-World Herald*; the *Rutland Herald*, Rutland, Vermont; and the *Saint Paul Pioneer Press Dispatch*. By examining local news, the student of community can understand how local action both reflects and determines global themes.

Throughout the preparation of this book, I was always encouraged by the generosity of many friends living in small towns who provided me with clippings, stories, and personal accounts.

Initially, this book began as an effort to update the 1990 edition of my book *Perspectives on the Small Community: Humanistic Views for Practitioners*. As I worked with my editors on this endeavor, we realized that the changes I was making were far too numerous and extensive and that the results had produced a new product. Nevertheless, some of the material contained in this book is the result of the combination of new research and work done for *Perspectives on the Small Community*. In this context, Roy Buck, professor emeritus of sociology at the Pennsylvania State University, deserves a special mention. He was particularly helpful in providing some text, critique, and background for the publication of *Perspectives on the Small Community*. I drew on his advice and many of his publications once again as I worked on this book. I also must acknowledge many former students at Penn State, but particularly Julie Parr, whose practice examples are still quotable.

I thank my editors at NASW Press, Paula Delo, Steph Selice, and Will Schroeder, who provided good-humored effort and advice on the editorial side. Heather Trammel ably transcribed tapes and typed for many hours, helping me meet various deadlines, and Anne Grant copyedited the manuscript with patience.

Last but not least, I want to acknowledge Provost Milton Glick of Arizona State University for believing in the concept of the scholar/administrator. I could not have finished this work without a sabbatical leave, and I am grateful for the support I received from my university.

Introduction

Over years of teaching community theory and practice to generalist social work students and decades of work with small-town practitioners, I drew from a variety of textbooks to cover essential community content. Many of those textbooks were excellent examples of the comprehensive writings of community workers and organizers, and I, like my students and colleagues, derived much useful information from them. Nevertheless, the more I worked on interventive strategies, the more I realized that, in order to make sense of them, it is important to build on theory, because theory helps explain the perspectives offered by those who exhort us to action.

It was with this in mind that I wrote *Perspectives of the Small Community*, which appeared in 1990. In the decade since it was written, I have observed that in spite of the many positive changes in social work education and the new communal spirit of the times, many students and young practitioners are still not internalizing the ideal of community that current interventions attempt to support.

Most authors of community workbooks assume that readers have the broad experience necessary to illuminate the intricacies of the debate about the concept of community. Furthermore, they assume that students training to practice in small communities have a strong attachment to the ethos of communal life.

Those assumptions very often prove wrong. *Close to Home: Human Services and the Small Community* is an attempt to give social work students and practitioners not only an understanding of the theory of small communities but also a broader perspective on the meaning that small communities have for those who live in them. Unless they can understand the phenomena that surround them, practitioners will not be able to intervene effectively. Without a strong sensitivity for what the small community has to offer to its citizens, they will not be able to help its residents. Finally, small-town practitioners must have a way to explain and anticipate community behavior not just as manifestations of the folk but also as behavior that can be understood in the context of the necessities, pleasures, and values of units of social interaction. This book is intended to bring students and practitioners in the field as close to the small community as those who live in it.

To transcend the classic debate over what constitutes a rural community, a debate based primarily on demographic dimensions, I have chosen to use the term "small." Many communities, including neighborhoods in cities, share the social, cultural, and psychological characteristics of "small" communities. This book focuses primarily on those social and cultural characteristics—thus, the choice was to use the term "small." Many of the communities addressed will be rural in the demographic sense, but the content of the book is not exclusively rural. Because many urban residents come from rural backgrounds, in spite of residing in neighborhoods in large metropolitan areas they maintain the types of relationships that are characteristic of small towns. I believe that people with a recent agricultural history continue to support what social scientists may view as rural attachment, even in cities. A story by Preciado Martin (1996) about her experiences in the barrio in Tucson, for example, clearly illustrates that hypothesis. This and other stories give life to my points throughout the book.

Social developments and other topics of public discussion through the 1990s helped clarify and narrow the parameters of this book. The use and misuse of the term "community" to apply not only to geographic places but also to relationships established in cyberspace led me to conclude that the focus of the book must be the unit of human organization that allows for face-to-face interaction. Without disassociating it from the technological changes that have affected geographic communities, this book will concentrate on the small community as the milieu (often but not always geographical) that gives meaning and cohesion to patterns of daily life for those who live in real communities. To do more would be to move beyond what it is possible for any book to cover. Though the influence of virtual communities is acknowledged, therefore, it is not treated in depth.

Finally, the book attempts to provide at least a glimpse of a posture that is common among postmodernists: a philosophy of valuing differences and a suspicion of single paradigms or grand theories. To engage the reader in discovery, the book offers a variety of ways of looking at small communities.

All the chapters of the book contain both information from interdisciplinary research on important areas of community theory and literary or journalistic excerpts to illustrate the issues discussed. The excerpts, themselves entertaining, are often captivating illustrations of small-town life. Changes through the decades in both the perception and the lifestyles of small towns and villages are explored. From the protagonists of fictional as well as real events, the student of community can learn to feel like people in small towns, empathize with their joys and dilemmas, and perhaps evolve a more realistic yet positive view of nonmetropolitan life. Because social work and other helping arts, products of the industrial world, have seldom dealt sympathetically with small communities, literary and journalistic examples can make a tremendous difference in a practitioner's outlook. Literature can also broaden the practitioner's ability to see these communities differently.

This book is organized somewhat differently from its predecessor. Instead of requiring the reader to search through the book for the examples that illustrate key concepts, the excerpts are inserted throughout the text. A concluding chapter brings the material closer to application. In addressing community-oriented practice, it constitutes in many ways a practical epilogue.

Chapter 1 is devoted to helping the reader view differently both theory in general and community theory in particular, placing literary contributions in the context of theory. In discussing the concepts of "small" and "rural," it expounds on various ways of viewing small communities. Additionally, it illustrates key controversies preoccupying small town residents today. It offers some answers to the questions of why we are still concerned about small communities, how they are changing, and how, in postmodern fashion, their ancestries are being rediscovered and reinterpreted.

Chapter 2 clarifies concepts essential to the understanding of the word "community." Focusing on Gemeinschaft and primary relationships, with Gesellschaft as the contrast, it details the attributes of Gemeinschaft as the personal community that was for many decades equated with an idyllic image of the town. The chapter includes excerpts from both "romantic" writers of community and those whose visions were more ambivalent. They also illustrate how Gemeinschaft can be found in cities.

Chapter 3 looks at the basic psychological and cultural elements of communal life. It discusses how communities are bound by horizontal and vertical ties that link their inhabitants and those that link the community with the outside world. The influence of history and of the physical environment is addressed. Finally, variables that can be used to further understanding of the concept of community are reviewed.

The idea of community as a personal solution or an answer to anomie is explored in Chapter 4. Community practitioners need to understand some of the personal reasons that people embrace communal causes. It would be difficult to explain the devoted work of volunteers or the active participation of community members in meetings without an awareness of the personal meaning and satisfaction they derive from such activities.

Chapter 4 provides a sociopsychological understanding of what community means to individuals, illustrating for social workers how different people seek different forms of satisfaction through communal relationships.

Chapter 5 focuses on the specific variable of power as a driving force in communal life. Because the subject of community power, influence, and leadership always has been central to political science, basic concepts from political science and sociology can be highly meaningful to social workers in small communities. Models of power distribution in a small town and the relationship between the policy decisions and the distribution of power are discussed in Chapter 5.

> Nor less I deem that there are powers
> Which of themselves our minds impress;
> That we can feed this mind of ours
> In wise passiveness. (Wordsworth, cited in George, 1904, p. 83)

How power plays out among various community actors is crucial in the life of the small community because it affects not only collective decisions but also how people perceive each other, rely on each other, defer to each other in social situations, or work together to find common cause.

Chapter 6 addresses the long-standing dilemma of the interrelationship between localities and larger political or geographic units, an issue that has received the attention of both philosophers and government officials. The matter of allegiance to the locality, the region, or the nation has not been easy to resolve. Can individuals belong in any meaningful sense to vertical communities, those beyond locality, or do people identify with only the small unit of Gemeinschaft? The nostalgia of locality and localism coupled with the political mood of the 1990s has given this century-old debate new dimensions.

In the field of social welfare, politicians and scholars have persistently debated the relationships among various levels of government. The appropriate role of federal or central, state, and local governments in relation to all matters of governance, but particularly social welfare, always has been contentious. Practitioners at the local level—which is where practitioners are most likely to find themselves—need to understand the premises underlying these controversies. Furthermore, social workers at the local level need to overcome the often negative attitude of policymakers toward small localities; they need to appreciate local language in its richness. Chapter 6 provides the historical and philosophical background needed to understand the frequent tensions between professionals and community residents; it discusses centralization and localism as they have affected and continue to affect small communities.

When my book *Perspectives on the Small Community* was published in 1990, American culture had moved from looking outward, being concerned with societal forces, to looking inward, pondering on the intimate forces that propel individuals to continue. That was in the 1980s. Increased emphasis on microlevel or clinical intervention attested to societal concern with individual adjustment; the importance of understanding "the collective" as nourishing individuals and nations had decreased. The previous book pointed up the shortcomings of this trend. But during the 1990s the pendulum swung again in the direction of family and community. This book reflects the new swing. Chapter 7 captures how practitioners are building community in small towns today. It also offers them new ways of analyzing their roles as we move into the new millennium.

At the end of the 20th century, we have discovered that anonymity and accountability might be tied, and that while we may not be able to postulate a stance that explains all situations or solves all problems, we might be able to propose a practical ethic of communal life to help us be more accountable in our daily lives. As Kathleen Parker put it humorously in a recent column about life in her small town, civility seems to be indirectly related to anonymity and accountability.

> The effect of the anonymity that comes with larger populations is to diminish accountability. In my new town, which shall remain unnamed lest my neighbors send me packing, everyone's accountable. Everybody knows everybody's business, which is not a good thing if you're up to no good, but a grand thing if you need help. (Parker, 1998, p. B7)

This book is intended to encourage students and practitioners in small towns to reevaluate much they may have taken for granted and reassess much they may have tended to let alone.

CHAPTER 1

Community Theory for Practitioners

Theory as Explanation

I began my 1990 book, *Perspectives on the Small Community*, by stating that "practitioners who do not have a solid understanding of the theory behind practice principles inevitably will flounder when they try to apply those principles, their interventions reduced to mere attempts to apply a technology" (Martinez-Brawley, 1990, p. xxi). Today, as social work has become more technical than ever and as more of our textbooks focus more pointedly on technique, I believe my concerns in 1990 were well founded. In terms of community practice, the assessments and actions of practitioners who are unable to make theoretical connections lack the substance provided by generalizable explanations, even if the assessments are correct. As our community practitioners launch into their careers at earlier ages, often with fewer years of experience living in communities as citizens, without any understanding of community even as a theoretical construct, they will relate to isolated events, often missing a complex web of causal factors related to them. Without a theoretical grounding, discussions of practice in community are likely to lack the integrative framework needed to give meaning to isolated occurrences. Similarly, without a strong belief in or a positive feeling for the communities the professional is supporting, social intervention on their behalf is likely to be meaningless.

The flourish of community practice that occurred after 1990 corroborated the need for practitioners to be grounded in a solid understanding of the elusive concept of community. Since 1990, community has become almost a catchall permitting entrepreneurs, academics, practitioners, and lay people to design a variety of programs, some solid and respectable, others raising serious concern. It has become very clear that the activity associated with communities often is not based on much understanding of this difficult but magnificent construct.

In what for many generations of community workers has been a classic training textbook, Ross (1955) stated, "Just as the caseworker must know a great deal about individual psychodynamics and the process of interviewing, so the community . . . worker must know a good deal about the forces in the community which make for or hinder community integration" (p. 101).

The community worker must have not only knowledge about the community but also an appreciation for what "community" means to people at both an affective and an intellectual level. In this book, references to a "small community" are not restricted to communities of particular population size. What matters is the nature of the social interaction and sentiment among community residents. As can be seen in many environments, particularly in the United States, even a community of as many as 50,000 people can have small-town characteristics.

The concept of "small" as used here is, then, not solely or even primarily a demographic concept. In fact, "small" was selected to avoid the debates that often surround the word "rural." Whereas the concept of "rural" often is used in the social sciences to identify demographic, economic, social, or sociocultural differences, the concept of "small" is used here to imply a judgment based on the fusion of those elements. Many of the controversies over the use of the term rural through the decades pivoted on the different importance given to demographic, economic, social, and sociocultural elements. The U.S. Census Bureau uses the term rural only in a demographic sense—a place is classified by the Census Bureau as rural when it has a population of 2,500 people or fewer. Fuguitt (1995) suggests that whether economic and sociocultural characteristics are associated with demographic conditions is an empirical question: Each rural place has its own economic and sociocultural identity to be assessed by the trained observer.

The Census Bureau also distinguishes metropolitan and nonmetropolitan counties by population. Metropolitan areas can include not only big cities but also their suburbs, whereas nonmetropolitan areas are less densely populated. Yet in many parts of the United States, adjacent to large cities are areas that are very rural in the social, cultural, or interactional sense. Because the focus of this book is more on sociocultural distinctions, the term chosen to describe the communities studied is "small." The communities may be rural. They may be suburban. They may even be pockets of the metropolis. What they share, however, is a way of life, a pattern of relationships among their citizens, and a history and a place in the country's imagery.

Empathy for the small community is not easily developed among human services professionals. Generally, social work and other helping careers have had an urban orientation; the small community, the village, the countryside, the hinterland have seldom been presented in a positive light, if discussed at all. Analyses by social workers have often dwelt on the more rigid class structure of small towns or villages or on the problems of depopulation or economic stagnation.

One social work student asserted that most students and practitioners she knew criticized the ideal of communal life in small towns as too restricting. The idea that anyone might derive psychological satisfaction from living in a small town with its inevitable prejudices, intolerance, and rejection of outsiders was considered preposterous. However, is rejection always and only a small-town characteristic? Does prejudice appear only in small towns? Are small towns, in fact, more or less rejecting or prejudiced than anywhere else? Certainly recent coverage in the press about harassment and killings in large metropolitan areas would contradict those assumptions.

The more important question is how committed human services practitioners are to working with the small town and helping it change its different attitudes. Even those sympathetic to the small town often dwell on its less positive aspects. For example, the recent film *The Horse Whisperer* (Redford, 1998), purportedly celebrating the bucolic in Montana, leaves viewers with the idea that a smart person who chooses to stay in town will inevitably get involved with the wrong person and not reach full potential. Even the sympathetic view of country life in the film does not lead to a pro-small-town conclusion. To be sure, small towns have their share of problems, but it is hard for practitioners who have no understanding of small-town strengths to help small towns survive and grow strong.

I am promising a book that will convey theoretical principles to generalist social workers. Theory is simply a name for explanations that help us all make sense of the world. It must be understood that theories of community do not provide prescriptions. Theory at the community level simply provides explanations to support professional judgments. It is precisely because of its explanatory capability that community theory can integrate contributions from the humanities, which do not have prediction as one of their goals.

Students and new professionals often frown at the thought of theoretical discussions. Yet occasionally, when they encounter clear explanations of existing phenomena, they are pleased to recognize that theory helps them make sense of the world. Research courses tend to emphasize that theory serves to describe, explain, and sometimes even predict a course of events. Many who have learned this in relation to the natural sciences have come to accept that there is a certain amount of rigor and prediction there, but even when the explanations that are encountered in the ambiguous professional world are good, the response among learners and novice practitioners is inevitably surprise. For example, social work students never cease to be amazed that Ferdinand Tönnies's constructs of Gemeinschaft and Gesellschaft—basic concepts from sociology—still can be used to anticipate the behavioral styles of certain communities and the actions of their residents. The notion of community as giving identity is valuable in explaining the behavior of individuals in place communities (geographic) as well as nonplace communities (clubs, associations, even Internet groups, though the last will not be discussed here).

The idea that theory provides useful explanations is reinforced by many writers who have recently begun to emphasize the interactive nature of social work theory and practice.

> So far, I have argued that social work itself is interactive because it responds to clients' demands on service affecting workers and that theoretical development [sic] reflect this, because theories are rejected or amended as they fail to deal with the demands actually made.
>
> To take this further, theory must also develop in response to demands made by clients on agencies and workers affecting the interpretation or acceptance of theoretical ideas. Since theory is a statement of what social work is and prescribes what social workers should do in various situations, it follows that the nature of social work and its theory are defined, not by some independent process of academic development and experimental testing but by what social workers actually do. And that is created by their reality, the demands made by clients in the context of the basic values and social structures established within the occupation of social work. A modern social work theory must therefore respond to the modern social construction of reality. (Payne, 1991, pp. 21–22)

Because social work theory is not only interactive—worker–client—but also reflective—self-search and discovery—students and young professionals can correlate their personal search for social identity with their own community behavior (whether action or inaction). By discovering the personal meaning of theoretical explanations, they corroborate Kuhn's statements (1962) that "the process of learning theory depends upon the study of applications" (p. 47).

All disciplines possess

> a system of internally consistent propositions which describe and explain the phenomena that constitute the subject matter of that discipline. This system is called a body of theory. The function of all [good] science is to construct theories about the what, the how, and the why of the natural world. There is some current misunderstanding regarding this function of science, many laymen believing that only philosophers theorize and that scientists stick close to facts. . . . In this connection it will prove clarifying if I were to distinguish between two levels of knowledge. . . . On the first level are . . . facts called empirical generalizations; on the second . . . are the explanations or interpretations of these facts called theory. (Greenwood, 1961, p. 75) [bracketed addition mine]

The explanations and interpretations of the small-community phenomena that constitute the core of this book are theories in the sense that they are based on reality as observed not just by social scientists but also by writers, journalists, humanists, and laypeople. Although these descriptive explanations (theories) are diverse—and sometimes opposing—they represent the reality of community and the beliefs about community of many participants and observers. A lot has been learned in the past 25 years about how knowledge is built. Although much of this knowledge did not permeate social work until recently, today lessons have been learned from how constructivism sees knowledge built. In a very interesting study of paradigms in qualitative research, Guba and Lincoln (1994) state that for constructivists,

> knowledge consists of those constructions about which there is relative consensus (or at least some movement towards consensus) among those competent (and, in the case of more arcane material, trusted) to interpret the substance of the construction. Multiple "knowledges" can coexist when equally competent (or trusted) interpreters disagree, and/or depending on social, political, cultural, economic, ethnic, and gender factors that differentiate the interpreters. These constructions are [subject to continuous revision], with changes most likely to occur when relatively different constructions are brought into juxtaposition in a dialectical context. (p. 113)

Although it might be difficult to visualize how these kinds of musings can offer practitioners guidelines for intervention in complex situations, it is evident that social work knowledge is built by understanding, interpreting, and reinterpreting the constructions of many people. Critical theorists believe that "knowledge consists of a series of structural/historical insights that will be transformed as time passes" (Guba & Lincoln, 1994, p. 113), and this is so for community practitioners as well. The theories practitioners believe in and the premises they adopt will govern their observations, choice of conclusions, and policy recommendations but will be ever changing, enriched by experiences and new understandings. Theories influence perceptions; new perceptions shape new practice.

From a critical theory or constructivist perspective, it is easier to accept that not all explanations or theories on which practitioners act come from the social sciences. In other words, if theory can change because the prevailing consensus changes, and various points of view can be incorporated into a search for better explanations, then all disciplines, sciences or not, can contribute to a better understanding of the world. If theory can be understood to provide an effective means of comprehending the universe in a dynamic way, then many current community dilemmas are explained well by literary writers, journalists, and laypeople. For example, Thomas Wolfe wrote that "fiction is not fact, but fiction is fact selected and understood, fiction is fact arranged and charged with purpose" (1929, p. i). For the professional student of communities, it would be a mistake to interpret theory narrowly as comprising only statements from the traditional social sciences.

In 1990, when the predecessor of this book was published, social work had not yet questioned traditional interpretations of the scientific. It had not even questioned measurement as the only way to arrive at satisfactory generalizable explanations. Today, social work has moved beyond that point. The writings of Gergen (1994), Hartman (1994), Howe (1994), and Sheppard (1995) on different ways of knowing have at least minimally opened up questions that social work dared not ask in the past. Furthermore, in the social sciences postmodernists have taught us about the importance of context to our understanding of reality. Although skeptics among postmodernists might reject any form of representation of reality, others do not go to that extreme (Rosenau, 1992). At the very least they employ science more critically and less naively than previously (Rosenau, 1992). Postmodernism, critical theory, and constructivism have brought about a broader acceptance of and appreciation for the qualitative that emerges from the contributions of a wider and more diverse audience. Because philosophy, history, literature, and journalism certainly can help us describe and relate to phenomena, they should have an important place in the social sciences. This book is predicated on that premise.

Addressing the contributions of novelists to community studies, Bell and Newby (1972) suggested that humanistic works, such as John Marquand's *The Point of No Return* (1949), have often illuminated dimensions of small-town life that social scientists miss. Warner, a social scientist who like Marquand dealt with the town of Newburyport, Connecticut, (1949) missed in his five-volume scholarly work *Yankee City* (Warner, 1963) many of the points Marquand's hero Charles Gray made about social mobility in New England towns (Bell & Newby, 1972). Agatha Christie (1950, 1963), observing English village life in her village mysteries, and John Mortimer in *Paradise Postponed* (1984) also contributed to community studies. More recently, Susan Allen Toth in *Blooming: A Small-Town Childhood* (1990) and Howard Owen in *The Measured Man* (1997) clarify historical and current race relations in a Southern town, while Patricia Preciado Martin in *El Milagro and Other Stories* (1996) speaks beautifully of a childhood spent in a growing city among people with a small-town ethos. Penelope Fitzgerald in *The Bookshop* (1997) continues in the tradition of English village stories. Countless other stories enrich our theories of community; as social scientists it is essential that we use their contributions to broaden our perspectives.

To feel the pulse of small towns across America, we will tour through the decades with poets, novelists, and journalists, and we will learn from community studies. Zora Neale Hurston in *Mules and Men* (1935) provides a privileged understanding of life in a small black community in Florida circa 1930. Mary Helen Ponce in *Hoyt Street* (1993) offers wonderful insights into small-town life in a Hispanic community on the fringe of a California metropolis. Patricia Preciado Martin (1996) offers true insight into life in a Southwestern barrio on the verge of becoming a city—for although Preciado Martin describes life within the city of Tucson, the rural ways of many of its Hispanic inhabitants still prevail. T. R. Pearson's novels (1985, 1987) transform the daily activities of the residents of a small North Carolina town into significant indicators of the reality of provincial life. And in Jonathan Raban's *Bad Land* (1997), we tour prairie railroad towns.

The narratives of humanists discuss communal, social, and psychological dilemmas not very different from those social workers encounter every day. These narratives can enhance the ability of professionals to listen to, interpret, and become actors in the stories of their clients and their communities. Literature offers an unparalleled pool of descriptions that can help social workers understand small towns.

Personal Values and Community

A major concern in preparing this book was deciding what from the humanities and the social sciences would help human services professionals make sense of the real world of the small community. These concerns echoed those of Ross (1955): "What do we need to know about the community which will help those who are concerned about developing a kind of community life in which people feel a sense of belonging, participate in the life of the community, achieve a set of common understandings, and work cooperatively at their common problems?" (p. 102). The question exposes the positive aspirations of community practitioners, particularly those who work in small towns and villages. For them, community is an identity-giving entity, a personally meaningful sociological unit that relies heavily on the primary interaction of its members. Because of their concern with human relationships, human services practitioners in small towns are naturally oriented toward Gemeinschaft, which is characterized by common understandings, mutual interdependence, and a nourishing sense of personal meaning and participation. Bell and Newby (1972) once observed that behind the objective facade of sociologists who study community "lurk value judgments, of varying degrees of explicitness, about what is the good life" (p. 16).

For most proponents of strong community ties, the good life is attainable in the intimate small community. This value assumption is consonant with the cultural orientation of those who actually live there. (The fact that scientific assumptions are not value free is a point made by the constructivists.) For instance, Garrison Keillor (1997) epitomizes the ethos of small communities, the philosophy of people in many rural towns across America, when in speaking about the good life in mythical Lake Wobegon, he writes, "In Lake Wobegon, you learned about being All Right. Life is complicated, so think small. You can't live life in raging torrents, you have to take it one day at a time, and if you need drama, read Dickens. My dad said, 'You can't plant corn and date women at the same time. It doesn't work'" (p. 3).

One of the objectives of this book is to illustrate through the use of literary and journalistic excerpts the strength of communal ties that give hope and that fuel conceptions of the good life in small communities. This book presents small-town values as reported by people who share them rather than just by academics who theorize about them. If the literature, scholarly and lay, is indeed a cultural barometer, people continue to long for the positive aspects of small-town living. Even in these days of massive corporations, business takeovers, medical conglomerates, and the like, people still search for small-town human closeness. The sense of anomie created by the large impersonal organizations of early industrial society is no longer considered admirable. In large cities or beyond them, the term community is a banner for "goodness." Clearly, citizens are engaged in an often frantic search for meaningful community. This search fulfills psychotherapeutic as well as social needs. In personal terms, people are looking for intimate community to relieve the external pressures of their complicated lives. Anomie can only be combated by a strong sense of personal interdependence.

Though perhaps not as noticeably as in the 1970s and 1980s, today citizens searching for convivial solutions are flocking in large numbers to small towns and rural areas not only in the United States but also in many other industrial countries. There has been a resurgence of village life in England and Wales. Even in Scotland, where remoteness often made villages less attractive, people are going back to the Highlands and Islands communities they once abandoned. In continental Europe, where village life was not embellished by the "country squire" tradition of England, people are reviving abandoned villages. For example, in Catalonia, Spain, I discovered that many people are refurbishing once-abandoned medieval villages, settling in them, opening businesses, and trying to recreate an intimate environment, often against the odds of diminishing services. So also in France and Italy, where the press has expressed a concern about how people from the English-speaking world, particularly the United Kingdom, were settling in once-remote agrarian provinces. Many of the most successful recent novels and travel books reflect the rebirth of country locations and manageable businesses throughout the world (Mayes, 1997; Mayle, 1994; Parks, 1993). When people can choose where to live, unburdened by the demands of earning a living—as do retirees, writers, and others whose jobs can be located anywhere—small towns and villages provide the sense of belonging to true communities. This makes small towns all the more deserving of attention from social workers.

The personal search for community is not limited to small rural towns. In cities people have gravitated to revitalized older neighborhoods, which resemble the small towns of the hinterland. People gravitate to small, personal communities. Inner cities now provide tax incentives to families who want to relocate there. Young people buying and refurbishing old houses are attracted not only by those incentives but also by the nostalgic possibilities of bringing up children with the more personal support of neighbors. Inner-city neighborhoods now offer "tours" of refurbished houses, reflecting keen historical interest.

Academic interest in small communities has come full circle. In the 1930s and 1940s sociologists and anthropologists carried out community studies mostly in small towns, and some interest in rural and small towns was retained through the decades. Today, the discovery of community values has been extraordinary. Politicians, social workers, teachers, funders, have all have discovered that without an external glue to tie people together, strong values do not survive.

The thrust in the late 1990s has been to return to environments that help maintain a strong America. The cry has been for "community schools," "community in the schools," "community as a solution to crime problems," and "town watches." All of these trends reflect the discovery, at least at the emotional level, that the ties that bind people to interdependent ways of living are important for the survival of the country. In *Membership and Morals*, essentially a treatise on the morality of associations, Rosenblum (1998) writes about how individuals feel motivated to live up to their potential and generate friendly feelings and trust. Her statements about associations echo with truths about community life in general. Our assumptions about associations and communities are based on centuries of experience with how we have all learned to be social creatures:

> Individuals are motivated to live up to the ideal of their station as a result of ties of friendly feeling and trust. Reciprocity is key and members must do their share. Since associations have diverse ends and embrace different things as contributions, individuals must find arenas suitably adjusted to their abilities and wants, where their specific capacities and talents are appreciated. They must have some place where their notions of the good life are affirmed. (Rosenblum, 1998, p. 61)

So the recent emphasis on communal values and communal identities, on ties that bind individuals together and help them overcome social disorder, is well founded, the product of a long tradition. Because ideal communities have always been personal, small, and strong on human interaction, small towns have epitomized the ideal. By extension, as we shall try to illustrate, intimate associational ties within boundaries of neighborhoods, even in large cities, constitute another type of community that we will address.

Local communities, communities as primary interaction, will be our central study. This is not to say that social workers should disregard non-place communities or communities as social categories. It would be misleading to suggest that non-place communities, such as ethnic and otherwise unique groups like professions do not fulfill many human needs. Although practitioners must recognize that non-place communities provide purpose and cohesion to individuals, they must also recognize that the ties that bind people vertically beyond the local setting—along state and national lines, or in professional or occupational structures—are often bureaucratic and thus, in a sense, do not reflect as clearly the community value of personal interaction. This book offers those who are preparing for or already practicing social work in small towns a useful theoretical scheme and a repertoire of literary and journalistic illustrations. With these tools, they can analyze communities of primary interaction and learn from the opposing perspectives about them.

Illustrations of Change

The excerpts that follow are intended to provide contemporary corroboration of change through the words of journalists who report current small-town events and developments. The first piece, from the *Dallas Morning News* (see excerpt, "A Country Comeback," p. 13), discusses the new migration from metropolitan to micropolitan areas, showing very clearly that "way of life" is the attraction. It describes how the small agricultural town of Comfort, Texas, has been transformed and how it is expecting, with mixed emotions, more transformations. The article presents not just an idyllic view of a Main Street lined with antique stores but also the advantages and disadvantages of small towns; it also discussed the issue of services and retirees.

Those who come to rural areas are greeted, by and large, by the pleasant attitudes of the people there, their helpfulness and their welcoming spirit. That is why they have come. Retirees also have been drawn to many of the rural areas in the West, particularly those in the Southwest where the climate is mild and is not a factor in their daily comfort of their daily lives. But there are still issues to be recognized and addressed.

Growth has occurred very unevenly in rural areas of the United States during the past decade. The Western states have attracted many people in recent years, especially Colorado, Arizona, and certain parts of Texas, where construction is booming and where broad expanses of cotton and cattle land have been transformed into housing developments. States that have not partaken of the growth include North Dakota, Kansas, and Michigan. Even within states, population retention has been uneven, as the following excerpt from the *Dallas Morning News* points out.

It is also important to mention that the people returning to rural areas are not only from one ethnic or socioeconomic group. The *Chicago Tribune* (August 1, 1996) noted, for example, that a changed rural South is luring blacks from the North. Although popular understanding is that blacks migrated from the rural South to the cities of the North and remained there, the reality of black migration has included a new effort at returning to the rural South. As blacks have improved their incomes, asserted their social positions, and expanded their economic and employment possibilities, many of them are returning to the rural South, the home of their ancestors, to work as managers of national or local companies or in state government or health organizations. Some have returned as retirees to simply enjoy the rural communities they were once forced to abandon.

> From the rich soil of the Delta to the red clay of Georgia, African-Americans who migrated North during the 1940s, 1950s and 1960s are returning to the land they loved, in a region vastly different from the sharply segregated area they had left decades earlier.
>
> "I had always looked forward to returning back to my roots," said retired school librarian Lynette Williams, who, with her husband Boyce, moved back to her hometown of Union, Ala., four years ago from Chicago. . . .
>
> Her sentiment is echoed by many black who are returning to their southern hometowns from such cities as Detroit, Buffalo, Cleveland and New York. In small towns throughout the South, the new homes or house trailers that dot the hot, dry landscape belong to retired couples who have moved back home. The northward migration was officially over by the mid-1970s, when the South began to see more blacks return than leave, but the most recent U.S. Census figures are dramatic: Between March 1993 and March 1994 more than twice as many blacks moved South than headed North. . . .
>
> Again, the diverse populations returning to rural areas are having to face their fair share not only of rural pleasures but also of frustrations. Many white residents are opposing the politically active blacks who are now involved in government in many of the small Southern towns. Also, many of the returning blacks, now accustomed to city amenities, now are concerned about the lack of city services in many small towns in the rural South. The important thing is that many of the returnees now lead the efforts to improve things (*Chicago Tribune*, August 1, 1996, section 1, p. 1).

The second text illustration, "Last Resort?" (see excerpt, p. 17), was published in the *Yakima Herald-Republic*. It features the small town of Roslyn, which was the site of the television show "Northern Exposure" (where it was called Cicely, Alaska). The piece focuses on development—always controversial in a small town or a rural area. There has always been tension between preservation of the environment and the economic forces that push for development in an effort to create jobs. The problem transcends national boundaries. Recently, villagers in France complained about the large numbers of English settlers who had arrived in Provence and were making that area lose its uniqueness.

Similarly, in many parts of the United States, economic needs dictate development, yet congruent development—development that addresses

[Text continues on page 16]

A Country Comeback: Rural Texas Counties Rebounding from Years of Population Loss

COMFORT, Texas—Jim Lord lived in a prestigious Atlanta neighborhood five years ago. A computer executive, he drove a Mercedes-Benz and shopped frequently at the mall.

If anyone had told him he'd move to a small town in the Texas Hill Country, "I'd have said you're nuts, absolutely nuts," he says today.

Now that he lives in this town of 1,554, he drives a Ford van with 124,000 miles on it and spends his money at the general store. He extols his friendly neighbors and relaxed pace.

His conversion to small-town life is not unique.

After a decade marked by a stagnant or dwindling population in much of rural Texas, today many areas appear to be on the rebound. During the 1980s, 98 Texas counties, primarily rural, lost population. But from 1990 to 1992, only 24 counties lost population, according to a report from Texas A&M University.

The population uptick mirrors a national trend, but experts caution that the figures do not signify the return of the family farm. In fact, farm residents are so few nowadays—less than 2 percent of the population—that the U.S. Census Bureau no longer counts them in its annual population survey.

"It is not that rural, agriculture-dependent areas have suddenly revitalized," cautioned Dr. Steve Murdock, rural sociology professor at Texas A&M. "It is that many rural areas have changed."

In 1995, rural residents are as likely to run antique stores as they are to run tractors. And rural Texas is no longer synonymous with cowboys and cattle, farmers and 4-H.

The reasons for the transformation, besides births and an improved statewide economy, include:

- Urban refugees seeking a more relaxed lifestyle.
- Technology making rural life more viable.
- Urban sprawl reaching further into the country.
- Nontraditional rural business growth, such as tourism, retirement centers and prisons.

In Comfort, changes are readily apparent at the Ingenhuett general store, established 1867. Proprietor Gregory Krauter doesn't sell much hen scratch anymore. He does ring up a lot of watering-can rosettes for antiques dealers on his battered old cash register.

Comfort is still "very much agricultural," Mr. Krauter said. "But not predominantly like it used to be."

Instead, new businesses center on tourism.

"Christmas in Comfort," for instance, is a festive weekend similar to others that pop up across the state year-round. According to the Texas Department of Commerce, tourism is increasingly important in rural areas. Visitors spent almost $2.3 billion in nonmetropolitan counties in 1993, according to the department, up from more than $1.9 billion in 1989.

At Mr. Krauter's store, that translates into more business. And, he said, "It's changed the type of customer."

Today's customer may likely be someone just passing through. "There are a lot more people around that you don't know," Mr. Krauter said.

In addition, the people coming to stay—64 migrants in 1990–92—are different from rural residents. Instead of farmers and ranchers who work the land, "They already have their wealth," noted Mr. Krauter's mother, Gladys.

Mr. Lord and a partner, for example, bought the Comfort Common, a bed-and-breakfast operation, with money earned in the computer business. Down the street, Dr. Bob Potter, a part-time orthodontist, operates Antiques on High.

Moving in with Money

That's not unusual for city people who settle in the country, said Dr. Kary Mathis, professor of agricultural economics at Texas Tech University. "People who don't have money can't afford to move from wherever they are," he said. "People who have moved from urban areas to a rural area already have money."

Because their backgrounds and occupations are different from traditional small-town residents, so are the newcomers' attitudes, experts said.

Urban refugees often "have a different set of values, wants and needs than people who have lived there out of sight and mind," said Dr. Greg Taylor, program leader for community development with the Texas Agricultural Extension Service.

In some parts of the country, those attitudes have clashed, Dr. Taylor said.

For example, urban refugees often want to "ranch the view" instead of the land, or may have different views on environmental issues. When Atlanta media mogul Ted Turner considered buying a New Mexico ranch to raise buffalo in 1993, local ranchers formed a foundation to purchase the land to ensure its continued use as a cattle spread.

City folk also may "bring urban notions of services with them," said Calvin Beale, senior demographer with the U.S. Department of Agriculture. "They want better schools than are there and better shopping, and they want the trash picked up and to be on the sewer line."

"Not Real Anymore"

That worries longtime residents of Comfort, an unincorporated area that offers minimal services. They also worry that the influx of newcomers will turn their hometown into a tourist trap.

. . .

Swallowed Up

It may not be. Many small Texas towns that once functioned as agricultural-supply centers have been swallowed by urban development, along with surrounding farms and ranches. Since 1980, the Census Bureau has changed the designation of nine Texas counties from "nonmetropolitan" to "metropolitan," a distinction that reflects urban sprawl, according to the Texas State Data Center.

Statistics show that counties next door to metropolitan areas grow faster than more remote counties. Still, even relatively isolated areas are attracting urban refugees.

Edwards County Judge Nevill Smart marvels at the city folk buying ranches in his part of Texas, 150 miles northwest of San Antonio. "They move out here from the big city," he said, "and they think they're in heaven."

Mr. Smart works in Rocksprings, a town of 1,441, known as the nation's Angora capital. He sees the newcomers, who typically buy pleasure ranches of 100–150 acres, as a mixed blessing.

"I've got a 13,000-acre ranch that's been in my family since the turn of the century," he said. "From under that hat, I think it's a bad thing because it's taken some of the best country in Edwards County out of production.

"On the other hand, I own the Rocksprings Abstract and Title Co. here. And they bring us a lot of business. We make money off of 'em. I put that hat on and it's great."

Edwards County attracted 230 newcomers from 1990 to 1992, but not all of them are urban refugees. Rural counties, particularly those in the Hill Country, also have benefited from retirees relocating to the area, experts said.

Texas has a band of so-called "retirement destination" communities stretching from East Texas through the Hill Country into South Texas. Retirees "want to go to small towns, yet have the benefits of urban areas," said Dr. Taylor, the development specialist.

Benefits for Retirees

For older people, those benefits include sophisticated medical care, which now is more widely available in the country, thanks to modern technology. Today, for example, rural physicians may consult with colleagues in larger cities through telecommunications.

That same technology also broadens the labor force in rural areas by making more skilled job opportunities available, said Michael Brown, chairman of the telecommunications committee for the Texas Rural Development Council. . . .

Dickens County, located 60 miles from Lubbock, has successfully bucked [the depopulation] trend.

During the '80s, Dickens was one of the few counties in the nation to lose over 25 percent of its population, said County Judge Woodie MacArthur Jr.

Mr. MacArthur, who moonlights as a farmer and rancher, watched with dismay as the county declined. In his hometown of Spur, stores were boarded up and locked. Public-school enrollment fell, dropping the local district from Class 2A to 1A for extracurricular activities. Churches adjusted their budgets as congregations dwindled.

Desperate, Mr. MacArthur and others lured the only industry interested in the area—a maximum-security prison.

Once, he would have been impeached for broaching such an idea, Mr. MacArthur said, but, "The county was at the bottom."

The prison, which is owned by the county and run by a private corporation, contracts with the state to house 489 prisoners. When it opened in 1990, some 80 new jobs made an immediate impact in the county of about 2,600 people.

From 1990 to 1992, Dickens County gained 67 migrants, a population gain of almost 1.2 percent.

Businesses on the verge of closing stayed open. Houses were built. A hardware store opened. Now apartment construction is under consideration because, "We've got a housing shortage," Mr. MacArthur said.

Despite the county's achievement, Mr. MacArthur harbors no illusions of a population boom. Halting the population decline was the goal, he said.

"When you're losing 25 percent in 10 years, just staunching the blood flow was something," he said.

Experts say Mr. MacArthur's caution is well-advised.

Two years of population gains are too little to tell if the shift will last. As quickly as people move to small towns—for economic opportunity or quality of life—they can leave, experts stressed.

"I don't think any town could consider itself secure," said Dr. Mathis of Texas Tech. "Let's go through another rural, agricultural, oil area recession or depression—and see what holds on, what lasts."

SOURCE: Jennings, D. (1995, January 22). A country comeback: Rural Texas counties rebounding from years of population loss. *Dallas Morning News*, p. 1A. Reprinted with permission of the *Dallas Morning News*.

[Text continued from page 12]

both the preservation of the countryside and the fulfillment of economic needs—is hard to come by. Even development for high-tech industries requires construction and often an infrastructure that is not easy to attain without some destruction of the natural landscape. In "Last Resort," issues of economic survival through the creation of resorts are highlighted. Resorts, generally accessible to the affluent, bring a great many economic resources to the countryside, particularly to areas of natural beauty where extractive industries like mining and logging are no longer located.

Development—particularly rural development—has always been of interest to social policymakers throughout the world. The controversy in the developing world has been the level to which economic development can be fostered in order to ameliorate hunger without leading to the total destruction of culture or of environment. The same question has only recently been posed for the developed world, however. Taylor (1994) pointed out that

> Development practitioners have not realized the significance of the environment as a diverse resource system that includes humans; or understood the interrelation (protective, regulative and productive) between humans and the environment. Furthermore, western development experts failed to understand culture/nature interactions in various social fields; specifically the religious/cultural and social imperatives in which humans identify and relate to the environment. Conventional development thinking—dominated by a school of economics concerned with specific growth paradigms, cost effective strategies and, in general, the establishment of a set of global "market friendly economic policies"— tended to externalize the environment, to isolate and separate it from humans. In development planning this created a competing ideological space as in the symbolic distinctions "forest and farm, and bush and settlement (the former wild, uncivilized and backwards—the latter domesticated, civilized and, importantly, developed)." (p. 111)

Although this perception of development as antagonistic to the environment is still pervasive—and in many instances true—the dilemma is much greater. There are real issues of economic survival of remote communities that often can be addressed only through development. The most accepted alternative is one that does not preclude development as a source of positive enhancement of the livelihood of locals, but also does not detract from the conservation of open spaces, resources, and attractive ways of life. The next excerpt illustrates the dilemma.

[Text continues on page 20]

Last Resort?

Northern Kittitas County—In a matter of hours, a friend would be buried in the cold, mountain earth that once sustained this area's mining and logging.

Dressed for the funeral, Nick Henderson braked his topless Jeep Wrangler at a stop sign on historical Pennsylvania Avenue. He could have just as well been waiting to pay his last respects to Roslyn.

The street, aside from a chain saw's howl somewhere in the surrounding forest, was as quiet as the leaves changing colors.

Henderson said his hometown, which only two years ago was flourishing as a tourism mecca for legions of "Northern Exposure" fans, "is dying, whether we like to admit it or not."

"We need good jobs," he lamented.

Good jobs, hundreds of them, and a strong economy are what Bellevue-based Trendwest Resorts is promising as part of a $350 million plan for the largest destination resort in the Pacific Northwest.

Henderson was among the first locals to be hired by Trendwest this year. As the resort is built over the next 20 years, he said, it will require carpenters, groundskeepers, computer technicians, managers, security guards, chefs, busboys and maids.

If completed, the MountainStar resort and residential area will be bigger than Roslyn and the nearby communities of Cle Elum and Ronald combined. It would bring an estimated 300,000 to 400,000 visitors to the area every year, Trendwest said.

"Our children will have something to stay for," said Cle Elum Bakery owner Davene Osmonovich. "And new faces will be coming into our businesses."

But researchers of the timber-to-tourism "New West," warn that big development and newfound prosperity usually arrive with unintended consequences: population booms, traffic snarls, culture clashes and inflated real estate prices, among them.

At risk, they say, is the small-town serenity that lured urban refugees to the country and kept many descendants of the early pioneers from fleeing.

"These towns need to be absolutely careful to put their hopes and expectations for the future in separate baskets," said John A. Baden, a former logger and University of Washington economics professor who writes about the contemporary American West. "If they don't, there will be some big disappointments."

. . .

It's here—7,400 acres of former commercial timberland [where] Trendwest hopes to start construction on MountainStar Resort next summer.

The company's plans call for a 550-room hotel to be erected first. Eventually, 800 condominiums, 3,200 homes, golf courses, historical parks, hiking and biking trails, campgrounds, a restaurant and a conference center will be added over the next two decades.

Like the scenery, [Henderson] said, Trendwest will offer economic security "that'll be forever."

But some local residents don't share his enthusiasm.

The Ridge Committee, made up of local environmentalists, worries the resort will bring water shortages, traffic headaches and too many low-scale service jobs. After a decade of fighting Plum Creek Timber Co.'s logging practices, the group now finds itself in the seemingly awkward position of wanting the site to be kept as commercial forest land, with limited harvesting.

In an open letter to residents, Ridge said it accepts that some development will occur, but that it would be irresponsible "to write Trendwest a blank check."

"We can't afford the taxes, the housing inflation and the mess that such an unrestricted romp would create," the group said.

. . .

Unable to provide jobs for its young, the Old West of lumberjacks, miners, cowboys and farmers has been fading from much of the American landscape since the late 1960s, according to scholars.

. . .

Between 1990 and 1995, the mountainous, wooded region of Deschutes County, Ore., for example, added 20,000 residents to its 75,000 population. The county seat, Bend, has kept pace by widening roads, adding 1 million gallons of water reserves annually and restoring the old downtown shopping district. A metro transit system is being considered to help alleviate traffic problems.

. . .

Building a resort is bound to accelerate the slow exodus to the mountains into a tidal wave of growth, said Baden, who oversees research at the Bozeman, Mont.,-based Gallatin Institute, a nonprofit organization dedicated to studies of the contemporary American West.

David Povey, a professor of planning and public policy at the University of Oregon, warned the era is not long off when local government and planning decisions will no longer have its roots in Northern Kittitas County.

"Now is the time to figure out what is sacred to them and their towns, and then try to set the course to preserve it," he said.

The new pioneers, he said, will bring distinctly urban values and habits with them. They'll eventually want urban services such as art galleries, stockbrokers, fast food and movie houses.

If the people of Cle Elum don't want the Golden Arches towering above their church steeples, they'd best take steps to stop it now, Povey said.

Washington State University rural sociologist Anabel Cooke said some level of friction between the old and new West is inevitable. "There's almost always a power struggle when old timers and newcomers try to share the same piece of paradise," she said. "The newcomers usually win."

Gary Tewalt, a 67-year-old excavator who has lived in Sisters, Ore., since birth, has experienced the pitfalls of an Old West town rebuilding on modern-day dreams of gold.

Before the Black Butte resort was launched in the early 1970s, Tewalt said, Sisters was hardly more than a gas station, grocery store and a few darkened sawmills along State Route 20.

Now, he said, Sisters—once a blue-collar enclave—has been overrun by "millionaires." He complains they've taken over City Hall, bought nearly every available acre of decent real estate and laid cultural siege with Beamers, Big Macs and Baby Joggers.

. . .

Mary Andler, the 77-year-old daughter of a Yugoslavian coal miner and curator of the Roslyn museum, was around when "coal was king," before World War II. . . .

She pointed out a tattered black and white photo of Roslyn 60 years ago, when it was a vibrant town of 5,000. Look out the window to see it today, struggling with a population of 930, she said.

From 1990 to 1995, Roslyn's historic storefronts moonlighted as fictional Cicely, Alaska, on the television series "Northern Exposure." Then the show went south in the ratings and was canceled.

This summer, far fewer tourists—or "Looky Lous," to use the local pejorative—turn off Interstate 90 to click pictures of the Roslyn Café's oasis mural and buy T-shirts, key rings and postcards. Many businesses open only on the weekends.

. . .

In July, the Kittitas County unemployment rate was 5.7 percent, compared with 4.4 for the state. No one believes there are any permanent jobs left to squeeze out of the area's major employers: the U.S. Forest Service, the county, the state Department of Transportation and Plum Creek.

Enter Trendwest. The company—whose annual sales hit $100 million last year—operates 19 smaller vacation resorts, including sites at Lake Chelan, Leavenworth,

Ocean Shores, Discovery Bay, Lake Tahoe, Long Beach, Birch Bay, Whistler (in British Columbia) and in Mexico and Hawaii. It also developed Oregon's Eagle Crest and Running Y resorts. Its condominiums, marketed under the Worldmark name, are run on a time-share basis. Figures from the American Resort Development Association show that time-share purchasers are typically over 45, with an annual household income of more than $80,000 and married, but with no children at home.

But to Baden, that profile demonstrates why local residents should worry. "These are well-off transients, who are in no way dependent on the local area," he said. "They'll probably look down on the indigenous. Of course, they will."

Trendwest says MountainStar, named by a local couple in a contest, could eventually bring about 950 jobs to the area, with a total annual payroll of more than $90 million.

. . .

According to Deschutes County Commissioner Nancy Schlangen, Trendwest so far has a solid track record in Redmond, also a long-suffering former mining town.

"They donate to roads, parks, children," she said of the company. "They've drawn other businesses to town. And civic pride is way up."

She said Trendwest also has successfully used a water-recycling strategy [there] that's similar to the one planned for MountainStar.

In Kittitas County, any potential environmental problems or impacts on schools and roads will be worked out in an environmental-impact study, which is in its preliminary stage, said Trendwest Senior Vice President Mike Moyer.

At the same time, he said the company is challenging the notion that ecology and economics must live apart. Or that resorts are a pantheon for the wealthy. . . .

Already, Trendwest has promised to leave 56 percent of the forest land untouched by bulldozers, developing it instead as a pub-

lic park for hikers, horse riders, mushroom pickers and mountain bikers.

Moreover, the conversion of the land from forestry to a resort would generate about $1.5 million in property-tax revenue alone for the entire county, Moyer said. The fully developed project, he said, would cause the county's assessed valuation to shoot up $1.2 billion and force tax rates to drop.

Yet in Deschutes County, where the value of a family home has climbed from $84,600 to $188,150 in 15 years, lower tax rates haven't translated into smaller tax bills.

"People are paying more because development and an influx of people have made the cost of property go up," said Helen Sherman of the Deschutes County Assessor's Office. The actual taxes on a family home in the county have nearly tripled since the early 1980s.

. . .

In July, Trendwest opened its first MountainStar office in Roslyn, inside what used to be a service station. Administrative offices fill half of the newly carpeted headquarters. The other half houses the public-relations operation, headed by Cle Elum City Council member Jennifer Beedle.

Beedle answered a question before it was asked: "It's not a conflict of interest. You see, I excuse myself from meetings when Trendwest business comes before the City Council," she explained.

. . .

Kittitas County planners are expected to take at least a year to review Trendwest's book of blueprints, maps and applications, submitted in March.

Until then, Cle Elum restaurant owner Lexi Vallone will wait anxiously. Once convinced that "change wasn't going to happen in my town," she's now converted and confident Trendwest will be healthy for both the local economy and environment. . . .

So what if the community is buffeted by some cultural cross-currents, said Julie Cohn, a Cle Elum insurance agent with cold blue eyes and hot pink earrings. At least smoke-belching factories or mobile home parks won't be going on that forest land, she said.

She likes the idea of her home-town becoming a destination spot, where wads of cash from tourists will energize the sagging economy. As it is in the movies, "if we build it, they'll come," she said.

"Let 'em come," she said, flashing the thumbs-up sign. "Let 'em come."

SOURCE: Rose, J. (1997, August 31). Last resort? *Yakima* [Washington] *Herald-Republic.* Reprinted courtesy of the *Yakima Herald-Republic.*

[Text continued from page 16]

History as Theory

Veblen (1994) suggested in an early essay that "the country town in America is one of the greatest institutions" because it has helped shape public sentiment and give character to American culture. Lingeman (1980), in one of the best historical reviews of small-town America, discussed the distinctive traits unique to each small town in the United States, traits that have often been determined by an idiosyncratic history. Sometimes, history and geography combined to stamp a particular small town. Alone or in combination with other elements, the historical factor is essential in understanding the broad range of culture and personality in the thousands of American small towns.

Social workers need to understand historical forces if they are to understand small towns. History closely reflects culture. Consequently, learning the historical record of a town is learning its culture, the ethos of its people, its power structure, and the forces that determine it to be what it is. What good historical research teaches us is that history, just like sociology, is an interpretative enterprise (Tuchman, 1994). Scott (1989) suggested that history is not just about facts or about truth:

> By history, I mean not what happened, not what truth is out there to be discovered and transmitted, but what we know about the past, what the rules and conventions are that govern the production and acceptance of the knowledge we designate as history. My first premise is that history is not purely referential but it's rather constructed by historians. Written history both reflects and creates relations of power. (p. 681)

What is important to understand, as historical accounts are offered to complement other social science and literary accounts is that all these pieces woven together can give the practitioner a way of explaining, interpreting, and reinterpreting the context of practice.

Social workers more than other professionals are aware of the relationship between individuals and their culture. Generalist social workers must confront the intertwining of psychological and cultural variables as determinants of lifestyles, the choices people make, and their patterns of personal activity. The same connection exists between communities and their culture (culture interpreted to include people, places, sense of time, and other processes). Arensberg (1955), an anthropologist, hypothesized that communities are basic units of organization and transmission within cultures. They facilitate cultural adaptation to nature. They offer the social relations through which survival is ensured from generation to generation. For Arensberg, as for many others, there is a correspondence among cultural constructs, the physical form of a community, and its historical record:

> Mumford demonstrated that for each cultural advance in European life, a new form of the city emerged. The medieval borough around market and cathedral, urban counterpart of the manorial village, expressed the high Middle Ages; the baroque capital of parade avenues, palaces, and places d'armes mirrored the absolutist national states; the sooty tangle of factory and slum and the residential segregations of the withdrawn squires on the hill in mill towns and mill cities matched the industrial and railroad age. Each community town (here "city") was unique just as the age, which the anthropologist calls "culture," was unique. . . . We can thus expect American culture, in its many subcultures of region and age, to show similar correspondence in forms. (1955, p. 1144)

Arensberg's speculation that there is a correspondence between the geography and history of a particular region and its forms of habitation is corroborated by Lingeman (1980) and Smith (1966). In *As a City upon a Hill*, Smith relates to the New England towns where somber Puritans determined the structure. Though they had left England, they often repeated what was familiar to them. The men who created the New England town, with its strong sense of collective decision making and Puritan values, were the ascetic young men and stern elders who had arrived on the New England shore in search of solace. Lingeman (1980) said that nowhere else in the colonies did the town form implant itself as firmly as it did in New England. New England towns became the cradles of democratic participation and decision making in American culture.

Other regions had their own special characteristics. Lingeman (1980) describes the Southern settlement as quite different.

In the south, settlement followed a markedly different course, one in which towns played a minor role, save for a few seats of government and important ports such as Baltimore and Charleston. This variant southern pattern stemmed from different geographical conditions, religious ideals, and agricultural practices. To be sure, the settlers of both regions were English and, at least initially, under charters of the London Virginia Company. But differing social, cultural, and geographical mixes produced contrasting societies in the new world—two unique pools of social genes that produced two variant American cultural strains. These strains would eventually intermingle in the democracy of the western frontier to produce a new hybrid America, even as the two societies were on the collision course that produced the Civil War. (p. 15)

The later Western settlement was even more particularly unique, as well as uniquely American.

Arensberg proposed an early ecological perspective for local communities. He suggested that the historical background and the social relationships of particular groups during particular periods became explicit in the physical forms communities took. For Arensberg (1955), the New England town illustrated the principles of his theory:

The eminent colonial historian Wertenbaker accepts the derivation of the New England town from the manorial village of the champion country of East Anglia, whence most of the Puritans came, a derivation established by Homans. In East Anglia, the village in turn was a local specialization of the open-field village of the North European plain. It was brought into newly opened Fenlands by Angles and Saxons from the Elbe mouth and was of a settlement pattern, village type, and agriculture quite different from that of once-Celtic western Britain and even from that of nearby once-Belgian and Jutish Kent. Nothing prevents inventors in a New World from elaborating, adapting, formalizing already familiar, even unconscious, heritages. In fact, that is the way anthropology tells us most cultural evolution (*anglice* "invention") proceeds. The urbanizing Puritans rationally planning new settlements in the wilderness were elaborating ancestral cultural materials and, as we shall see, every other American pioneer community did likewise. (p. 1148)

A similar thesis was proposed by architectural analyst Darley (1978) in her study of British "villages of vision" from a contemporary planner's perspective. Her descriptions, like those of Arensberg, illustrate the relationship between the history and beliefs of the founders or planners and the layout of the community. Discussing how the Cadbury family started its industrial village, she wrote:

> In 1861, as Saltaire took form in its valley outside Bradford, George Cadbury took over the family tea and coffee firm. He had spent much of his spare time working in Sunday Schools and had a Quaker conscience for the welfare of others and an unusually clear sight of what needed to be done to improve life for his employees.
>
> However, it was not until later, when the firm moved out into the countryside to a new large factory, that the situation offered itself for a real advance, not merely in the smaller details but for a change in environment. The essential difference between Cadbury's plans at Bournville and others, before and after, was that they were designed not merely as improved industrial housing, but as improved housing—equally suitable for office workers as for packers in the chocolate factory. The planning was revolutionary; low density suburban villa development was the starting-point with large detached housing replaced by various cottage forms, both terraced and semi-detached. . . .
>
> Physical fitness was one of Cadbury's prerequisites for a contented employee . . . enormous emphasis is laid on groups of men doing press-ups and women doing gentle gymnastics. . . . Cadbury [also] thought that employees could achieve a measure of independence and self-sufficiency, as well as health, by cultivating their own vegetables, and he rightly felt that gardening was the perfect antidote for repetitive work. (pp. 137–138)

An understanding of the historical development of communities in particular areas is valuable. Through the decades the physical layout of communities tied together history, economics, and landscape; it also captured philosophies and action plans for the future. The choice of building material and the distribution of buildings in the landscape both speak of the identity of the community and the life of its members. Regional differences in these instances can be important.

In the New England towns, communal values and religious control were of the utmost importance. As towns began expanding outside New England into the Midwest, economic factors dominated. Yet as Smith (1966) pointed out, many New England traditionalists attempting to revive the religious purity of the early New England migrated to the Midwest. These settlers formed islands of stability in a heterogeneous stream of immigrants. In his very important history of small-town America, Lingeman (1980) gives the example of a town in Ohio, Greenville, and its development through the years. After capturing a variety of points in time, he reaches 1870:

> A photograph taken ca. 1870 would probably depict a blur of activity. Sixty new buildings were in the process of construction; and there was industry—a foundry and machine shop and a steam planing mill—as well as finance—a building and loan association. The streets were graded and lined with shade trees, and more beautification in the form of parks was in the offing. Schools were in permanent buildings now, and Greenville High School, completed in 1868, accommodated 100 students. . . . Fraternal organizations abounded—the pioneer society, the Sons of Temperance (the rights of temperance in the middle west went hand-in-hand with the disappearance of pioneer ways), the Masons, the Women's Christian Temperance Union, the Y.M.C.A., the Darke County Bible Society, and the Patrons of Husbandry. It was a stable town. (p. 171)

In Greenville married life was the norm, divorces were low, and illegitimacy was rare. The historical record reported that these virtues were because of "family honor being highly estimated" (Lingeman, 1980, p. 171). Clearly Greenville in the 1880s was a peaceful, pretty Midwestern town that was confident of its future.

The settlement of the Great West came, according to historical record, in a series of peristaltic waves beginning in the 1840s and continuing for the rest of the century. "By 1890 the great movement west was over, ending in a final hurrahing stampede of boomers into the Oklahoma territory, a rash of humanity that created entire towns in an afternoon" (Lingeman, 1980, p. 174). But this did not mean that all the new territory had been settled and that there was little left for the adventurous.

In *Bad Land* Jonathan Raban (1997) talks about the settlement of the prairie, a vast extension of land extending roughly from Chicago to Seattle. Raban reviews how the rectangular survey of the West began circa 1784 with Thomas Jefferson. He talks about the land ordinance of 1785, a project that reflected the "French Enlightenment temper of Jefferson's mind" (Raban, 1997, p. 58). He discusses how ambitious the land ordinance was in its attempt to survey the great western desert, or the prairies. Raban takes us on a tour of various settlements, beginning with those that were established as the railroad moved westward and ending with his own westerly tour past the very religious settlements of eastern Washington and on to Seattle. Raban encountered a large variety of people who told him stories about how the Bad Lands were settled by adventurers, immigrants, merchants, and other daring souls who took the offers of the railroad companies and accepted the challenges of tracts of land that they could claim.

By the time the prairies and the Western states (primarily Nevada and California) were settled, Eastern cities had already been established with a very clear identity. The movement West created a lore rich in drama and myth. In the mid-1800s, the gold rush to California created mining towns that had their own unique characteristics. Virginia City, Nevada, was one town that many historians chose to describe; it was immortalized by the fact that Mark Twain had lived there as a journalist. Another journalist, J. Ross Browne, visiting Virginia City in the mid-1800s, described the town:

> Frame shanties, pitched together as if by accident; tents of canvas, of blankets, of brush, or potato sacks and old shirts, with empty whiskey bottles for chimneys . . . everywhere, scattered broadcast in pell-mell confusion, as if the clouds had suddenly burst overhead and rained down the dregs of all the flimsy rickety, filthy little hovels and rubbish of merchandise that had ever undergone the process of evaporation from the earth since the days of Noah. (J. Ross Browne, quoted in Lingeman, 1980, p. 199)

The saloon keeper was the pinnacle of Virginia City society as described by Mark Twain. He was widely deferred to and constantly in demand to serve as alderman or state legislator. In mining camp society, "the rough element predominates"; thus members of the traditionally honored professional groups back East—lawyers, doctors, editors, bankers—"found themselves socially on par with the gambler, the desperado, the speculator, the miner who had struck it rich" (Samuel Clemens, quoted in Lingeman, 1980, p. 201).

Through these examples of historical development, it is easy to see how useful the social worker will find the history and stories behind small communities. They often provide insights that are impossible to develop otherwise. All who wish to function successfully within small towns need to be mindful of the possibilities that looking into the past can offer.

Gathering Information: Community Centers

A corollary of the physical distribution of people in towns and of the understanding that history provides is the idea of *centers*. A center is a locus of interaction for people in the community (Freilich, 1963). Freilich, an anthropologist, suggested the identification of centers to facilitate the study of human interaction in communities. He was interested in centers because they provided, for the anthropologist, a way of identifying culture-based local interaction within a geographic spot where information could be collected and where information could also be distributed to the members of the community.

Experience in local communities, whether small towns or city neighborhoods, suggests that the same notion of center can be useful for assessing interactional patterns in small communities today, not only in nonindustrial societies but in the industrial world. For example, in one farming town I know, the locals meet every morning at the coffee room of a local hotel. First, businesspeople frequent the coffee shop; they have their breakfasts before opening nearby stores or offices at 9:00 a.m. The farmers meet in the same coffee shop at 9:30 or 10:00 a.m. when they come to town for business or shopping. Obviously, the coffee shop is an important community center; social workers who wish to establish relationships in the community would be well advised to use it.

Likewise, in many small towns, fire halls are powerful centers where people congregate to discuss community issues. In England, Ireland, and parts of Scotland, there is no better center for taking the popular pulse of communities than the local pub. Cafés or bars frequented by locals play the same role in towns and villages in the United States. Churches, markets, schoolyards, pubs, and coffee shops all can be centers that help the social worker understand the context. In many newly developing communities adjacent to large cities, the many coffee shops established by large chains like Starbucks can serve the same purpose. Many newcomers into an area with an ill-defined ethos gravitate to locations like these where they can perhaps connect with others.

In the same way, bookstores that are members of large chains like Barnes & Nobles or Borders that also offer places where people can sit down and talk have become centers to counteract the largely anomic responses of residents. Many of these bookstores are beginning to locate close to small towns, or at least in regional centers that may be frequented by residents of nearby small towns. Social workers, who often lack the influence that guarantees community backing for their endeavors, would do well to use the opportunity for interaction with the locals afforded by these informal local centers. An intellectual as well as a sympathetic appreciation of the nuances of local settings can greatly enhance human services workers' perspectives and can broaden their spheres of action.

Cyberspace as New Reality

No book on community theory would be complete without a discussion of cyberspace and new technologies, which are particularly important for the future of rural America. In rural America, the electronic world is now more than a way of communicating. It has become a livelihood for many, particularly those who have recently migrated to rural America and who represent the new blood that may be adding to the economic strength of communities. As we approach the 21st century, it would be very hard to deny the importance of computers to small towns. Computers have turned out to be powerful objects that create new positive and negative realities for those who have either fallen in love with them or discover them as opportunity enhancers. Turkle (1995) describes the situation as follows:

> In Freud's work, dreams and slips of the tongue carried the theory. For Douglas, food carries the theory. For LaCanne, the theory is carried by notes. Today, life on the computer screen carries theory. Here is how it happens. People decide that they want to buy an easy-to-use computer. They are attracted by a consumer product—say a computer with a Macintosh-style interface. They think they are getting an instrumentally useful product, and there is little question that they are. But now it is in their home and they interact with it every day. And it turns out that they are also getting an object that teaches them a new way of thinking and encourages them to develop new expectations about the kinds of relationships they and their children will have with machines. People decide that they want to interact with others on a computer network. They get an account and a commercial service. They think that this will provide them with new access to people and information and of course it does. But it does more. (p. 49)

Turkle was particularly concerned with the new identities assumed by many people who participate in virtual communities, which are not bound by the limits of personal relationships, face-to-face interactions, and social recognition that geographic communities impose on people. Nevertheless, whether in virtual communities or simply in the use of the Internet to communicate with others, to sell products, to perform services, and so forth, the broad use of the computer has radically changed possibilities and expectations in rural communities.

For the better, computers have opened a multitude of avenues to be explored—from education to commerce to medicine. For the worse, they have created a sense of self-containment and often a lack of concern for other real individuals as people worldwide operate in the realm of cyberspace. However, whether we believe that computers have been primarily beneficial or primarily detrimental, they are here to stay. They will be a central force in the life of rural communities well into the next millennium.

In an interesting book, *City of Bits* (1995), William Mitchell provides a very full description that reads like the quick sequences of a movie. It illustrates our view of the world since the advent of the computer. Mitchell begins his description by taking the reader back to the preindustrial settlements of 1935. He recalls how as a boy in a small Australian town in what he calls a "dusty country school room with the songs of magpies swirling in on the scorching, eucalyptus-laden breeze" (p. 163), he relived Australian history by locating on a map how various settlements had been initiated on that continent: "We would take out our red plastic templates to trace maps of the island continent and its straggling rigorous systems into our blue-lined exercise books, then we would meticulously mark the tracks of England trailblazers and coastal navigators, locating the settlements that followed and inscribing the dates" (Mitchell, 1995, p. 163).

Mitchell describes how as a school child he learned of heroes who selected sites for settlement, of settlers who came to country places, of convicts and their settlements, of whalers and sealers in port communities, and many others who settled in the interior of Australia. He also learned how the railroad and telegraph systems spawned remote and desolate villages. All this learning was concrete—placed on a map, physically located—and guided by the physical presence of a teacher.

Mitchell (1995) moves swiftly on to the new world of computers and telepresence rather than physical presence:

> Fast Forward. The year is now 1994 and I am trying this text on a computer in my office at MIT. On the same screen, there is a video window open to the design studio upstairs where my students are working, and there are additional windows to studios at universities in St. Louis, upstate New York, Vancouver, Hong Kong and Barcelona. There's a small video camera on my desk so that the students can also see me at work. We are all interconnected by the Internet and the students in these different locations and time zones are working together on proposals for some new housing in an old area of Shanghai. . . . For the moment, at least, we scattered souls have become an electronically linked virtual community. Bodily location is no longer an issue; for me, the students in Hong Kong are as much a part of it as are those to be found within walking distance of my office. (p. 164)

The whole point of Mitchell's book is the reinvention of the human habitat—the fact that cyberspace is opening up opportunities and that we are entering an era of electronically extended bodies.

The repercussions of this phenomenon are tremendous for rural America. Although rural infrastructure may or may not be able to accommodate the pace of these new connections and discoveries, we have learned that the opening up of cyberspace can have at least partially positive consequences for rural America.

Illustrations of Electronic Communities

The two pieces that follow were selected to illustrate the fast-moving phenomenon of electronically connected communities. The first, published in the *Omaha World-Herald* (see excerpt below), is about how rural citizens use the Internet, which has opened up opportunities for school children and business people. The article illustrates how a teenager is using the Internet to create business opportunities for himself that might permit him to remain in rural Nebraska. Therein lies the dilemma: Rural Nebraska is attractive because of the sociopsychological characteristics of personal relationships, intimate interaction, and human support. However, to remain there, citizens must explore less individualized and far more technical ways of earning a living.

 Isolated No Longer: Teens from Rural Nebraska Use the Internet to Travel the World

HYANNIS, NEBRASKA—Amid the cattle pastures, irrigation systems and sandy hills of western Nebraska, computer technology keeps rural teens in touch with the world. Take, for example, Tanner Graham. With the click of his computer mouse, this 16-year-old from Ellsworth, a remote Sand Hills community along Highway 2, talks to an American soldier in South Korea. Tanner and his friend even have video hookups on their computers so they can see each other as they chat.

Tanner can query Internet trouble-shooting chat rooms and get programming answers from techies across the continent. In turn, Net-surfers can learn more about rural life by clicking on the Web pages Tanner has designed for Sand Hills businesses and communities.

"I can bring different cultures into my office," Tanner said as he scanned in photographs of the Hyannis Old Timers Rodeo for its home page. And, he said, he avoids the cacophony and traffic congestion of big cities.

Tanner can look out his window and see nothing but big skies and blowing bluestem.

Educators say computer technology helps rural students connect to people, places and ways of life outside their small communities. As students learn to use computers for everything from entertainment to entrepreneurial ventures, rural developers hope the trend not only provides better education but also helps keep young people on the farms and small towns of Nebraska.

"The technology has helped to expand their minds and open up their eyes to things beyond their communities," said Sue McNeil, a social studies teacher in Taylor, Neb. "It can be frustrating living in a small town where everything is the same. Students want to see bigger places and know the world outside.

Members of McNeil's current-issues class regularly correspond with students from a small high school in rural Kansas. McNeil hopes to broaden the experience by including students from an inner-city school in Boston.

Such exchanges can erase stereotypes and help both rural and urban students learn about each others lifestyles and values, she said.

Even the exchange with students of similar background has opened the eyes of Taylor senior Misti Griebel. Their school seems bigger and their lives more hectic, Misti said, "but they also deal with many of the same things we do."

Another classmate, Russett Switzer, only recently went online with her computer at home. She has chatted with students in India, Mexico and Switzerland.

"I was talking with this high school guy from Switzerland about soccer and he told me he speaks all these languages, German, French. So I typed back, 'Holy Cow' and he's like, 'What's Holy Cow?' He didn't understand that. I laughed," she said.

The appeal of worldwide communication is so appealing that many students spend more time in front of a computer screen than a television screen, said Kay Horstman, a teacher at Hemingford High School.

Russett is one of them. The Internet is so much better than television, she said. "It's more entertaining. It's real conversations with real people. It's a unique experience.

No one else is going to have your exact conversation. Television is fake."

And in the classroom, Horstman's students use the Internet for research. She also taught a class that participated in an e-mail exchange with teens in Australia.

"They learned that we're more similar than we think we are," she said. "They like sports just as much as we do. The girls still talk about boys and giggle. It seems so unknown to them. They have no idea what it's like in Japan or Australia. But in so many ways we are all the same throughout the world . . . They were able to view these other students as friends and liked being able to say, 'I have a friend across the world and we talk on the Internet.'"

Sean Kuhn, Horstman's student aide, often e-mails friends he met at a conference in Washington, D.C. He also likes to access chat rooms to find out how other people think and behave. "There's not a lot of real diverse opinions around here," Sean said of Hemingford, population 953. "Everybody pretty much is the same."

But on the Internet, people talk about anything and everything from a variety of perspectives. When chat-room talk turns to sensitive subjects such as religion, Sean can't help but share his Midwestern, Christian values.

"I used to be a keep-to-myself kind of guy. These type of discussions open up a lot of thoughts. Sometimes people can get pretty angry. But I've learned to look at life in a whole new way."

Rural developers see computer technology as not only opening minds but also as opening opportunities. They hope telecommunications keep young people from leaving their small communities for better opportunities in larger cities.

"Kids these days want more than a job," said Don Macke, executive director of the Nebraska Rural Development Commission. "Communities have to work to create careers for people. Technology can open so many doors that 15 years ago were not available. And that might help young people make the choice to stay."

That makes sense, although there is no national data to support such speculation, said Timothy Collins, director of Education Resources Information Center, a clearinghouse for rural education based in Charleston, W. Va.

"What technology can do is offer those kids who might otherwise have to leave an opportunity to stay in or near their home communities and become entrepreneurs using the new technology," Collins said.

And in western Nebraska, Tanner may be the best example of that. Technology has always been his friend. His computer kept him company growing up in Ellsworth. Internet access brought the world to his doorstep. And computers allowed him to start his own consulting and visual communications business, Sandhills Technologies.

Now, after Tanner's 30-mile drive home every evening from Hyannis High School, he finishes his homework, then goes to work designing Web pages or stationery. He currently is working on five Web sites and typically gets two or three calls a week from prospective customers. He also has taught an Internet class in Hyannis.

"I'm so backlogged," said Tanner, whose business cards describe him as a technical consultant.

"I love living in rural Nebraska, but by the same token it's very important for me to have a career in something that I love," he said. "I hope I can live here where it's safe and beautiful and have a career at the same time. Rural areas should have access to technology—because that's the only way I can do all of that."

SOURCE: Wright, K. (1998, September 20). Isolated no longer, teens from rural Nebraska use the Internet to travel the world. *Omaha World-Herald*, p. 1E. Reprinted courtesy of the *Omaha World-Herald*.

The second illustration (see excerpt below) was selected to show the use of the Internet even in a very remote area, among the Havasupai, a tribe near the Grand Canyon in Arizona. This article from the *Arizona Republic* describes how a consultant who worked with the Havasupai tribe to connect remote communities among the Supai in the Grand Canyon was recognized for his efforts.

 ## Tribal Computers Earn Award for Installer

Using mules to haul computers into the Grand Canyon is apparently a way to make friends out of wary neighbors.

Paul Deshler, a 32-year-old Flagstaff computer specialist, spent the past two years helping the Havasupai and Hualapai tribes install computer networks complete with Internet connections and Web pages.

To get the computers to Supai, the Havasupai Tribe's headquarters, Deshler and others had to strap them on the backs of mules and hike into the depths of Havasu Canyon, a side canyon to the Grand Canyon. There's a road to Peach Springs, the Hualapai Tribe's headquarters, so it wasn't nearly so challenging there.

For his efforts while working for the Colorado Plateau Field Station, Deshler received the U.S. Geological Survey's John Wesley Powell Citizenship Award in a ceremony recently in Reston, Va. The annual award is the highest citizenship honor handed out by the Geological Survey.

Three months ago, Deshler left the field station, a Geological Survey partnership with Northern Arizona University that does biological research, to take a computer programming job with Flagstaff.

Helping the two tribes log onto the information highway was a clear goal of the project, Deshler said, but forging communication partnerships with the tribes was the larger goal.

Necessity was the driving force behind Deshler's five-year effort to improve communications with the 23 tribes on the Colorado Plateau.

"Thirty-three percent of the land on the Colorado Plateau is owned by tribes," Deshler said. "To do this kind of research we needed to establish relationships with tribal environmental offices."

Five years ago Deshler was commissioned to meet with all the tribes on the Colorado Plateau to find out how capable they were of interacting using e-mail and the Internet. The idea was to find ways to open channels, allowing trust to be built up between tribes and federal researchers.

Five years and $30,000 later, three prototype computer networks have been set up—the third is on the reservation of the Jicarilla Apache, a small tribe in northern New Mexico. Each tribe has a Web page [and] e-mail capabilities and has had training sessions on how to use the Internet.

"We were doing this on a shoestring budget," said Deshler, the project's director, laborer, grant writer and general all-around make-it-happen guy.

"He's a really unique individual because he's got vision," said Mark Sogge, a Geological Survey ecologist. "If there's something he sees that needs to be done, he'll find a way to make it happen."

The director of the Geological Survey also had glowing praise.

"I am pleased to commend you on the work that you have done to bridge the cultures of Western science and American Indians on the Colorado Plateau," Director Charles Groat wrote in a Dec. 3 letter. "You have developed the respect and trust of the Indians and non-Indians with whom you worked.

"Probably more than any equipment, data or materials that you brought them, the trust is your paramount achievement."

Internet access has been a boon to the Havasupai Tribe, albeit one that has seen minimal use so far, said Marian Marshall, who coordinates water resource grants for the tribe.

"We do try to get in there every so often" she said. "We use it to check the weather and for some wildlife research."

Poor phone connections and limited training—many of the tribe's employees had scheduling conflicts when training sessions were offered—have made it difficult for tribal members to take full advantage of the Internet access.

"We're still learning about it," Marshall said. "I know how to use it, but I'm still apprehensive with it."

Marshall said she looks forward to more training opportunities.

Deshler said forces are at work to provide the tribes with high-speed connections. The program is also being expanded to other tribes.

SOURCE: Velush, L. (1998, December 29). Tribal computers earn award for installer. *Arizona Daily Sun*, p. 2. Reprinted courtesy of the *Arizona Daily Sun*.

Summary

In this chapter we have discussed how knowledge is built through interpretation and reinterpretation of phenomena and how history adds to that knowledge. For social workers in small communities, interpretation and reinterpretation have been essential throughout the 20th century. The wax and wane of the acceptance and the popularity of small communities in the national literature and press are well documented by demographers and historians. A practitioner's theories must be built on the broad understanding that all these perspectives provide. We have reviewed how perceptions and explanations of small-town phenomena have changed through the decades. Early in the 20th century, rural America had a fundamental place in the national economy and in the national ethos. During the 1920s and 1930s, the situation changed. Small-town dwellers were often apologetic about their roots and identity. In the 1950s America continued on its urban quest, but during the 1960s and 1970s there was a strong rediscovery of rural tradition. In the 1980s the farm crisis negatively affected population growth in many small towns throughout America. The importance of the small town became centered on values and the preservation of a way of life. Yet during the 1990s the technological revolution has further opened the possibility of reconciling economic and demographic phenomena with the preferences of many citizens for a small-town way of life. During the late 1990s the economic boom brought a level of security to many citizens in the United States and other parts of the world. Many individuals found themselves more economically secure and capable of earning a living outside the usual routine of jobs in days past. This phenomenon unleashed transformations that will have far-reaching effects on many rural areas in the decades to come.

CHAPTER 2

Understanding the Small Community

Beyond Mere Definitions: Gemeinschaft and Gesellschaft

A well-known student of community has suggested in her work that "trying to study community is like trying to scoop Jell-o up with your fingers. You can get hold of some, but there's always more slipping away from you" (Pelly-Effrat, 1974, p. 1). Although Pelly-Effrat's analogy refers primarily to the sociological research traditions that at various times have provided different, often antagonistic perspectives for the study of community, it also applies to the concept of community itself, which is difficult to define precisely in relation to groups of real people.

Because the focus of this book is on the small community, the definitional task is not as elusive because the parameters are more circumscribed. Most human services practitioners who work in small towns and villages are dealing with community in the sense of a location in which an array of activities—social, economic, and political—is carried out. Much like anthropologists, small-town social workers view their communities as microcosms of society coterminous with defined territorial and interactional boundaries. Although these boundaries vary with evolving goals, they are potentially identifiable for specific purposes.

In terms of culture, practitioners in small towns and villages view their communities as possessing unique characteristics, although they share in and send messages to the culture at large. In the context of small-town practice, locality as community is struggling for continued survival. It is therefore important to look at locality in historical terms to understand the new developments.

However, social workers often discover that influences flow in and out of the small community. Inside and outside institutions are interrelated and interdependent. What happens inside a local community is determined by and is a determinant of what happens outside. The exchange is dynamic. Particularly in the 1950s and 1960s, proponents of mass-society theory and speakers for the decline of community often dwelt on the complete absorption of the local community; mass-society theorists espoused the idea that, with modern transportation and communication systems, the differences between small towns and cities had been obliterated. They believed that in the modern world, villages and small towns had lost their autonomy, importance, and vitality. For example, Vidich and Bensman (1968) said of the governing board of the small U.S. town of Springdale (a pseudonym for a real New York town): "In almost every area of jurisdiction the board [of supervisors] has adjusted its actions to the regulations and laws externally defined by outside agencies which engage in functions parallel to its own. State policy, regionally organized fire districts, state welfare agencies, the state highway department—these agencies and others are central to the daily functioning of the village" (p. 115).

Mass-society theories popular in the 1960s caused a great deal of rethinking among politicians, policymakers of all kinds, and even corporations during the 1980s and 1990s. While decision making and budgets were decentralized during the 1990s, the economic complexities continue to affect the political responses of small-town leaders. The reality is that external bureaucratic forces still impinge on the life of small communities, but the problem is quite different. What was begun with decentralizing efforts under President Reagan continued under President Bush and gained greater momentum under President Clinton. Yet the message exchange between the small town and the larger outside institutions continues to be important. Howarth (1995) addresses the intense complimentarity of rural urban interaction. He states:

> The rural urban interaction is widely recognized, yet historians read it quite variously. Cultural critic Raymond Williams says urban values prevail because cities concentrate the force of economic capital. Landscape historian John Stilgoe emphasizes design, finding that layouts of rural farms and roads initially shape urban streets and houses, until those agrarian forms turn industrial, producing mills and factories that consume, rather than sustain resources. Biologist Edward O. Wilson takes a longer view, suggesting that urban parks may be efforts to preserve humanity's first home, the savannah: A rolling, grassy plain with few trees and no cultivation—as on the early American plains. (p. 15)

The fact is that there is an acute interaction between urban and rural environments. The more removed we are from our agrarian past, the greater the interaction. Those who have remained on the land or in the small towns across America must interact with the urban centers of consumption, be it for the marketing of products, for medical services, or other improvements in the quality of life which demand greater concentrations of population. Those who live in crowded urban environments must look to the countryside and the small towns to obtain relief from their absorption with industrial forces and from the stresses of a rhythm of life which is often contrary to natural human rhythms. Discussing the endurance of the "pastoral" in American literature, Howarth (1995), suggested that:

> Societies that invest in progress are deliberately courting change, and modernization inevitably brings the crowded, swifter pace of urban life. The pastoral monitors that social change: for all classes, it assuages fears of progress and posits a stable continuity in nature. To the critic William Empson, pastoral is a means of putting the complex into the simple, expressing intricacy clearly, which explains why the impulse waxes with a quickened pace of history. The pastoral endures because it travels well, adjusting to changes of style and substance. In a world now driven by ideology and information, pastoral reminds us of unmediated labor, the pleasure of raking leaves or stacking firewood. The view from a moving train or a car must be pastoral, to preserve our dream of unfallen paradise. (p. 28)

Howarth captures the interaction between small communities and the urban world in his perception of the complementary relationship between pastoral and urban. Though small towns depend on urban areas, so urban areas depend on the countryside and the small town. Yet at any one point in time, the internal forces shaping the small town are not always consonant with external forces. The preponderance of one or the other seems to be related to cultural, political, and economic moods that social workers must try to recognize and understand. To that end, we will highlight some useful concepts.

Certain theoretical constructs are useful because of their endurance. Tönnies's Gemeinschaft and Gesellschaft are examples. They are basic, useful terms because they embody a set of community attributes. For human services professionals, Tönnies's contrasting types of communities provide inarguably the most useful analytic tool; Bell and Newby's (1972) explanations of the concepts provide the clearest framework to apply. Bell and Newby succinctly described them as follows: "If there is a founding father of the theory of community . . . the label perhaps suits Ferdinand Tönnies more than any other individual. Tönnies's book *Gemeinschaft und Gesellschaft* (usually translated as *Community and Society*) was first published in 1887. It has provided a constant source of ideas for those who have dealt with the community ever since" (p. 23).

In Gemeinschaft, Bell and Newby went on:

> Community human relationships are intimate, enduring and based on a clear understanding of where each person stands in society. A man's "worth" is estimated according to who he is not what he has done. . . . In a community, roles are specific and consonant with one another. . . . Members of a community are relatively immobile in a physical and social way: individuals neither travel far from their locality of birth nor do they rise up the social hierarchy. In addition, the culture of the community is relatively homogeneous, for it must be so if roles are not to conflict or human relations to lose their intimacy. The moral custodians of a community, the family and the church, are strong, their code clear and their injunctions well internalized. There will be community sentiments involving close and enduring loyalties to the place and people. (p. 23)

The concept of Gemeinschaft has many social consequences. In analyzing the definition provided by Bell and Newby, a number of elements emerge. First, human relationships are intimate, enduring, and based on a clear understanding of where each person stands in society. This element is probably still important in many small towns throughout America. Bell and Newby stressed homogeneity because they were addressing very homogeneous environments. However, even in the very heterogeneous small towns across America, there still exists an understanding of who each person is, based on intimate relationships, reputation, or history.

Bell and Newby also say that worth is established by who a person is, not necessarily by what he or she has done. In the heterogeneous small communities of today, the definition of who someone is has been broadened slightly. A person may still be identified by historical or social position in the town or village, but class boundaries have become more fluid. Still, *gemeinschaftlich* (the adjective describing Gemeinschaft-type relationships) applies to relationships in small towns, even though more elements enter into the valuing of the individual today. Ever since the GI Bill, the class structure of rural and urban society in America has been changing in ways that would have been hard to imagine in the past. Homogeneity may persist as important, but the natural consequence of the growing diversity of ethnic, racial, and social groups throughout America has been to increase the heterogeneity of small towns. Furthermore, in certain regions homogeneous small towns may be inhabited primarily by minority groups. Leadership has also become broader as women have achieved more significant status in small towns.

The legitimate moral custodians of the community continue to be perceived as the church and the family, as Bell and Newby suggested. Recent emphasis on family relationships has strengthened that commitment. Commitments to family, to neighbors, to locality are still important as small towners define the ideal life. In many ways these values continue to be romanticized because without them a compass would be lost and people would wander without direction in our complex world.

For practitioners currently concerned with the small community, it is essential to recognize social bonds that give added meaning to daily life; the current search for community, not just in the United States but throughout the world, is a personal search for emotional support, cohesive networks, and fullness of life. The community people seek is not a place that stands out because of external attributes; it is the place where they have found a spot, the place to which they are pulled by their emotions.

> In a person's life, there's always some place that possesses them, I figure, some place that owns a chunk of your soul, and a person cannot dispute it or escape it, not even in her sleep. It's the place where desire begins, the place longing brings you back to. For me, that was the little town of Resurrection, right on the edge of the foothills called the Ozark Mountains, smack dab in the middle of the state of Missouri. It was the sort of no-count, nowhere place even the Lake of the Ozarks, Bagnell Dam, and all sorts of Methodists could not revive to a bedraggled glory. It had never been upclimbed, so there was never an appreciable decline, despite the sign outside town announcing: RESURRECTION, GATEWAY TO THE OZARKS, POP. 1523. The "gateway" business was new, but the population was about the same. We were fond of saying that those Ozark hills just south of us were as tall as any Rocky Mountains, you just had to realize that most of them were underground. And so it was for Resurrection. It was as big a town as a person needed, once you'd been there long enough. (Agee, 1997, p. 1)

Gesellschaft is the antithesis of Gemeinschaft, Bell and Newby (1972) proposed:

> Opposed to the concept of community was *Gesellschaft* (variously translated as "society" or "association") which essentially means everything that community is not. *Gesellschaft* refers to the large-scale, impersonal and contractual ties that were seen by the nineteenth century sociologists to be on the increase, at the expense of *Gemeinschaft*. Here is the central idea that runs through so many community studies: social change is conceptualized as a continuum between two polar types: *Gemeinschaft*

or community and *Gesellschaft* or society. For Tönnies, there are three central aspects of *Gemeinschaft*: blood, place (land) and mind, with their sociological consequences of kinship, neighborhood and friendship. Together, they were the home of all virtue and morality. *Gesellschaft*, however, has a singularity about it; in Tönnies's terms, "all its activities are restricted to a definite end and a definite means of obtaining it." This rationality is, of course, usually seen as a key aspect in the development of western capitalism. Indeed it might be claimed that in *Gemeinschaft* would be found what Max Weber calls "traditional" authority whereas *Gesellschaft* incorporates what he would call "rational-legal authority." (p. 24)

Although many sociologists have identified Gesellschaft as metropolis, Tönnies did not necessarily address settlements according to size; rather, he addressed the daily interactions among people. Thus, Rivera and Erlich's (1981) more contemporary use of the term Neo-Gemeinschaft to describe cohesive ethnic and minority metropolitan pockets is accurate because people interact in those units the way people interact in small towns.

Although the personalism associated with Gemeinschaft at one time gave the small community a bad name among proponents of more bureaucratic, rational ties, students of bureaucracy have since come to ascertain that the purported rationality of bureaucratic systems is not limitless but is rather bound to the integrity and independence of the individuals in the system. Nepotism, favoritism, and personal knowledge are not the monopoly of small town or other *gemeinschaftlich* environments. Most people function on the basis of some personal information.

What people seek is a level of comfort in association. The employer who seeks references on a potential hire is using the experience of others to ascertain the suitability of a candidate. Personal knowledge and relationships become negative primarily when they are used to exclude others. Although population size, density, and heterogeneity combine to produce a move in the direction of relationships that are less personalized, in real life people in large cities strive to replicate the more personal environments of small towns in order to combat feelings of isolation.

The concept of Gemeinschaft as used in a contemporary context must stress the psychological aspects of the ties binding individuals to the communal unit. Community may be a place but it is also the source from which groups of people derive a sense of personal identity. Using a sociopsychological approach still valid today, Clark (1973) suggested that it is neither territory nor function that keeps the notion of community alive; rather, it is the psychological elements: "Despite all the potential dangers, what has deprecatingly been termed community-in-the-mind must in fact be *the* springboard for any realistic examination of the phenomenon. It is how the members of the group *themselves* feel that is the basic concern" (Clark, 1973, p. 409).

Clark's contentions are exemplified by contemporary occurrences. People cope with the largeness of city life by finding smaller, more human-size communities, be they sports clubs, churches, or benevolent organizations. Sport and activity clubs have emerged as cities have become larger. The idea is to let people feel they belong somewhere.

There is in all human beings the need to care and be cared for (Noddings, 1984), and caring can only occur in reasonably intimate environments. In more institutionalized settings—what we here call bureaucratic circles—caring cannot occur; thus we work to make smaller or more intimate the circles of our "face community" interactions. Referring to the institutional but polite circles of collegial interactions, Noddings (1984) put it in very personal terms:

> I listen with a certain ready appreciation to colleagues, and I respond in a polite, acceptable fashion. But I must not forget that the rules are only aids to smooth passage through unproblematic events. They protect and insulate me. They are a reflection of someone's sense of relatedness institutionalized in our culture. But they do not put me in touch; they do not guarantee the relation itself. Thus rules will not be decisive for us in critical situations. (p. 46)

Although varying in intensity or degree, a certain amount of "community-ness" is apparent in many human groups that share social interaction. Some are bound by locale (the inhabitants of a town or the workers in a factory); others are not (ethnic groups, national professional organizations, unions). Researchers who study towns or villages often find that physical or political parameters are not necessarily coterminous with the boundaries of social interaction. Territoriality or geographic boundaries often must be transcended; the degree of cohesiveness and the pervasiveness of communal relationships differ depending on the extent to which members identify with a territorial area. In some cases, cohesiveness, support systems, and communal identity exist despite the apparent lack of territorial boundaries. In the case of migrant workers, for instance, community identity transcends the constancy of spatial parameters.

Despite our focus on the small communal unit with strong sentiment and generally with strong territorial ties, Pelly-Effrat's Jell-O analogy is not inappropriate. Exceptions to the elements of territory or even sentiment are readily found to keep one aware of the complexity of the subject.

What is not questionable is the need of individuals for communal ties, the need to "step out of one's personal frame of reference into the other's" (Noddings, 1984, p. 24).

The Small Community in Literature and the Press

The excerpts that follow present the small town in America through the decades. During the 19th century, the image of the small town for most Americans was predominantly Eastern. The small town was where most Americans lived; the environment was very familiar to writers. Most turn-of-the-century writers had experienced small town as a cohesive community and, positively or negatively, drew on those experiences in their work. Many literary treatises have analyzed the presence of the small town in American literature; one historian, Page Smith, in her classic *As a City upon a Hill: The Town in American History* (1966) pointed out that, until the first decades of the 20th century, the overwhelming scenery for American novels was the small town. In 1995, Hölbling, an Austrian, wrote that:

> The small town in US literature makes its appearance in the early 19th century, quite naturally, as an east coast town. . . . But it is New England women who, in a sense, invent the town as a literary landscape. Harriett Beecher Stowe is the first in a long line of women writers that extends from Sarah Orne Jewett and Mary Wilkins Freeman to Alice Brown and Edith Wharton, and then moves west around the turn of the century to include Zona Gale and Willa Cather. Some critics speculate that these women's exploitation of the town reflects the fact that a number of exceptionally intelligent and energetic ladies were marooned in towns that had lost their most enterprising and adventurous men. (p. 97)

But even if the loss of the adventurous men through wars, disease, and departure caused these women to feel confined, their perceptions of small towns were by and large idyllic. The small town is reflected as a caring place, the place where the post office, the general store, the farmer and his wagon, the friendly country doctor, the clergyman, are all central to life.

Through the years the picture of the small town has become much more ambiguous. As writers moved beyond New England to the Midwest and industrial towns, they no longer depict the small town as flawless. They come to the conclusion that "you can't go home again" (Wolfe, 1929). Nevertheless, just as the small town has remained an ever-present phenomenon in sociology, it has retained an attraction for writers. The illustrations that follow allow the reader to consider contrasts between early and more current depictions of the small town.

A Romantic Vision of Home Town

Booth Tarkington's *The Gentleman from Indiana* (1900) was first published in 1899; in it the small town is the place where moral principles triumphed in the long run, where community spirit not only existed but prevailed, and where people were able to create genuine and lasting relationships.

Plattville, Indiana, was a microcosm of society. As such, there was good and evil in the town. What was distinctive about Tarkington's depiction of the small community, unlike that of Sinclair Lewis, is that for Tarkington, good and integrity prevailed in the end without need for extreme compromise. Those virtues, however, coincided with the business interests of the town, a matter that made the book quite popular among contemporary middle-class readers. As Lingeman (1980) commented,

> Plattville, Booth Tarkington's seat of small-town folksiness in *The Gentleman from Indiana*, has a promoter drilling for oil—a former bunco artist who was reformed by the noble hero. This now-honest wildcatter does indeed strike oil, among the many happy endings in which the book abounds; and Plattville seems on the verge of moving to some vaguely defined higher plateau of prosperity without, of course, losing any of its deeply ingrained folksiness. Whether Tarkington's novel had any basis in fact is beside the point; its author, as an accomplished sensor of the popular mind, knew that his middle-class audience needed to believe in the happy ending of wealth from striking oil. (p. 339)

The Gentleman from Indiana is the story of John Harkless, a newspaper editor, and his involvement in the small town of Plattville. Harkless chose to return to Indiana after some years spent in the big cities of the East because "I always had a dim sort of feeling that the people out in these parts knew more, had more *sense* and were less artificial, I mean—and were kinder, and tried less to be somebody else, than almost any other people anywhere" (Tarkington, 1900, p. 182). Harkless had returned to Plattville in search of Gemeinschaft. He did not accuse city folk of cruelty or disloyalty, but he did not feel that the city was *his* community. He needed a personal community. So, when Harkless by chance stumbled on *The Herald*, he bought it.

The plot centers on Harkless's crusade against the rowdiness and vice of the nearby shantytown at Six-Cross Roads and his involvement in local politics. He is deeply committed to cleaner political activity and to eliminating the less desirable element of Plattville, the "hooded Whitecaps." His adventures against the hooded Whitecaps "anticipated the organized violence of the Ku Klux Klan in Indiana two decades later" (Goist, 1977, p. 16). In this sense, *The Gentleman from Indiana* can be viewed as social and historical prediction.

At one point in the novel, Harkless is nearly beaten to death by the hooded Whitecaps; after a long convalescence he recovers and, showing the strength of his community ties, he returns to Plattville. During his absence, he had been nominated for Congress amidst great jubilation. Unlike Carol Kennicott in Lewis's *Main Street* (1920), who "reluctantly acquiesced to a town whose values she [could] only partially share" (Goist, 1977, p. 17), John Harkless realized his ambitions and ideals "within the context of the homey, middle class qualities of small town" Plattville (Goist, 1977, p. 17).

Although a sense of the romantic and ideal pervades Tarkington's writing—the town is gathered together to welcome its "hero"—anyone who has participated in a small-town welcoming parade even recently will recognize pervasive communal elements, elements that, although often ignored by social work practitioners, must be understood and appreciated. An excerpt from *The Gentleman from Indiana* (see excerpt below) illustrates these elements.

 ## The Great Harkless Comes Home

The Harkless Club of Carlow wheeled into Main Street, two hundred strong, with their banners and transparencies. Lige Willetts rode at their head, and behind him strode young William Todd and Parker and Ross Schofield and Homer Tibbs and Hartley Bowlder, and even Bud Tipworthy held a place in the ranks through his connection with the "Herald." They were all singing.

And, behind them, Helen saw the flag-covered barouche and her father, and beside him sat John Harkless with his head bared.

She glanced at Briscoe; he was standing on the front seat with Minnie beside him, and both were singing. Meredith had climbed upon the back seat and was nervously fumbling at a cigarette.

"Sing Tom!" the girl cried to him excitedly.

"I should be ashamed not to," he answered; and dropped the cigarette and began to sing "John Brown's Body" with all his strength. With that she seized his hand, sprang up beside him, and over the swelling chorus her full soprano rose, lifted with all the power in her.

The barouche rolled into the Square, and, as it passed, Harkless turned, and bent a sudden gaze upon the group in the buckboard; but the western sun was in his eyes, and he only caught a glimpse of a vague, bright shape and a dazzle of gold, and he was borne along and out of view, down the singing street.

Glory! Glory! Hallelujah!

Glory! Glory! Hallelujah!

Glory! Glory! Hallelujah!

As we go marching on!

The barouche stopped in front of the courthouse, and he passed up a lane they made for him to the steps. When he turned to them to speak, they began to cheer again, and he had to wait for them to quiet down.

"We can't hear him from over here," said Briscoe, "we're too far off. Mr. Meredith, suppose you take the ladies closer in, and I'll stay with the horses. You want to hear his speech."

"He is a great man, isn't he?" Meredith said to Helen, gravely, as he handed her out of the buckboard. "I've been trying to realize for the last few minutes, that he is the same old fellow I've been treating so familiarly all day long."

"Yes, he is a great man," she answered. "This is only the beginning."

"That's true," said Briscoe, who had overheard her. "He'll go pretty far. A man that people know is steady and strong and level-headed can get what ever he wants, because a public man can get anything, if people know he's safe and honest and they can rely on him for sense. It sounds like a simple matter; but only three or four public men in the country have convinced us that they are like that. Hurry along, young people."

Crossing the street, they met Miss Tipps; she was wiping her streaming eyes with the back of her left hand and still mechanically waving her handkerchief with her right. "Isn't it beautiful?" she said, not ceasing to flutter, unconsciously, the little square of cambric. "There was such a throng that I grew faint and had to come away. I don't mind your seeing me crying. Pretty near everybody cried when he walked up to the steps and we saw that he was lame."

Standing on the outskirts of the crowd, they could hear the mellow ring of Harkless's voice, but only fragments of the speech, for it was rather halting, and was not altogether clear in either rhetoric or delivery, and Mr. Bence could have been a good deal longer in saying what he had to say, and a thousand times more oratorical. Nevertheless, there was not a man or woman present who did not declare that it was the greatest speech ever heard in Plattville; and they really thought so—to such lengths are loyalty and friendship sometimes carried in Carlow and Amo and Gaines.

He looked down upon the attentive, earnest faces and into the kindly eyes of the Hoosier country people, and, as he spoke, the thought kept recurring to him that this was the place he had dreaded to come back to; that these were the people he had wished to leave—these, who gave him everything they had to give—and this made it difficult to keep his tones steady and his throat clear.

Helen stood so far from the steps (nor could she be induced to penetrate further, though they would have made way for her) that only fragments reached her, but she heard she remembered:

"I have come home. . . . Ordinarily a man needs to fall sick by the wayside or to be set upon by thieves, in order to realize that nine-tenths of the world is Samaritan, and the other tenth only too busy or too ignorant to be. Down here he realizes it with no necessity of illness or wounds to bring it out; and if he does get hurt, you send him to Congress. . . . There will be no other in Washington so proud of what he stands for as I shall be. To represent you is to stand for realities—fearlessness, honor, kindness. . . . We are people who take what comes to us, and it comes bountifully; we are rich—oh, we are all Americans here!

"This is the place for a man who likes to live where people are kind to each other, and where they have the old-fashioned way of saying 'Home.' Other places, they don't seem to get so much into it as we do. And to come home as I have to-day . . . I have come home. . . ."

Every one meant to shake hands with him, and, when the speech was over, those nearest swooped upon him, cheering and waving, and grasping at his hand. Then a line was formed, and they began to file by him, as he stood on the steps, and one by one they came up, and gave him hearty greetings, and passed on through the court-house and out at the south door. (pp. 366–370)

SOURCE: Tarkington, B. (1900). *The gentleman from Indiana,* pp. 346–384. New York: Grosset & Dunlap.

Senator Glenn Comes Home to Ohio

There are many modern counterparts to the Great-Harkless-comes-home parade across small-town U.S.A. A recent one, one indelibly inked in the minds of citizens of New Concord, Ohio, was the return of John Glenn to the town of his youth after his second voyage into space (see excerpt below). The ticker-tape parade that welcomed him is the modern equivalent of a hero's welcome on Main Street.

Many small towns, as they celebrate their histories, revive their ancestries, and look for business opportunities in their historical richness, have resorted to celebrations to attract outsiders. While the return of John Glenn was not one of those, it shows how an important event of national significance can bring added life to the small town.

In the past, small towns have welcomed many back to their birthplaces. Some of those heroes came back to stay, having made contributions in the outside world but feeling that their real identities were in the small town. Others returned as martyrs, having offered their lives in service to their country. The historical place held in small towns for veterans and the pride in their contributions is clearly seen in county seats across America. Furthermore, the ethnic origins of many towns are clearly revealed when one reads the lists of those who gave their lives for their country. A visit to Occidental, California, reveals, for example, the influence of the town's Italian settlers. Italian names are prominent in the town's veterans memorial as well as in its buildings and local historical documents (Hill, 1998).

Senator Glenn came back periodically to New Concord to rejoice with the folks in his hometown, where they took pride in his contributions to the country and in his achievements. In small towns, more than anywhere else, the personal achievements of a local hero are celebrated as a collective event.

Thousands Turn Out to Honor Glenns in Hometown

Wrapped in blankets, gulping hot chocolate and coffee, and hovering under umbrellas, more than 5,000 people lined Main Street yesterday on a chilly afternoon to welcome their hometown heroes—77-year-old senator and astronaut John Glenn, and his wife, Annie.

Among those who arrived early to get a choice curbside seat along the parade route was Marie Boyd, 86, of New Concord, and her sister, Bettie Wilson, 70, of Caldwell, Ohio.

Boyd was in New Concord in 1962 when well-wishers turned out to welcome Glenn home after he became the first American astronaut to orbit the Earth.

Yesterday's event was to honor Glenn and his wife after he became the oldest astronaut to orbit Earth, which he did in late October and early November aboard the space shuttle Discovery.

"I'm proud of him. I live here, and I think we should come out to honor him," Boyd said. Her sister agreed. "He's a very good person and a good family man," Wilson said.

Other well-wishers said the parade and reception for the Glenns at their alma mater, Muskingum College, was a welcome diversion from the impeachment debate involving President Clinton and the U.S. bombing of Iraq.

"This was a very good thing. Just look at all the happy faces," said Renee Morrow, 17, a student at John Glenn High School and editor of the student newspaper.

Morrow had traveled to Cape Canaveral,

Fla., to cover Glenn's launch aboard the shuttle.

Morrow said she was thrilled to interview Mrs. Glenn, 78, who told her of her high-school romance with Glenn. "She said she knew in her junior year that he was the one for her," Morrow said.

Larry Miller, former superintendent of East Muskingum Schools, and a trustee of a project to create a center in New Concord to honor the accomplishments of Glenn and his wife, also was on hand for the hoopla. He was along the parade route 36 years ago on March 4, when New Concord staged a huge parade to honor the Glenns.

"They said there were 50,000 here. They were hanging from the trees," Miller said. His daughter, Christina McClanahan, of Canton, also recalled the 1962 parade, as a 4-year-old. "I remember getting squished and my mom saying to me, 'Isn't this fun?'" McClanahan said with a laugh.

At Muskingum College, more than 1,200 people gave the Glenns a standing ovation when Glenn, a retiring senator from Ohio, presented the school with a college flag that he carried with him on the spaceflight. Both Glenn and his wife attended the college in the 1940s.

The Glenns also fielded questions about his flight and some personal questions about their lives posed by students at John Glenn High School and Muskingum College.

Glenn joked that there was no truth to the rumor that NASA had turned him down for a spacewalk during the shuttle flight because "they were afraid I would wander off someplace," and he poked fun at himself for getting oatmeal on his glasses instead of his tie while trying to eat breakfast in zero gravity.

When the Glenns were asked for the secret of their more than half-century marriage, both said they are a team and always talk about the pros and cons of issues with each other and their children.

Glenn said the best answer to the question is two words. "We always finish every conversation with 'Yes, dear.'"

SOURCE: Hinchey, F. (1998, December 20). Thousands turn out to honor Glenns in hometown. *Columbus [Ohio] Dispatch.* Reprinted with permission from the *Columbus Dispatch.*

The Two Sides of Small-Town Life for Southern Blacks

In the essay "The Black Writer and the Southern Experience," Alice Walker (1983) discussed the sense of community reflected in the reminiscences of Southern African Americans. She recounted a story told by her mother of an episode that occurred during the depression when the family lived in a small Georgia town. Walker narrated how the family, who were sharecroppers, had to submit vouchers signed by local officials to collect flour (an item difficult to obtain), which was distributed for the government by the Red Cross:

> One day, [when] my mother was to go into town for flour she received a large box of clothes from one of my aunts who was living in the North. The clothes were in good condition, though well worn, and my mother needed a dress, so she immediately put on one of those from the box and wore it into town. When she reached the distribution center and presented her voucher she was confronted by a white woman who looked her up and down with marked anger and envy.
>
> "What'd you come up here for?" the woman asked.
>
> "For some flour," said my mother, presenting her voucher.
>
> "Humph," said the woman, looking at her more closely and with unconcealed fury.
>
> "Anybody dressed up as good as you don't need to come here begging for food." (pp. 15–16)

Walker said her mother refuted the accusation of begging by stressing that the government was giving away flour to those who needed it and that she needed it, but to no avail. Walker described the white woman's anger and her mother's humiliation as she and her children walked back into the street with no flour. But the point of the story was not to stress the humiliation or lack of "community-ness" reflected in the white woman's behavior; rather it was to highlight the communal feelings of other black citizens who responded to the family's predicament:

> "What did you and Daddy do for flour that winter?" I asked my mother.
>
> "Well," she said, "Aunt Mandy Aikens lived down the road from us and she got plenty of flour. We had a good stand of corn so we had plenty of meal. Aunt Mandy would swap me a bucket of flour for a bucket of meal. We got by all right."
>
> Then, she added thoughtfully, "And that old woman that turned me off so short got down so bad in the end that she was walking on two sticks." And I knew she was thinking, though she never said it: Here I am today, my eight children healthy and grown and three of them in college and me with hardly a sick day for years. Ain't Jesus wonderful. (Walker, 1983, p. 16)

Walker stressed how the story reveals the strength of people. People humiliated by the larger society used religion and the closer, more meaningful ties with their ethnic group as an antidote to bitterness. Walker commented that when she listened to her mother tell the story, the white woman's vindictiveness was less important than her Aunt Mandy's generosity or the group's sense of community.

Perhaps no Southern writer better conveys the sense of richness, cohesiveness, culture, and spirit of the small southern black town than Zora Neale Hurston, novelist and anthropologist. Her book, *Mules and Men* (1935), a collection of stories she gathered in her native community of Eatonville, Florida, is a mirror reflecting life in the small black Southern town of the 1930s.

In the essay "Looking for Zora" (1983), Walker suggested that Hurston's rich prose came from her rich experiences in Eatonville. "Not many black people in America come from a self-contained, all-black community where loyalty and unity are taken for granted. A place where black pride is nothing new" (Walker, 1983, p. 100).

The excerpt on page 49 is Hurston's description of her arrival in Eatonville as she embarks on an expedition to collect black folklore among those she knew and loved in a Florida country town of the 1930s.

The Barrio in Gesellschaft

In 1981, Rivera and Erlich analyzed the flourishing ethnic and minority communities of the inner city and concluded that the relationships among

[Text continues on page 50]

Arriving in Eatonville, Florida

As I crossed the Maitland-Eatonville township line I could see a group on the store porch. I was delighted. The town had not changed. Same love of talk and song. So I drove on down there before I stopped. Yes, there was George Thomas, Calvin Daniels, Jack and Charlie Jones, Gene Brazzle, B. Moseley and "Seaboard." Deep in a game of Florida-flip. All of those who were not actually playing were giving advice—"bet straightening" they call it.

"Hello, boys," I hailed them as I went into neutral.

They looked up from the game and for a moment it looked as if they had forgotten me. Then B. Moseley said, "Well, if it ain't Zora Hurston!" Then everybody crowded around the car to help greet me.

"You gointer say awhile, Zora?"

"Yep. Several months."

"Where you gointer stay, Zora?"

"With Mett and Ellis, I reckon."

"Mett" was Mrs. Armetta Jones, an intimate friend of mine since childhood, and Ellis was her husband. Their house stands under the huge camphor tree on the front street.

"Hello, heart-string," Mayor Hiram Lester yelled as he hurried up the street. "We heard all about you up North. You back home for good, I hope."

"Nope, Ah come to collect some old stories and tales and Ah know y'all know a plenty of 'em and that's why Ah headed straight for home."

"What you mean, Zora, them big old lies we tell when we're jus' sittin' around here on the store porch doin' nothin'?" asked B. Moseley.

"Yeah, those same ones about Ole Massa, and colored folks in heaven, and—oh y'all know the kind I mean."

"Aw shucks," exclaimed George Thomas doubtfully. "Zora, don't you come here and tell de biggest lie first thing. Who you reckon want to read all them old-time tales about Brer Rabbit and Brer Bear?"

"Plenty of people, George. They are a lot more valuable than you might think. We want to set them down before it's too late."

"Too late for what?"

"Before everybody forgets all of 'em."

"No danger of that. That's all some people is good for—set 'round and lie and murder groceries."

"Ah know one right now," Calvin Daniels announced cheerfully. "It's a tale 'bout John and de frog."

"Wait till she get out her car, Calvin. Let her get settled at Mett's and cook a pan of ginger bread then we'll all go down and tell lies and eat ginger bread. Dat's de way to do. She's tired now from all dat drivin'."

"All right, boys," I agreed. "But Ah'll be rested by night. Be lookin' for everybody."

So I unloaded the car and crowded it into Ellis' garage and got settled. Armetta made me lie down and rest while she cooked a big pan of ginger bread for the company we expected. (pp. 23–24)

[Text continued from page 48]

the folk in them were simply variations of those in the small town or village. Today, when suburbia extends to what were once small communities, we are faced with attempts to create Gemeinschaft in metropolitan areas. The spread of violence, intolerance, poor schooling, and lack of interest in positive communal pursuits have increased the emphasis governments and citizens place on the revival of inner-city neighborhoods as communities.

In 1997, for example, a plan in Los Angeles, California, targeted neighborhoods that were poor but showed promise as areas for improvement. The *Los Angeles Times* reported that the program sought to invigorate neighborhood groups that showed initiative in fighting crime (Newton, 1997). In one neighborhood, for instance, citizens sought the help of the Mayor's Office to enforce a curfew. While many of these community rebirth projects are triggered by crime-fighting initiatives, their results are often broader and more positive. The *Los Angeles Times* reporter interviewed a longtime veteran of neighborhood-building efforts:

> Lorene Melendrez, who has lived for twenty-three years in Highland Park . . . credits [the neighborhood projects] with a modest slate of improvement . . . but, she said, "Its more lasting impact was in helping draw the disparate elements of community together."
>
> Artists, preservationists, human service providers and residents all united to help develop and supervise those neighborhood improvements. Eventually, the group spent about $650,000—all of it had to go towards transportation-related projects—and once that effort was completed, Melendrez and others went on to form the Highland Park Community Development Corporation. The new community organization efforts throughout the country are focusing on discreet, reasonably well-defined areas, where citizens can unite with government in attempting improvements. (Newton, 1997, p. A17)

But the history of "community-ness" in barrios is much longer and filled with color than current accounts indicate. The story that follows (see excerpt, "El Milagro," p. 51) captures with precision life in a Southwestern barrio, probably around 1960. The author, a native of Tucson, brings to life rhythms that can still be felt today. While the "milagro" is part of a rich folklore, Preciado Martin's rhythms, the code-switching between Spanish and English, and the life she breathes into her narrative are uniquely enjoyable.

[Text continues on page 53]

El Milagro (The Miracle)

I could have told you that something out of the ordinary was going to happen in Barrio Anita that summer. Everything seemed milagroso: the way the light glanced off the faces of the people so that you saw your reflection in their cheeks; the way the dust motes twirled and eddied and settled like golden powder in the narrow streets; the way the leaves in the cottonwoods trembled and burned like green flames and lit up the lampless alleyways at night.

And who could explain the way the air moved? There was always a breeze, even in the doldrums of July. And those brisitas, sweet with the fragrance of carnations, spilling out of rusty tin cans, down windowsills, up walls, and across driveways—cut back every evening into enormous bouquets that perfumed the home altars in the humble adobe houses, only to reappear in the same abundance the next morning.

My abuelita's neighbor, Doña Hermela, grew tomatoes the size of pumpkins, and la Viuda Elías grew a squash so large it took her brother-in-law a whole morning to cut it up. Everyone for two blocks around had calabacitas con queso for dinner that night. And that's to say nothing of the chiles that grew in everyone's garden: one relleno was enough to feed four people! My Tata's cornstalks grew so tall and so broad that he set up a little stand and started charging everyone twenty-five cents to climb them, swearing on the cart of San Isidro that you could see the Río Santa Cruz from the top.

"Flaco" Miranda's cantankerous mule (never mind that the zoning commission hadn't allowed hoofed animals or barnyard fowl in the Tucson city limits since the forties) knelt down and let all the neighborhood buquis[1] ride him and swing on his tail without once showing his teeth. El Diablo, the aptly named one-eyed rooster in my abuelita's chicken coop, clucked like a Rhode Island Red and lay on all the eggs in the henhouse to keep them warm. My Nina's canary, Pedro Infante, sang "Barca de Oro" from beginning to end one morning and so startled my Nino that he set himself to whitewashing the house without even having to be asked.

My Tío Lalo, "El Rey de la Bacanora," excavated all the home brew that he had been stashing beneath the higuera[2] and handed it all out one Friday evening. He started accompanying my Tía Veva on her nightly novenas for the sick, the dying, the dead, and the resurrected.

Lest you think that things were getting a bit too serious, believe me when I tell you that homely Lupita, who hid behind her mantilla and missal at daily mass and spoke only when spoken to (and only to Padre Nuestros at that), bought a red dress, put a rose in her hair, and became the belle of the Del Río Ballroom at the Sunday tardeadas,[3] where one afternoon she won the "Grito"[4] championship away from "El Güero" Lionel and ran away with the bandleader to Los Angeles.

Anyway, the word got out, traveling like a dust devil through the alleyways of Barrio Anita. Everyone was talking about it: Sábado a las siete en la casa de Señora Sánchez.[5] No one stopped to inquire what or why, they just set themselves to polishing boots or shining patent-leather shoes, brushing the lint off their Sunday best sombreros, and putting their jackets and cloth coats out to air. Clouds of steam rose out of the windows of the houses all through the neighborhood as the housewives took to washing and boiling and bleaching and bluing and starching and ironing white shirts and dresses and blouses and petticoats and socks until they were as unblemished as newly confessed souls.

On Saturday—at six on the dot—we all thronged at Santa Rosa Park and began the procession to the house of Señora Sánchez. The parade stretched for blocks, winding all the way around El Paraiso Market where "El Chinito" Lee handed out free saladitos[6] and lemonade, across the tracks and past the Sagrada Familia Church. Father O'Brian, who was just finishing confessions and not wanting to miss anything, joined the tail end of the gathering still wearing his chasuble.

And what a crowd! It was quite a sight to see: the compadres in their shiny jackets; the niños in their Communion suits and dresses liberated from mothballed boxes for the occasion; the señoras somehow squeezed into their wedding dresses that had lain in cedar-lined chests through silver anniversaries; the teenaged girls in their quinceañera[7] duds kicking up the dust with stiletto heels; the vatos[8] perspiring from their thumbs; the abuelitas in their flowered, ankle-length frocks embroidered with punta de cruz; the viudas, in black polyester, de luto como siempre;[9] the viejitos with their ancient guitars, leading the way.

Who would have thought that Señora Sánchez, thrice married and never one to attend daily mass or complete a novena or hold a vigil, would have witnessed a miracle? But strange are the ways of the Lord, y a cada santo le llega su día.[10] Even the Monseñor, skeptical, took time and stopped by to give his blessing, staying for a few minutes to visit, sitting stiffly on the faded velveteen sofa and drinking Nescafé from a cracked cup.

When the crowd arrived at the house of Señora Sánchez, the radio was blaring rancheras from the screenless kitchen window. Ave María. Señora Sánchez had made menudo and empanadas and teswín, and had strung multicolored lights out of season from the clothesline to the corners of the house to the roof of the rattletrap garage. Her numerous children were passing out the food and drink in paper bowls and cups on little metal trays. The dirt yard had been freshly watered to keep down the dust, and it smelled of earth after a rain. Tea roses, blooming unexpectedly in midsummer, clambered over the rickety trellises, across the rooftop, and into the trees, scenting the evening air like a chapel. Señora Sánchez' faithful cast-iron stove, propped up by a mesquite log at a corner where it was missing a leg, was festooned like an altar. It held all manner of flowers, fresh and paper and plastic, and votive candles and holy cards and rosaries and family photographs and religious medals and myriad ofrecimientos and tokens of her neighbors' reverence and good will.

And there we found Señora Guadalupe Sánchez, presiding in the middle of the freshly raked corral, the piocha blossoms fragrant at her feet. Her bare head was crowned by a halo from the street lamp, her lips moved silently with reverent gracias a Dioses, her mottled and veined hands were folded prayerfully over her ample belly—while everyone pushed and pressed to see . . .

the face of Christ . . .

in the tortilla.

[1]Kids; brats.
[2]Fig tree.
[3]Afternoon dances.
[4]Shout (of enthusiasm, revelry).
[5]Saturday at seven o'clock at Mrs. Sánchez's house.
[6]Apricots soaked in brine and dried.
[7]A Mexican custom in which 15-year-old girls are presented to society.
[8]Young men, "dudes."
[9]In mourning as always.
[10]And every saint has his or her day (pp. 3–7).

SOURCE: "El Milagro (The Miracle)," from *El Milagro and Other Stories,* by Patricia Preciado Martin. Copyright © 1996 by Patricia Preciado Martin. Reprinted by permission of the University of Arizona Press and the author.

[Text continued from page 50]

Ambivalent Visions of Main Street

Even at the turn of the century, people had different perceptions of community. Although Tarkington offered a positive view of the cohesive Gemeinschaft where citizens realize their ideals and where the life of the soul and the body is nurtured, there is an alternative. During the 1920s and 1930s, a host of writers rebelled against the constrictions of Gemeinschaft as represented by small towns and villages across America.

Enduring Issues: Community and Culture

Few of those writers surpassed Sinclair Lewis (1920), whose *Main Street* epitomized the struggle of a young intellectual city woman against the suffocating forces of a small town. However, through various cultural waves, the rebellion against small-town provincialism of the 1920s changed again in the 1930s, a testimony of the wax and wane of small-town values in the culture at large. Lingeman (1980) commented:

> The sociologist Carl Withers recalled that in the twenties, the impact of *Main Street* caused small-town boys attending urban colleges to feel ashamed of their background and become objects of pity to their urban classmates. But in the thirties this attitude changed; small town boys were regarded as "true Americans," exemplifying the rural traditions that had suddenly become so attractive (at a distance) to the students from the city. (p. 394)

What characterizes Lewis's fiction is its endurance. Although the story takes place between 1912 and 1920 when Carol Milford, a young city college graduate, marries Willi Kennicott, a provincial doctor, and arrives to settle in Gopher Prairie, Minnesota (population 3,000), Carol Kennicott's plight has been reenacted through the succeeding decades in many provincial towns. The often suffocating social environment that Carol perceives in Gopher Prairie has often been encountered by social workers who take jobs in small towns, unaware that just as community nourishes one's soul, community can also limit one's horizons.

Community is tightly bound to *culture*, the traditions, institutions, people, and places that mold the life of a particular locale, region, or nation. It is unrealistic to expect that a group of people who have been contented with a way of life for decades or even centuries would readily welcome innovations, even if potentially more satisfying. Human nature clings to the known. Social workers must learn that just as the inevitable process of physical growth represents a threat to the integrity of the child's or young adult's ego, so the often inevitable striving for change and development within communities represents a pull of forces, a painful struggle for survival.

Another element of Carol's struggle in Gopher Prairie that is contemporary is the ambivalence that characterizes her search for community. On the one hand, Carol is searching for the simplicity of a former time; on the other, she is fascinated by the intellectual excitement and liberal views of a new age. As Goist (1977) pointed out, Carol's "yearning for community is clearly not merely a local matter. Though many of her efforts are misdirected, Carol's hope is that what she can accomplish in Gopher Prairie be linked to a worldwide struggle for freedom and comradery among all peoples" (p. 28).

Carol Kennicott wants to strengthen vertical ties, which can weaken the horizontal ones. In Carol's mind, individuals who actively search for the satisfactions of community are looking for higher universal values, hoping to find them all embodied in a single communal entity; of course, that is what Carol cannot find: "I believe all of us want the same things— we're all together, the industrial workers and the women and the farmers and the Negro race and the Asiatic colonies, and even a few of the Respectables. . . . We want our Utopia now and we are going to try our hands at it" (Lewis, 1920, pp. 201–202).

Carol rebels against the small town, and for a time Washington offers her a momentary sense of community. She finds her own people and is gratified by intellectual stimulation. Yet in the end Carol returns to Gopher Prairie. The city had offered her a community of interests; the town offers her stability, which, after her fling with excitement, she can more readily tolerate. As Goist (1977) commented, "The town . . . stands for a community of stable familiarity. Carol [chooses the town] essentially, not because she loves the town, or even likes it much, but because it is a familiar environment to deal with. She has decided she can maintain a critical stance without waging war with the town as she had done previously" (p. 29).

Carol's episode probably is rewritten in the lifescripts of millions of contemporary small-town residents. Social workers in small towns probably will come in contact with many Carol Kennicotts, whose invaluable help and wisdom can be activated to make community life better. Social workers may easily identify with Carol Kennicott because they recognize that all individuals are ambivalent about the virtues of their communities and that they both rebel against and yet adopt their mores.

An excerpt from *Main Street* (see "My Dear," p. 55) provides a lively description of an episode that leads to Carol's improvising—or perhaps formulating—a theory of social change for the Gemeinschaft. Confronted

[Text continues on page 58]

My Dear, You Really Must Come to the Thanatopsis This Afternoon

She had often been invited to the weekly meetings of the Thanatopsis, the women's study club, but she had put it off. The Thanatopsis was, Vida Sherwin promised, "such a cozy group, and yet it puts you in touch with all the intellectual thoughts that are going on everywhere."

Early in March Mrs. Westlake, wife of the veteran physician, marched into Carol's living-room like an amiable old pussy and suggested, "My dear, you really must come to the Thanatopsis this afternoon. Mrs. Dawson is going to be leader and the poor soul is frightened to death. She wanted me to get you to come. She says she's sure you will brighten up the meeting with your knowledge of books and writings. (English poetry is our topic today.) So shoo! Put on your coat!"

"English poetry? Really? I'd love to go. I didn't realize you were reading poetry."

"Oh, we're not so slow!"

Mrs. Luke Dawson, wife of the richest man in town, gaped at them piteously when they appeared. Her expensive frock of beaver-colored satin with rows, plasters, and pendants of solemn brown beads was intended for a woman twice her size. She stood wringing her hands in front of nineteen folding chairs, in her front parlor with its faded photograph of Minnehaha Falls in 1890, its "colored enlargement" of Mr. Dawson, its bulbous lamp painted with sepia cows and mountains and standing on a mortuary marble column.

She creaked, "O Mrs. Kennicott, I'm in such a fix. I'm supposed to lead the discussion, and I wondered would you come and help?"

"What poet do you take up today?" demanded Carol, in her library tone of "What book do you wish to take out?"

"Why, the English ones."

"Not all of them."

"W-why yes. We're learning all of European Literature this year. The club gets such a nice magazine, *Culture Hints*, and we follow its program. Last year our subject was Men and Women of the Bible, and next year we'll probably take up Furnishings and China. My, it does make a body hustle to keep up with all these new culture subjects, but it is improving. So will you help us with the discussion today?'

On her way over Carol had decided to use the Thanatopsis as the tool with which to liberalize the town. She had immediately conceived enormous enthusiasm; she had chanted, "These are the real people. When the housewives who bear the burdens, are interested in poetry, it means something. I'll work with them—for them—anything!"

Her enthusiasm had become watery even before thirteen women resolutely removed their overshoes, sat down meatily, ate peppermints, dusted their fingers, folded their hands, composed their lower thoughts, and invited the naked muse of poetry to deliver her most improving message. They had greeted Carol affectionately, and she tried to be a daughter to them. But she felt insecure. Her chair was out in the open, exposed to their gaze, and it was a hard-slatted, quivery, slippery church-parlor chair, likely to collapse publicly and without warning. It was impossible to sit on it without folding the hands and listening piously.

She wanted to kick the chair and run. It would make a magnificent clatter.

She saw that Vida Sherwin was watching her. She pinched her wrist, as though she were a noisy child in church, and when she was decent and cramped again, she listened.

Mrs. Dawson opened the meeting by sighing, "I'm sure I'm glad to see you all here today, and I understand that the ladies have prepared a number of very interesting papers, this is such an interesting subject, the poets, they have been an inspiration for higher thought, in fact wasn't it Reverend Banlick who said that some of the poets have been as much an inspiration as a good many of the ministers, and so we shall be glad to hear—"

The poor lady smiled neuralgically, panted with fright, scrabbled about the small oak table to find her eye-glasses, and continued, "We will first have the pleasure of hearing Mrs. Jenson on the subject 'Shakespeare and Milton.'"

Mrs. Ole Jenson said that Shakespeare was born in 1564 and died 1616. He lived in London, England, and in Stratford-on-Avon, which many American tourists loved to visit, a lovely town with many curios and old houses well worth examination. Many people believed that Shakespeare was the greatest playwright who ever lived, also a fine poet. Not much was known about his life, but after all that did not really make so much difference, because they loved to read his numerous plays, several of the best known of which she would now criticize.

Perhaps the best known of his plays was "The Merchant of Venice," having a beautiful love story and a fine appreciation of a woman's brains, which a woman's club, even those who did not care to commit themselves on the question of suffrage, ought to appreciate. (Laughter.) Mrs. Jenson was sure that she, for one, would love to be like Portia. The play was about a Jew named Shylock, and he didn't want his daughter to marry a Venice gentleman named Antonio—

Mrs. Leonard Warren, a slender, gray, nervous woman, president of the Thanatopsis and wife of the Congregational pastor, reported the birth and death dates of Byron, Scott, Moore, Burns; and wound up:

"Burns was quite a poor boy and he did not enjoy the advantages we enjoy today, except for the advantages of the fine old Scotch kirk where he heard the Word of God preached more fearlessly than even in the finest big brick churches in the big and so-called advanced cities of today, but he did not have our educational advantages and Latin and the other treasures of the mind so richly strewn before the, alas, too offtimes inattentive feet of our youth who do not always sufficiently appreciate the privileges freely granted to every American boy rich or poor. Burns had to work hard and was sometimes led by evil companionship into low habits. But it is morally instructive to know that he was a good student and educated himself, in striking contrast to the loose ways and so-called aristocratic society-life of Lord Byron, on which I have just spoken. And certainly though the lords and earls of his day may have looked upon Burns as a humble person, many of us have greatly enjoyed his pieces about the mouse and other rustic subjects, with their message of humble beauty—I am so sorry I have not got the time to quote some of them."

Mrs. George Edwin Mott gave ten minutes to Tennyson and Browning.

Mrs. Nat Hicks, a wry-faced, curiously sweet woman, so awed by her betters that Carol wanted to kiss her, completed the day's grim task by a paper on "Other Poets." The other poets worthy of consideration were Coleridge, Wordsworth, Shelley, Gray, Mrs. Hemans, and Kipling.

Miss Ella Stowbody obliged with a recital of "The Recessional" and extracts from "Lalla Rookh." By request, she gave "An Old Sweetheart of Mine" as encore.

Gopher Prairie had finished the poets. It was ready for the next week's labor: English Fiction and Essays.

Mrs. Dawson besought, "Now we will have a discussion of the papers, and I am sure we shall all enjoy hearing from one who we hope to have as a new member, Mrs. Kennicott, who with her splendid literary training and all should be able to give us many pointers and—many helpful pointers."

Carol had warned herself not to be so "beastly supercilious." She had insisted that in the belated quest of these work-stained women was an aspiration which ought to stir her tears. "But they're so self-satisfied. They think they're doing Burns a favor. They don't believe they have a 'belated quest.' They're sure that they have culture salted and hung up." It was out of this stupor of doubt that Mrs. Dawson's summons roused her. She was in a panic. How could she speak without hurting them?

Mrs. Champ Perry leaned over to stroke her hand and whisper, "You look tired, dearie. Don't you talk unless you want to."

Affection flooded Carol; she was on her feet, searching for words and courtesies:

"The only thing in the way of suggestion—I know you are following a definite program, but I do wish that now you've had such a splendid introduction, instead of going on with some other subject next year you could return and take up the poets more in detail. Especially actual quotations—even though their lives are so interesting and, as Mrs. Warren said, so morally instructive. And perhaps there are several poets not mentioned today whom it might be worth while considering—Keats, for instance, and Matthew Arnold and Rossetti and Swinburne. Swinburne would be such a—well, that is, such a contrast to life as we all enjoy it in our beautiful Middle-west—"

She saw that Mrs. Leonard Warren was not with her. She captured her by innocently continuing:

"Unless perhaps Swinburne tends to be, uh, more outspoken than you, than we really like. What do you think, Mrs. Warren?"

The pastor's wife decided, "Why, you've caught my very thoughts, Mrs. Kennicott. Of course I have never read Swinburne, but years ago, when he was in vogue, I remember Mr. Warren saying that Swinburne (or was it Oscar Wilde? but anyway:) he said that though many so-called intellectual people posed and pretended to find beauty in Swinburne, there can never be genuine beauty without the message from the heart. But at the same time I do think you have an excellent idea, and though we have talked about Furnishings and China as the probable subject for next year, I believe that it would be nice if the program committee would try to work in another day entirely devoted to English poetry! In fact, Madame Chairman, I so move you."

When Mrs. Dawson's coffee and angel's-food had helped them to recover from the depression caused by thoughts of Shakespeare's death they all told Carol that it was a pleasure to have her with them. The membership committee retired to the sitting-room for three minutes and elected her a member.

And she stopped being patronizing.

She wanted to be one of them. They were so loyal and kind. It was they who would carry out her aspiration. Her campaign against village sloth was actually begun! On what specific reform should she first loose her army? During the gossip after the meeting Mrs. George Edwin Mott remarked that the city hall seemed inadequate for the splendid modern Gopher Prairie. Mrs. Nat Hicks timidly wished that the young people could have free dances there— the lodge dances were so exclusive. The city hall. That was it! Carol hurried home.

She had not realized that Gopher Prairie was a city. From Kennicott she discovered that it was legally organized with a mayor and city-council and wards. She was delighted by the simplicity of voting one's self a metropolis. Why not?

She was a proud and patriotic citizen, all evening.

SOURCE: Lewis, S. (1920). *Main street* (pp. 124–128). New York: Harcourt, Brace. (Note: The title of this excerpt does not appear in the original version.)

[Text continued from page 54]

with the presumptuousness of the local cultural club discussing all the English poets at once, Carol wonders whether to erupt and charge the members of the Thanatopsis Club with their ignorance and lack of sophistication or whether to introduce her own point of view incrementally.

A Current Issue: Gays in Small Towns

Those who are considered in one way or another different often do not fare well in *gemeinschaftlich* environments. Carol Kennicott found out that incremental changes were essential for survival. Other groups might find that even incremental changes will not prevent their rejection. Nevertheless, most people who remain in small towns want to maintain their hopes alive, whether they be members of ethnic minorities or of groups with different sexual orientation. The excerpt "Gay in a Small Town," from the *St. Paul Pioneer Press-Dispatch*, reports on an incident at Mankato State University in Minnesota (see excerpt, "Gay in a Small Town," p. 59). The article reports the comments of many members of the gay and lesbian community, including advocates from large gay organizations. It is clear that people who are seen as different can experience many hardships in small towns. Yet what is worth observing is that their identities as small-town residents and their values do not weaken with hardship.

A Contemporary View of The Industrial Small Town

The Industrial Revolution took its character perhaps primarily from the transformation and growth of the towns and villages that had been associated in England with the production of textiles. Until the later 1700s, that had been mainly a cottage industry. In towns like Lancaster or Manchester or many villages in the South Pennines, cloth was produced in small, scattered mills or by women working at home in the countryside. But a dramatic transformation occurred in the late 18th and early 19th centuries in England, a phenomenon that later spread to the Midwest and South of the United States.

Arensberg (1955) wrote that the mill towns or factory cities born in Britain spread "like any other cultural ware" throughout the United States and reached their peak around 1925 (p. 1144). But American industrial mill towns had a very different social structure. The social relationships that had characterized many agricultural small towns were transformed. After 1925, Arensberg continued, although no longer spreading with vigor,

[Text continues on page 61]

Gay in a Small Town

Last October, after gay and lesbian students held "Coming Out Week" at Mankato State University, members of a secretive group called Zero Tolerance tacked up fliers around campus proclaiming "Getting Back In The Closet Week"—a celebration of anti-homosexuality.

The fliers said, "Get your [expletive deleted] back in the closet." They advised people to identify homosexuals, " . . . point them out to everyone you know . . . publicly express your shame, anger and hatred for those who commit sodomy, violate God's laws and spread AIDS."

One flier said, "Don't be afraid to apply a little force if necessary."

According to the Gay and Lesbian Community Action Council's Anti-Violence Program, there were 49 reports of violence and harassment toward the gay male, lesbian, bisexual and transgender community in greater Minnesota in 1995. This is an increase over 1994, when 26 nonmetro incidents were reported.

Constance Potter, Anti-Violence Program coordinator, estimates that fewer than 15 percent of all incidents are reported. Though the Minneapolis-based Anti-Violence Program has encouraged gays and lesbians in rural Minnesota to report, fear of retribution remains a powerful deterrent in isolated areas.

Indeed, autumn was an uneasy time for some in the Mankato area. Fear surged unexpectedly, like a wind gust that surprises brittle leaves into eddies of motion. Jeff Langstraat remembers one harrowing day last September.

"I've got bumper stickers on my car that make it pretty obvious that I'm probably gay and my political inclinations are slightly to the left. And as I was driving, a car passed me and they feigned driving me off the road," says Langstraat, 27, a Mankato activist. Among the stickers on his red Toyota: "Homophobia is a Social Disease."

"I am a lot more aware of my surroundings here," Langstraat says. "I check over my shoulder a little bit more. I'm a lot more conscious of my actions than I am elsewhere, simply because I know what goes on."

To combat this kind of fear, gay, lesbian, bisexual and transgender people from around Minnesota will gather this weekend at the 1996 OutFront Conference in Alexandria. One work group scheduled to meet at the conference is the Greater Minnesota Rural Organizing Institute, comprised of people concerned about anti-gay discrimination and violence in rural areas.

Marcy Westerling worked as a neighborhood organizer in St. Paul in the early 1980s and now runs the Rural Organizing Project in Scappoose, Ore.—an organization created to counter anti-gay sentiment in that state. Westerling will hold a workshop at the OutFront Conference that she hopes will help gays and lesbians in rural Minnesota live more open, less fearful lives.

"For most of us, it's this commitment to wanting to live in our communities that's combined with a much newer commitment to try to figure out how to live our lives openly. And there's tremendous fear and confusion about how to do that," Westerling says.

"Traditionally, our urban communities have a much higher percent of gays and lesbians, and if you ask these gays and lesbians where they were born, many of them talk about their rural background. We've kind of created these safe havens if you relocate, but for so many of us, we want to live in a rural area or small town. That's what our values are."

Westerling says gays and lesbians are politically "getting our butts kicked" in small towns across the country. However, they feel hopeful because grass-roots organizations are getting the message out that "it's not OK to be racist, it's not OK to be sexist, it's not OK to be homophobic."

. . .

Marj Carol, 53, a folklorist from Two Harbors, says that as bad as things can be for lesbians and gays in Duluth, things are worse in Iron Range communities. Carol and Stolle recall an incident from 1993 when Aurora was planning its music festival. Two lesbians living near Grand Rapids were on the verge of offering their land for the festival when they learned that a well-known homophobe lived just a few miles from them.

Fearing violent retribution, the women backed out.

"When the governor's task force went to Grand Rapids, they had like over 100 Bible-bangers show up, and this [same] man . . . was standing up and making threats and saying [gays and lesbians] should all be killed," Stolle recalls. "The governor's task force said that Grand Rapids was the most homophobic city in Minnesota."

So many rural gays and lesbians remain closeted, isolated and fearful. And young people who believe they may be homosexual feel there is no one to talk to who will be nonjudgmental.

"It's really tough when we get calls from young people who say, 'Well, as far as I know, I'm the only gay person in my town of 300 or 1,000,'" Stolle says. "The kids who do call have gotten brave enough to call here or it seemed like an option to them to try to find out what's going on in Duluth, and if they could get transportation here and maybe talk to someone."

Carol says that while she is very open about her sexual orientation, she is also careful.

"I don't think I would be standing in my front yard necking with somebody. But I'll sure walk arm-in-arm down the street," she says.

Carol doubts anyone in Two Harbors really gives two hoots about such things.

Dewey Stuve will tell you that they do give a hoot about such things in Mankato. Stuve had never had problems getting by in his hometown until October 1991, when he was diagnosed with AIDS.

He had been hospitalized in Mankato with a temperature of 107 degrees and at one point was clinically dead. Doctors were mystified at first, but they eventually asked the right questions of Stuve and ordered the right tests.

Stuve's doctor confessed he did not feel qualified to treat an AIDS patient and recommended Stuve migrate to the Twin Cities and be treated at the University of Minnesota.

"When I was first diagnosed, I didn't know where to go. There was nobody here to help me," says Stuve, 34.

"I found out later that there were doctors [who took AIDS patients]. There are like 200 people in the area with AIDS, but the majority of them are heterosexuals, women and children. The government offices here in town were unwilling to gear me in the right direction. 'Move to the Cities, you'd be happier up there.' No, Mankato is my hometown. I'd be happier here with my family."

Stuve has been "out" since high school and had never felt threatened or discriminated against. Suddenly, he felt that people were trying to push him aside. Ironically, he says, the straight community has been more supportive of him since his diagnosis than the gay community has.

"I'm so open about my sexuality, and I can go into anywhere—any bar in this town—and know half the people in there and they all know I'm gay. But the rest of the gay community is so closeted that they know me but they won't approach me out of fear of association. Guilt by association," says Stuve, who jokes that city friends doubt his "gay credentials" because he fishes, hunts elk and bear, and dislikes the color salmon.

While Stuve has not been victimized in Mankato because of his sexual orientation, he knows of people who have.

"I've heard horror stories from guys and women who've gone to college here about being beaten up by their roommates or being physically threatened," says Stuve, whose family roots in the area go back 100 years.

"I've known people, they'll move back to the Cities because of the fear of being hurt in Mankato or being threatened by roommates or being threatened by people on campus," Stuve says.

SOURCE: Barbieri, Susan. (1996, January 26). Gay in a small town. *St. Paul Pioneer Press*, p. 1A.

[Text continued from page 58]

the mill towns continued to leave their mark on the social structure of many communities. Among these, Arensberg wrote, was their use of space:

> This use of space is telltale. Far from being merely chaotic and lawless, the "unplanned" form the early industrial cities of American took was a new and distinctive (if unlovely) community form. The new use of space gives us the typical banded and stratified zonal ordering.
>
> . . .
>
> This use of space bands and zones the middle-class dwellings and the middle-class shops in the middle and crams the mills and the warehouses and the industrial warrens of factory workers and immigrant hands in the narrow blighted bottoms which once were marketplaces and the cross-roads of the older towns. It creates a new assemblage center in the rail-road station and the "downtown center" about it and a new pattern of withdrawal whereby the same railroad or the avenues—pushing out the "Main Line"—put the better off and higher occupations of the common factors on which all depend in progressively farther removed residential blocks. It makes visible in external display these graded and successive zones of better or worse neighborhoods and mirrors perfectly an open-class system's scalar stratification of incomes, of power, and of prestige in the zonal successions one sees moving inward from withdrawn garden suburb to blighted tenement district. (p. 1158)

Novelists like Sherwood Anderson also observed the vast changes that had taken place as a consequence of industrialization. Writing in 1919, Anderson commented:

> In the last fifty years a vast change has taken place in the lives of our people. The coming of industrialization, attended by the roar and rattle of affairs, the shrill cries of millions of new voices that have come among us from overseas, the going and coming of trains, the growth of cities, the building of the interurban car liens that weave in and out of town and past farm houses, and now in these later days the coming of the automobiles has worked an enormous change in the lives and in the habit of thought of our people of Mid-America. (pp. 70–71)

Anderson had much to say about those changes, not all of it negative. He noted, for example, that the new structure had brought with it improvement in the sophistication of the citizens: "Much of the old brutal ignorance that had in it also a kind of beautiful childlike innocence is gone forever" (Anderson, 1919, p. 71).

In the 1920s Robert and Helen Lynd studied Muncie, Indiana. Their report, *Middletown*, as we shall note repeatedly throughout this book, became a classic. Because their sponsor was the Institute for Social and Religious Research, one of their clear interests was how small towns coped with social change and the role of occupational or class structure in that change. The Lynds believed that the small town was the key to progress in America; although later disappointed, they concluded that in spite of the changes of industrialization, "Democracy was not dead or doomed in the small town" (Van Holthoon, 1995, p. 37).

A much more contemporary view of the industrial small town was provided by Peter Davis in his description of Hamilton, Ohio. In *Hometown* (1982), Davis provided shrewd descriptions of the spirit, "the sentiment" of a midsized industrial community. Unlike earlier 20th-century writers, Davis did not sing only of the beauty and supportive networks of Gemeinschaft. In true sociological and journalistic fashion, he was a realist who recognized that small and midsized communities were plagued by problems. Davis (1982) recognized that, however cohesive, these communities were divisive; however nourishing of an individual's social needs, they also could be punishing:

> As for Hamilton's being split into factions, the West and East Sides never liked each other, blacks and whites have been uneasy for over a century, rich and poor have been estranged since the town's first industrial, John Woods, refused to give his employees a five-cent-a-day raise in 1836. Hamilton's mayor, Frank Witt, worried about the city's divisions in the late 1970s. Just forty, he was a three-term mayor already and had an eye that fixed itself well beyond Hamilton. Both his friends and enemies expected higher office for him; God only knew where he would go from here. "Remember this and you'll know Hamilton," Mayor Witt said as a January afternoon darkened outside his flag-decked, municipally correct office in the City Building. "We are a deeply fragmented community. We're nice to each other so much of the time we get the idea that's all there is. But since the problems and misunderstandings remain pretty consistent year after year, I have to assume we don't actually like each other as much as we claim to. Maybe nice is what you have to be or you'd be swinging at each other all the time. Still, if you don't recognize your

divisions, it's going to be pretty hard to heal them." The bright, ambitious young mayor—shrewd, handsome, supple—was perfectly in tune with his predecessors who, in the 1890s, were already mourning the loss of a sense of community in Hamilton. (p. 17)

Davis's *Hometown* is a statement of the permanence of the industrial town as a form of American community, the permanence of its problems, and the permanence of many of its patterned solutions. In Hamilton, there is stability in change. Just as communities did in the past, Hamilton often finds elements of cohesiveness or common cause in its own fragmentation—a sad but true reality.

Does that mean that it lacks socially redeeming qualities? No. It simply means that Hamilton is far from perfect. It simply means that, apparently, the perfectly harmonious community, always a yearning in the hearts of citizens, was even at the turn of the century hard to find.

I went to Hamilton not so much looking for as assuming change. The prevalence of change is a given in America. Yet what I found was an astonishing, striking, virtually genetic resemblance between Hamilton's past and its present. The desire to sell, build, expand, advertise, migrate, win, get more for the children—all of this has been in Hamilton for over one hundred fifty years. Dazzled by the vividness and clutter of technology, Hamiltonians themselves remark on how much has changed in the town. Buildings are replaced, everything runs by computer, people are ciphers. Sidewalks are no longer safe, everyone gets mad at his neighbor too easily, public officials are dishonest, kids leave town if they get an education. Yet each of these complaints echoes one in the nineteenth century. The bootlegging city marshal of the 1870s is mirrored in the sheriff who in the 1970s was convicted of embezzlement, conflict of interest, and income tax evasion. The rapid pace of change disturbed those Hamiltonians of the 1890s who longed for "the gentler days gone by" when families stayed together, indeed for their own youth: "The maypole surrounded by a bevy of girls dressed in every color of the rainbow, a beautiful sight that reminded many a heart, whose youthful throb had become chilled, of the merry times of long ago." New buildings were condemned for shoddy workmanship; fighting in the streets made evening walks perilous.

As for technology, Hamiltonians proudly and somewhat fearfully recorded the "radical changes" that had made the 1890s different from the early nineteenth century—the railroad, telegraph, telephone, electric light, microphone. These made them feel they lived in a time the world had never known, and of course they were right. But so had their own grandparents been right when they declared that canals, steamboats, and daguerreotypes had changed the world forever. (Davis, 1982, pp. 14–15)

Hometown is seen as a microcosm of society. Although Davis did not deny the interrelationship of the town and the world, he emphasized the self-sufficiency of the many social networks of its inhabitants. The inhabitants of Hamilton act through many social institutions. If horizontal ties are strong, if a sense of "we-ness," usefulness, and satisfaction is achieved, it is precisely through those various roles and tasks internal to the community itself, rather than through associations with the outside world. For Davis, Gemeinschaft, imperfect as it might be, is alive and struggling.

Davis (1982) focused on social stratification and factions emerging from class and occupational structure. Other kinds of disagreements often plague even the happiest of places. The same question that fascinated the Lynds in the 1920s—whether the small town can deal with change—still preoccupies many writers and decision makers today. Bill Welch, a former newspaper editor now mayor of a prospering small college town in central Pennsylvania, writes wittily about citizen reactions to proposed changes that would affect municipal efficiency. Local government, as we shall discuss further in chapters 5 and 6, is central to the happiness of local citizens. For most Americans, the guarantee of the pursuit of happiness has always been an active promise best put into practice within the local community as the vehicle for individual fulfillment and improvement. But regardless of promised improvement, rational decision making is not always the most salient characteristic of citizens arriving at decisions. Traditions, commitment to old boundaries, habit, and perhaps the popular wisdom that makes small-town dwellers believe in the tried and true all play a part in slowing even the best-intended innovations.

The excerpt reprinted on page 65 was originally prepared as testimony by Mayor B. Welch from State College Borough, Pennsylvania, before the Local Government Committee of the Pennsylvania House of Representatives. It addresses cooperation among many close municipalities. Lurking behind the reluctance to accept municipal consolidation are feelings of local pride, local autonomy, and perhaps access to decision makers. In many Eastern states, including Pennsylvania, municipalities have historically been the first layer of government through which citizens can make their opinions count. De Tocqueville commented on the local community as the primary political unit and the main virtue of the American Republic (de Tocqueville, 1899). There is a price to pay for the maintenance of any virtue, even a democratic one. The difficult process of change in municipal government addressed by Welch is but one example of what occurs in all areas of community life.

Welch's testimony provides a preview for the issues of localism and centralism that we will analyze further in chapter 6. While recognizing the strengths of the local, he leads us through an examination of its potential weaknesses. Interestingly enough, here is a local government official calling for more decisive central action, if by central we mean state government (in the case of Pennsylvania, the *Commonwealth*). Welch proposes enticements to local communities for doing what might be hard to do—an old but decisively pragmatic remedy for reluctance. Whether you agree or disagree with Welch's calls for efficiencies, his testimony will provide a solid basis for discussing consolidation, mergers, and reordering or redistricting in a variety of areas, from municipal government to schools and hospitals.

Finally, Welch reminds us of the all too common temptation of calling for more planning—or the parliamentary equivalent, more study committees—when facing tough decisions. In Welch's words, "The Central Region has had the heck planned out of it over the last 35 years and the result still includes much that we do not like—traffic congestion, loss of prime farm land, a spreading uglification" (1999, p. 8). Readers may find it refreshing to hear about the exaggerations of bureaucracy from a public official!

 ## One Nation, Too Divisible

Welcome to State College, a community divided against itself. Visitors, indeed most residents, are not aware of those divisions. They see the beauty, prosperity and energy that gives us our nickname. But the divisions created by our municipal boundaries are real. They create an invisible maze that zig-zags through our Happy Valley.

To better navigate that maze, five townships and the borough of State College cooperate in the Centre Region Council of Governments to provide services from fire protection to recreation to code enforcement. By all accounts, ours is one of the most effective councils of governments in the commonwealth. Yet it is a tortuous way to govern. For elected officials and COG staff members, it often is torturous as well.

I served as a member of the COG during my four years on State College Borough Council. I was chairman of its Finance Committee for two years. As a newspaper reporter and editor, I covered the formation and growth of the COG and its forerunner regional planning agency. Thirty-some years ago, I wrote the newspaper series on our very first regional plan, the Kendree Shepherd Report. Before becoming a reporter, I had a brief career as a codifier of municipal ordinances. And I now serve as de facto mayor of Greater State College—elected by citizens of the Borough but called upon for community activities and events throughout the Centre Region.

I have had more experience of Pennsylvania municipal government than any one person probably ought to have. Based on that experience, I offer the following observations and suggestions:

- Most citizens believe that municipal boundaries were established by God Almighty, right after he handed the Ten Commandments to Moses.
- Most citizens don't know where those boundaries are, but believe that they are sacred.
- Most elected officials know exactly where the boundaries are, and believe that they are holy.
- Citizens from across Pennsylvania communities work well together in the same offices and schools, attend the same churches, synagogues and mosques, make beautiful music together in choirs and bands, give to the United Way and the local hospital. But when the issue is municipal and extends across those boundaries that are so readily crossed by faith, hope, and charity, we fight like the calico cat and the gingham dog.
- Municipal boundaries, some of which pre-date the Revolutionary War, often are no longer aligned with communities, many of which overflowed old boundaries in the post-World War II demographic shift from town to suburbs.
- Pennsylvania lacks an effective process by which old boundaries can be redrawn to accommodate new circumstances.
- The answers to our municipal challenges do not lie in more planning. The Centre Region has had the heck planned out of it over the last 35 years and the result still includes much that we do not like—traffic congestion, loss of prime farm land, a spreading uglification. We do not need more planning; we need more effective decision making by elected officials.

To do this requires that we increase the size of the playing field and reduce the number of players. That is, we need to combine our existing municipalities into larger entities that can deal effectively with boundary-busting problems such as traffic and sprawl. "Urban sprawl," by the way, is something that seems to happen in other municipalities; in our own, it is often "welcome growth."

- One-third of Pennsylvania's municipalities have fewer than 1,000 residents, less than my small neighborhood in the borough of State College. This fragmentation severely limits local governments' ability to deal effectively with the most important issues facing their communities. Such limits, in turn, deeply frustrate those involved in the process, and undermine citizens' confidence in government's ability to solve problems such as sprawl. It is in the Commonwealth's interest to reduce the number of municipalities it deals with. It is in the citizens' interest to have municipalities large enough in population to provide adequate services at a reasonable cost.

The more than 2,500 municipalities in Pennsylvania's 67 counties make up a Gordian knot that no one can untie. The knot must be cut, as Alexander the Great is said to have cut the inextricable knot of King Gordius.

The power to do so rests with the commonwealth. It has cut such a knot before, when it combined tiny school districts in each municipality into larger and more efficient jointures some 40 years ago. The enormous controversy attending that process mostly is forgotten—unless you lived through it—but the benefits are with us still.

Like school districts, municipalities are creatures of the commonwealth. I look for statewide leadership on municipal consolidation simply because so many of us seem unable to trust our local neighbors who happen to live on the other side of that invisible maze. The truth is that many citizens act like our towns and townships are rival sports teams, rather than neighbors. A state mandate for municipal consolidation would cut thousands of Gordian knots across the commonwealth.

"Consolidation" may not be the best term to describe a reordering of Pennsylvania's municipalities. It has come to have ominous overtones for some. I would suggest a term with which citizens, if not legislators, may be more comfortable: "redistricting."

A fair and orderly redistricting of Pennsylvania municipalities can be carried out by a combination of mandates and incentives. Were I advising King Gordius on building a friendlier knot for our Commonwealth, I would propose the following steps:

- Establish municipal redistricting as a priority for the Commonwealth.
- Set a seven-year deadline for municipalities to realign themselves into units better reflecting communities of interest or size of population. Citizens of such new municipalities should enjoy a direct financial benefit for taking this progressive step—perhaps a modest reduction in their state personal income taxes over a three-year period. (One hopes this would not be equated to vote buying.) In local communities that do not meet the deadline, there would be no tax benefit and the Commonwealth would require electors at a referendum to chose from among several optional forms of government. Samuel Johnson pinpointed the power of such deadlines some 200 years ago. He wrote, "When a man knows he is to be hanged in a fortnight, it wonderfully concentrates the mind."
- Give municipalities the flexibility and resources necessary to do the job. For example, set up a process whereby

citizens of two or more municipalities can create redistricting study committees to propose new boundaries and appropriate forms of government for the new municipality.

- Enable such plans to be advanced in two or three phases, as approved by referendum in the participating municipalities. Strengthen municipalities' ability to frame what citizens and/or their elected representatives determine to be the key questions for a referendum ballot. (Earlier in this decade, elected officials of the borough of State College and the townships of College and Patton developed a fragile proposal for consolidation that could not go forward because the county deemed the ballot question to be "advisory.")
- Provide a means whereby only a portion of a municipality may be included in a new combination. For example, the six Centre Region municipalities could be reorganized as a city and a primarily rural township. This would require the division of several municipalities, to the ultimate benefit of their citizens, I believe. Of course, they may not agree. This brings me to a key point.
- "No one loses" would be a worthy slogan for municipal redistricting. It also is an attainable goal if the transition is spread over a period of years.
- An effective transition will require that some policies and practices be maintained within the boundaries of existing municipalities for a period of years. For example, when school districts were combined, so were school boards. My father presided over a 33-member State College Area school board during a transition period of several years, until a seven-member board could be elected. The more difficult the adjustment—for tax rates, staffing, and zoning, to cite three always-controver-

sial elements—the longer the transition period should be.

Whatever path we take toward reshaping our municipalities and their governments, the process must be entirely open and entirely public and as open-ended as a seven-year deadline allows. Our fellow citizens demand and deserve no less. Thanks to the invisible maze, seemingly

routine government actions can take decades. Seven years seems prompt.

SOURCE: Welch, B. (1999). Testimony to the Local Government Committee of the Pennsylvania House of Representatives. Reprinted as *One Nation, Too Divisible* in the *Centre Daily Times,* July 6, 1999, p. 8. Reprinted courtesy of the author.

Summary

This chapter has shown the intimate relationship between local community and culture, between local history, local heroes, and the sense of belonging that makes people want to live where they are known. Yet the illustrations woven throughout the chapter do not all portray the small town as an idyllic place. Small towns have been, since their inception, places where human nature has shown its best and its worst. They can provide support and understanding as well as rejection. Yet there is something that makes them endure. In this age of impersonal communication, scant relationships, and services that transform us into mere numbers in a massive universe, small towns still make our daily rounds human. Take, for example, the town of Topsham, Maine, population 10,000, where there are only 70 paid employees carrying out the affairs of government. The town relies on volunteers, from gardeners to lawyers, from graphic designers to engineers (*Parade*, May 1, 1994, p. 20). When the town needed a new vacuum cleaner, no complicated requisition system had to be followed. One of the volunteers hunted for a discontinued model that cost the town much less than a current model and provided a very useful service. As Topsham's town manager tells it, in Topsham people want to help.

Even those who have written somewhat satirically about small towns recognize their value and beauty. Bryson, a native Iowan, having traveled through many American small towns, wrote in 1990 about reaching his state, where he knew he belonged:

> In the fading light, I drove almost randomly around northeast Iowa. Every couple of miles I would pass a farmer on a tractor juddering along the highway, heading home to dinner. . . . It was Friday, one of the big days of

the farmer's week. . . . He would wash his arms and neck and sit down with his family to a table covered with great bowls of food. They would say grace together. After dinner the family would drive into Hooterville . . . and watch the Hooterville High Blue Devils beat Kraut City 28–7 at football. The farmer's son Merle Jr. would score three of the touchdowns. Afterwards Merle senior would go to Ed's tavern to celebrate (two beers, never more) and receive the admiration of the community for his son's prowess. Then, it would be home to bed and up early . . . to go hunting for deer. . . . I was seized with huge envy for these people and their unassuming lives. It must be wonderful to live in a safe and timeless place, where you know everyone and everyone knows you, and you can all count on each other. I envied their sense of community, their football games, their bring-and-bake sales, their church socials. And I felt guilty for mocking them. They were good people. (p. 193)

Social work as a profession has been a formalized and often bureaucratic response to the demise of intimate communities. Yet social work as a profession has probably supported and idealized family values and community networks like few others. Social workers in small communities need to help citizens reclaim their ability to capitalize on close ties. Yet social workers also must guard against the forces of conformity that can make small towns become very exclusionary. The Carol Kennicotts of this world are but the surface of the phenomenon of exclusion in small towns. The illustration about gays and lesbians makes that clear. Social workers must advocate for those who are marginalized and must not lose sight of the many others who find joy and happiness in small-town relationships. Like the farmer described by Bryson, the values of the people who are happy in small towns are timeless, and many of these people can extend their support to the cause of social work. Social work needs to be ready to embrace them.

CHAPTER 3

The Ties that Bond, the Dimensions that Explain

Horizontal and Vertical Ties

People have been fickle in their affections for the small community. Small towns or villages where people not only dwell but find meaning for their private and social lives have been seen as a source of felicity because of their "community-ness"; however, they have also been seen as a source of unhappiness because they can be divisive, suffocating, and stultifying.

Writers have gone from one extreme to another. At the turn of the 20th century, the small town or village (the Gemeinschaft) was seen as the only community, while the city (the metropolis and its interest groups) was seen as anti-community. With industrialization, from the 1920s through the 1950s, the city was viewed as the only truly liberating unit of social interaction. During the 1960s, the pendulum swung again, and the small town, the village, the county seat, became redeemers of anomie. The decline of agriculture as a central economic force in the 1970s and early 1980s elicited a general concern about the fate of small towns. Since then, advances in technological and mass communications may account for yet another shift of sentiment in favor of small towns. However, these pendulum-like mood swings are not so much rational as related to cycles in history, people's preferences, and even literary fashion.

Early social sciences studies of community made value judgments about the virtues and predictable patterns of life in small towns, which generally were viewed as epitomizing Gemeinschaft. Bell and Newby (1972) perceptively suggested that "sociologists . . . have not always been immune to the emotive overtones that the word community consistently carries with it" (p. 21). During the first three decades of the 20th century, students of community in its *gemeinschaftlich* sense identified with small towns or villages, guarding their integrity and deploring their decline.

Until the 1950s, the prevalent social science concept was that Gemeinschaft, and therefore community, was only found in non-urban environments. Urbanism was perceived to destroy cohesiveness, mutuality, and community. As late as 1937, the National Resources Committee in the United States (cited in Nisbet, 1953) commented that:

> The urban mode of life tends to create solitary souls, to uproot the individual from its customs, to confront him with a social void, and to weaken traditional restraints on personal conduct. . . . The tenuous relations between men, based for the most part upon a pecuniary nexus, make urban existence seem very fragile and capable of being disturbed by a multitude of forces over which the individual has little or no control. (p. 16)

In the United States, the rural town tended to evoke images of harmony. For centuries, in Britain, particularly in England, all the attributes of the gentleman were associated with the country town, while the rest of the population of small towns was generally ignored. Murdoch and Pratt (1997) have suggested that in Britain, terms such as "rural" and "countryside" "always seemed to enshrine those timeless qualities that make this 'sceptered isle' forever 'England'" (p. 51). They also addressed how differences in the idyllic geography and culture of rural Britain were for long obscured. Clearly, the phenomenon of rural and countryside idealization was not confined to the United States.

As long as the idyllic village or country town prevailed as an ideal, the emphasis was on self-sufficiency and on the internal patterns of relationship within small towns. In other words, the set of relationships we label "horizontal ties" was of center interest in the study of these towns.

During the 1960s, community was reconceived to recognize the impingement of national forces—an important step in acknowledging the complexities and the systemic interrelationships of various-size places today. Perhaps the most influential representative of this school of thought was Roland Warren. Warren (1963) pointed out that "local units" have two distinctive types of systemic ties: horizontal and vertical. The horizontal ties stress local community linkages. The vertical ties relate to the nexus between local institutions and the outside world.

Strong horizontal ties clearly were discernible in the early 20th century when less industrialization, simpler patterns of existence, and a minimal degree of bureaucratization tended to enhance the importance of local community networks. Much of the popular literature on "place" communities highlighted the microcosmic dimensions, the horizontal patterns, of community existence. A sense of inner control, functional versatility, and mastery of the community's destiny through horizontal relationships was pervasive in the early literature on community. The pre-industrial community was primarily local and place-bound in a way it can never again be, given modern communication systems.

In a number of works Castle (1995) pointed out that American rural institutions have been always faithful to the problems they were created to address. This is not to say that society—with its problems—does not change, but Castle recognized the original good fit between strongly local institutions and earlier forms of social organization. Similarly, Hobbs (1995) discussed the foundations of local social organization in America:

> Two features of rural America have historically contributed most to its distinctive forms of organization: the dominance of the family farm and the initial rural industry (and the dominant national industry until the early 20th century) and the prevalence of geographically separated small settlements. Before improved mobility and greater market penetration, the two characteristics were interdependent—most of the small settlements existed to serve the needs of the surrounding farm population. The settlements became farm towns. Social organization and other social attributes reflected those conditions. The interdependence of farm and town also fostered and reinforced agrarianism as a dominant, pervasive, and persistent rural value.
>
> The dispersed settlements and their local and economic roles became identified as community, which was equated in the minds of many with a territory and a pattern of common identity and cooperative relationships. Although the idea of community connotes different meanings . . . , community was in the early rural context, simultaneously a description of locality, purpose, and a statement of value. (p. 373)

In spite of the return to localism and the movement to enhance the importance of local government as the institution closest to the people, local communities could not return to the way they were at the turn of the century. Our current efforts to enhance horizontal ties in communities are very different from those of the early 20th century. Then, the idea was self-containment, survival within fairly self-sustaining local units of government and interrelationship among local people. At that time, standardization was neither important nor enforceable when distances were great, central government remote, and differences among localities fairly marked.

As time went by, certain institutions gained national importance, bringing a movement toward standardization. Hobbs discusses some of the institutions that responded to standardization because "standard patterns of response . . . excite standard institutional environments" (Hobbs, 1995, p. 386). Local variations among social institutions were reduced in favor of greater uniformity, the result of professionalization, state regulation, and other pervasive efforts at improvement.

> One of the earliest distinctive rural organizational forms was the one-room country school, an organizational adaptation to farming and a dispersed rural population. . . . It was, in fact, the need for farm children to provide labor on the farm that established what was to become the nation's school calendar and length of the school day. The school day began after farm children had helped with morning farm chores and ended early enough for children to repeat their ritual in the evening. . . .
>
> Until about 1920, schools were mostly locally financed and therefore locally controlled, although states had established departments of education and were supporting "normal schools to provide professional teacher training." But the state and the federal role in financing (and regulating) education was minimal. . . . Succeeding decades, however, have witnessed an inexorable process of rural schools incorporated into a national education institution. The rationale for incorporation has been rural school improvement. . . . What followed had a great effect, not only on rural schools, but on rural neighborhoods and communities as well. (Hobbs, 1995, pp. 386–387)

The efforts of national and state governments to consolidate the schools in order to improve their services and modernize their offerings have had extraordinary influence on expanding the geographic size and outreach of many local communities. Just as the schools began a movement toward standardization and created ways for local communities to strengthen vertical ties, often at the cost of horizontal linkages, so have other modern institutions. During the 1970s and 1980s, regional medical centers were created to replace the local hospitals that were disappearing, and to attend to what were in essence community needs. In spite of the continued concern for the importance of local ties to the psychological makeup of individuals in communities, the strength of horizontal ties has diminished. Today, vertical ties are of the essence even in the strongest local milieu.

Strengthening Vertical Ties

From the 1950s through the 1970s, horizontal patterns gave way to vertical ones. "The relationships through which [local units] are oriented to the larger society beyond the community . . . constitute the community's vertical pattern" (Warren, 1963, p. 237). Warren asked whether there was "a discernible set of relationships to extra community systems which was sufficiently general to be called a pattern of organization" (p. 238). Of course, government ties and the linkages of banks, chain stores, factories, and even churches attest to the existence of a pattern of interrelationships between local and central. Clearly, communities must be viewed not only from the perspective of their microcosmic dimensions (horizontal ties) but also from a macrocosmic perspective (vertical ties). The macrocosmic perspective stresses the dependence of community units on other units in the larger society.

As we discussed, in the horizontal community model:

> Individuals and families who share the same locality associate in neighborly fashion with others in the immediate vicinity. A unifying basis of interest underlying such association is that of the common locality. . . . Such important functions as production and distribution, socialization of the young, social control, and mutual support are performed largely within the locality by such relatively undifferentiated groups as family and neighborhood. . . . The families share a common interest in that they are units of economic production, as in the earlier American preindustrial rural community. (Warren, 1963, pp. 59–60)

The illustrations selected for this chapter highlight a variety of aspects of small-town life and relationships ranging from religious feelings to personalism in the small-town judiciary.

In the illustration (see excerpt, p. 75), Kathleen Norris (1993) perceives small-town people as generous, even when they practice the ancient art of gossiping. In a later excerpt in this chapter (see p. 98), small-town religion and the communal ties of gossip make for a less benevolent situation. Both illustrations foster impressions that are within the realm of possibility, the first generous, the second punitive. As students of small communities, we need to understand that people can make positive and negative use of any activity, including gossip—which is, after all, a way of disseminating news in small towns.

In the vertical model,

> [the] contrasting situation is a differentiation of interests among people in the locality and differential association based on the respective interests. The individual often turns away from other individuals in his immediate locality and associates himself with individuals from other localities on the basis of selective interests. (Warren, 1963, pp. 59–60)

In the early 1960s, Warren felt, as industrialization and urban growth pervaded the United States the vertical model was becoming far more

[Text continues on page 77]

The Holy Use of Gossip

> It is the responsibility of writers to listen to gossip and pass it on. It is the way all storytellers learn about life.
>
> —Grace Paley

> If there's anything worth calling theology, it is listening to people's stories, listening to them and cherishing them.
>
> —Mary Pellauer

I once scandalized a group of North Dakota teenagers who had been determined to scandalize me. Working as an artist-in-residence in their school for three weeks, I happened to hit prom weekend. Never much for proms in high school, I helped decorate, cutting swans out of posterboard and sprinkling them with purple glitter as the school gym was festooned with lavender and silver crepe paper streamers.

On Monday morning a group of the school outlaws was gossiping in the library, just loud enough for me to hear, about the drunken exploits that had taken place at a prairie party in the wee hours after the dance: kids meeting in some remote spot, drinking beer and listening to car stereos turned up loud, then, near dawn, going to one girl's house for breakfast. I finally spoke up and said, "See, it's like I told you: the party's not over until you've told the stories. That's where all writing starts." They looked up at me, pretending that it bothered them that I'd heard.

"And," I couldn't resist adding, "everyone knows you don't get piss-drunk and then eat scrambled eggs. If you didn't know it before, you know it now." "You're not going to write about that, are you?" one girl said, her eyes wide. "I don't know," I replied, "I might. It's all grist for the mill."

When my husband and I first moved to Dakota, people were quick to tell us about an eccentric young man who came from back East and gradually lost his grip on reality. He shared a house with his sheep until relatives came and took him away. "He was a college graduate," someone would always add, looking warily at us as if to say, we know what can happen to Easterners who are too well educated. This was one of the first tales to go into my West River treasure-house of stories. It was soon joined by the story of the man who shot himself to see what it felt like. He hit his lower leg and later said that while he didn't feel anything for a few seconds, after that it hurt like hell.

There was Rattlesnake Bill, a cowboy who used to carry rattlers in a paper sack in his pickup truck. If you didn't believe him, he'd put his hand in without looking and take one out to show you. One night Bill limped into a downtown bar on crutches. A horse he was breaking had dragged him for about a mile, and he was probably lucky to be alive. He'd been knocked out, he didn't know for how long, and when he regained consciousness he had crawled to his house and changed clothes to come to town. Now Bill thought he'd drink a little whiskey for the pain. "Have you been to a doctor?" friends asked. "Nah, whiskey'll do."

Later that night at the steak house I managed to get Bill to eat something — most of my steak, as it turned out, but he needed it more than I. The steak was rare, and that didn't sit well with Bill. A real man eats his steak well done. But when I said, "What's the matter, are you too chicken to eat rare meat?" he gobbled it down. He slept in his pickup that night, and someone managed to get him to a doctor the next day. He had a broken pelvis. . . .

There was the woman who nursed her husband through a long illness. A dutiful farm daughter and ranch wife, she had never experienced life on her own. When she was widowed, all the town spoke softly about "poor Ida." But when "poor Ida" kicked up her heels and, entering a delayed adolescence in her fifties, dyed her hair, dressed provocatively, and went dancing more than once a week at the steak house, the sympathetic cooing of the gossips turned to outrage. The woman at the center of the storm hadn't changed; she was still an innocent, bewildered by the calumny now directed at her. She lived it down and got herself a steady boyfriend, but she still dyes her hair and dresses flashy. I'm grateful for the color she adds to the town. . . .

We are interrelated in a small town, whether or not we're related by blood. We know without thinking about it who owns what car; inhabitants of a town as small as a monastery learn to recognize each other's footsteps in the hall. Story is a safety valve for people who live as intimately as that; and I would argue that gossip done well can be a holy thing. It can strengthen communal bonds. . . .

Gossip can help us give a name to ourselves. The most revealing section of the weekly Lemmon Leader is the personal column in the classified ads, where people express thanks to those who helped. . . .

Often these ads are quite moving, written from the heart. The parents of a small boy recently thanked those who had remembered their son with:

> prayers, cards, balloons, and gifts, and gave moral support to the rest of the family when Ty underwent surgery. . . . It's great to be home again in this caring community, and our biggest task now is to get Ty to eat more often and larger amounts. Where else but Lemmon would we find people who would stop by and have a bedtime snack and milk with Ty or provide good snacks just to help increase his caloric intake, or a school system with staff that take the time to make sure he eats his extra snacks. May God Bless all of you for caring about our "special little" boy—who is going to gain weight!

No doubt it is the vast land surrounding us, brooding on the edge of our consciousness, that makes it necessary for us to call such attention to human activity. Publicly asserting, as do many of these ads, that we live in a caring community helps us keep our hopes up in a hard climate or hard times, and gives us a sense of identity.

Privacy takes on another meaning in such an environment, where you are asked to share your life, humbling yourself before the common wisdom, such as it is. Like everyone else, you become public property and come to accept things that city people would consider rude. . . .

At its deepest level, small-town gossip is about how we face matters of life and death. We see the gossip of earlier times, the story immortalized in ballads such as "Barbara Allen," lived out before our eyes as a young man obsessively in love with a vain young woman nearly self-destructs. We also see how people heal themselves. One of the bravest people I know is a young mother who sewed and embroidered exquisite baptismal clothes for her church with the memorial money she received when her first baby died. When she gave birth to a healthy girl a few years later, the whole town rejoiced. (pp. 69–76)

SOURCE: Excerpts from *Dakota*. Copyright © 1993 by Kathleen Norris. Reprinted by permission of Ticknor & Fields/Houghton Mifflin Co.

[Text continued from page 74]

prevalent. In the 1980s and 1990s, in spite of a national movement toward devolution to more local units, as new technologies became more pervasive vertical linkages were intensified. While many vertical linkages stress control and standardization, many others facilitate the very existence of dispersed communities. Of course, because technologies require an appropriate infrastructure, smaller places might still have to rely on more traditional ways of relating.

Be that as it may, the influence of communication networks has been marked. Hyman, Gamm, and Shingler (1995) discuss the "teleological" society in rural areas and small towns:

> A teleological society would use the new technologies differently than would a super industrial society. For instance, a super industrial society would use the new technologies to increase surveillance and control of citizens, whereas a teleological society would use new technologies to broaden opportunities for participation in political and social arenas. Such applications are certainly important for rural citizens, who often find that the distance of their communities effectively excludes them from state and national politics. It is more difficult for rural Americans to attend speeches, rallies, and other forms of political participation that are historically urban centered. The increased control and decentralization of both economic and political units of the teleological paradigm places greater responsibility at local levels. Modern technology can increase the capacity of local governments and local industries to manage their communities and companies. . . . Decision support and expert systems can enhance the capacity of smaller units to manage the planning and governance of local organizations. Improvements in decision-making technologies can thus strengthen the managerial capacities of rural governments and organizations. (p. 100)

Discussing the influence of new means of communication in rural Australia, Cheers (1996) recognizes how in a continent or a country with a large land mass, communication technology has changed how rural people do many tasks, from agricultural work to reaching markets to accessing human and medical services. He points out that new networks have made it possible for communication-based industries to move into rural areas. However, Cheers also notes how some of the same technologies have eroded the primary networks that characterized the countryside. Thus, the vertical linkages that tie communities to the outside continue to increase, though for different reasons and in very different patterns from those that might have been anticipated in the 1960s.

Ties with the larger world through the Internet or any other asynchronous system challenge many of the values and assumptions of rural living. Communication through these means is disembodied; people talking to each other do not need to "know" who the other person is, whether the person comes from the "right" or "wrong" side of the tracks, whether the person occupies a "respectable" place in society, or even whether the other is a real person or a devised persona (Mitchell, 1995). Through the new modes of communication, anomie is not to be feared; it is, in fact, sought. Local ties are diminished. Global ties become the norm. Quite a modern rural dilemma!

From a social-welfare perspective, vertical ties were always emphasized. The legacy in social welfare was of the Depression years, when local communities were overwhelmed by the intensity of need. Moreover, against the background of the 1960s, when so many social programs were instituted, social workers favored the infusion of central resources, often at the expense of local control. Strong vertical ties accommodated the larger role of benevolent and affluent forces outside the community.

Even today, local decisions in the social welfare field are tied to state and federal institutions. Consequently, local communities are particularly vulnerable to the infiltration of outside forces, rewards, and deterrents. Most social workers believe that local communities, although autonomous, are heavily influenced by the values prevailing in the culture at large, by outside political trends, and by policy actions of state or federal government. Today, community livelihoods are deeply affected by the decisions of large conglomerates, the demands of outside markets, and the regulatory powers of national organizations. Most economists would agree that, after the Industrial Revolution, the destinies of local folk became intimately related to the destinies of their nation and the world. With the advent of asynchronicity, relationships and communications are often tied to a disembodied global audience. However, the existence of vertical ties does not mean that local communities have lost their meaning or importance in the lives of their citizens.

Current Considerations for Practitioners

In much of contemporary social science literature, *place*, undeniably an important dimension of cohesiveness, is not always viewed as a prerequisite of community. Clark (1973) suggested that "to argue that place influences community is a very different matter from assuming that certain geographical units or areas are synonymous with it" (p. 398). Yet though place cannot be viewed as the single ingredient of community, it is still an important element.

An examination of a rekindled interest in community as a unit of social service intervention across the nation reveals that, for psychological, identity, and practical reasons, community members are restricted by place considerations. While the development of linkages among interest groups, support groups, etc., through electronic means has enhanced vertical ties, place is still very important for the most vulnerable populations: the young, the old, and the poor. In a personal communication (October 20, 1982), Roy Buck, a professor from the Pennsylvania State University, suggested that vertical ties alone cannot build communities. "Community organization, emphasizing as it does collective autonomy and responsibility, interdependency and individual insufficiency, faces people away from vertical and formalized systems of authority and service." He added that if one sees community "as an alternative to emphases on individualism, self-sufficiency and mass society ordered by comprehensive legal, rational authority," then community is by definition local. Given these presuppositions, community organization is for Buck "a strategy for translating vertically sponsored programs into the fabric of day-to-day community life. As community organization matures, the vertical dimension (centralization) gives way to increasing reliance on local autonomy. Funding and other resources are generated close to home, so to speak," with community becoming more a horizontal phenomenon. Vertical ties are seen at best as seed from which community building must be generated.

Buck recognized the problems inherent in his position. In the diverse American society, the vertical system is not only strong but often is needed to mitigate the lack of resources in many local settings. In the 1990s there has been a return to the locality as an important component in social service delivery. The decentralization of budgets from federal to state governments, the emphasis placed on the smallest unit of administration, have resulted in an emphasis on local communities that is sometimes but not always realistic.

For small-town social workers, the consideration of vertical as well as horizontal ties is essential to an understanding of how to proceed in certain circumstances. Although some social service projects will quickly capture the local imagination, others might more effectively draw support from the external ties of the community. One of the most delicate assessments a practitioner must make is deciding when to reach outside the community for support. As Buck pointed out, vertical ties may weaken horizontal ones. Yet practitioners often must seek vertical support for funding, expertise, or simply legitimacy, particularly when the issues are controversial. Although most organizing efforts in the long run must rely on local support, they can at times be effectively expedited by outside trends.

The mutuality of influence and the delicate balances between the local community and the larger society, between the microcosm of the locality and the macrocosm of the nation, are apparent. All communities have identifiable cadres of both local and cosmopolitan influential people. The local powerful actors will facilitate horizontal linkages, intracommunity relationships; the cosmopolitan influential people will be instrumental in making the transition from the local unit to the society at large, whether it be state, region, country, culture, or world. Though new communication systems have enhanced the global connections of local influences, even now some prefer to circumscribe their sphere of influence to more local face-to-face relationships.

The local practitioner stands at the point where the vertical system meets the horizontal. "This is the point where policy is transformed into action. It is here that the worker must perform the magic of 'taking a recipe and baking a cake'" (personal communication with R. Buck, professor from the Pennsylvania State University, October 20, 1982). Social workers face concrete problems that carry the unique mark of the community in which they arise. They need to understand the intangible as well as tangible factors that shape the characters of their communities. They need to be as interested in the horizontal ties binding community members as in the vertical ties connecting professionals with the social provisions they interpret.

Social workers thus need to be skilled applied ethnographers. They need to be able to see the world and assess its problems the way those whom they are trying to serve would—not necessarily to agree with them, but to define clearly the present point of reference in the sociocultural mosaic.

Personalism in Horizontal Ties

One of the characteristics of small communities is that they maintain strong horizontal ties. People there must perforce relate to one another on fairly close terms. There is not enough distance for the kind of impersonality that might be possible in larger cities. Yet the lack of distance necessitates a level of intimacy that aids survival. One way or another, people are more likely to get involved in what professionals like to call "dual relationships," various roles converging. The professional cannot be detached from the client, for the client or customer might be a professional at times. The grocer can be a merchant today but a parent tomorrow, a scout leader the next day, and even a priest or minister on another occasion. The local official can perform the tasks of a functionary one day and the personal tasks of a citizen the next.

The interconnection of individuals may be most evident among those professions where confidentiality and detachment are valued in the name of objectivity. Among social workers, the assumption is that if the worker knows a client on personal terms, the worker cannot be "objective" about that client. This is not always the case; personalism has been the object of much controversy among small-town practitioners. It is almost impossible to find a worker who actually lives in a small town who can claim no knowledge of most clients outside official circumstances.

The same problem arises for members of other professions. An excerpt from the *Dallas Morning News* (see excerpt, "A Question of Judgment," p. 82) illustrates clearly a judge's dilemma. On the one hand, Judge C. C. "Kit" Cooke is viewed by the citizens of the small town as fair, caring, committed to the law, and balanced in his actions. On the other hand, when the interests of a large company were at stake, he was accused of being partial, of having conflicting interests, and of not having met his professional responsibilities. While it is impossible to ascertain what exactly happened, the article illustrates the professional dilemmas quite clearly.

Human services professionals struggling for balance must be realistic in their assessment of dual relationships outside the very big cities, when they are appropriate and when they are not. While the new *Code of Ethics* (National Association of Social Workers [NASW], 1996) does make special provision for people who practice in rural areas, the ethos of the profession tends to safeguard the interests of bureaucracy. Our professional traditions are urban; they require that small-town social workers carefully clarify for themselves their roles vis-a-vis their clients. As the article on Judge Cooke suggests, in the end it is all a matter of good judgment.

In human services professional decision making, rules cannot be substituted for professional decision making and good judgment; rules cannot respond to all the difficulties of relationship that can emerge in small towns. Because complexity often increases in inverse relationship to the size of the unit, a social worker's care in judging how to function in it must increase accordingly.

Minimal Essential Elements of Communal Life

Many of the natural desires of people can be satisfied through communal ties. One is the desire for *solidarity* or cohesiveness—the wish to live in a total and visible collective entity. Another desire is for *engagement*, that is, significance—the wish to confront one's surroundings and find the meaningful extensions of one's ego. Another desire is for *dependence*, that is, security—the wish to satisfy and be satisfied.

[Text continues on page 84]

A Question of Judgment: Small-Town Familiarities Pose Possible Conflicts

When State District Judge C. C. "Kit" Cooke surveyed his Cleburne courtroom at the start of a civil fraud case earlier this year, he saw a familiar face among the lawyers about to make their arguments.

An old friend and former colleague on the bench, John MacLean, was representing the plaintiff, David's Supermarkets of nearby Grandview. That wasn't unusual, though, since Mr. MacLean had argued dozens of cases before Judge Cooke over the years.

In fact, it is rare that the judge doesn't know one or both parties appearing in his court. A popular figure in this small Johnson County town of 22,000 just south of Fort Worth, he is involved in numerous community activities, including Boy Scouts and Little League. So he never thought of announcing his friendship and past business ties with Mr. MacLean, and the trial proceeded.

On Monday, the judge's lapse hit him full force: A visiting judge—sitting in Judge Cooke's own chair—reversed a $211.2 million judgment against the defendant, Fleming Cos. Inc., and ordered a new trial. The ruling was the outgrowth of an attack Fleming launched against Judge Cooke the day after the verdict, claiming his relationship with Mr. MacLean and his client led him to favor their side of the case. The verdict was tainted, the company claimed and demanded Judge Cooke step aside—which he did two days later in a passionate public letter.

The surprising turn in the case is a vivid example of how tough it is for small-town judges to walk the line between friendship and fairness—and how vulnerable they are to attacks on their integrity and impartiality when they do.

Trying cases involving friends is "almost unavoidable or otherwise you would have visiting judges trying every case"—an ex-pensive if not impossible proposition, said Judge John Boyd, a former state district judge who served for years in a small West Texas town. He said he even hears cases involving members of his church. Besides, he and other judges say, it's rare that small-town judges will step aside, simply because they feel they are elected to try cases, not pass them off to other judges. Stepping aside is a subjective matter. It's "really a matter of judgment," he said.

The acid test, judges say, is simply whether or not they believe they can be fair.

But Judge Cooke's predicament shows how difficult answering that question can be in a small town.

David's Supermarkets, a 23-store regional grocery store chain, sued Fleming last year alleging that the wholesaler had pushed David's to the edge of bankruptcy by overcharging. Small, independent chains like David's can't buy products directly from manufacturers and must rely on wholesalers to give them a fair price. David's claimed, among other things, that Fleming did not pass along some of its manufacturers' discounts.

David's lawyers could not have been more pleased to have their case tried just down the road from its corporate headquarters by an area judge and jury. Fleming's lawyers, at the time, didn't object either.

After the jury returned their staggering verdict, however, Fleming staged a Dallas press conference to claim that Judge Cooke was friends with the plaintiff's lawyer, Mr. MacLean, and that 11 years earlier had borrowed $2,985 from David Waldrip, one of the largest shareholders in David's Supermarkets.

Fleming's lawyers, in their argument for a new trial on Monday, repeated their allegations: "The judge had a responsibility to say David Waldrip did me a favor and loaned me money. It's inconceivable to me that didn't happen," said John Hill, a lawyer for Fleming. A judge should avoid even the appearance of impropriety, he argued.

Fleming argued that it didn't know the extent of Judge Cooke's relationships and business deals with the plaintiff and that either the judge or one of David's lawyers had a duty to disclose them.

They pointed to Judge Cooke's letter issued after he removed himself from the case: "Even though it was an oversight, I fully admit that this transaction should have been disclosed. I have no material wealth. I do, however, love the law. I would never do anything that would in any way cast a shadow of a doubt on the integrity and independence of the judiciary."

'I made a mistake'

The judge refused to be interviewed for this story, but one of his close friends, John Harrison, publisher of The Cleburne Eagle News, said that Judge Cooke has been devastated "both professionaly [sic] and personally" by this case. "He takes his job seriously. . . . He told me right after this happened: 'I made a mistake; I wasn't thinking. At the time it never occurred to me.'"

Those who know Judge Cooke, 49, say he is a smart judge, quick-witted and nobody's fool. He drives a Dodge Ram pickup, wears cowboy boots and hat, but no one mistakes him for just a slow-talking country judge.

Last year, he was one of only four judges in the nation asked to lecture New York state judges on how to handle capital murder cases. He was named Cleburne's Citizen of the Year in 1995 and ran unopposed for judge during the last election.

Judge Cooke's problems began years earlier when he and long-time friend Mr. MacLean hit on an idea to help the judge out of some financial problems.

Most of the judge's savings were tied up in his modest brick home that he was having trouble selling. So in 1985, Judge Cooke sold his home to Mr. MacLean for $200,000, and then nine months later Judge Cooke

bought the house back for $300,000. Fleming referred to this transaction as a "property flip."

"Everyone knew about it," said Mr. Harrison, who published a story about the deal. "And these dealings he has had in the past with David Waldrip were a matter of public record in a bankruptcy filing."

Mr. MacLean said that he has known Judge Cooke for 20 years and that Cleburne's two state district judges know most of the lawyers and many of the litigants. "You just can't build a wall between you and the bar. . . . You are allowed to have friends."

The loan owed to Mr. Waldrip and all the judge's other debts were detailed in a September 1989 personal bankruptcy filing after some stock investments collapsed.

Mr. Waldrip said although he was acquainted with Judge Cooke, they "are not friends; we go nowhere together and we belong to nothing together. I might see him at the courthouse, and I know who he is."

He said a loan officer at First National Bank asked him to personally loan the judge the money. "I never even talked to him when that loan was made. They made it read like we were close friends. . . . It was nothing, $2,900. That is nothing."

A change forever

In Johnson County with a population of about 100,000, for example, there are only two state district judges. None of the state's legal organizations contacted keep data on the number of times state district judges step down from a case.

Mr. MacLean, a former state district judge in Cleburne, said his brother-in-law frequently tried cases in his court and "never did I hear anyone complain. It never became an issue. I think it's that way in all small towns. When you are in that courtroom you are not at a social gathering or bar banquet. The rules change as soon as you enter the courtroom."

State District Judge Wayne Bridewell, Johnson County's other state judge, said a judge does not decide a case based on who the litigants are but rather on the facts and the applicable law.

Judge Bridewell said that although he often knows the parties to a lawsuit, he'll step aside no more than two or three times a year. And in those instances, it's because he has direct knowledge about the cases.

"Normally I wouldn't even bring it up (knowing one of the lawyers) unless there was a question about it," said Judge Bridewell. "A judge in a small county wants people to know they have had their day in court and they have been fairly dealt with whether the judge has ruled in their favor or not."

But Fleming's lawyers cite several examples of what they consider to be unfair treatment by Judge Cooke.

"These issues raise the suspicion of partiality, and judges are supposed to avoid even the appearance of impropriety," said Fleming's spokesman Shane Boyd.

Supporters of Judge Cooke say over the years, many friends of the judge have come into his court only to find the judge just as tough on them as those he doesn't know. For example, William T. Padon, who has known the judge for years, said during a 1981 divorce proceeding the judge ordered him to give some 70 percent of his estate

to his estranged wife. The fact that Mr. Padon and the judge were friends and fellow members of the local Masonic lodge seemed to make no difference, he said.

"I think he was fair to both of us," said Mr. Padon. "I think he's a good judge, and I think he would have been all right in the Fleming case."

No matter the outcome of this case, Mr. MacLean and others say the criminal justice system in Cleburne and Judge Cooke specifically have been changed forever. He said judges and lawyers in Johnson County will become a lot more formal with each other, or as one lawyer said: "less friendly." There will be, Mr. MacLean said, a different attitude, because many of the county's lawyers and judges feel like this case has cast a shadow on all of them.

As for Judge Cooke, he said: "I'm sure he will isolate himself more, which I'm not sure is healthy. This has weighed heavily on him because his integrity has been questioned, and that is really all you have, your reputation."

SOURCE: Deener, B. (1996, June 26). A question of judgment. *Dallas Morning News*, p. 1D. Reprinted with permission of the *Dallas Morning News*.

[Text continued from page 81]

The essential elements of communal life are revealed through the lay as well as the scholarly literature. These elements exist whether social workers believe that community requires an interactional space or whether they stress the non-spatial elements. Clark (1973), after detailed discussions of those elements, concluded that "the strength of community within any given group is determined by the degree to which its members experience both a sense of solidarity and a sense of significance" (p. 409). According to Clark, those essential elements of community were recognized in MacIver's early assertions (1924) that "life is essentially and always communal life. Every living thing is born into community and owes its life to community" (p. 209). Community is not circumscribed to the sphere of social interactions; it permeates the visceral and psychological spheres of life. "Community is. . . sentiment," MacIver said (1924, p. 209); although the term sentiment might not be entirely unambiguous, it seems to be the best available to describe the phenomenon of community because it emphasizes the importance of members' self-perception rather than observers' perception.

Because these essential elements of community life are clearly manifested in the interactions of the residents of small communities, they cannot be ignored by human services practitioners. The elements are *solidarity*, *significance*, and *security* (Clark, 1973). Although *solidarity*—cohesiveness or "we-ness"—can be found in both large and small units, in place and non-place communities, the degree to which it can be observed in the small town is often greater. Residents of small towns speak of "we, the people of Clover Hill" or "we, the friends of Township Square" as if there could be no question about the authoritativeness of the "we."

A sense of *significance* must permeate those manifestations of collective behavior that help perpetuate the idea of community. Acts such as public citizen awards, both in towns and communal associations, celebrate the significance of individual contributions. Perhaps the search for significance has sparked the continued movement of citizens to small towns and villages where undramatic contributions to community are recognized by their fellow citizens. A sense of *security* is derived from this mutuality of communal relationships, from the familiarity of the environment, and, more obviously, from the affection and support of friends and neighbors.

However, the emphasis on communal behavior in contemporary society has been cyclical. Thus solidarity, significance, and security often have been hidden behind individualistic strivings. As early as 1976, Philip Slater wrote a critique of the American obsession with privacy, individualism, and freedom from interdependence that he had observed in the 1950s and early 1960s and to which he saw the "flower children" movement of the 1960s responding. Slater pointed out contradictions that faced the American of the 1950s and 1960s that rendered the average citizen somewhat schizophrenic. On the one hand, Americans pursued competition, success, and material gains; on the other, they sought associations, freshness of air, and communal backyard talk.

> Suburbanites who philosophized over the back fence with complete sincerity about their "dog-eat-dog world," and what-is-it-all-for, and you-can't-take-it-with-you, and success-doesn't-make-you-happy-it-just-gives-you-ulcers-and-a-heart-condition, were enraged in the six-

ties when their children began to pay serious attention to these ideas. To the young this seemed hypocritical, but if adults didn't feel these things they wouldn't have had to fight them so vigorously. The exaggerated hostility that young people aroused in the "flower child" era argues that the life they led was highly seductive to middle-aged Americans. (Slater, 1976, pp. 10–11)

The elements of romanticized village life that seduced the American middle class probably account for the popularity of such British village novels as those of E. F. Benson (1977), Agatha Christie (1950, 1963), and E. M. Delafield (1931). The recent fascination with James Herriot's "vet" stories (1985) set in the Yorkshire dales illustrates this point well.

The contradictory streaks in the American character were obvious: Individualism was in a constant tug-of-war with the desire for community. Many predicted that the emphasis on individual competition of the 1950s would result in a reversal of philosophy in the 1970s. In the 1980s, many sociologists predicted that the emphasis on individualism and the relative egocentrism of the early 1980s would bring another about-face in the 1990s.

In 1986, Schorr admonished that it was important to move our society toward community. Corporatism, in his view, was sharpening class conflicts.

These are developments that most Americans would surely wish to avoid. But, even if they do not come to pass, it is important to undo the increasing fragmentation of our society (alienation and anomie, sociologists say) which is expressed in passivity, in violence turned inward—suicide and family abuse, for example—and in crime. (Schorr, 1986, p. 20)

To some extent, society was paying a hard price for impersonality, in many more ways than had been predicted. Slater (1976) had suggested that collectivism has always been "the more usual lot of humans. Most people in most societies have lived and died in stable communities that took for granted the subordination of the individual to the welfare of the group. The aggrandizement of the individual at the expense of his neighbors was simply a crime" (Slater, 1976, p. 9). Etzioni (1989), proposing an expansion of the communal perspective, contrasted the "I" model of relating with the "we" model wherein the individual is perceived as interdependent with the community.

The most pervasive common elements of community are not just the product of social scientists' empirical observations but have been stated by many observers of the human condition. Interdependence is an important biological, psychological, and sociological concept. What community provides is the opportunity for satisfying the need for affiliation by living interdependently. Besides, the smaller the community, the less "caring" and "significance" that can be purchased as services and the more horizontal ties and interdependence become central. Norris (1996), writing about Benedictine monks, points out that living in community is still an experiment, even for those who have done it away from the tensions of the mundane world, such as monks. The struggle to live up to communal values, to be cohesive, to derive significance, to be healthily interdependent, entails constant acts of discovery. As a serendipitous welfare lesson, consider what St. Benedict has to say about what it means to live communally in a humane way: "Whoever needs less should thank God and not be distressed . . . ; whoever needs more should feel humble because of his weakness, not self-important because of the kindness shown him. In this way, all members will be at peace" (Norris, 1996, p. 19). Reviewing the contemporary philosophical foundations of social welfare and redistributive justice, we encounter the same idea in Marx: To each according to his need; from each according to his means.

Addressing contemporary concerns about raising children, Hillary Clinton (1996) highlighted the elements of cohesiveness and security needed to bring up the next generation. The very title of the book, taken from an old African proverb, "It takes a village," brings together the essential elements of solidarity, engagement, and interdependence.

And The Remote Villages Survive . . .

The small-town revival is not just an American phenomenon. In many parts of the world, small towns retain their importance, providing the opportunity for making a living to those who are strong and capable of surviving their remoteness. As we have discussed, the English village has always played a prominent role in English imagery and literature, sung by poets and novelists as the idyllic place where country life reaches its pinnacle. In fact, efforts to conserve the village and its environment preceded current environmental efforts. The more remote villages in Scotland and Ireland did not enjoy the same reputation. And those that lived on mining activities or that housed mills where textiles were produced often declined very rapidly with the demise of those industries.

The English village today, whether in the South or the North, has often been transformed. From the quaint 18th and 19th century landscape that provided a means of livelihood for many working people, it has become gentrified, and often affordable only by the very rich. The same

situation has occurred in the more densely populated parts of Scotland—
for example, the quaint fishing villages of the East Neuk in Fife, which
have experienced a rebirth and considerable gentrification.

In the more remote parts of Scotland, this has not been the case. In
spite of the boom caused by the discovery of oil in the North Sea, many
islands in the north of Scotland retain their crofting economy, which makes
for a very precarious life (Chapman & Lloyd, 1996). In a recent story
about the Orkney Islands, that remote chain due north from John o Groats
into the North Sea, Bill Bryson (1998), writing for *National Geographic*,
captured the beauty of the land and the resiliency of its citizens. The
Orkneys still carry the rhythm of life in very remote centers. Similar
rhythms could be documented in parts of Canada and Australia, to speak
only of the industrial, English-speaking world. In addition to remoteness,
or perhaps because of it, the strong horizontal ties that bind people in
villages become very apparent. People in remote areas often view the world
in different terms. Bryson, for example, tells of one Orkney citizen who
did not consider his place lonely because "the postman came every day"
(1998, p. 50). People rely on each other for very basic services and human
contact. They must rely on each other to survive the adversities of in-
clement weather or poor crops or lost animals or plain loneliness. A conversation between Bryson and the minister of the Orkney Cathedral, St.
Magnus, confirms this sense of separateness:

> "Oh, yes, it's a different world here," he agreed without hesitation. "And
> mostly in good ways. I came here from a district in Glasgow so rough that
> when people went to bed at night they locked their inside doors as well as
> the outside ones. Here when they talk about crime prevention, they mean
> not leaving your car keys in the ignition overnight. We are also a long
> way from the seat of power here—closer to Norway than to London—
> which contributes to a sense of separateness." (Bryson, 1998, p. 50)

Some time ago, I spent some time on the Isle of Barra, another island
in the Outer Hebrides on a remote chain in the Munch. The social worker
on Barra served about 3,000 people dispersed in two or three settlements.
The horizontal ties that bound people were evident, not only in the way
outsiders were viewed—the presence of any new individual on the island
was noted and actively welcomed or rejected—but also on the functioning of the social worker. Individuals knew where she lived, knew what her
husband did, relied on her for social work services and general overall
caring, and relied on the capabilities of her family to further support the
citizens. On the other hand, she was able to rely on them, ensuring that

her children would always be cared for by the watchful eye of the community and that her needs would be met in very interdependent ways (Martinez-Brawley, 1986).

In a recent work, Burnett (1996) reviewed the complexities involved in defining who is an "incomer" and who is not defined as one in Uist, another remote island in the Outer Hebrides. Her work focused on women incomers and their identities, particularly as they attempt to reconcile their "status of difference and legitimate sense of belonging in the rural community" (p. 18).

Remoteness as a dimension in social work services and as an important variable that affects how people are bonded is also addressed by Cheers (1999) in his book about social care in Australia. Cheers defines remoteness as a multidimensional variable incorporating a number of elements such as limited access to larger population centers, public and private services, and public and private decision-making processes that affect the lives of the residents of the community. He also cites the lack of solid physical infrastructure (roads, water, power, etc.), the limitations of lifestyle opportunities, and the lack of opportunities and services to improve the quality of life of people (Cheers, 1999).

In continental Europe, the village has always been part of the life experience for most people. In Spain, for example, most city dwellers hail from villages or provincial towns and often return to them every week or month to visit relatives, oversee ancestral houses—be they humble or prosperous—have Sunday meals with older relatives who have stayed back, and experience the close networks of small towns (Martinez-Brawley, 1991). In France and Italy, countries with strong agricultural ties, village life has always been important to culture. What is notable is that in recent years, the villages of continental Europe—particularly in Spain, France, and Italy—have attracted many newcomers from foreign countries, including affluent retirees and intellectuals (Martinez-Brawley, 1986b). A similar situation can be seen in Mexico, where remote towns like Alamo or San Miguel de Allende have become favorite spots for American citizens longing for a simpler or more intimate life.

While these trends are never devoid of real challenges and contradictions that social workers must address, they demonstrate a general fascination with the days of more manageable environments and a way of life closer to the soil. Those readers who want to experience how fiction writers have captured this new and rapidly growing movement of revival of villages in Continental Europe can read, among many others, the works of Mayes (1997), Mayle (1994), or Parks (1993). These works provide delightful entertainment, cross-cultural experiences, and a satisfying sense that even the remote villages are resilient enough to endure the changes of coming as well as past centuries.

> The ideal approach to my new hometown is first to see the Etruscan tombs down in the flatland below the town. There are tombs from 800 to 200 B.C. near the train station in Camucia and on the road to Foiano, where the custodian never likes the tip. Maybe he's in a bad mood because he spends eerie nights. His small farmhouse, with a bean patch and yard-roaming chickens, coexists with this *tomba* that would appear strangely primordial in the moonlight. A little uphill, a rusted yellow sign is all that points to the so-called tomb of Pythagoras. I pull over and walk along the stream until I reach a short lane, cypress lined, leading to the tomb. There is a gate but it doesn't look as if anyone ever bothers to close it. So there it is, just sitting around a stone platform. Niches for the upright sarcophagi look like the shrine at the bottom of my driveway. The ceiling is partially gone but enough of the curve is left that I can see the dome shape. I'm standing inside a structure someone put together at least two thousand years ago. (Mayes, 1997, p. 146)

Communities as Illustrative Microcosms

For generations, anthropologists have studied communities in primitive villages and other environments. In the anthropological tradition, and probably because of the nature of field observations, the anthropologist has tended to identify community with a place in which a whole array of activities—social, economic, and political—are coterminous with defined territorial boundaries. Pelly-Effrat (1974) suggested that writers of this orientation make a "claim (whether or not it is explicit) that the community under study represents a microcosm of the total society or some important segment of the society" (p. 6).

Community as a microcosm of the society at large has been one of the respected research traditions of sociology as well as anthropology. In the United States, this orientation was prevalent among sociologists in the 1920s when Lynd and Lynd (1929) published *Middletown*. It remained popular among British sociologists—Williams (1964) and Pahl (1966) both shared it. With an anthropological bent, Frankenberg (1957) produced a number of landmark studies about a small town in Wales and about British communities. He emphasized that special activities such as weddings and christenings bound the communal microcosm.

Architects and urban planners, too, have used this approach to study communities, particularly "planned" communities. The very idea of a planned or a utopian community arises from the belief that community can be potentially self-contained. Although communities have been studied as microcosms, they still can be influenced by outer community forces. Planned communities and utopias often survive or fail because of outside influences. However, the emphasis of those who study communities as microcosms is on the potential of their microcosmic forces to illustrate, in reduced scale, the gamut of human experiences.

Unfortunately, community studies in sociology were unduly maligned when sociological investigation turned quantitative. Ruth Glass (1966) labeled those qualitative studies "the poor sociologist's substitute for the novel" (p. 148), and as Bell and Newby (1972) reported, "Ruth Glass' criticisms went further than this. She also castigated community studies for their 'innumeracy'" (p. 13)—a lack of figures that bothered the budding scientific sociologists. Yet community studies had extraordinary humanistic and scientific merit. They read like novels, a quality not to be casually dismissed; they documented social history; and they provided accessible blueprints for professional practitioners to follow in their studies of other specific communities.

Community studies in sociology were criticized because of their holistic approach—their tendency to describe all aspects of town life—a tendency that greatly curtailed the possibility of making statistical inferences. However, it is precisely this tendency that renders them useful to social workers, just as novels can teach them a great deal. For example, Keillor's *Lake Wobegon Days* (1985) painted a microcosm of human existence in a small community.

Non–social scientists are in fact making explicit their interest in the notion of community as a microcosm of society. Searching for a community where he could find a variety of social dimensions on which to base his novel *Hometown*, Peter Davis (1982) visited the chief of the Demographic Statistics Branch of the Population Division of the U.S. Census Bureau:

> Tell me [he said to the chief], where can I go to combine categories of social research with techniques of storytelling? Where I can observe activities the way an anthropologist might, as Robert and Helen Lynd did in *Middletown*, and then tell about them as Sherwood Anderson did in *Winesburg, Ohio*? Stories of marriage and morals, work and leisure, politics, crime, punishment, religion, caste and class. Stories of real people

using not only fact but fantasy, not only information but impression, attitude, legend—diverse tidings that disclose particular truths in a community. (p. 10)

After much thought and search in the catacombs of the Census Bureau, the leading demographer responded:

> "You have to find a place," [the demographer] said, "big enough to have everything its people need and small enough so you can figure out what the hell is going on." The town should be northern enough to be industrial, southern enough to have a gently rural aspect, western enough to have once been on the frontier, eastern enough to have a past. No single integer can ever contain the whole, but it can contain processes that reflect those other integers.
>
> In concluding his story, Davis tells us that having searched most diligently the myriad of Census documents until dark befell the labirynthine nook in the Census building, the demographer finally pronounced, "You could do worse, . . . than to go to Hamilton, Ohio." (p. 11)

The tendency to theorize that urbanization destroys the folk community and that to find community as a microcosm one must avoid totally urbanized centers undergirds traditional community studies. Redfield (1941) exemplified this tendency in *The Folk Culture of the Yucatan* and, as Bell and Newby (1972) criticized, framed his questions so that it appeared that folk societies were necessarily and always more organized than cities. However, social workers and other human services professionals have not suffered from Redfield's tendency. On the contrary, folk (small) communities until recently held no interest for human services professionals, who tended to focus on urban community dynamics. Recently, however, local communities have become more appealing to social workers, who felt their dynamics merited closer scrutiny. Political, economic, and demographic forces, as well as the rebirth of volunteer and self-help local efforts in the provision of social services, have helped expand the interest of social workers and other human services generalists beyond the impersonal parameters of Gesellschaft into the strong networks of Gemeinschaft (Conklin, 1980).

"Community implies having something in common. . . . Those who live in a community have overriding economic interests which are the same or complementary. They work together and also play and pray together. Their common interest in things gives them a common interest in each other" (Frankenburgh, 1966, p. 238). Often, at least for the purposes of study, it is easier to find oneness and complementarity in smaller units. Thus, social science examples of community as a microcosm have tended to focus on small towns.

Many of the selections in this book clearly illustrate that writers have perceived place communities as microcosms of society. Inasmuch as human services workers emphasize the interconnections among the political, economic, educational, and social aspects of community life, they too support the perception that communities are microcosms of the total human experience. As Bell and Newby (1972) aptly stated, community studies of the holistic variety are after "reality" described and analyzed as "totality." They stress a certain style of research, of direct observation and reporting. Viewing community as a microcosm of society implies selecting, perhaps by default, a naturalistic or field-based research method and an interdisciplinary orientation, both of which are beneficial to practice.

Variables as the Focus of Community Research

In addition to those social scientists who have primarily used the ethnographic or field observation approach to community as a microcosm, there are those who have emphasized a single dimension (often called a variable) or several related dimensions. This approach assumes that although many dimensions appear in community, they are not all equally salient in all communities. Thus, some communities might be particularly fruitful for studying community power, others might be propitious for examining social needs, and still others might be excellent for analyzing decision making. This more particularistic approach to the study of communities often gives the neophyte practitioner the impression that, for those investigators, community is not an integrated unit but the juxtaposition of distinct variables of unequal weight.

The study of a single dimension, aspect, or variable in communities, which is common among sociologists and political scientists, is an approach aligned with the positivistic research tradition. In this tradition, knowledge is built through "building-blocks," discreet bricks that add to the edifice of knowledge. Unlike those using the holistic approach, the single variable researcher attempts to understand communities with the lenses of "disinterested scientists, as informer[s] of decision makers, policy makers, and change agents" (Guba & Lincoln, 1994, p. 12). If not used to the exclusion of other perspectives, this approach can also be a useful way to learn about communities. Hunter (1953), for example, looked at his city of study from the perspective of its power structure. He examined its *elitism*—the pyramidal distribution of power and decision making in the community, in which a few people at the top influence decisions in many spheres of life. Political scientist Dahl (1961) isolated *pluralism*—an urban pattern of decision making in which many influential people on equal footing in the community strata influence decisions, but only in their own specialized areas of operation.

Wellstone (1978), in a study of Rice County, Minnesota, criticized the lack of democratic pluralistic decision making in small communities. Unfortunately, while this is true, studies that focus on democratic decision making through majority rule often fail to see, or overtly ignore, the consensual elements of decision-making in small towns. On the other hand, in the past, leaders often spoke of consensus when what they really had was the approval only of the elite. Current consensus tends to reflect broader participation, even in small towns. It becomes quickly evident that in complex social situations, single variables are hard to isolate. There is an attenuating factor in every situation that cannot be ignored. Yet, for positivists, more comprehensive pictures are attained only cumulatively, through the analysis of isolated variables. Wellstone (1978) uses the single variable approach, but his search for the distribution of power within a rural community leads him to more holistic conclusions.

Pelly-Effrat (1974) warned that it is more fruitful to conceive of community as a "multidimensional ordinal variable" (p. 21)—that is, several factors compose a community. In attempting to understand community through studies that emphasize specific variables, social workers should keep Pelly-Effrat's admonition in mind and not be misled into thinking that the single variable under consideration itself represents the "community-ness" of the unit being analyzed.

It is important for all human services practitioners to study power, authority, and influence within communities. The implications of these notions for service delivery are obvious and fundamental. Yet community social workers must remember that, although community decisions might be based on power relationships, not all community behaviors are. History, traditions, idiosyncrasies, beliefs, prejudices, and geographic and environmental factors all converge to influence the outcomes of communal events.

Practitioners can seldom afford to subscribe to single definitions. They need to look at their small towns and villages from at least six perspectives, asking many questions to determine what to assess.

- Is the community-of-mind coterminous with a place, and if so, what are its boundaries? The importance of locality should not be under-

or overestimated. "Community-ness" cannot be imposed on localities; it develops through the exercise of relationships through time.

- What are the systemic ties of the community? How strong are the horizontal or local ties in the political, economic, educational, service, and other fields? How affected is the community by external forces (vertical ties)? Because the small-community practitioner in the helping fields might need to strengthen the horizontal ties, it will be important to determine specific areas of social interaction where such efforts are likely to be fruitful. This might require identifying the strongest horizontal ties or the weakest vertical ones.

- How does the community rate in terms of cohesiveness, engagement, and interdependence among its members? What does the sense of belonging do for individuals in the community? Practitioners need to consider solidarity, sentiment, and significance.

- How holistic are communal relationships? Are communal activities derived from a view of the community as a microcosm? If so, what kind of picture can be painted of this microcosm?

- How has this community developed through the centuries or the decades? How evident is the local or regional mark in its development? How unique is its background? Are its physical characteristics congruent with the current patterns of interaction of its members?

- What are the specific dimensions or variables that could be looked at to create a full picture? For example, are power relationships so obvious or important that they deserve special study? What about patterns of social class interaction? In most small communities, power and class relationships can be very strong, but the historical forces, properly understood, will shed more light than mere surface analysis.

All in all, practitioners must consider all these ingredients in assessing the nature of their small communities and identifying the forces that will affect their interventions.

Small-Town Religion

The importance of religion and the church in small communities is well documented (Larson, 1978; Levenberg, 1976). For example, in New England, historically "the minister had a powerful role to play in the town. This presence was required by law, and if a minister had not actually been a leader in the town's founding, the town made it its first order of business to bring in a suitable person" (Lingeman, 1980, p. 42). Although in the early New England towns the church and the minister, as moral guardians of the community, were part of the social hierarchy of the town and constituted a powerful judiciary, in the modern small town, church and minister constitute only informal sources of community sanction.

The church and religion took on different personalities in different parts of the United States because of the historical forces that shaped their establishment. The early Puritan churches in New England "banned music and other trappings of popishness; the congregation sat rigidly upright . . . as waves of scholarly rhetoric about divine love and eternal damnation rolled out over them from the pulpit" (Lingeman, 1980, p. 42). But not all church life in the early New England town was easily controlled. Quarrels often arose over money, the seating of parishioners, and the degree of moral enforcement the minister could exert upon his congregation. Yet dissenters had little choice but to conform or move away. Even after the most cruel witch hunts had passed, dissenters were not viewed benevolently (Lingeman, 1980).

The Southern church, however, flourished under different circumstances. Unlike the settlers of New England, who were steeped in Puritan Congregationalist ideals, the colonists of Virginia brought with them the established Church of England. The setting was more elaborate. There were parishes and vestries. These colonists did not make town and congregation one, as the Puritans did in New England (Lingeman, 1980).

As time went on, initial characteristics developed into differences. New Englanders for a long time continued to legislate "sin" through temporal laws; public morality was often linked to religion. In the South, "vices" like alcohol and tobacco were more tolerated, although Southerners were "prone to revival-meeting purgation" (Lingeman, 1980, p. 75), a tradition revived in the contemporary prose of Valerie Sayers (1987) in *Due East*.

The excerpt from Sayers's novel (see page 98) is highly symbolic, in many ways a caricature of what many perceive to be small-town religion. Sayers expertly captures the tone of a revivalist southern church.

The story in *Due East* is uncomplicated. Mary Faith Rapple, the narrator and central character, a sad 15-year-old young woman, lives alone with her father, for whom she keeps house. Mary Faith's parents were religious people, Baptists, who had always conformed to the rather strict mores of their religious community. Early in the story, Mary Faith gets pregnant by the adopted son of a Roman Catholic family. The youth kills himself without knowing about Mary Faith's predicament. Jesse Rapple, Mary Faith's father, prefers to believe that the father is Stephen Dugan, another Roman Catholic who employs Mary Faith to help in adult education classes. Mary Faith defiantly claims to be immaculate and refuses to be "helped out" of her situation.

When Jesse finally reconciles himself to Mary Faith's pregnancy, he wants to do what is right and what his devout Baptist wife would have done. He asks Mary Faith to get dressed up and takes her to church. Although Sayers focuses perhaps too heavily on the punitive aspects of small-town religion, she has captured the imagery and cadences of a sermon in a revivalist small-town church.

The Midwestern and Western churches had a different origin. Bender (1978) suggested that by the time the West began to be settled, the Ordinance of 1787 and the U.S. Constitution had established freedom of religion, so "people of a town could set up a church in any of the religious faiths they fancied" (Lingeman, 1980, p. 115). The multiplicity of faiths resulted in quarrels and discontent, but the ease with which new towns could be settled relieved the "pressure-cooker effect of . . . Puritan theocracy" (Lingeman, 1980, p. 115). As time went on, the westward movement was a community-building movement (Bender, 1978). Men and women moved West in the company of kin and friends, often from the same place of origin. Frequently, churches and other voluntary associations provided the glue necessary to hold individuals together in community. "Churches provided essentially uniform standards for behavior and community participation that could be, and were, replicated in town after town in the Middle West . . . . To a considerable extent . . . the churches were at once centers of religious and social life, advocates of public order, and schools for group and community leadership" (Bender, 1978, p. 97).

Many of these historic religious orientations are found in contemporary small towns, as the revivalist orientation of the fictitious sermon Sayers (1987) uses (pp. 131–143) to show the unbending standards of a Baptist church in a southern community demonstrates. The many stories of Lutherans and Catholics Garrison Keillor (1985) recounts in *Lake Wobegon Days* speak of the ethnic and social ties of religious groups in small Midwestern towns where the church served to preserve remnants of national or ethnic identity brought to America by European immigrants.

At the same time, the church helped create almost instant local communities among people who otherwise would have been strangers. Being a Protestant of one of the prevailing groups or a Roman Catholic gave groups within remote yet thriving communities an "intimate core of experience" (Bender, 1978, p. 97) that would have been hard to create otherwise. The church helped, intentionally or unintentionally, in building strong com-

[Text continues on page 101]

Services

Dr. Beady fussed with his big sleeves and gazed out over the congregation. He looked out of place at the front of the church—everything in First Baptist is fifties-modern, from the walnut-veneer empty cross to the walnut-veneer pulpit that looks like it was made by the Zenith Corporation after they were done making television cabinets—but Dr. Beady is straight out of the nineteenth century. He is the kind of preacher who tiptoes into choir practice, wearing a cheap black suit and his hungry rat's smile, and pulls up ten-year-old boys by the collar if he finds them acting up. That night I had a feeling he had his small black eyes directly on me, but I told myself not to play up the paranoia. I was trying to decide whether to wait for Stephen to call me. I could wait forever, with his guilt.

Finally the choir had done its bit, and Miss Christobel Hawkins had sung her solo (flipping her blond hair over her shoulder at the end of every bar), and the deacon had done his bit, and Dr. Beady rose to preach. The last few Sundays he had been pushing faith: faith that there would be a good tomato crop this year, faith that the building fund would grow tenfold by the end of the summer, faith that California would not fall into the sea. The bulletin board outside had given the title of the Wednesday night service—the short sermon—as "Our Duty in the Community." I was pretty sure it was another tidy way of getting at money. But as soon as Dr. Beady began to speak, I knew I was in trouble. When he was seated, listening to the choir with one finger pressed against his temple, I had had the sensation that he had picked me out to avoid. His eyes darted around and up, to everyone in the congregation but me. He started in his low nasal whine, the whine that would work up to a fever pitch.

"The sinner," he said. "What must we ask of the sinner?" All around me I could feel the electric buzz that Dr. Beady set off when he began to speak. In a few minutes, people would drift away, would stop listening to him, but for now, he had them; he had them lined up naked with their legs spread apart and they were trying to shield themselves. He loved those words sin and sinner: he sloshed them around in his mouth like wine and then spat them out, all over the congregation.

"The sinner has a debt to pay to the community," said Dr. Beady, and all the Baptists of First Baptist snuck peeks at their neighbors out of the corners of their eyes. "The adulterer," Dr. Beady went on, and we all settled in, anticipating the best. "The adulterer must go back to his spouse and beg her forgiveness." He paused. "The employee who has pilfered must go back to his employer and make restitution." Big pause. "The fornicator" (here he took a deep cleansing breath and came out of it at the other end with a bellow) "the fornicator must stop his immoral actions and begin anew on a pure path." He swallowed gasps of air, and so did the congregation. We had made it past fornicators. Dr. Beady squeezed his eyes up again to circle them over the sinners below, and again I felt that he met everyone's eyes but mine.

Suddenly he began again, off-beat, catching us off-guard. "But *what*," he said, "but *what* do we do when the sinner not only refuses to pay off this debt to those he has sinned against? What of the sinner who refused to say to the community: I am sorry? What do we do with the sinner who is proud of his low deeds? What do we do with the drug addict who parades his weak character through our streets?" We all tried to imagine junkies marching down River Street. "*What* do we do with the drunkard who will not give up his bottle?" Winos parading down River Street! "What do we do with the adulterer who will not return to wife and children, but goes on in his sinful ways? Or the teenager who *flaunts* her promiscuity?" I felt my father stiffening beside me. No one had drifted off this time: we all followed Dr. Beady like sheep, and he was building up for the slaughter.

He pulled in another cleansing breath. "*I will tell you what we can do,*" said Dr. Beady. "We can confront that sinner. What has become of us, in 1981, that we are afraid to confront the sinner? What has become of us that we can no longer say to those who have gone astray: 'You are wrong. You are doing e-vil. You re-pulse me.' Why can we no longer say that?" We all shrank back in our pews. "I will *tell* you why. We can no longer say that because we are afraid. Because our society, yes, our media, our schools, tell us that it is all right for our children to drink liquor, to pop pills, to engage in the sacred marriage act when they are fourteen and fifteen years old. They have *frightened* us into acquiescence." He mopped his brow, but didn't look at all acquiescent. His face had the glow of proud red anger it took on for all his sinning sermons, and the glow shone out among the congregation.

When he began again, he dropped his voice, and I could feel my father's stiff arm lean forward, as if to catch his words. All over the big white church women leaned their shoulders forward to hear how they could regain their righteousness and lose their acquiescence. "We have an example," said Dr. Beady. "We have an example," whispered Dr. Beady, "of this in-ab-il-i-ty to face sin in our community today. I mean *today*, this very day, this Wednesday, in this hot June when we are thinking of our air conditioners and our sprinklers and when we should be thinking of bigger things, of sin that must be confronted." People leaned back an inch or two: it was one thing to confront sin, but another to be made guilty about an air conditioner in Due East, South Carolina. Dr. Beady rolled on, unperturbed. "We have this very day," he said, "witnessed the local media giving coverage to, giving encouragement to, what it should have been deriding." There was a sucking in of breath all over the church. The local media consisted of three radio stations, two of which played country-western and one of which played easy-listening; the educational TV station on UHF that nobody ever bothered tuning in to; and the Due East *Courier*. Dr. Beady meant the Due East *Courier*. For a minute I thought that even Dr. Beady couldn't do *this*, that he had never gone so far as to point a finger at an individual from the pulpit. He had hinted at those who didn't support the church, but he had never dropped hints about one who sat below his nose. About me. My father's hand had knotted into a fist. He was leaning forward again, almost to the next pew.

Dr. Beady looked around him and made a great show of relaxing his shoulders, of relaxing his whole body. We all knew this phase: when he was out of the buildup, out of the anger, and down to the conversational, I-don't-mean-to-scare-you-by-any-of-this-I'm-just-one-of-you-folks-too phase. Now his voice would be as smooth and as thick as treacle. "I don't know how many of you know exactly what I am talking about," he said. Conversational. "I'm not one of those preachers who thinks we should point the finger directly at anyone. Remember Jesus! Remember what he said about casting the first stone! Read your Bible. Read John, Chapter Eight, verses one through twelve." He laughed a little conversational laugh and hung his hands over the edge of the pulpit. "You know," he said, and now he stared directly at me, eye to eye, Dr. Beady's beady black eye thinking it was boring through me, thinking it was scaring me. "You know, when I was a boy, the preachers did not hold back at anything. When I was a boy, if you were caught chewing gum in church, the usher would come over and pull you up by the elbow and escort you down the aisle for all to see. Once," and he laughed again, mirthlessly, "once a young visitor to our small town upstate arrived in the middle of summer." We all of us realized we were in for a detour—Dr. Beady would take us back on a ride through his boyhood—and there was settling in all over the church.

"We were not a proud community," he went on. "Our fathers were farmers mostly, eking out a living from soybeans or peaches, but when this young visitor arrived at our church we all took notice. We were all dressed in our best—maybe not a very fancy best, maybe our shoes were run down, but they were polished; maybe our suits were worn thin, but they were pressed—we were all dressed in our best, but this young lady arrived at the front steps of our church dressed in shorts. Dressed in *bermuda* shorts." He calmed himself back into the conversational. "It was a hot day, a hot Ju-ly day, but I remember the look of my mother and the other good women of our community as they spied this young girl coming up the steps in her bermuda shorts. My mother, and all her friends, were wearing white gloves, and modest dresses with long sleeves, and their best shoes, and they blushed when they saw this young thing coming up the steps of the *house of our Lord* in her bermuda shorts. I will never forget the blushes, the shame those good women felt. When the one who should have been feeling shame bared her legs on a Sunday morning for all to see." He bowed his head in shame, and we all bowed our heads.

"I'm sure the good people of this community would blush, too," said Dr. Beady soothingly. "Even in the nineteen-eighties. Even in this day when anything goes. Even in this day of the drug addict, and the drunken driver, and the topless dancer, and the pregnant teenager." He bore down on me again. "*What do you think our preacher did?*" he roared. Then he stopped and composed himself. "This is what he did. Our minister was just arriving to enter the back of the church, but when he saw this young girl outside *the house of our Lord*, dressed in bermuda shorts, he had one of the ushers call her aside, and he took her back with him to the side entrance of the church. I suspect he told her she would have a special place for listening to the sermon, because she was a visitor. I suspect, in her pride, that she was flattered by his attention. Imagine that scene, if you will." He paused to let us all picture it. "Perhaps you can *imagine* what happened when it came time for our minister to deliver the word of the Lord. Can you imagine it?" He let us imagine it. "Can you see our preacher bringing this young girl out in front of the congregation, and telling her what he thought of her disrespect? Perhaps you can't imagine that in 1981, but that is what happened. That is indeed what happened. Our preacher told this girl what he thought of her immodesty, what he thought—and he wasn't afraid to say it, not in nineteen *fifty-one*—what he thought of her *sin* of coming to Sunday services dressed in a pair of bermuda shorts."

Suddenly I was aware that my father had put his arm around my shoulder, lightly—not leaning me toward him or squeezing him, but just resting it there, something he'd never done before—and I saw Dr. Beady's eyes veer away from us. All the tension that my father had put into listening to the sermon, fighting the sermon, was gone. He just had his arm around me. I had never felt that sensation before, the sensation of being borne up by him. (pp. 132–137)

[Text continued from page 97]

munities; however, it also helped to split them along denominational lines that still persist.

Lingeman (1980) commented that the Western pioneers were prone to disputes over fine points in the Bible, a matter well illustrated by Keillor's story (1985) of his own denomination, the Sanctified Brethren, "a sect so tiny that nobody but us and God knew about it" (p. 101). Keillor said of these disputes:

> Scholarly to the core and perfect literalists every one, they set to arguing over points that, to any outsider, would have seemed very minor indeed but which to them were crucial to the Faith, including the question: if Believer A is associated with Believer B who has somehow associated himself with C who holds a False Doctrine, must D break off association with A, even though A does not hold the Doctrine, to avoid taint?
>
> The correct answer is: Yes. Some Brethren, however, felt that D should only speak with A and urge him to break off with B. The Brethren who felt otherwise promptly broke off with them. This was the Bedford Question, one of several controversies that, inside of two years, split the Brethren into three branches. (p. 105)

Although the separation between Roman Catholics and Protestants is slowly fading in many small towns, it cannot be taken for granted. Recently, a conciliatory Lutheran pastor, addressing a local Roman Catholic congregation in a rare exchange of pulpits in the town of Remsen, Iowa, said to the congregation:

> We laugh at things which hurt. And when we think seriously about the gulf that has separated this pulpit from the ones a couple of blocks away, we're more likely to weep than laugh.
>
> I still wince when I remember the sermons preached during my childhood 25 years ago. Our pastor would dish one up every now and then when our fervor was lagging. The sermon always said that the Protestants were right, thank God! and that Luther had discovered the Bible, recovered the Gospel and uncovered corruption in high, holy places. The sermon was like a pre-game pep-talk, an oratory before battle. We would stand up after the sermon and sing, "A Mighty Fortress Is Our God." We sang aggressively, defiantly, and passionately. After all, it was the national anthem of heaven, wasn't it? Our battle song, for we were the good guys. (Herzberg, 1985, p. 3)

Horizontal ties are often manifested through the relationships that people build in their churches, with the organized church in its spiritual sense and with the community of the church or the individuals who attend it in the more social sense. In a chapter entitled "Getting to Hope" in *Dakota, a Spiritual Geography*, Kathleen Norris (1993) describes the ambivalent relationship that country churches have with the organized bureaucracy of the church:

> Perhaps it's not surprising that so tiny a rural congregation is not often well served by the larger church of which it is a part. For all the pious talk of "small is beautiful," church bureaucrats, like bureaucrats everywhere, concentrate their attention on places with better demographics; bigger numbers, and more power and money. The power of Hope Church and country churches like it is subtle and not easily quantifiable. It's a power derived from smallness and lack of power, a concept the Apostle Paul would appreciate, even if modern church bureaucrats lose sight of it. (p. 165)

But church in rural areas is community. Again Norris (1993) illustrates this thought:

> "It doesn't matter what religion they are," says one long-time member. "The Lutherans and Catholics tell us that Hope is important to them, too, and becoming more so. We're the church in the neighborhood." A former pastor said of Hope Church, "It seemed that whatever was going on, a farm sale or a funeral or wedding, Hope was a part of what happened in that community." A measure of this may be seen in the annual vacation bible school for children which is attended by both Lutheran and Catholic children. (p. 162).

Norris describes how well cared for the church in Hope is. The sanctuary and the outhouse are always freshly painted. The small church is attractive; standing alone in the prairie, it is a landmark that attracts the eyes of any visitor.

One of the assignments Norris had as she wrote her book was to preach in a monastery, in the small church at Hope, and also in a town church. After a sermon she had preached on the meaning of advent in terms of the tangle of pain and joy in preparing for birth and death, she comments:

> The difference between the two churches on that Sunday confirmed what I had begun to suspect: The people of Hope Church were less afraid than

the people in town to look into the heart of their pain, a pain they share with many monasteries, which also have a diminishing and aging population. When these people ask, "Who will replace us?" the answer is, "Who knows, maybe no one," and it's not easy to live with that truth. The temptation is to deny it or to look for scapegoats. The challenge is to go on living graciously and thankfully cultivating love (pp. 173–174).

What Norris was describing is the situation of many rural communities and their churches that have learned that with population swings many of their cherished institutions die, or at least slumber, often for decades. The centrality of the church as an institution in rural communities cannot be denied. It must be considered (Ostendorf, 1987).

Summary

In this chapter, we have looked at the importance of horizontal ties in the small community. The ties that bond are those linkages that make people feel they belong in a particular place, enhancing the cohesiveness of a community. Many view these ties as liberating; many find them restricting.

The community seen as a microcosm allows the student of community to view it holistically, understanding its interconnections. There are minimal essential elements of communal life that surface to the fore in all analyses. Without the sentiments of solidarity or "we-ness," meaning, or significance, individuals will not feel *in community*. Certain institutions (or places) add to the sense of belonging. Because the church is one of the most significant institutions in rural community life, it was given special attention.

CHAPTER 4

Community as a Personal Solution

Searching for Identity and Meaning

Modern individuals are plagued by anomie and disorientation. Feeling that control over their destinies has been lost, they are struggling with their sense of selfhood. "Surely the outstanding characteristic of contemporary thought on man and society is the preoccupation with personal alienation and cultural disintegration" (Nisbet, 1953, p. 3). With varying degrees of sophistication, all people ask, Who am I? What is the purpose of my being? What is the meaning of my existence?

In their quest for solutions to the puzzles of their lives, people turn to community because their preoccupation with insecurity is accompanied by a growing regard for the merits of community. Increasingly, people in the late 20th century are seeking to escape the normlessness of individualism and secularism that once propelled many to the metropolises. Nostalgia has become a major theme of American society. "It is plainly a nostalgia, not for the greater adventurousness of earlier times but for the assertedly greater community and moral certainty of the generations preceding ours" (Nisbet, 1953, p. 31). Nostalgia, of course, can be a wonderfully positive concept if used as a source for reflection, learning, or making accommodations. It can be a dangerous concept when used as an exclusionary way of longing for things that never really existed. Buck (1980) warns of the dangers of unrestrained nostalgia merging with prophecies of "millenarianism" for "last times," "last days," "the end."

People turn particularly to community because the family is perceived to be weakening. Because of the processes of civilization and industrialization, the family is growing smaller, less orthodox, less encompassing, less capable of satisfying individual needs. Roszak (1978) lamented the apparent contradiction of the reduction of the family unit in a world where all other societal institutions are expanding:

> I began . . . with the lament that our world has become "too big." But there is one institution that has become too small, and that is the family. It has wasted away to the bare minimum and is desperately in need of expansion. In fact, this is not an exception to our thesis: it is a corollary. Things have gotten too big at the expense of basic structure. Some of these structures—the neighborhood, the village, the community of work—have simply been driven into the ground as obstacles to big system efficiency. The most basic structure of all, the family, lingers on. It remains a biological necessity. . . . The family is tolerated—but only in its most denatured, nuclear form. It might be an axiom of our thesis: the bigger the industrial apparatus, the weaker the family. The one subtracts its human resources from the other. (p. 152)

The family also is becoming less permanent and more transient because of the pressure of modern living. Although permanence is not a virtue per se and should not be made a social fetish, chronic impermanence results in anxiety; as a result, people experience disquieting feelings of loneliness and disconnectedness.

Permanence to some extent challenges individuals to solve problems that emerge from the situation, rather than run away from them. It is similar to the challenges faced by long-term marriages. It is not that the people in them are more virtuous; it is that they have faced problems with a view to resolving them rather than dissolving the bond. When mobility was limited, people could not escape their extended families or communities of origin easily; consequently, they tended to focus more on resolving tensions, developing tolerance for each other, and carving acceptable ways of sharing. So it is with the search for communities. Those who need community need also support and permanence.

In the middle of the city of Phoenix, Arizona, lies the small community of Guadalupe. Guadalupe is inhabited primarily by members of the Yaqui tribe and by Mexican-Americans. It is built in the mission style around a wonderful adobe church, next door to which is the traditional gathering place for Yaqui ceremonies.

The town of Guadalupe, which has a long history, is in many ways at odds with the surrounding luxury of the city of Phoenix. The inhabitants of Guadalupe are traditional. They follow their ways, their Yaqui traditions, their Mexican traditions, their Catholic practices. While the town accommodates many religious denominations and groups, it has remained traditional. The story that follows tells of a native son who becomes a doctor and returns to Guadalupe to repay the community. It is touching not only because his professional practice is respectful of traditional customs, but also because of his sense of social responsibility.

 ## "Humble" Health Clinic Gets New Space: Guadalupe Doctor Encourages Patients to Use Non-traditional Healing

While recently looking through a patient's files, Dr. John Molina was reminded how far he's come since the day his free health clinic opened in August 1995. "My mom and I sat in an empty room with a couple of folding chairs and waited," he said. After treating his first patient, he only had scrap paper on which to take notes. The scrap paper is still in her file.

Molina, a Guadalupe native who grew up a few blocks from Las Fuentes Health Clinic, paid the electric bills out of his personal checkbook for the first year.

Times have changed. In March, the clinic will move from its original, 800-square-foot building to an adjacent 1,800-square-foot one. With the new space, dentistry will be available for the first time. Although the clinic now has five employees and a $400,000 annual budget, Molina still says, "We're a humble place."

In Guadalupe, the home-grown clinic works. It's a place where the doctor understands if patients want to first treat themselves with teas and snake powder, where patients can be comforted by pictures of the Virgin of Guadalupe and a crucifix in the examining room and where patients pay only if they can afford to.

It was years ago when Molina was going door-to-door as a social worker that he decided the town needed a clinic. Although the low-income, Hispanic-Yaqui community of about 5,000 is surrounded by cities with numerous doctors, he realized many residents were unable to afford medical care, had no transportation to a doctor's office or were intimidated by a typical, sterile, suburban doctor's office.

Molina eventually obtained a medical degree from the University of Arizona, specializing in obstetrics and gynecology, and while working for Indian Health Services in Phoenix, decided to open a part-time free clinic in Guadalupe. The patient load grew from 350 the first year to about 800 the second and about 3,000 in the third year. Last year, Molina made doctoring at the clinic his full-time job.

"For me, it's been fascinating watching it develop to this size," he said. "It really changed me. [The patients have] made an impression on my life. . . . This is where I want to stay."

The town's main health problems are diabetes and drug and alcohol abuse. He estimates about one-fifth of the residents are diabetic and 40 percent have the potential to develop the disease. The clinic helps diabetics keep up with their medicine and treats respiratory infections, provides cancer and diabetic screenings and other outpatient services. "We've treated women who haven't had Pap smears [tests for cervical cancer] in five years," he said.

Although many doctors steer clear of alternative therapies, Molina is moving in that direction because his patients come from a culture that has relied on herbs and rituals for thousands of years. Some Guadalupe residents will still consult Molina only after they've treated themselves with herbs. And even after he prescribes drugs, many continue with herbal treatments with Molina's approval.

"I encourage it unless there are problems," he said. "Medicine tends to be evidence-based. If there's no proof to it, if it hasn't passed a double-blind test and been published, you shouldn't do it. Yet you see results of a lot of healing without evidence."

He recently spent several weeks learning about alternative medicine from Leon Acosta, a longtime Guadalupe healer who died in November at age 91. Molina said Acosta taught him to get to know his patients and to "let a higher energy do the healing."

"I learned more about healing from him in three weeks than I did in medical school," Molina said. "People have to believe if it's going to work."

He plans to offer acupuncture, therapeutic touch and cranial manipulation. He also wants to plant a "healing garden," featuring Sonoran Desert plants, next to the clinic.

"This is all similar to what these people are used to," Molina said.

The clinic depends on donations and seems always to be short of money. The gray carpet is frayed, the furniture mismatched and there's a donation box on the counter. The clinic began charging patients a nominal amount on Jan. 1 based on their income.

Molina gets a lot of volunteer help from nurses, medical students and some physicians, including a cardiologist who visits once a month.

But he still needs money, more volunteer physicians and medicine samples. About 70 percent of the medicine the clinic provides comes from donated physician samples, those little promotional packets of prescription medicine doctors get from pharmaceutical companies.

Even though state and federal funds are available, he prefers to do without them because of the paperwork.

"My goal is to stay as far away from government funding as I can," he said. "It's unpredictable and takes a lot of energy. That was my lesson from the tobacco law."

Molina was counting on a year's worth of funding from the state tobacco tax to fund indigent care for residents outside Guadalupe. But he got only six months worth. Still, he plans to keep treating those people through the end of the fiscal year.

Molina also turned down the chance for a $50,000 block grant from Maricopa County that could have helped finance remodeling of the new clinic. If he had to wait for the county's money, he said construction couldn't even start until the summer.

"It would have become a bureaucratic nightmare," Molina said. "It's a lot of paperwork. The staff can make better use of its time taking care of patients."

The clinic relies heavily on private grants. Major supporters include Avnet Inc.'s Computer Marketing Group, National Relief Charities Foundation, Pascua Yaqui Tribe and St. Luke's Charitable Health Trust.

"By relying on community support, it creates a relationship and closeness. . . . It develops a sense of community," he said. The Tempe Governors Board, a civic group that promotes health care, has decided to give the proceeds, an estimated $50,000 of its Feb. 6 Tempe Governors Ball to the clinic. Molina plans to use that money to convert the current building into a dental clinic.

But even after the clinic moves from its tiny 1950s building, he plans to keep the crucifixes and Virgin of Guadalupe pictures and to maintain a humble home environment.

Molina, dressed in khaki pants and a blue denim shirt, said, "The best compliment I ever received was, 'You just don't seem like a doctor.'"

SOURCE: Beard, B. (1999, January 17). "Humble" health clinic gets new space: Guadalupe doctor encourages patients to use non-traditional healing. *Arizona Republic*, pp. EV1–EV2. Reprinted courtesy of the *Arizona Republic*.

In moral philosophy, thinkers often connect communal living with ethical principles. "MacIntyre (1984) traces moral action to communal tradition. It is when individuals are embedded in communal life, and develop self-identifying narratives that render them intelligible to others and to themselves, that moral action is possible. It is because of the self-identifying narratives and their embeddedness in communal life that the individual can be held morally responsible" (Gergen, 1994, p. 103). Similarly, in a recent book about monastic life Norris (1996), using the tools of the keen observer and teller of stories, discusses the communitarian ideals of monasteries. Monasteries are about the oldest continuous form of communities built not only on religious beliefs and moral commitments but also on the principles of unity, cooperation and cohesion. Yet, as Norris points out, their sense of community does not require uniformity. "Monasteries have a unity that is remarkably unrestrained by uniformity; they are comprised of distinct individuals, often memorable characters, whose eccentricities live for generations in the community's oral history" (Norris, 1996, p. 63). This is not to say that the challenges of heterogeneity in communities are not present in monasteries. Norris states that they are very evident, but the important commitment is to resolve them in the unity of community. Useful lessons can be drawn by today's heterogeneous communities from the "unity without uniformity" principle illustrated by Norris.

In our contemporary world, the smaller the family becomes, the more individuals search for purpose and meaning in the larger collective, in contrived groups, and in artificial or utopian communities. Alternative arrangements that take the place of Gemeinschaft flourish for a variety of people. For many of both the old and the young in search of community, for example, shopping malls have become *the* community. Judicial controversy has even arisen over whether malls are private property or part of the community like any park, airport, or downtown square. For many people, shopping malls are the only community they experience. Keyes (1973) wrote of what he found in a shopping mall, Whitman, that he describes as "an honest to goodness community dominated by kids but not limited to them" (p. 120):

> The heart of this community wasn't the dip-in-and-outers, the dilettantes who only showed up on Saturday. The real Whitman community was the people who hung out there virtually everyday, and had for years, the people with some commitment to the place.
>
> One widow, seventy-eight years old, has her breakfast every morning at 10 in [a mall department store], then [sits] around on the benches before

having some milk at 1 and returning to an empty house. She'd been coming to Whitman for four years, and really enjoy[s] the kids. . . . They tell jokes and sit around. And the kids return the affection. (p. 120)

Individuals often find that a variety of "contrived" environments become their community and fulfill a need where family might not exist or might have failed. An article in the *Atlanta Constitution* mentioned interest clubs as a way to help "people cope with the largeness of city life by providing smaller, more human-sized community" (Long, 1987, p. 38). Keyes (1973) commented that "an ideal community would be like a good family: the group from which one can't be expelled. Or like Robert Frost's definition of home—'the place where when you go there, they have to take you in'" (p. 168).

This is one of the reasons for the success of modern therapeutic communities (Weight Watchers, Alcoholics Anonymous) and, on the negative side, gangs. In these communities people may err, but when they return to the group, they are in community. They are at home; they are taken in; new pacts for responsibility are drawn and past ways forgotten. How many people can do that in their own families? People search for personal communities, hoping that in community they might find others who will accept fully their strengths and foibles. In turn, people are prepared to accept the strengths and weaknesses of others. Human services professionals must understand the forces that propel individuals to participate in communal activities. Those who work with groups or clubs will see these artificial communities as fulfilling the roles that natural communities once played.

To remain healthy, all communities, whether natural or contrived, need to be able to achieve unity without uniformity. When groups aim at uniformity, they can become dangerously excluding; true communities make room for differences. Small communities in particular have historically accepted and in their own ways accommodated the roles played by different people. They may not always have devised egalitarian roles for all, but they learned to accommodate eccentric people, unique elders, poor people, and those who were in other ways different. The real task of communities is not to make differences disappear or to create artificial symmetries. The real task of communities is to make differences complementary so as to achieve successful interdependence.

Interdependence in communities has been the theme of many social service projects that have tried to bring people together to help each other. The "patch system" that was tried in Britain in the 1980s and in some parts of the United States in the 1990s offered valuable lessons. In the late 1970s, the 1980s, and the early 1990s, many local British social services departments advocated the decentralization of services to small units called "patches," in which generalist workers attempted the "fusion of statutory work with voluntary action in the community" (Hadley & McGrath, 1980, p. 1). The patches and their networks of statutory and voluntary efforts tried to create more real and helpful interdependence (Martinez-Brawley, 1981). This was also the central premise of "community care" (Walker, 1982) and of "community social work" (National Institute for Social Work, 1982). In principle, community social work supports and enhances the personal, identity-giving role of the community. A true patch was a communal unit that had been identified as meaningful for residents and workers. Patches covered areas as dissimilar as rural Herefordshire and inner city London, but their common rationale was:

> . . . the abandonment of existing assumptions about the automatic supe-riority of the large-scale bureaucracy as the principal mode of organisation, . . . [the] readiness to explore the potential of more decentralised, flexible structures; a broader, more open definition of professionalism which has room to recognise the full potential of lay workers . . . ; acknowledgment of the present contribution and future potential of the community to provide a whole range of services for itself; the right of local communities to share in decision-making about service priorities and methods of pro-vision. (Hadley & McGrath, 1980, p. 10)

Though many of the patches of the 1980s were dismantled when the political ethos changed in the late 1990s, many continue to draw on the interdependence of workers, customers or clients, volunteers, and all other community residents. The patch worker recognizes that the community itself is a personal solution and a meaningful environment for many. In practicing, the patchworker is willing to apply this recognition. Although the social worker does not necessarily view patch work as a panacea, the concept does begin to recognize the central role of community in the life of service workers as well as clients. With the patch model, human ser-vices workers can no longer remain the "anonymous persons from county hall, dropping in from outer space" (Jones, 1980, p. 16).

People find meaning in their social roles within communities; they find meaning in participatory responsibilities. "The more we retreat into homebound self-sufficiency and isolation," said Darley (1978) of the Lon-don Courtland Institute, "the more we hear of 'the community'" (p. 9). People who are not anomic are busy, active, coping, living, winning, or losing—but never disengaged. People who are not anomic find meaning in helping the larger collective; they find meaning in being helped or cared for by those with whom they share community. In fact, community often takes over (or is sought to do so) what once were solely individual or familial cares.

Concern over children, as a theme that dominated the 1990s, recognizes the community's role in the personal lives of parents and children, and accepts community functions that at other times would have been deemed intrusive. The community is viewed, sometimes appropriately, sometimes not, as a psychological answer, a personal solution. In a television interview with parents who had joined a "tough love" group as an answer to their child-rearing problems, one of the fathers emphatically asserted, "Parents do not raise children, communities do" (Donahue, 1982). Hillary Clinton's book (1996), *It Takes a Village*, revolves around the principle of community responsibility for the raising of children. The enormous growth of support groups, from farmer granges to La Leche Leagues for young mothers, attests to communal needs for well-being that cannot be met by individuals.

But our age is an age of ambiguity and contradiction. While on the one hand we speak loudly about the collective role in parenting or the importance of the community in raising children, on the other we continue to regulate responsibility away from the very few who have a sanctioned role in guiding children. Because of concern about abuses, our laws and regulatory practices have mandated that as citizens, we turn away from each other. Can members of a community, any community but particularly a *gemeinschaftlich* community, act on their implied role as child raisers? Would the parents of the child accept the friendly corrections of a stranger who might meet with the behavior of a child who needs guidance in the supermarket, for example? Would our own regulations permit teachers to behave as guiding forces to the best of their personal judgment? Do our current procedures encourage parents to confide their child-rearing frustrations before they become overwhelming, or do they curtail such confidences? As generalist practitioners expecting the community to play its supporting role, we must be aware that there are many contradictions inherent in our philosophy. Community members are often baffled by those contradictions, and it is the role of the worker to clarify and reconcile them.

Providing another illustration of the search for personal support from the collective, Keyes (1973) wrote about W. H. Auden's return to Oxford:

W. H. Auden recently left New York City and returned to England, to Oxford. The British poet said that he regretted leaving his adopted home of more than two decades, but explained: "It's just that I'm getting rather old to live alone in the winter and I'd rather live in community. Supposing I had a coronary. It might be days before I was found."

"At Oxford," he said, "I should be missed if I failed to turn up for meals." (p. 145)

Keyes suggested that for him, as for Auden, the attainable community is "the place where it is safe to be known" (p. 145). That kind of community has the advantage of being plausible in a variety of settings, from a village to a town, from a commune to a bar or church. Keyes continued his comments on Auden:

Auden fingered what, for me, is the minimum criterion of being in community, of being known: that my absence, as well as my presence, be noted. . . .

Such a community is more than many of us have—a place where we're recognized as a unique name, face, and set of quirks. Where we can go everyday and be sure of finding familiar faces.

But there's that next level, the one Auden mentioned, of also being missed when absent. (p. 145)

Some old-time residents of the megalopolis seek Gemeinschaft in their neighborhoods. Others flock to the small town searching for that personalized sense of being missed when they do not show up, of knowing the daily cadences as they go about routine activities. What millions want, reported a *Newsweek* article, "is a piece of the simple life: friendly, slow paced, basic, safe, a return to community on a human scale" (Morganthauw, 1981, p. 27). Garrison Keillor (1997) offers a perspective on "being missed" that is important to the sense of belonging. When one can enter a restaurant and order "the usual" or know that the server will remember a favorite dish, one has encountered an effective antidote to anomie.

Community as Psychosocial "Salvation"

Some people join communes or utopian collectives to share philosophies; there they sometimes find in the communal effort, their lost sense of self, the personal "salvation" they seek. The idea that community could spell salvation is not new. The term salvation is used here metaphorically to mean deliverance of an individual or group from psychological or social destruction, or preservation of the person or group from danger, loss, or difficulty. Although salvation is not used here in any religious sense, communities often have given individuals the same support religious beliefs give others. Smith (1966) suggested that the New England covenanted community, perhaps the cornerstone or model of American communities in other regions, represented a truly religious experience, not just in the dogmatic sense but in the sense of feeding the inner lives of its members. Such a community "was intensely communal in that it turned inward toward the interior spiritual life of the community; it was, however, remarkably dynamic, creating surpluses of human energy that were discharged increasingly against an intractable environment" (p. 12). The combination of potential for individual fulfillment and external, pragmatic viability made the covenanted community a success as a personal solution for those who embraced it.

Centuries after the decline of covenanted communities, the community as a personal solution was expressed in the themes of philosopher Josiah Royce, one of the great American idealists:

> Royce came to his concern for the great community by his own Western experience as a child and young man growing up in the Gold Rush Town of Grass Valley, California. Apparently, the violence, the deceit, the crime, and the greed [of individuals he encountered as a young man] caused Royce enough irritation to set his thoughts on constructing a theory of community by which men could live not only in peace with one another, but in service and personal creativity. (Allemand, 1976, p. 48)

Royce proposed that "only the consciously united community . . . can offer salvation to distracted humanity and can calm the otherwise insatiable greed and longing of the natural individual man" (Royce, 1916, p. 49).

Contemporary ethicists view community as the source of moral action. MacIntyre moves the locus of moral action from the individual to persons in relationships: "We cannot . . . characterize behavior independently of intentions and we cannot characterize intentions independently of the settings that make those intentions intelligible both to agents themselves and to others" (MacIntyre, 1984, p. 206). Gergen (1994) moves the argument even further when he states:

> Moral action is not a byproduct of a mental condition, a private act within the psyche, but a public act inseparable from the relationships in that one is (or has been) participating. According to this account, morality is not something one possesses within, it is an action that possesses its moral meaning only within a particular arena of cultural intelligibility. One participates in the cultural forms of action as in a dance or a game; ques-

tions of why one is moral or immoral do not require a specifically psychological answer any more than questions of why one moves in three-quar-
ter time when dancing a waltz or plays tennis with balls rather than
shuttlecocks. Such actions can be fully understood as sequences of coor-
dinated action within particular communities. A moral life, then, is not
an issue of individual sentiment or rationality but a form of communal
participation. (p. 103)

This philosophic position, supported by the constructivists, grounds
moral action within culture and community tradition rather than absolute values. It lends credence to the belief that communities can enhance
or corrupt the moral identity of individuals. It also lends credence to our
current interest and concern with ameliorating crime, abuse—whether of
children, women, or elderly people—and other forms of antisocial behavior by encouraging not only individual moral development but also the
health of communities and the strengthening of cultures. Gergen's position that moral life is not an issue of individual sentiment would support
popular practices such as community-oriented approaches in social work.
However, the same position can also be understood to support the attenu-
ation, if not the denial, of individual responsibility. As Gergen (1994) put
it, "Rather than punish the immoral agent, one's concerns move outward
to the form of interaction that render the problematic action intelligible,
desirable, or possible. It is not individuals who are ultimately blamewor-
thy, but extended patterns of relationships" (p. 110).

On the positive side, traditional communities play an important part
in defining identity, maintaining nonanomic practices, and stressing normative behavior. They bind the members through a strong sense of what
came before or through a strong personal commitment to maintaining the
culture—rituals, lore, and folklore. Ethnic group practices that emphasize
a sense of who the individual is, given a role in group rituals, also function
as an antidote for the sense of normlessness and confusion that often plagues
modern societies. The more traditional Indian tribes in Arizona, for example, offer their members a continued sense of belonging by adherence
to the rituals that have been, through the ages, a mark of tribal continuity.
Among the Hopi in Arizona, even among tribe members who would be
considered "modern" because they dwell and earn a living outside the reservation, the maintenance of ritual has great significance.

An excerpt from an *Arizona Republic* article (see "Modern Couple,"
p. 115) describes Hopi ways deeply imbedded in local culture. It represents both the best of community as personal solution and a view of history that is alive in a culture kept vibrant through practices and storytelling.

"Modern Couple Follows Old Trail" tells of a Hopi couple who decided to get married the traditional way. Hopi culture is not on the surface. It permeates the life and the environment of the reservation residents. Traditions are strong and cultivated with care. Even such currently successful art forms as the Kachina dolls that draw heavily on Hopi traditions have to respect the sacredness of their roots. While Kachina dolls may abound in the large art centers of the world, an invitation to a Kachina dance ceremony is still a special honor. The isolated mesas on the Hopi Reservation tell clearly of the wonders of cultural preservation.

Because of modern pressures, many Hopi have left the reservation to earn a living outside. Yet they still return to the reservation in search of solace and to affirm their traditional, ancient, and sacred ways of life. The wedding ceremony is one of those ancient traditions.

Modern Couple Follows Old Trail

The bride walked up the hill, barefoot in the dusty driveway, wearing a manta, the black one-shoulder dress of the Hopi maiden. Her eyes downcast, Delight was beautiful, dignified, somber; a modern woman following an ancient tradition.

She carried a basket of blue corn meal tied in a cloth. With her were her two daughters, Mariah, 3, and Miranda, 5, and her female relatives. . . .

Delight Dalton and Frank Poocha grew up on the Hopi reservation. She is from the most traditional area, Third Mesa, and speaks the Hopi language. Frank's mother, Idella Poocha, a fifth-grade teacher, is Pima. His Hopi father, Fritz Poocha, was a day school principal at Polaca and Moencopi. . . .

When Frank's father died, he left each son a cow for their weddings. But there were to be no Hopi weddings for Frank's brothers; they all married Navajos and didn't have the ceremony. When Frank and Dee were joined in a civil marriage at Phoenix City Hall a year ago, Frank's mom gave them a dinner. Dee's family arrived with multiple truckloads of food, in the traditional way.

And the two families began planning the wedding Frank's late father wanted.

Delight, 35, and Frank, 34, have been together for six years. They live in central Phoenix with their daughters, a chow named Buffy, and Hopi baskets on the walls of their home. . . .

So why a Hopi wedding?

"It's good for us," Frank said. "We are in that era where our culture is the connecting link. Either we learn and continue the religion, or it's gone." The realization makes him feel almost desperate, he added. . . .

He said the next two generations are crucial.

"We grew up on the reservation doing all the things little Hopi boys and girls do. But now we have to teach our little kids how to be as Hopi as they can, trying to teach them a way of life."

Frank and Delight's wedding was part of the teaching, and it involved many family members. . . .

Once the couple agreed to the wedding, they had little say in it. Almost every weekend for a year, they made the five-hour trip from Phoenix to Hopiland, helping get ready.

The work seems endless.

"We more or less have to prove that our family is worthy of having him," Delight said of the massive food exchanges that are central to Hopi weddings. "In Hopi tradition, when the man gets married, he belongs to me."

By tradition, during the opening part of the wedding, the bride grinds corn at her mother-in-law's home while the men weave her wedding robes in the kiva. Corn is sacred to the Hopis. . . .

The ceremonial parts of a Hopi wedding usually last at least a week. This one was compressed into three days over a long weekend.

On Friday afternoon, the arrival of the bride at the home of the groom's mother was the first major event of the Hopi wedding. . . .

Frank was waiting, still wearing his work gloves. He had been chopping wood and doing strenuous preparation, waiting anxiously. He hadn't seen his wife and children in almost two weeks. They had been in Hotevilla, working just as hard.

In procession behind the bride were a line of 20 pickup trucks stretching down the highway. The bride and daughters entered her mother-in-law's home and were seated to one side. . . .

Delight's family was ready to pay for Frank.

Her family paid two years' worth of corn harvest to Frank's family, and there is more to come to pay off the debt of her robes.

"We think it'll take three years," said Delight's sister, Lynn Nuvamsa, who was one of the family members who kept track of donations. "We're shooting for a year and a half."

Thus do Hopi weddings stretch backward and forward in time, forming a complex web of obligatory preparation and payback.

The trucks following Delight backed up to the front porch. Unloading began with piki bread. The traditional tissue-like bread of the Hopis was folded in the square style for weddings, instead of the usual rolls. So much piki was stacked against one wall under plastic that the mound was the size of a tall single bed. Several of Delight's female relatives slept in the room with it that night to safeguard it.

Next came ten 30-gallon barrels of blue corn meal, and enough five-gallon buckets of corn meal to fill three-quarters of the floor space of the room where Delight stayed. Each barrel and bucket represented weeks of backbreaking work over the past year. Delight's family had divided up the work: the harvesting, shelling, washing, coarsely grinding, roasting the corn in big cauldrons, and finally grinding it into blue cornmeal.

Next came "lazy flour," as one auntie called it, smiling as she said it. Sack after 25-pound sack of Blue Bird white flour was passed down the chain of men unloading it, 35 sacks to each truck. There were seven or eight trucks full.

The flour was too heavy to store in the mobile home, but it had to be passed through the home.

With each item that came into the house, the men said, "Kwa kwai," and the women said, "Askwali." Both expressions mean "thank you."

The sacks of flour emitted puffs of white as they were tossed down rows of hands, out a window and into trucks belonging to the groom's relatives. . . .

Last were the baked goods, a boggling array of cakes, pies, yeast breads, cookies, doughnuts, brownies, quick breads. Goods filled waiting shelves in the back room, top to bottom, stacked.

The food was Delight's dowry, donated by her immediate family and clan family members. It would be divided up among Frank's family members who helped with the wedding.

"Askwali, askwali," Delight said. The unloading of 20 trucks took an hour. There was a palpable sense of quiet pride.

Delight was now *me-we*, the in-law. She had been accepted by Frank's family.

In a Hopi wedding, the bride's family brings the hearth-oriented goods, showing their prowess as homemakers with huge amounts of flour, cornmeal, baked goods. The groom's family takes back to her village the supplies a hunter would bring: meat, firewood, clothing, groceries. . . .

After the unloading and stacking the first evening, Friday, the big meals commenced.

Behind the house, 20 feet of cooking fires and a windbreak had been set up. A fire pit was dug, and an outdoor kitchen constructed. . . .

An outdoor dining tent sheltered seating at tables for about 45 people. Indoors, guests sat on the floor around tablecloths covered with food. . . .

As the sun set, lights twinkled on the mesa above.

Long before the sun came up Saturday morning, juniper and piñon pine smoke rose from the cooking fires, and a rooster crowed somewhere between the house and the mesa. Frank and Delight and the girls knelt in the living room over tubs of warm water to have their hair symbolically washed. . . .

The water was saved to take back to Hotevilla, where Delight's mom used it to mop the floors, a symbolic marking of the space. Frank had a brief, chilly ritual bath on the front porch in a washtub, and after it, Delight's mom gave him a blanket.

The family sat together, cornmeal applied to the faces of Delight and the girls. They also held ears of corn. Family members took turns rubbing small amounts of cornmeal gently on their arms. Delight's hair was in two pigtails wrapped with yarn and her bangs cut on either side in the traditional married-woman style. Then there was a lull, as the participants waited for the sunrise.

"I think they're going to throw the corn stuff at the sun," one of the teenagers in attendance told another. She was right. Accompanied by their mothers, Delight and Frank walked toward the sunrise and tossed cornmeal, an offering with a prayer to the sun. . . .

Breakfast was as big a spread as the meal the night before. . . .

After breakfast, the men left for the mesa with bundles that contained the ceremo-

nial bridal clothing. They went to the kiva, to smoke and pray over the robes.

About 50 women in aprons sat on the floor to make two ceremonial wedding blue-corn dishes.

Both were made with the same filling of blue cornmeal and a little sugar, mixed in tubs with hot water to the proper consistency. Stuffed into rehydrated corn leaves and tied into triangles, they became *tsukuviki*. Fashioned into slender rectangles and wrapped in corn husks with double ties, they are called *somiviki*. Both were boiled and served at subsequent meals.

Delight, wearing a lace-trimmed apron over her black dress, still barefoot, led the preparations with her mother. She had never made any of these dishes before, but she was the perfect bride, intent and patient. Mandy, in an apron just her size, made the blue corn dishes with her mother and grandmother, serious and focused beyond her years.

Delight also prepared *pik-ami*, a pudding of sweet corn flour and sugar. That dish was put into the fire pit and covered to bake overnight. . . .

At noon, Delight's paternal Sun Clan aunts and her maternal Corn Clan relatives went into action. They drove up to the mesa, unloaded food from trucks, and passed it down the ladder to the men in the underground kiva with the robes.

When the men returned two hours later, they were fed again.

Special hominy had been soaking since dawn in four big washtubs. Frank's relatives had cracked and dried each piece of hominy by hand for a special wedding stew. Cooked with diced mutton, the kernels flowered like popcorn.

All day long, food was exchanged. The Hotevilla contingent brought blue corn in buckets for the tsukuviki and somiviki; dried ears of corn were placed in the empty containers for them to take home. Frank's relatives brought over clothes they had made and basket after basket of groceries, to be taken the next day to Delight's village. . . .

At the wedding dinner of cracked hominy stew, no soda pop was served, in deference to the stricter traditions of Third Mesa.

Sunday morning dawned, and soon thereafter Delight and her daughters had a final ceremonial hair washing. Frank and Delight were exhausted from lack of sleep, but this was the last big day.

Breakfast featured the sweet pik-ami pudding. And for the first time there were as many men as women, Frank's deer clan and immediate family relations.

Sheets were spread on the floor for the dressing of the bride. Delight wore her black dress. Over their little-girl clothes, Mandy and Mariah were dressed in long-sleeved dresses made for the occasion.

Over the dresses the girls wore their own black mantas, one-shoulder maiden dresses secured with a red, woven belt that had to be wrapped and tucked a certain way. The men put the sashes on Delight and the girls.

Two women worked on each side of Delight to put her hair into the married-woman style, wrapped with yarn. The emotional meaning of the ceremonies was now coming home to Delight, who kept swallowing a lump in her throat.

The dressing took a long time. . . .

Working patiently, aunties dressed the girls' hair in a short-haired version of the Hopi maiden butterfly style, wrapping yards of yarn around each section of hair, fanning it out at the top and bottom.

Special shoes and leggings made of perfectly white buckskin were fitted onto Delight and each girl. A cloth shawl with lace trim was tied around each one's shoulders.

"It's time for your Hopi makeup," one of the aunties told Mandy. The faces were gently powdered with cornmeal.

Then it was time to don the *ovah*, the white wool blankets, with tassels on the corners to represent corn and fertility. Prayer feathers had been attached in the kiva.

Delight explained before the wedding that the robes were "my ticket to heaven." They have a dual purpose: The robes that the Hopi bride wears at her wedding will someday serve as her shroud.

The men stepped forward to the ovah, two holding each one by the corners. As they unfolded them, cornmeal from the religious ceremonies in the kiva puffed into the air like pale smoke. . . .

Delight then made a thank-you speech, her poise cracking for the first time. "Askwali," she started. Then she said in Hopi, "I want to thank everyone who has labored very hard in order for this to happen, and because of that, we are very happy. We are finishing beautifully."

The men stepped forward, one by one, to talk to the couple. Tears rolled down faces throughout the room, and even those who didn't speak Hopi were affected. The speakers talked about family, and love, and how to live the Hopi life. They gave practical advice, too, such as avoidance of alcohol. After each person spoke, cornmeal was tossed in a trail toward the open door.

The talks went on . . . everyone was sobbing.

It was beautiful.

They were married.

By the time the talks were finished and hugs exchanged, Frank's family's trucks were loaded and ready to roll to Hotevilla. There was meat already butchered, and several live sheep in a trailer.

In addition to more flour, loads of groceries, and a load of firewood, there was one truckload of bags of clothing, shawls, and dresses for Delight and the girls, much of it handmade.

Delight carried the traditional bride's "suitcase" of woven reeds, rolled around the ceremonial sash, its hanging tassels symbolizing rain.

The group assembled . . . Frank and Delight walked down the hill, married in the Hopi way.

They drove to Hotevilla. They unloaded. They ate another big meal.

Frank's uncle gave him a blanket. Later that evening, Delight's relatives tried on her wedding robes and she showed them all her shawls. She gave a shawl and meat, flour and groceries to each of those who had contributed.

The wedding obligates the couple to return to the reservation even more often. Since Frank now belongs to Dee's family, he will be responsible for planting and harvesting crops for them each year, carving kachina dolls for his girls, taking care of his wife and the womenfolk in her family.

Delight's robes have to stay in her mother's home until they are all paid for, years down the road.

Only when that happens will this Hopi wedding be over.

SOURCE: Walker, J. (1999, January 17). Modern couple follows old trail. *Arizona Republic*, p. A1. Reprinted courtesy of the *Arizona Republic*.

Utopian and Alternative Communities

American utopias had their antecedents in Europe. Darley (1978) traced the origin of many to the difficulties and failures experienced by many Britons in their quest for perfect community. In utopian experiments, many of these quixotic seekers of community were gratified in their dreams while providing realizable blueprints for not only architectural but also sociopsychological communities:

> The theorists whose writings abounded with schemes veering from the hare-brained to the potentially workable fell foul of many obstacles and the higher the aims of the community builder, the further they might fall . . . many of the ideas lay dormant and in a more advanced social climate could be readopted. Advance was very slow. . . . Industrial experiments were often merely marginal improvements, concentrating in early days on better education and facilities than the norm. Inevitably each step advanced the standards and gradually the aspirations of the social reformers were realized.
>
> Allied to the comparatively simple aims of improved housing and conditions came the far more complex theories of environmental community reform. . . . Effecting revolution in environment was one way to influence future living conditions. All idealists of varying persuasions, they set precedents and provided practical examples of workable communities which had immense influence abroad and in this country. (Darley, 1978, p. 11)

Kanter (1972), a student of visionary communal movements in the United States, provided yet a broader review of the historical search for community. She suggested that utopian communities have been the response to three forces: religious, politico-economic, and psychosocial. Religious communities often emerged when separatist and Pietist sects sought closer contact with God and each other. In the past, "spiritual ideals [for such groups] were preeminent. Communism was adopted at times only through economic necessity to permit the community to retreat to its own territory to live and practice together. Often these groups coalesced around a single charismatic figure" (p. 4). Examples of utopian experiments in the origins of the United States were the Quakers and the Amish, and later on the Shakers, the Amana, and the Mormons.

Although many Old Order Amish communities in, for example, Pennsylvania, Ohio, Indiana, and Iowa, are not utopian in the conventional sense, they are spiritual or idealist and represent a continuation of successful earlier communal experiments, now translated into a way of life for the group. Collective efforts intertwined with religious beliefs related to the non-use of machinery have been successful in helping Old Order Amish communities survive and succeed in these hard times for modern agriculture (Logsdon, 1986).

> The Amish have been a people of the plow for more than three centuries. An agrarian tradition and a love of the land have shaped their distinctive faith and culture in many ways. The farm provided a crib for nurturing large families and stable marriages, a locus for work, and a haven from the vices of the larger world. Indeed, some analysts have argued that only a rural context could sustain the sectarian ways of Amish life. (Kraybill & Nolt, 1995, p. ix)

But the Amish have moved with the times. They have moved from successful agriculture to successful entrepreneurship. Though they appear aloof from the hustle-bustle of modern life, they have been successful in the 20th century using their rural way of life as a point of departure. Yet hard work, cleverness, and simplicity in the way undertakings are pursued remain central to Amish life.

What makes their society fully communitarian is their stress on interdependence. Buck (1980) suggested that:

> Amish identity and socialization are developed and reinforced by acceptance of interdependence. Being needed, as suggested earlier, grounds Amish personhood. Therefore, reciprocity is basic to Amish socializa-

tion. Brotherly concern and bearing one another's burdens weave through the Amish life web and contribute mightily to strengthening the total fabric of Amish culture. (p. 34)

Other types of utopian community emerged out of politico-economic concerns because of increasing dislocation and poverty in the wake of the Industrial Revolution. Like the religious communes, they were inspired by the social creed of reformers who sought "in the small socialist community a refuge from the evils of the factory system" (Kanter, 1972, p. 5). Places like New Harmony (1825–1827), the Wisconsin Phalanx (1784–1850), and Brook Farm (1814–1847) were inspired by the social philosophies of idealist reformers Horace Greeley, Robert Owen, Charles Fourier, and Etienne Cabet.

A large number of modern communes, many founded on Eastern mysticism, also are the result of psychosocial forces. Rejecting society's emphasis on achievement and material gains, these communities seek to provide their members with a place to grow, experience intimacy, and realize their potential. For the truly utopian groups, all modern institutions are considered "sick" and "are felt to be instrumental in promoting the neurotic behavior at the root of our most pressing social problems" (Kanter, 1972, p. 7). During the 1960s, many utopians approached community in the spirit of social experimentation. Nonviolent communities, rooted in Ghandian philosophy, appeared all over the world. Their central theme was respect for all human beings and a strong faith in the concept of Ahimsa (Sibley, 1977). Many peaceful communities inspired by Gandhi and his followers strive to achieve freedom and fulfillment through peaceful, nonviolent methods. They aim to achieve the spiritual development of individuals and the evolution and welfare of human society (Mohan, 1972).

In the spirit of environmental experimentation and congruence with the physical world, architects like Paolo Soleri created model communities (Cosanti and Arcosanti in Arizona) that respect and harmonize with the ecology. These artistic and environmentally conscious communities continue their mission today, supporting the lives of the few people who work and live in them (Soleri, 1964).

Initially successful but short-lived communal settlement efforts were common in the 1970s and 1980s. Unfortunately, what are personal solutions for some people are personal offenses for others. For example, a group of followers of the Bhagwan Shree Rajneesh, an Indian guru who settled in the village of Antelope, Oregon, apparently offended the citizens of Antelope, who were mostly retirees. Having exhausted the usual measures to keep the newcomers out—zoning laws, building permits, the courts, and even a referendum to dissolve the city—the old-timers finally decided to abandon the village to the new group. The Rajneeshees captured, through elections, the office of mayor and a number of city council posts. They even voted to change the name of the town.

In 1985, the Bhagwan encountered serious trouble and emigrated to escape legal entanglements in the United States. During subsequent legal proceedings, followers voted to change the name of the town back to Antelope in an effort to patch up relationships with the locals. Although the conduct of such modern communities may be rejected by many citizens, their cohesiveness, strength, and, often, their economic success deserve attention (Fitzgerald, 1986).

The notion that these alternative communities or "new *Gemeinschaften*" are personal solutions is highlighted by those who perceive them as performing functions once carried out not just by communities but by families:

> Scaling down the industrial leviathan means building bigger families— or rather bigger households. It is not more children we need in families, but more family we need in the life of every child: more adults to share the home and participate in parenting the young. And such families are being built, as experimental models with many shapes and under many names. We hear them spoken of these days as communes, collectives, rural homesteads, ashrams. (Roszak, 1978, pp. 152–153)

Roszak (1978) evaluated these new communes as follows:

> We are living through a period of exuberant communitarian experimentation, one of the great episodes of the Utopian tradition. . . . The fluidity and variety of experimentation is immense, and it moves on many fronts at once, challenging our concepts of child rearing and sex relations, work and property, authority and freedom, privacy and participation, consumption and distribution. (p. 153)

However, he cautioned, "one has to be tentative, not simply because the communes are new and untested (not all of them are) but because our society at large and many communitarians themselves, no longer possess a fixed standard of success and failure to work by" (p. 153). An example of abuses of this search for community as a personal solution occurred in the Reverend Jim Jones's community in Georgetown, Guyana, where fanaticism led to the suicide/massacre of hundreds. Unfortunately, in the American heterogeneous culture, many of those who search for meaning in new, sometimes esoteric, communal experiences may be seeking personal meanings they have never before experienced. Unlike Israel or China, the United

States has had little experience with communal alternatives such as kibbutzes, whose founders also were builders of a community at large.

Unfortunately, in some cases, the common bond that ties certain communities together (for example, some skinheads, the Aryan Nation, the Church of the Creator, and so on) has been intolerance and hatred toward other groups of people, who may be different from them in color, faith, belief, or lifestyle (Harowitz, 1993; Sears, 1989; Van Bienna, 1993). Fairly recently, the Randy Weaver siege in Ruby Ridge, Idaho, the Murrah Building bombing in Oklahoma City, and the Freemen of Montana terrorized citizens across the nation who wondered why militia groups would act out their paranoic violent ideologies against their own nation and communities (Overholser, 1995; Rosenberg, 1996; Stern, 1996a; Thomas, 1976). We have no appropriate theories to help us understand the ideologies of hate (Stern, 1996b).

Although the search for community as a personal solution shares many of the characteristics of the utopian movements described by Kanter (1972) and Darley (1978), the search takes place not only in communes or utopias but also in ordinary towns and villages across the United States. People who have now joined that search for community are not only intellectuals, social philosophers, utopian supporters, or religious mystics, but also insurance salespeople, entrepreneurs, teachers, farmers, and civil servants. The search for personal meaning in community is widespread all over the industrial world.

Community and Size

Community as a personal solution can be found more readily in an intimate unit. Even during the early 1960s, at the height of the national captivation with large-scale systemic linkages and vertical communities, residents identified with their local communities, as Dean (1967) showed in her study of five Midwestern towns: "From the social-psychological point of view, most Americans do not live in 'the nation' or 'the total society'; they live in towns and cities. . . . For most Americans, then, their local community of residence still constitutes the microcosm in terms of which the national community is comprehended and evaluated" (p. 6). *Gemeinschaftlich* ties cannot materialize in large environments. Keyes (1973) described this problem for Americans:

> The benefits of small scale have been ignored too long by Americans. . . .
> A manageable size has been considered irrelevant to the quality of our

human institutions. The convenience of collected resources, the efficiency of long assembly lines, large hospitals, schools, and factories have taken priority. One analysis of a variety of writings on America found that love of size, of bigness, was something generally agreed upon as unique to this country. It has a lot to do with our loneliness.

We may have come "together" to fight World War II; Texans may feel an intense relationship to their state and when I went to see the Rockets play basketball, I felt very much a San Diegan. But such feelings of "community" are all in the abstract, and generally pass. The other members don't know me, nor I them. (pp. 173–174)

Communities in the abstract have been a recent middle-class piece of wishful thinking, suggested Bellah and his colleagues in *Habits of the Heart* (1985). The middle class with its emphasis on rationality, technical rules, and occupational hierarchies has encouraged an emphasis on universal rules (Bellah, Madsen, Sullivan, Swindler & Tipton, 1985). But universal communities do not exist. All real communities are particularistic and encumbering. And even those who would like to feel "unencumbered" in their professional lives prefer to be in community in their personal lives, thus the constant dilemma many Americans experience between being "place bound" and in community, or "place free" and not in community. Bellah proposed that the "constituted self," that is, the self that is encumbered but connected to others, is always in community.

Traditionally, it was the virtues indelibly associated with friendship that were central to the "habits of the heart." It is also part of the traditional view that friendship and its virtues are not merely private: they are public, even political, for a civic order, a "city," is above all a network of friends. Without civic friendship, a city will degenerate into a struggle of contending interest groups unmediated by any public solidarity. (Bellah et al., 1985, p. 116)

The Manageability Issue

For these civic-minded friendships to occur, people have to live within environments of manageable size. Sheer physical unmanageability curtails the ability of individuals to maintain the memory of community, another important ingredient of community relationships. In the same sense that Gergen (1994) traces the moral self to community, Bellah and his colleagues (1985) suggest that the conception of what the good person is, is based on the memory of virtue and character learned from the narratives of communities.

The need to identify with a manageable communal unit is not just an American phenomenon. In most countries, people identify with a province, a region, a county, or a village—a unit of manageable size. Because size can be overwhelming, most people attempt to break it down for the purpose of ready identification and familiarity. In Britain, although local differences might appear to be less pronounced given the small size of the country, any keen observer of human nature will quickly discover that, at least from a psychological viewpoint, people from the North of England identify with the North, people from London are clearly Londoners, and Scottish and Welsh people relate not only to their nations but also to local areas within them. The lore and pride of nation, region, and locale are beautifully illustrated by a story told often in the Outer Hebrides of Scotland:

> I grew up with the legend that the Good Lord made the world in six days, and despite what people like Charles Darwin and David Attenborough have had to say on the subject, that's the way that the bit of me I like best, likes to believe it. If only for the tail end of the legend which goes on to say that when God was resting, as everybody should, on the seventh day, he suddenly discovered that he had completely forgotten to use one last handful of jewels which he had meant to place in some exotic area like the Caribbean. However, rather than break the Sabbath more than was necessary, he just opened a window in heaven and threw the jewels out without even bothering to watch where they fell. Some cynics claim that he still doesn't know but that, in fact, they strung themselves out along the north-west coast of Scotland forming the long line of islands now known as the Outer Hebrides.
>
> I was born in the second island from the top. At least we call Harris an island, and even the Post Office calls it "The Isle of Harris," but, geographically, it is only a tall mountain range which separates it from what is called, also inaccurately, the Island of Lewis. Be that as it may, a Harrisman is a Harrisman, and a Lewisman is a Lewisman, and neither would have it differently! (Macdonald 1983, p. 6)

Recently, scholars, environmentalists, and economists have discussed the advantages of manageable size from an ecological perspective. When Dean (1967) studied her five communities, she had a definite orientation toward the value of vertical community linkages for economic growth. Nevertheless, her findings supported the view that if place community is to act as a personal solution, there must be an optimum size beyond which the community cannot grow because psychological ties are lost. Social workers have been caught between commitment to the local, cohesive community unit (the "philosophy of community") and professional training that has emphasized the merits of vertical linkages to larger and more resourceful systems. They have questioned the "community of manageable size" because, unfortunately, the equation has read:

small community = insularity, discrimination, nonservice ideology

The very idea of psychotherapeutic interventions was based on a rejection of the personal, horizontally bound environment. Because rationality and impersonal objectivity were to prevail in psychotherapy, size did not matter. In a study of the culture of therapies carried out in the 1970s, Veroff, Koulka, and Douvan (1981) concluded that in most therapies common in the United States, individuals were searching for self in contractual relationships that are not those of real life. Modern psychotherapies attempt to cure people by detaching them from their communities and from relationships; most other forms of self-renewal, such as shamanism, faith healing, or prayer, attempt to restore individuals by bringing them back into interdependence with the community.

For social workers to be effective in small communities, they must transcend their own stereotypes, reexamine their commitment to impersonal, rational therapeutic models, and dispassionately scrutinize the relationship of the client to a viable human community. It is not that small communities will all be positively psychotherapeutic, or that manageable size will be the answer for all people, but they and their clients will be better served if they can realistically recognize the strengths and weaknesses of communities of manageable size.

Decentralization and manageable size are prerequisites for building personal communities in which individuals can find a sense of significance—an important element in combating anomie. Large communities are not intrinsically bad but, as E. F. Schumacher (1973) contended, for every kind of activity or endeavor there is an appropriate scale:

> What I wish to emphasize is the duality of the human requirement when it comes to the question of size: there is no single answer. For his different purposes man needs many different structures, both small ones and large ones, some exclusive and some comprehensive. Yet people find it most difficult to keep two seemingly opposite necessities of truth in their minds at the same time. They always tend to clamor for a final solution, as if in

actual life there could ever be a final solution. . . . For constructive work, the principal task is always the restoration of some kind of balance. Today, we suffer from an almost universal idolatry of giantism. It is therefore necessary to insist on the virtues of smallness—where this applies. (If there were a prevailing idolatry of smallness, irrespective of subject or purpose, one would have to try and exercise influence in the opposite direction.) (pp. 65–66)

What might be an efficient structure for economic gains in the modern industrial world might be altogether meaningless or counterproductive to individuals who are seeking personal or psychosocial solutions to the problems of their existence.

If what people are seeking is community as a personal solution, their disconnectedness will not be remedied in large units in which they continue to experience a lack of personal significance. Rather, it is in the smaller units that people can probably best achieve recognition and social support. However, if the limitations the community places on an individual's freedom result in unhappiness and estrangement, a small community is not the solution. Social services workers need to identify the community that the client finds personally manageable and meaningful. Child welfare workers trying to capitalize on community resources or enlist significant populations cannot deal with communities that are geographically dispersed.

One study of preferences for personal social services among farm families addressed the issue of location (Martinez-Brawley & Blundall, 1989):

> Assuming that the family decided to consult a professional helper or social agency, [family] members were asked to discuss their preferences for location of the agency. A helpful hint was given: would you prefer it to be inside or outside your local community?
>
> Overall, most families stated that they would prefer an agency within their local community. The families did not want to drive more than 30 miles. In relation to the specifics of the locale, most people expressed a preference for multiservice type buildings, suggesting that no one would then know why the family (or person) was going into the building. (p. 518)

Professionals cannot in a vacuum calculate the size of the "ideal" community, or provide generalizable prescriptions, but, as Schumacher (1973) advanced, in practice they must consider the element of size in assessing a situation, and learn to trust their intuition or clinical judgment.

The issue of the appropriate size of a city has fascinated philosophers and planners through the centuries. Ebenezer Howard, precursor of the English and perhaps even the American New Towns movement in the late 19th century, offered his blueprint for the ideal "Garden City." Howard wanted to create a Garden City that would combine the best elements of city and country; he proposed the maximum number of 30,000 people to inhabit a nucleus of 1,000 acres surrounded by an agricultural belt of 5,000 acres (Petersen, 1968, p. 160). Other philosophers and planners from Josiah Royce, the 19th century idealist thinker, to Benton MacKaye (1962), the 20th century conservationist, also struggled with the ideal size of cities. Perhaps the lack of successful prescriptions attests to the validity of Schumacher's proposition that people really do not know what is right—although, at least in relation to community as a personally meaningful unit, experience has shown that for most people the community unit should not be too large. "A real community for me, a safe one," wrote Keyes (1973), "can't be comfortable with too many members. There's definitely a limit to the size of the group in which I can feel comfortable" (p. 175).

Qualitatively, the sense of personal identity derived from communities of a manageable size is different from the sense of identity that can be derived from larger units, such as professional or ethnic communities. Gemeinschaft gives individuals inner direction; but the community of interest addresses the outer image: It gives individuals direction in relation to others.

At the level of Gemeinschaft, people become familiar with each other's quirks. Each person's identity becomes recognizably public. Lives are experiences shared in all their facets. Keyes (1973) illustrates how public identities emerge in small towns:

> I wrote the final draft of this manuscript in a little California town called Comptche. To call Comptche a town is a presumption. Downtown consists of one small store and post office. . . . Comptche's few score residents are scattered on outlying farms.
>
> Though I'd find it hard to live here the year round, several things impress me about Comptche. The store owner asks for no I.D. to cash a check. She knows who I am. Though the post office is tiny, and the postlady anything but a model of brisk efficiency, I find myself far more sure than in the city that she will get my letters where they're going. The postlady knows me, my name, where I live, why I'm here, and the fact that I'm always getting magazines Postage Due. I get a much greater feeling of trust from that than from the brisk professionalism of the vaguely familiar faces at one of six counters of my post office in San Diego.

> One time, a sign appeared on the post office bulletin board saying: "The wedding is on for July 21st." The next day that sign was down and another had taken its place, reading "The wedding is postponed till July 28th." Nothing more. *That's* being known. (p. 173)

In the community of interests, only one aspect of people's lives is shared with the collective—each person becomes known in a single-dimensional way (for example, by professional accomplishments or benevolent deeds). In Gemeinschaft each person becomes known for the sum total of his or her idiosyncrasies.

Post offices have been notoriously accurate barometers of the connectedness of communities, centers through which individual members become known to their community. These identity-givers on occasion have demanded loyalty from community members. Margolis (1980) told of a local post office that demanded unqualified support; community members reciprocated, putting their cash on the line:

> The rural post office frequently helps to reduce isolation and sustain community. Such connections are far from abstract. When the residents of Lemont, Pennsylvania, opposed a plan to move their post office from the town's center to its outskirts . . . , so strongly did the citizens of Lemont feel about the location of their post office that when push came to shove, more than 300 of them donated $8,000 for work the contractor had already undertaken on a new objectionable site; it was the Postal Service's price for calling off the project. (p. 28)

Because they are small and individuals are known, personal communities often make serious demands on their citizens. Yet people continue to search for communities of a "manageable size." The communities that continue to grow, as reported by sources for national statistics and by the press, are small rural towns with accessible economic resources, such as high-tech industries or proximity to metropolitan centers where work is available. Although people might resign themselves to work in impersonal environments, they still prefer to live in highly personalized ones.

In the past decade, a number of gated communities have developed throughout the United States. These "communities" have attempted to create a sense of manageability of space—though many have argued that they are artificial and have been only attempts to keep people out. While the latter is true, the fact that gated communities have sprung in rural as well as urban environments leads us to think that the search for intimacy, meaning, and manageability can also be a factor for their popularity.

Development costs aside, these gated communities try to offer a sense of connection in the physical space. Few achieve their goal because they often lack natural centers where people can actually interact. More successful are the "planned" communities—more a product of the 1960s and 1970s that offered manageable space often combined with places of work, schools and social centers (e.g., Columbia, Maryland, or Reston, Virginia).

Parochialism and Size

Because size is an important variable in the maintenance of personal solutions, community members often keep outsiders at bay. Perhaps the rejection of outsiders by small-town dwellers is based on a desire to keep the numbers small to avoid a loss of local identity. The tension between "insiders" and "outsiders" in small communities often gives meaning to social interaction. The tension must be seen in both functional and dysfunctional terms, for both the individuals and the group. To maintain community, even the most progressive individuals safeguard manageability.

In *Dakota*, Norris (1993) talks about her return to North Dakota, the home of her ancestors. She makes it clear that hers was not the typical return of the "back to the lander" where one acre and a cow makes for a farmer. Her own family had owned a farm in Western Dakota, where she had inherited 160 acres. The move "was one that took me deep into the meaning of inheritance, as I had to try to fit myself into a complex network of long established relationships" (Norris, 1993, p. 3).

Later in the book, Norris discusses how, in spite of her roots, she was viewed as an outsider in the little town of Lemmon where she had settled: "In the spring of 1984 a woman in her early thirties said to me: 'You don't understand this town because you're an outsider. You don't know what it was like here twenty years ago. That's what we want; that's what we want to get back to'" (Norris, 1993, p. 45).

In spite of the profound trauma throughout the country in 1964, and the difficulties that all citizens would encounter as political clashes spread throughout the nation, Norris suggests that its inhabitants considered Lemmon a little paradise in Western Dakota. Norris (1993) recounts how, as the local citizens kept on talking, she felt both grief and anger at their rejection of the outside world:

> I began to wonder where her magic boundaries lay: family? town? the
> state line? Even I, who had roots here, who spent my childhood summers
> learning to swim in the WPA pool, playing monopoly with neighbor-

hood children on a picnic table in my grandparents' backyard, I'm to her an outsider, a serpent in her Eden, because in defining the town's problems I refer to the world outside: the national economy, regional demographics. I'd spent too long exposed to the world outside to really love the town she longs to see as a Norman Rockwell portrait come to life, a triptych with neat white edges. (p. 46)

The reluctance of small-town citizens to recognize that "outsiders" come in many varieties, to realize that many outsiders may be insiders in many ways, is not only characteristic of small towns but is often explained by a deeply felt sense of insecurity from having been left out of the national picture, from having been often bypassed and unrecognized by the outside world.

> Small town insecurity often takes the form of an exaggerated sense of our own importance. A minister [in Lemmon] was criticized in an anonymous letter to her superiors at the state level, for doing volunteer work for the American Cancer Society. As a survivor of a particularly deadly form of cancer, she had been honored by the Society and asked to take on some speaking engagements in the area. She saw this as a valid form of ministry. But her critics couldn't image that her work might reflect well on their church; all they could see was that she was taking time away from them. By these standards, if being honored by the Cancer Society is bad, receiving the Nobel Peace Prize would be much worse. (Norris, 1993, p. 57)

The tension between recognizing those who make the town important in the eyes of the outside world, and clinging to the security of clear boundaries is not only explainable, more importantly it is predictable. Social workers need to be very aware of this ambivalence. Being a professional in a small town can make an individual suspect. The professional brings in the outside world, the values of those who are, in the view of locals, "cosmopolitans." Again, Norris (1993) refers to this:

> Small-town people know that professionals, especially those who have or seek exceptional credentials, are likely to live among them for a short time before moving on to a place where they can earn more money and advance their careers. Their differentness often shows in needs that cannot be met locally. A clergyman, for instance, who is in the process of obtaining a Ph.D. from Clairmont in Ancient Biblical Studies is able to

live in Lemmon only because the South Dakota State Library can provide through interlibrary loan the hundreds of books and articles he needs,
including texts in Ethiopian free of charge. (p. 57)

Locals in small towns know that these professionals will spend only a
short time with them, and even those who intend to stay cannot readily
prove it. Thus are tensions generated.

Minority communities often are cautious of newcomers and outsiders,
just as majority communities are of minorities. Although people who have
been ostracized might be expected not to ostracize others, all communities
protect themselves from outside forces. Among minority communities,
particularly those that welcomed large numbers of immigrants recently,
being an outsider can have many negative consequences. Local newspapers repeatedly described a raid in which police tried to identify and arrest
undocumented Mexican immigrants in the primarily Hispanic community of Chandler, Arizona. In that community, on that particular occasion, the status of outsider created legal difficulties and discomfort for the
new immigrants. The *Tribune* commented on the feelings of many Hispanics in the town about the police. While some Hispanics have not
changed their daily activities, given the raids, others, whether or not native to the town, have. As the reporter commented, "Some say they now
feel like outsiders in the community. Others say that their mistrust of police runs so deep they want nothing to do with them" (Grado & De Isasi,
1998, p. A1).

The literature is full of colorful accounts of conflicts between insiders
and outsiders in communities. In some, the outsiders are frowned upon for
their new, strange, perhaps progressive ideas. In others, they are disregarded as eccentric when their ways do not coincide with the ways of the
locals. In minority communities, outsiders are guarded against, sometimes
because those who experience the solidarity of origin and who have a common language can only tenuously tolerate the impact of outsiders. In other
communities, insiders have developed their own code of legitimacy, which
they guard jealously. In an interesting novel, Dorothy West (1995) describes insiders and outsiders in an African American community. This
novel describes the very subtle distinctions that were made on the summer island between those who truly belonged, insider old-timers, and those
who did not quite belong, outsider newcomers:

Though money was as important in the Oval [the residential area for all
African American families] as in any other upper class community, it was
not the determining factor in distinguishing between majors and minors.

The distinction was so subtle, the gradation so fine drawn, that only an Ovalite knew on which level he belonged, and an outsider sometimes wasted an entire summer licking the wrong boot. (p. 7)

Outsiders have a distinct status—sometimes positive, sometimes negative—in small towns. Visitors are clearly identified as outsiders and treated differently. In *Bad Land*, Jonathan Raban, sitting at a café in a small town in Eastern Montana, overhears a discussion between one elderly man "toying with a plate of liver and onions" and the family in the booth immediately behind him. The conversation was about Raban: "The man eyed me intently for a while, then said: 'Looks like a stranger to me, too.' He spoke loudly, with a happy solipsism of the very deaf. 'Yeah. He looks to me like he's just come off the railroad'" (Raban, 1997, p. 301).

In contrived community environments like communes, residents often protect themselves from a heavy influx of outsiders not just for philosophic reasons and insistence on compatibility of goals, but also because of the intrusion that outsiders represent. Students of the commune movement of the late 1960s and 1970s noted that many of the communes that survived protected themselves from "permanent intruders." Berger (1981) described this behavior in a somewhat typical rural California commune:

The Ranch is not the kind of commune that is easily accessible or open to anyone who wants to crash—as, for example, Morningstar Ranch was, a place whose very openness and accessibility brought it widespread publicity (and disaster) in the early phase of the commune movement. . . . The Ranch protects its privacy rather well. . . . Although the signs at the gate to its access road are not encouraging ("No Trespassing"), visitors may be welcomed if they are friends of someone who lives there, or even friends of friends, but they are generally not welcome to stay for very long, at least not without considerable discussion. (p. 24)

Similar exclusionary practices exist elsewhere. For example, in an article about the rebirth of small towns across America, Reese and Malamud (1981), two *Newsweek* reporters who noted a 32 percent growth in the population of Peterborough, New Hampshire, between 1970 and 1980, wrote that:

The influx of people has forced the town to grapple with the question of growth. Partly due to the persistence of newcomers, Peterborough adopted zoning laws in 1970. Now, says Paul C. Cummings Jr., 67, publisher of *The Peterborough Transcript*, one of the two town newspapers, "No board has more life-and-death power in the town than the planning board." As a result, Peterborough has no flashing neon signs, no McDonald's and it retains the look and mood of a Grover's Corner. But Peterborough's slow growth policies have a less fortunate consequence: most housing is too costly for those who hold jobs in the area. (p. 28)

The dilemma is real—the town is trying to protect its size. The very characteristic that makes the town desirable also makes it rejecting. Town clerk Stella Sumner said that those who come to Peterborough are "searching for peace and quiet. They want closeness, [a] sense of belonging" (Reese & Malamud, 1981, p. 28). Yet, in maintaining this quality, which is the greatest asset of the town, the conflict between newcomers and old-timers may be exacerbated.

Some interesting examples of conflict between newcomers and old-timers occur even in inner-city *barrios.* In an Arizona *barrio* that used to be in a rural area but is now in the city of Glendale, tensions were recently exacerbated by the practices of new immigrants (Amparano & Shaffer, 1997). This is a well-established Mexican-American *barrio,* where the neighbors continue their Mexican celebrations and the residents pride themselves on their style of life. As newcomers arrived in the *barrio* from countries south of Mexico, customs and cultures collided. Unfortunately, as has often happened in the United States, those already assimilated feel embarrassed by the poverty or the rural ways of the new immigrants and thus reject them. This situation has occurred through the decades among a variety of groups, but currently it is particularly clear in the Western states.

The parochial ways of small communities can be supportive as well as rejecting. New arrivals in Gemeinschaft prize the tangible sense of concern that is often apparent. "This place has all the qualities of a small town. You smile at people and they are supportive," reported a newcomer to Crested Butte, Colorado (Morganthauw, 1981, p. 29). A couple who moved to an upstate Pennsylvania farm struggled through the bitter winter with meager resources but learned respect for the taciturn compassion of their neighbors who, in their own quiet and reserved way, responded to emergencies no matter how they felt about the newcomers. On the other hand, many more newcomers have observed how "neighborly courtesy doesn't always mean acceptance" and some migrants to small towns find themselves ignored and end up being resentful. "In Crested Butte, the town's cadre of older Croatian miners keeps its distance from the big-city arrivistes, and older newcomers can be hard on still newer arrivals" (Morganthauw, 1981, p. 29). Neighborly pleasantry does not always mean a welcome; in many places, people are "newcomers" for a long time.

In the 1980s most small towns were in a quandary: Development was often the only way to survive the exigencies of the 20th century, yet the influx of outsiders that comes with development often threatened the town's identity. Crested Butte, a silver boom town whose historic buildings are protected, had experienced unprecedented growth because of its privileged mountain location, attractive to skiers and people who enjoy fishing.

> Pro-development residents say Crested Butte could become "the next Aspen"—which is precisely what the town's preservationist majority aims to prevent. People from large cities like Crested Butte for its quaintness and want it to stay that way, says Ann Vitti, who owns a ski-togs shop in fast-growing Mt. Crested Butte and favors the pace there. Nothing's going to stay small and quaint anymore, I'm afraid. Preservationists like Gil Hersch, who publishes a weekly newspaper in Crested Butte, prize their town's easy tempo and ready access to the outdoors. "I work 25 or 30 hours a week and spend the rest of my time in the back country," Hersch says.
>
> The preservationists are meanwhile fighting on a wholly separate front as well—a rear-guard action against a huge molybdenum mine on nearby Mount Emmons, the picturesque peak that forms a backdrop for the town. The project, now under state review, wants to attract mine workers into Gunnison County, a prospect that Crested Butte views with dismay. "There's a lot of elitism in Crested Butte, and I think there's an underlying bias against industry," says Joseph Blumberg, a spokesman for the mining company. "They remember what they left, and they don't want Crested Butte to look like Newark." (Morganthauw, 1981, p. 37)

But for the starkness of its choices, Crested Butte could be any of many American small towns: Its future is at stake but its residents are divided between ideals and survival. For example, 25 years ago, many small Florida towns were homogeneous hamlets struggling for survival. Today, those who lived there treasuring peace and tranquility can barely protect themselves from the intrusions of buildings and people.

A similar phenomenon occurred elsewhere in the West in the late 1980s and the 1990s. Development in Arizona, for example, was catapulted by numbers of new residents moving both from very prosperous states like California and from the less prosperous northeastern corridor. New buildings in Arizona spread briskly, and vast areas of land that had been cotton and hay farms became new communities. The tension is incredible. Yet business-minded state leaders tend to welcome development as a sign of prosperity, even while the managers of smaller communities fret about the threat that such large numbers of outsiders present to their way of life.

On the relationship between rapid growth and stress, State College, Pennsylvania, the hub of a countywide Standard Metropolitan Statistical Area (SMSA) but still very much a small town, was once identified as the "least stressful city to live in." A local columnist published a tongue-in-cheek commentary on the newfound fame of the town that he rightly called the "wet-behind-the-ears newcomer to the world of SMSA's." The columnist bemoaned the changes that had occurred in this once small college community as a result of growth. Regardless of whether the town was seen by others as low stress, the columnist regarded growth in itself as stressful and offered insightful comments tailored to the memories of insiders:

> I am an expert on stress, having held one of the most stressful jobs (executive editor of this newspaper) and one of the least stressful (editor to the nation's stamp collectors) in our low-stress city. The former task cost me my hair. The latter, inexplicably, has given me an ulcer. Actually, I can't blame the latter ailment on my employment. I think it results from the changes taking place in our community, which may be the least stressful of cities but which is a city nonetheless.
> For low stress you should have been here when:
> - There were no one-way streets.
> - There were three traffic lights.
> - The only organized activity between Memorial Day and Labor Day was the Alpha Fire Company parade and carnival. . . .
> - No one locked their doors.
> - You could get a hand-brewed Coke at Hoy Brother's General Merchandise for six cents.
> - There was no way to get from here to New York City.
> - There was no scheduled air service.
> - There was no fast food, only the tasty slow variety served up by the Penn Hi-Boy, J & L Barbecue and Fred's Restaurant.
> - Stores had wooden floors.
> - There were only two malls, both of them on campus and both of them elm-lined.
> - Teen-agers hung out at PeRo's on West Nittany Avenue and at Prexy's pool hall in Boalsburg.
> - Stress was something in an engineering textbook. (Welch, 1986, p. B4)

Newcomers have been difficult to resist but even more difficult to welcome. Many old-timers leave as newcomers enter a town because the character of the town they know changes with the arrival of new people, and the security the familiar landscape provided fades with those changes. Yet without newcomers, many towns would die. How to keep small towns alive without changing their character entirely is a dilemma that preoccupies both citizens and government officials.

Tension and parochialism in small communities are exacerbated by the issues related to development. Incompatibility between business interests, which often support development, and local interests, which often try to maintain the spirit of small town, is very clear. It becomes particularly apparent in rural neighborhoods close to large metropolitan areas, where farmers often refuse to yield to development. An article in the *Arizona Republic* (Ingley, 1997) relates how a farmer in the city of Chandler refuses to yield to the influx of construction workers building new developments:

> On one side of the road, cows are placidly munching hay. Across the way, construction workers are furiously hoisting beams, pounding nails and hanging drywall as house after house goes up in what used to be fields. . . .
>
> But a sign warns anyone who might become [the farmer's] neighbor that this is a working farm: "Notice home buyers: Agricultural fragrance, insect pest and dust possible within 1 mile of dairy." (p. A1)

The same article from the *Arizona Republic* presents the conflicts of outsiders and old-timers in terms of preservation of an environment. As we have seen, many old-timers in small towns feel that their way of life is threatened by the influx of outsiders. Development translates that influence into actions that overwhelm pristine rural environments.

In the excerpt on page 138, also from the *Arizona Republic*—though it could have appeared in a number of Western newspapers—the dairy farmer on the fringes of rapidly expanding Phoenix tries to protect his farm, but recognizes that his fight might not last long.

These are dilemmas especially for social workers in small towns because often they are at the core of the discussions and are forced to take sides on issues that are very problematic. For example, new immigrants in small towns tend to affect professionals in one way or another. While it is the role of the professional to maintain a balance of perspectives, the tension in many of these situations makes that a real challenge.

Although *parochial* simply means belonging to a parish or a locale, *parochialism* has come to mean narrow in scope and in spirit. Yet a parochial attitude can include pride of place, which is an essential dimension

[Text continues on page 139]

Dairy Farmer Refuses to Yield to Subdivisions

On one side of the road, cows are placidly munching hay. Across the way, construction workers are furiously hoisting beams, pounding nails and hanging drywall as house after house goes up on what used to be fields.

Dairy meets development—it happens time after time, and the farmer pulls up stakes.

Not Richard Dugan.

Subdivisions are growing closer every day to his dairy on Dobson Road in Chandler. The Motorola plant lies within sight of his herd.

But a sign warns anyone who might become his neighbor that this is a working farm: "Notice home buyers: Agricultural fragrance, insect pests and dust possible within 1 mile of dairy."

Dugan, 49, works his own 25-acre dairy and his retired father's 75-acre spread as one unit with 1,300 cows. His five brothers, who used to have dairies on surrounding land, have all sold out and moved to Casa Grande or Maricopa. They all wanted to expand, and there just wasn't any room.

Why has Dugan stayed?

"The facility is still economically viable," he explained. And his 77-year-old father doesn't want to sell out.

Back in the 1980s, Chandler's rapid growth worried Dugan so much that he ran for City Council. He was mayor from 1988 to 1990. But the houses just kept going up, and the farmland kept going under.

"I couldn't come up with a solution," he said. "The compromise was to get as much open space as we can."

The pungent smell of the dairy drifts over to the neighborhood where Beth Stewart's family lives.

"I'm from Kansas," she said. "You're not going to get a complaint from me." And not from her sons, 6 and 4, who love seeing the cows.

Among her neighbors, however, "everyone else complains," she conceded.

The dairy was there first, her husband, John, pointed out indignantly.

"Did they not see the cows when they bought the house?" he asked.

Indeed, sales agents for the subdivision say some potential home buyers back off once they realize there's a dairy close by.

For those who wonder, Dugan has another sign: "Notice: This dairy is not moving now or in the foreseeable future."

His office at the farm has floor-to-ceiling shelves displaying a collection of miniature tractors and farm equipment.

A clock with the slogan "Any time is milk time" has cows instead of numbers on the quarter-hours.

Despite his bravado, Dugan realizes that time eventually will run out on the dairy.

He figures that the facility has another two decades left. But once it isn't economical, he said, "What are you going to do? You've got to move on."

About that time is when he expects his prediction for Chandler to come true: It will be a small town with no agriculture.

SOURCE: Ingley, K. (1997, May 14). Dairy farmer refuses to yield to subdivisions. *Arizona Republic*, p. A1. Reprinted courtesy of the *Arizona Republic*.

[Text continued from page 137]

in a healthy community. It can also mean exclusion. Because many small towns fear outsiders (particularly racial minorities), decisions are often made that hurt town possibilities for renewal.

Community in its most manageable size and *gemeinschaftlich* dimensions always challenges social workers. They value openness, free access, and the routine welcoming of outsiders to social institutions; yet, inevitably, they are faced with making decisions that are exclusionary. Practitioners exclude people from services when provider organizations can no longer absorb new arrivals efficiently. Practitioners withdraw support from stronger clients when numbers grow overwhelmingly. When commitment to community survival clashes with inclusionary philosophy, social workers must be prepared to make judgments that are inspired not by arbitrary whims or discrimination but by pluralistic values. In the future, efficient professional intervention may be determined by how much social workers can support diverse groups in their searches for uniquely personal solutions. Social workers may well have to become interpreters of the ideal of community and advocates of the satisfaction of community building.

Social work does not have a proven record of success in helping build nurturing communities. Human services professionals have often found themselves drawn into a web of tensions. Because they try to relieve the distresses of the displaced, they have not been able to get either the approval of old-timers or the full confidence of newcomers. In efforts to be helpful to newcomers and the distressed, social workers in disregarding old-timers' fears have perhaps aggravated antagonisms, creating battles of will that no one could win. Social workers might be more successful if they acknowledged a community's desire to maintain collective control.

This acknowledgment does not mean condoning the prejudicial exclusions of certain groups or the capricious monopolizing of resources. Rather, it means that social workers must become realistic about the limitations of growth. As environmentalists have learned, one need not be for or against growth, but attuned to the idea of responsible growth—a concept social workers have tended to disregard in their professional fondness for vertical ties. Growth is often counterproductive to community sentiment, as some illustrations here show. However, social workers slowly are realizing that meaningful community ties are not imposed from without or willed by well-meaning practitioners. As they are built slowly by "average" folks, they require much nurturing. Community in the modern world is a complex evolving, active concept that because it defies many existing assumptions requires constant reinterpretation.

Communities and Freedom

Just as communities of manageable size enhance a person's sense of meaning, belonging, and social support, they also demand much greater conformity and more broadly restrict personal freedom. Many urban dwellers today are the product of a generation that rebelled against the restrictions of community. The desire for freedom is part of the very fiber of the lives of citizens today; yet it has resulted in the anomie many people now seek to remedy.

People who move to the Southwestern states are often in search of old-fashioned values that they believe the industrial Northeast has abandoned. In the illustration on page 141, Roberts, of the *Arizona Republic*, presents a different type of conflict between newcomers and outsiders. Here, the conflict occurs within a big city. The story illustrates the losses—in terms of money and capacity—that communities can experience when they are seen as unfriendly and aloof. It is a fitting illustration of what community means to people and how far people will go in search of personal meaning.

Although most current local communities might not be as extreme in their parochialism as those depicted in Robert's story, or, for that matter, in the early literature of Anderson (*Winesburg, Ohio*, 1919), Lewis (*Main Street*, 1920), or Masters (*Spoon River Anthology*, 1915), they still are strict. And the smaller the size of the community, the stricter the rules for the behavior of community members. Much of the struggle between insiders and outsiders in Gemeinschaft concerns issues of authority. By virtue of their experience in a setting, old-timers demand a degree of deference, respect, and adherence to prevailing codes of behavior—even in permissive atmospheres—that newcomers are often unwilling to grant. Some of the communes that emerged in the 1960s disbanded precisely because of tension between community and conformity. Early commune members wanted to share the "joy" of community but wanted also to give full expression to their individual freedom. With few exceptions, the reality was that the communal activity limited individual freedom. It necessitated accommodation. "To deny the relations between community and conformity, to call them two different things," wrote Keyes (1973), "is to make community that much more difficult to achieve" (p. 182).

For many generations now, people have been conditioned to hold fast, at least intellectually, to a philosophy of individualism, believing that happiness can only be found in release from ties, in what might be perceived erroneously as complete freedom. Nisbet (1953) documented how many 18th and 19th century liberal reformers forced an almost artificial dichotomy between individuals and society:

[Text continues on page 142]

Valley of the Shun: Newcomers Isolated by Neighborly Ways

I looked into the mirror the other day and staring back at me was part of the problem.

It was a few weeks ago, after I spent several hours with Joyce and Karen Gorycki. Just before they left town.

They came to Arizona, like so many others, looking for a new life. A fresh start. Some small measure of freedom from the memories of a massacre that forever changed them.

But then, just 10 months after coming here to begin again, Joyce and Karen Gorycki left Arizona.

Indifference drove them away.

You've probably read something about the Goryckis—Joyce and James and their daughter, Karen.

A few years ago, they were a quiet little family living on Long Island. James sold business forms there for 24 years. In May 1993, he was transferred to the Manhattan office and every afternoon he took the 5:33 train home to Mineola.

Six months after he started the commute, on Dec. 7, 1993, a gunman opened fire in the third car of the 5:33. When it was over, 25 commuters had been shot. Six of them died. One of them was James Gorycki.

He was one stop away from home.

His daughter, Karen, was 10 at the time. She remembers watching the story unfold on the evening news and watching the front door, waiting for her dad to walk through it. . . .

The next days and months were hard as Joyce and Karen lived through losing James, as the horrible last moments on the 5:33 were reconstructed, as the bizarre ramblings of the gunman were recounted.

Sixteen months later, Colin Ferguson was sent to prison for life and it was time to begin again.

James and Joyce had always talked about coming to Arizona some day. They had family here and a love of the landscape. So a few months after the trial, Joyce and Karen

Gorycki left New York for Arizona and a new start. . . .

They didn't think much of it when they didn't meet many people around their Scottsdale neighborhood those first few weeks. It was August, after all, and much too hot for hospitality.

By October or November, however, nothing had changed. Neighbors waved as they went by, of course, but not with any genuine interest.

Lots of newcomers can tell you about that wave. It usually comes right before you punch a button to cruise into the garage and disappear into the house and your own life.

We can be that way in Arizona, I'm told. Connections aren't easily made here.

The Goryckis made a few friends at church but elsewhere it was hard. The isolation was tough. So was school. Karen was teased every day about her accent. Few people made much of an effort to get to know her.

"This neighborhood to me is like living in an isolation camp," Joyce said. "It's very unfriendly. They don't want to know you. I'm not used to that."

So one day not long ago, they packed up and they left.

I drove home on that day thinking about the Goryckis and about Arizona and how it can be a lonely place.

Then I saw him: an older man walking his dog. He does that a lot, I realized. For two years, he's lived next door and I don't even know his name.

That's when I realized it.

Joyce Gorycki, when she talked about how unfriendly Arizona can be, was talking about me. . . .

Lots of cities have the same problem. But it's worse here, because of the walls we build and the space we expect—when you spread out the way we do your time is spent in a car, not on a sidewalk.

And it's also worse because people come

and go here. It's hard to invest much time in getting to know people you figure will be gone soon.

It's not that people aren't polite. They wave and they usually speak if they pass you on the sidewalk. But then they walk on by. They look through you and they walk on by. . . .

I could read off a long list of people with similar stories. From Brenda, who left New York two years ago; from Kelly, who came from California last August, from Bill and Cathy and Claire and Maria.

And from Jo, who is making plans to leave here for the same reasons the Goryckis left.

We don't mean to be that way, of course. People who have lived here awhile will attest to the warmth of the Valley.

But I keep thinking of those other people, the ones who've been here only a short while. The ones who find Arizonans remote, who find the Valley a lonely place to live.

They'll adjust, I guess. Or they can try to change things.

Ginny Gillespie is trying. She bought a bench and a chair for her front yard and when it gets cool, she plans to be out there to greet whoever comes by.

"I'm thinking maybe somebody will come by walking the dog and stop and pass the time of day," she said.

Madelon Rosenbaum, who moved to Scottsdale two years ago from New York, is trying. She wants to start an informal network for New Yorkers who are new to town.

John Nichols is trying, too. He set out to grow a real neighborhood out of his Scottsdale subdivision a few years ago, knocking on doors to begin to bring people together. Now, they have an annual yard sale, a block party and even better, a connection.

It's probably not that hard to achieve. It requires getting out of your house—whether you've been there a month or a decade—ringing a doorbell and introducing yourself to a neighbor. Even if it's just so they'll know who you are if they ever need help.

I know I'm going to try, and I'm already making progress. I've learned my neighbor's first name—it's Larry—and I invited him and his wife over to dinner a few weeks back.

They couldn't make it, but it's a beginning, at least.

And I'll try it again.

SOURCE: Roberts, L. (1996, August 4). Valley of the shun: Newcomers isolated by neighborly ways. *Arizona Republic*, pp. H1–H2. Reprinted courtesy of the *Arizona Republic*.

[Text continued from page 140]

The demands of freedom appear to be in the direction of the release of large numbers of individuals from the statuses and identities that had been forged in them by the dead hand of the past. A free society would be one in which individuals were morally and socially as well as politically free, free from groups and classes. It would be composed, in short, of socially and morally *separated* individuals. . . . Freedom would arise from the individual's release from all the inherited personal interdependences of traditional community, and from his existence in an impersonal, natural, economic order. (Nisbet, 1953, pp. 226–227)

Freedom as complete release from ties is not a viable alternative be-cause it denies part of the human condition. "An individual," wrote Slater (1976), "is a motley collection of ambivalent feelings, contradictory needs and values, and antithetical ideas. He is not, and cannot be, monolithic, and the modern effort to pretend otherwise is not only delusional and ridiculous, but also acutely destructive, both to the individual and to society" (p. 36). In *Caring,* Noddings (1984) speaks of circles of caring that expand outwardly from the individual. Community is but one of those circles of care. If we want to be cared for and care for others, our position in the circles cannot be anomic. Our freedom, by the nature of the relationships, is thus restricted. Noddings conceives of the situation as follows:

> As we move outward in the circles, we encounter those for whom we have personal regard. Here, as in the more intimate circles, we are guided in what we do by at least three considerations: How we feel, what the others expect of us, and what the situational relationship requires of us. Persons in these circles do not, in the usual course of events, require from us what our families naturally demand, and the situations in which we find ourselves have, usually, their own rules of conduct. We are comfort-able in these circles if we are in compliance with the rules of the game. Again, these rules do not compel us, but they have an instrumental force that is easily recognized. (p. 46)

The important point Noddings makes is that, as we reap the benefits of caring in the circles of community, we are constrained by rules. Though these rules do not necessarily force community members to limit their freedom, they present options that, if the members feel positively about the community, are limiting in and of themselves.

Contemporary studies in social psychology and the experiences of millions have revealed that people cannot be self-sufficient in social isola-tion, that their "nature cannot be deduced simply from elements innate in the germ plasm, and that between man and such social groups as the fam-ily, local group, and interest association there is an indispensable connec-tion" (Nisbet, 1953, p. 229). The philosophy of individualism might have been an answer at a time when institutions like the family and the com-munity required that individuals hold on to tradition and conformity. Currently, however, the main psychological malaise seems less the *suffoca-tion* of belonging than the overwhelming *lack* of belonging. Individualistic incentives—whether to increase production, to improve the human con-dition, or to free one's time—become important only in the context of meaningful social relationships.

John Dewey (1930) wrote that individualism often "ignores the fact that the mental and moral structure of individuals, the pattern of their desires and purposes, change with every change in social constitution" (p. 81). Dewey considered it absurd to suppose that the ties that hold individuals together in religious, political, artistic, domestic, or educational organizations are merely external. For Dewey, such ties affected the mentality and character of individuals, enhancing their disposition. Dewey saw negative conformity not as the result of too much communal interaction but rather as the result of an inner void. "Conformity is a name of the absence of vital interplay; the arrest and the numbing of communication. . . . It is the artificial substitute used to hold men together in lack of associations that are incorporated into inner dispositions of thoughts and desires" (pp. 85–86). Yet he saw a positive side to conformity when he suggested that "conformity is enduringly effective when it is a spontaneous and largely unconscious manifestation of the agreements that spring from genuine communal life" (p. 87).

Small towns often find a special social role for the nonconformist member—the town's eccentric. In Tilling, E. F. Benson's (1977) fictional "picturesque" village somewhere in the south of England, the very strength of one of the characters, "Quaint Irene," was that she was a gifted young painter who wore breeches and close-cropped hair and smoked a pipe. T. R. Pearson (1985) described the "peculiar" characters of his small North Carolina town with acceptance and even pride. He told of the advancing eccentricity of one community member:

> That was the day Miss Pettigrew stopped being just peculiar. She'd been peculiar ever since I'd heard of her and ever since I'd known what being peculiar meant, but now, when folks spoke of her they would say she was Not Right, which was an advancement of a sort. The town of Neely had seen a blue million peculiarities in its history, but those among its citizenry who were genuinely not right were rare and cherished. (p. 10)

The Hispanic tradition has a special place for eccentricity. Authors like Mary Helen Ponce (1993), Sandra Cisneros (1984), Patricia Preciado Martin (1996), and Ana Castillo (1994) all narrate stories of eccentric characters who had a special place in the heart of their communities. "La Loca" is often a central character. La Loca may be someone who is afflicted by seizure-like episodes but who could also have other powers, such as foresight or a special skill with animals.

Other current novelists also speak of magnificently colorful personages who are accepted within the heart of communities. In a very popular novel, *Where the Heart Is* (1995), Billie Letts depicts a sympathetic eccentric in a small Oklahoma town who rescues a pregnant teenager who has been abandoned by her boyfriend. The novel tries to place in the context of community in the heart of Oklahoma, not only kind eccentrics but also individuals of diverse backgrounds. Names that carry their own ethnic rhythms—Whitecotton, Nation, Goodluck, Husband—are central characters. Lett's story confirms that though small towns do limit freedom, they also confirm that individuals may find fulfillment in accepting limitations. What such small towns illustrate is the interrelationship of individualism and interdependence. Just as we are constrained by the small community, we are also emancipated by it.

In *Hoyt Street*, a novel by Mary Helen Ponce (1993), the author, currently a professor at California State University–Northridge, recalls her childhood in a neighborhood outside Los Angeles. The notes about the book state that many people asked her why she writes about Pacoima. Pacoima, a place she recalls was never called a town, was said to be infested with "gangs and drugs" (Ponce, 1993, p. ix). Ponce really had no answer other than that she needed to write, she persisted in writing about the place she calls her "Macondo"—a reference to Gabriel Garcia Marquez's mythical town. The book offers us the best of communal history. It tells of a life fulfilled by relationships to neighbors, to friends, to relatives. As Ponce (1993) recalls:

> The town of Pacoima lay to the northeast of Los Angeles, about three miles south of the city of San Fernando. The blue-gray San Gabriel Mountains rose towards the east; toward the west other small towns dotted the area. Farther west lay the blue Pacific and the rest of the world. The barrio, as I knew it, extended from San Fernando Road to Glen Oak Boulevard on the east, and from Filmore and Pier Streets on the north. We lived in the shadow of Los Angeles, twenty-odd miles to the south. (p. 3)

The excerpt is one of many wonderful stories that highlight how children are raised in community. Meaningful relationships are established not only with members of the immediate family but also with friends and neighbors. Each member of the community provides support to the child, who grows up in a nutured, healthy way. Each relationship binds the child emotionally to the community. This excerpt below, from the chapter "Sacrifice," tells of the Catholic childhood of a Mexican-American in Pacoima.

Sacrifice

Most Thursday evenings I accompanied Doña Luisa to Guardian Angel Church to pray el rosario. Church was only a block away from my home; I knew every bump and ridge along the path, most of that I had helped make. Once the first bell rang, Doña Luisa removed her apron, threw it atop the trunk in her bedroom, and called to me "Es tiempo para el rosario."

"I know, I know! Just let me kick the ball to Concha."

"And wash your face, eh?" she would caution in Spanish, her voice hoarse and low, "Lávate la cara."

I ran indoors, Concha's voice bouncing off the ball as she and my friends continued to play in the street. In the bathroom I shoved Josey aside, closed the door, and splashed water on my grimy face. I ran a damp towel over my knees, then grabbed a dress that did not appear too wrinkled. I knew well that one should wear clean clothes to church as a sign of respect. If time allowed I ran the family comb through my curly hair, plunked my favorite beanie on my head, and off I went to meet Doña Luisa.

Doña Luisa's dress rarely varied; she got ready in minutes. Other than to run a comb through her grey hair and pull a dress over the white naguas that clung to her skinny frame, there was little else she could do. She kept a black shawl handy on a peg near the door. In one swift motion she yanked it off and wound it around her head and skinny shoulders. She sometimes changed her shoes, which amused me. For although she was always after me to look clean for church, Doña Luisa was not too fussy about herself. She inevitably went to church in her scruffy everyday shoes, shoes that had seen better days.

We would leave soon after the second bell rang, not wanting to be late. I trudged along behind Doña Luisa, trying not to envy my friends still in the street. My beanie secured with bobby pins snitched from Trina, I sometimes ran ahead of Doña Luisa, skipping over the huge rocks in the street, then ran back. But mostly I walked alongside this dear woman, trying to keep up with her long strides. As she walked, she appeared to slide forward; her slender torso was constantly striving to catch up with her legs. Near the front door she would pause, waiting for me to catch my breath, then she would take my hand and lead me down the main aisle to our favorite pew, three rows back.

Few people, other than the Trinidads, Doña Luisa, and I, attended Thursday's rosary. On Hoyt Street most folks went only to Sunday mass, except when someone was dying; then whole families filled the pews, only to disappear again. My friend Nancy said that the rosary was boring, the prayers repetitious. She preferred the misiones held in the fall, when we got to light candles and listen to the visiting missionary screech about Satan, hell, and damnation.

Another reason the church was half-empty on Thursdays was because "Inner Sanctum," a radio series of spooky stories, came on at the very time our pastor was reciting the rosary. The program began with a squeaky door that sent chills up and down my arms.

Once ensconced in my seat, I would begin to fidget, but I was quickly silenced by Doña Luisa. At home she allowed me to be loud and sassy, even to talk back, but church was another matter. In The House of God, we were told in catechism, one should act accordingly. Tired of waiting for the priest to appear, I would sit back to contemplate poor Jesus of the Bleeding Heart, whom I had known for all of my five years, surprised that in all this time he had not bled to death.

Doña Luisa rarely had to coax me to attend the rosary; I was more than willing. Going to la iglesia got me out of washing the supper dishes. As I slid out the kitchen door, leaving her to clear the table and wash the dishes, Trina would give me a dirty look.

"You think you're so holy!"

"No, I don't!"

"I saw you take a nickel from . . ."

"Liar! I didn't steal . . ."

"You better tell that to the priest."

The thing is, I liked church! I liked to be inside the quiet building filled with the smell of incense. I enjoyed looking at the flowers arranged by Mrs. Barrera, a kind lady whom I liked. She had no children of her own, only a nephew who now and then visited. When I arrived extra early for rosary, she let me watch her fix the flowers. I helped to fill vases with fresh water and clean the flower stems.

"Take off the extra leaves. Like this, see?"

"But they look bare!"

"Sí, but they last longer."

Doña Luisa appeared to resent the attention I gave Mrs. Barrera. When I returned to the pew, a wilted flower in my hand, she would snort and purse her lips, and be slow about letting me get past her naguas and dark dress. Once, upon taking my seat, I saw tears in her eyes and quickly put my hand in hers to reassure her that she was the person I loved most. She took my hand, raised it to her lined lips, and kissed it. I sat looking at my hand, which felt warm. When next I glanced at Mita, her eyes were dry. (pp. 98–100)

SOURCE: Ponce, M. H. (1993). *Hoyt Street: Memories of a Chicana childhood* (pp. 98–104). New York: Doubleday. Reprinted with permission of the University of New Mexico Press.

Professionals in small towns are often bothered by what they perceive as their inability to speak their minds for fear of antagonizing locals. Discussing this, Norris (1993) asks:

> How do we tell the truth in a small town? Is it possible to write it? Certainly, great literature might come out of the lives of ordinary people on the farms and ranches and little towns on the Plains, but are the people who farm, the people working in those towns writing it? The truth, the whole truth, tends to be complex, its contentments and joys wrestled out of doubt, pain, change. How to tell the truth in a small town, where, if a discouraging word is heard, it is not for public consumption? (p. 79)

Norris fully discusses the dilemma of the writer or the artist living in small towns. She believes that too often local history is written to reveal much about the writers but not the true story of a region. Many small town people need to cling on to a way of presenting life in ideal terms. Norris understands the need of those people to avoid conflict and to preserve their integrity. Under these circumstances, the truth is not such a high priority. Furthermore, the truth is colored by context. Like people anywhere else, those who live in small towns want a good story. "A good story is one that isn't demanding, that proceeds from A to B, and above all doesn't remind us of the bad times, the cardboard patches we used to wear in our shoes, the failed farms, the way people you love just up and die. It tells us instead that hard work and perseverance can overcome all obstacles; it tells lie after lie, and the happy ending is the happiest lie of all" (Norris, 1993, pp. 85–86). Social workers, who often deal with unhappy endings, need to develop an appreciation for a good story. One way of warding off the unpleasantness, the decline, even the demise of many communities, is to tell a good story.

At all three levels of community living—the city, the neighborhood, and the family—individuals encounter restrictions on their freedom (Zablocki, 1971); they are aware that belonging and "community-ness" might, in the long run, represent curtailment of freedom, but not necessarily curtailment of their social potential. The fullest potential of human beings is realized in associations and communal efforts. The blossoming of organized religion itself speaks of people's desires to strengthen the associative aspects of creed. The enduring meaning of many religious groups cannot be divorced from the sense of earthly security and meaning they provide. Their communal messages and rituals help ease the individual's sense of isolation and validate communal traditions.

Although those who seek Gemeinschaft might intellectually understand the restrictions that communal living will place on them, at a deeper, affective level, they have difficulty comprehending what those limitations mean for their own individuality. To be "in community" is to be part of other people's lives.

More often than not, community members seek knowledge without malevolent agendas. For those who have grown used to anonymity, the realization that others can curtail their behavior may be difficult to face. Commenting on Peterborough's newcomers, *Newsweek* (Reese & Malamud, 1981) quoted a native: "The biggest problem for many newcomers is simply adapting to Peterborough's old fashioned ways. . . . In a small town you cannot always speak your mind" (p. 28) or remain unidentifiable. For better or for worse, one's private actions are, in a general sense, communal actions. "The Peterborough Transcript," reported *Newsweek* (Reese & Malamud, 1981), "now lists births to unwed mothers along with marriages and deaths—while the town's annual report includes those who fail to pay their taxes" (p. 28).

Social workers have not always been trained to understand, be sympathetic to, and respond appropriately to the freedom-eroding aspects of life in small communities. The education of practitioners has either ignored the real demands that community membership makes of social workers or has been generally critical of its restrictions. Social work education has wanted to recognize community but has failed to acknowledge the personal consequences of everyday living in real communities. Moreover, the individualistic emphasis of that education has taught students to react negatively to community demands. In a sense, the current trend toward Gemeinschaft and practice in local units has caught professionals by surprise; they often cannot respond appropriately to what are in essence natural corollaries of practice in community.

Some rural practitioners are aware of these dimensions. From them, social workers can learn what it means to practice in community:

> Social work in a rural setting offers the practitioner a variety of delights and difficulties because of the visibility of both client and worker. . . . The mental health center, where I have worked for 1½ years, averages 300 cases per year. To give an idea of what that means for visibility of client and practitioner, when I went to a son's Little League game, I found three children on his team who were known to me through the clinic. As the season wore on and my family and the client's families spent evenings at the ball park together, the usual professional image was impossible to maintain. In a small community, we are, above all, neighbors. (Fenby, 1978, p. 162)

Though the sharing process required in real community living can enhance the social worker's credibility as a human being, for those who persist in surrounding professional relationships with an evasive mystique, practicing "in community" is not likely to prove satisfactory. Being in community modifies, where it does not curtail, the freedom of social worker as well as client. Yet the understanding and sharing that both parties experience by their mutual communal experience can enhance both the professional relationship and the sense of satisfaction the social worker and client derive from the contact.

Human services professionals in the community may observe that the more a person fears being affected or controlled by or dependent on others, the more that person suffers psychologically and socially. People who pathologically fear being governed or who, like adolescents, react adversely to the mere idea of dependence, feel such helplessness that they often become *more* dependent, requiring greater control or care—as is often the case with those who are institutionalized.

It would be impossible for a social worker truly invested in community to maintain the traditional distance between social worker and client that is often dictated by bureaucracy. Given the current emphasis on service delivery at the local level, social workers must demystify the nature of the professional relationship. The current demand that human services workers work with the community, using volunteers from the community, requires that they look closely at the impositions on people's freedom this model represents. Fenby (1978) illustrated well what working in community really means in practice: "Just as neighbors are often my clients, so also I am often theirs. When I go to a shop or for professional advice or to see my child's teacher, I am quite likely to run into someone I know as a client. The roles are reversed. Now I am the seeker and they are the helpers. Because of this, it is virtually impossible to maintain the role of the omnipotent therapist" (p. 163).

This impossibility makes the human services professional's role in community all the more demanding. Community demands are not just positive; they can be negative. Public disclosures of private matters, gossip, prejudgments are inevitable reality that people encounter when they seek to live and work in "personal" communities. Yet Community curtailment of individual freedom is not unlike social workers' curtailment of client self-determination. Both freedom and self-determination exist not in a vacuum but within the parameters of social demand and gregarious coexistence, aided and abetted by local cultural norms.

Communities of Interest

Other types of community in which people partially satisfy their needs for identity and significance are occupational/professional, affiliational, and racial/ethnic communities (or "communities of interest"). The relationship between local community and other structured communal units has interested scholars for decades. Simmel (1950) studied secret societies and extreme political parties; Zablocki (1971) studied the relationships among members of the Bruderhof, a religious sect then in its third generation. Other social scientists have explored the unique ties that bind, for example, members of labor unions, businesses, and churches (Riesman, 1955; Rosales, 1997; Santino, 1989; Williams, 1987). Scholars have found that communal linkages must be translated, qualified, and changed in analyzing communities that are dispersed within the larger society. These communities, largely voluntary, take on personalities different from natural communities, where association among the members is sometimes voluntary, sometimes involuntary.

The analysis of the more unusual forms of communal units is outside the scope of this discussion. Writing in the *Encyclopedia of Social Work* (Martinez-Brawley, 1995), I addressed in great detail communities resulting from extreme groups. The focus here is on the professional/occupational and racial/ethnic communities, the communities most likely to attract the attention of social workers. Whether at the national or local levels, a professional community, according to Goode (1957), is a

> community without physical locus, and like other communities with heavy in-migration, one whose founding fathers are linked rarely by blood with the present generation. It may, nevertheless be called a community by virtue of these characteristics: (1) Its members are bound by a sense of identity. (2) Once in it, few leave, so that it is a terminal or continuing status for the most part. (3) Its members share values in common. (4) Its role definitions vis-à-vis both members and non-members are agreed upon and are the same for all members. (5) Within the area of communal action, there is a common language that is understood only partially by outsiders. (6) The community has power over its members. (7) Its limits are reasonably clear, though they are not physical and geographical but social. (8) Though it does not produce the next generation biologically, it does so socially through its control over the selection of professional trainees, and through its training processes it sends these recruits through an adult socialization process. (p. 194)

These characteristics also apply to racial/ethnic communities, except for producing the next generation, because racial/ethnic communities, producing their next generations biologically, are unable to choose or train their members in any selective sense. Some of these characteristics also apply to gender-specific and sexual minority communities.

For many people in modern society, occupation or profession constitutes a source of identity, significance, and community as a personal solution. Though many observers (Arensberg, 1955; Bender, 1978; Simmel, 1950) noted that the concept of community of interest has historically been seen at best as a poor substitute for other forms of community and at worst as an interference with a more continuing order, communities of interest offer rewards that differ from those of the intimate Gemeinschaft. In this regard, the complexities and tensions that affect the personal identity, social relationships, and political life of modern day Americans cannot be underestimated.

> Although it is common to speak of Americans as national citizens in the twentieth century, because they are involved with social organizations of national scale and with status referents in a national system of stratification, it is clear that distinctive patterns of culture, whether based upon class, ethnicity, religion, local tradition, or family heritage, affect the way

in which particular individuals or groups relate and have related to national institutions. . . .

By focusing on the shift from community to society, from personal to
impersonal forms of social organization, historians have largely overlooked
these complexities. What needs to be explored is the interplay of various
kinds of statuses and orientations over time in a bifurcated society. (Bender,
1978, pp. 117–118)

Small-town people learn to live in a bifurcated society, sometimes quite
painfully. There is a kind of social relationship that characterizes small-
town and local life; it is quasi-intimate and even when it angers or limits,
it feeds the need to belong. There is a different kind of social relationship,
more impersonal and definitely *gesellschaftlich*, that must be applied to communities of interest. The best way to learn these differences is often by
participation in both types at the local level.

Consequently, it is perhaps at the local level that the affiliational community offers its members the most. Generally, most members of occupa-
tional/professional and racial/ethnic groups claim participation in
affiliational communities on a national or even worldwide basis (for example, the Jewish, black, Hispanic, medical, or social work communities).
Yet, it is at the more circumscribed level of the region or the immediate
locale that identity ties are strongest. For example, although individual
lawyers or social workers will express solidarity with the worldwide professional community, they are likely to be more concretely identified with
the professional community of their particular area, because it provides a
more tangible system of support. Freeman (1973) wrote that, despite what
some authors have claimed, those people who joined the women's rights
movement were not "atomized and isolated" from intermediate structures
between the family and the nation, but rather participated in intermediate communication networks—in communal networks. "The most serious
attack on mass-society theory was made by Pinard. . . . He concluded that
intermediate structures exerted mobilizing as well as restraining effects on
individuals' participation in social movements because they found communication networks that assisted in the rapid spread of new ideas" (p.
41). Historical data corroborate the existence of communal intermediate
ties, at least in the United States, even among the precursors of the women's
rights movement who met at Seneca Falls, New York, in 1890.

Within the closely related ethnic groups, Hispanics in the United
States, for example, have tended to identify themselves with particular
regions of origin (Puerto Ricans, Mexicans, Colombians, Cubans), thus
creating their most cohesive community sentiments. This is a matter of

political concern for those who see the need for broad unity of subgroups in attaining political goals. This has been changing recently with the influx of large numbers of Hispanic immigrants.

Sense of personal identity is nourished through a number of concentric spheres of communal participation. At the most global level, a person might experience some sense of community by identifying with the goals of a worldwide or national group. At the state or regional level, a person might express solidarity with yet another more meaningful set of symbols and aspirations. At the more circumscribed local level, a person's community identity is translated into a personal set of rewards and obligations. A Hispanic American, for example, experiences different degrees of collective identity at the national, regional, local, and specific subgroup levels. Although his or her sense of identity might be enhanced by embracing membership in the national Hispanic or Latino community, the person might gain further support from shared experiences at the regional level (for example, Mexican Americans in the Southwest), or at the local or subgroup levels (Chicanos in San Jose, Puerto Ricans in New York City, Cubans in Miami, and Colombians in Washington, D.C.). Likewise, African Americans might identify with West Indian or Caribbean as well as African communities. Local, regional, and national groups represent sources of strength and identity, but the degree of binding of the communal ties varies with the level and consequent intimacy of the interaction.

Traditionally, social scientists have viewed participation in an affiliational community as antagonistic to participation in Gemeinschaft. They have seen the cultivation of ties to communities of interest as evidence of a decline of other forms of community. Zablocki (1971) lamented that:

> For many people, the neighborhood or home town has given way to the community of interest. With the automobile and the telephone, it is probably easier for people of common interest to find one another, and spend time together, than ever before in history. Such communities of interests are a kind of intentional community, but they fall short of satisfying the human need for communal relationships. For one thing, an individual characteristically belongs, not to one, but to a number of different communities of interest. Since relationships between members of such interest groups tend to be sequential and transitory, their members tend to avoid becoming deeply dependent on one another. Another problem stems from the fact that communities of interest often have no physical center or boundaries. . . . This sort of community lacks any sense of permanence beyond the motivations of individual members. Under such circumstances one would not expect to find the kind of friendship and belonging that

comes from the sharing of pains and pleasures over a long period of time. . . . The major problem seems to be finding some way to . . . rid themselves of some of the surplus freedom with which their senses have been overwhelmed. (pp. 293–294)

Some of Zablocki's concerns are probably well-founded—many people, unable to find psychosocial solutions for their anxieties in more intimate communal forms, might seek to find solace in the community of interest. However, participation in one or many communities of interest can also be seen as complementing rather than supplanting membership in Gemeinschaft. The thousands who have flocked to small towns and villages probably are members of a variety of affiliational, occupational/professional, and racial/ethnic communities, yet they still seek the ties of solidarity and significance that are found in intimate, traditional, multi-interest groups.

When the now-rejected notions of the "melting pot" in American society were in vogue, strong identification with racial/ethnic communities was seen as a threat to successful engagement in more "normative" communal units. Such symbols of identification as language and rituals among members of racial/ethnic communities were discouraged; to belong to both the ethnic and the traditional community of localities was considered suspect. Many lived in ethnic Gemeinschaft, bypassing altogether the issue of biculturality because their radius of personal commitment was to the community of residence alone. Having experienced rejection, racial/ethnic groups used their shared sense of hardship as a tool for building the cohesive protective communities their members required for survival. Just as the outside world frowned upon contacts with members of ethnic pockets, attempts by members of ethnic groups to make commitments outside the group were regarded with reservation. "Hillbillies" huddled together in the safety of special neighborhoods or bars; Hispanic Americans had their *barrios*; African Americans, their "harlems."

As American societal emphases have shifted in the direction of recognizing and appreciating pluralism and diversity, people have begun to recognize that membership in racial/ethnic communities, similar to membership in a community of interest, need not exclude members of a particular group from sharing in building of community with diverse people. Today, people must rise to the challenge of building meaningful, accepting communities within pluralistic structures, a need that transcends the boundaries of the United States. The enhanced sense of racial/ethnic consciousness of all groups should be used to help build nurturing, yet diverse communities. The communities of the new millennium will need to be not just tolerant of outsiders but appreciative of differences. They must recognize unique cultural traditions, yet be open to enrichment. It is perhaps in the achievement of these complex goals that human services practitioners who are well prepared to understand communities can play a facilitative role.

Summary

In this chapter, we have discussed how communities provide people with meaning and a sense of belonging and well-being. Sociologists and psychologists see a positive sense of community as a balancing force for anomie, the sociological disease of contemporary individuals. The enormous growth of support groups—from farmers' to mothers'—attest to the need people have for finding units of social interaction that take on community responsibilities when "natural" communities do not offer support.

The larger the unit of social interaction—such as large cities—in which people live their daily lives, the more people seek intimacy and solidarity from groups that recreate the natural community environment. Although the typical inhabitant of megalopolis might find it difficult to explain, many people today are willing to trade their free and anonymous environments for the greater warmth of the more restrictive small community.

In small towns, everyone knows everyone else's habits, their quirks. Many television watchers were fascinated by *Cheers*, the television show that depicted an inner-city bar where "everyone knows your name." It is not uncommon for a member of a small community to have daily *Cheers*-like experiences. In many small towns men in particular enter bars and get their customary drinks served without having to ask. In *Northern Exposure*, the television show set in the fictional Alaskan town of Cicely, a range of characters illustrates how citizens in small towns participate in each others' happiness and distresses. The very popular Lake Wobegon books of Garrison Keillor show quite vividly the sense of meaning and significance small towns give their dwellers, whether they are experiencing trying circumstances or rejoicing in communal celebrations.

People search for community as psychological healer or personal solution. Utopians have created artificial communities on religious, sociopolitical, or philosophic grounds. Some utopian experiments—the Amish and the Amana, for example—have been successful. Others have been fraught with tensions resulting from the influx of outsiders into unprepared small towns.

Community as a personal solution apparently can only be found in an intimate unit. Many towns attempting to protect their size have discriminated against outsiders. Although protection of size does not justify exclusivity, social workers need to understand the threat that the influx of outsiders might represent to many small-town residents. People are threatened not only because of their parochial views but also by the loss of community that results from expansion.

Small-town dwellers are willing to surrender some individual freedom for a sense of significance—the relationship between belonging and conformity is positive. Yet, although small towns and villages demand conformity, they have been known to tolerate peculiarity. Eccentrics often have played important social roles within the structure of relationships in small towns.

People can satisfy their need for identity in occupational/professional and racial/ethnic communities that enhance the sense of meaning and significance of their members. Although vertical communities have not been the object of study, they affect the local scheme. Generally, people who belong to large racial, ethnic, professional, or other types of vertical communities also identify with local units that fulfill their need for identity and belonging.

CHAPTER 5

Power, Influence, and Leadership in the Small Community

The study of specific variables in communities has been common among sociologists. Power, authority, influence, leadership and decision making— the central themes of this chapter—are variables that have been considered pivotal in a number of community investigations. As early as 1929, Helen and Robert Lynd, although not trained as sociologists, carried out their famous study of Middletown. The Lynds adopted the methodology of British anthropologists to produce a holistic study of Middletown—Muncie, Indiana—which turned out to reveal a great deal of detail on community life. The aspects studied—the daily patterns of people's lives, who married whom, who owned a car, who taught in schools—began, coincidentally, to open the door for the study of single, discrete variables.

Studies of small towns continued to appear throughout the thirties. In the early 1940s Lloyd Warner published a series of studies of Newburyport, Massachusetts. Warner's findings in *The Social Life of a Modern Community* (1941), *The Status System of a Modern Community* (1942) and other volumes stressed how industrialization had done away with craftsmen as a class with its predictable social mobility. In *Democracy in Jonesville: A Study of Inequality* (1949), Warner portrayed a small town in Illinois where large numbers of Norwegian immigrants were being assimilated into elite Yankee ways but where the class system remained rigid in spite of the overt commitment to democracy and equality.

A large number of community studies and novels have explored the class structure of the South. Dollard's *Caste and Class in a Southern Town* (1949), Davis, Gardner and Gardner's *Deep South* (1941), Rubin's *Plantation County* (1951), Lantz's *People of Coal Town* (1958) and many others paved the way for more sociological studies in which researchers of class structure and community power attempted to identify from that base other community characteristics. The classic example was perhaps Hunter (1953), who sought to understand Regional City (thought to be Atlanta): "I shall be using the concept of community as a frame of reference for an analysis of power relations. This is done because of a strong conviction that the community is a primary power center and because it is a place in which power relations can be most easily observed" (p. 11).

Social workers have learned that a thorough knowledge of the people and the structures that promote or interfere with community decision making is essential to their understanding of community units and to their professional functioning. Thus, the study of power, influence, and leadership is central to the preparation of community social workers. In small communities across the United States, an understanding of the intricate patterns of power relationships is a prerequisite for effective practice.

The Basic Concepts

A distinction should be drawn between *power*, the abstract capacity, the potential to affect the course of events in particular communities, and *influence*, the concrete, operational capability of actually swaying the course of specific actions. For many years, the study of community power and influence was obfuscated by confusion between the two concepts. In the late 1960s, students of community clarified their meanings. "Power refers to potential but not necessarily exerted influence. Influence is conceived as the making of decisions that cause change" (Magill & Clark, 1975, p. 35). *Powerful actors* are people who have the potential to exert influence; *influentials* are people who do exert influence; *leaders* are people who exert influence by mobilizing others to join in their causes. "Leadership refers to a complex process whereby a relatively small number of individuals in a collectivity behave in such a way that they effect (or effectively prevent) a change in the lives of a relatively large number" (Freeman, Fararo, Bloomberg, & Sunshine, 1968, p. 189).

Although powerful actors, influentials, and leaders can be the same people, the attributes of power, influence, and leadership are not necessarily embodied in a single individual. Whether they are in a given instance indicates the degree of elitism or pluralism in a particular community. Certain approaches to the investigation of power holders in a community, for example, *reputational studies*, help identify powerful actors; others, such as *decisional studies*, render information on influentials and leaders.

In his study of power, race, and privilege, Wilson (1973) proposed the use of two terms for the concepts of power and influence. They were "power ability"—what here is called "power"—and "active power"—what here is called "influence." The influence or active power of one group over another is not simply the result of overt efforts. The behavior of subordinates (whether individuals or groups) can be modified by what they perceive to be the influentials' power ability or command of power resources:

> Broadly defined, power resources have to do with the properties that determine the scope and degree of the group's [the superordinates' or influentials'] ability to influence behavior. These properties could include high social status, reputation for power, capability to bear arms, control of political office, control of mass media, wealth and land ownership. . . . Generally, inducement and persuasion resources are applied by groups that have placed themselves in a position whereby they can often influence another group without resorting to threats or penalties (i.e., constraint or pressure resources). (Wilson, 1973, p. 16)

The perception that an individual or a group has power or access to power resources may reinforce existing patterns of power distribution, a situation common in small communities where perceptions are easily discerned. Saul Alinsky (1971) observed that power is not really what a group has but rather what its enemies think it has, thus stressing the complicated relationship between power, the abstract capacity, and influence. That power and influence are affected by public perceptions is a fundamental point social workers need to understand. Inertia on the part of workers, clients, or community members is often related to their perceptions. If a group perceives itself as noninfluential, it is rarely possible for it to muster enough energy or to tap enough resources to take action. Often the social worker must modify perceptions to encourage even modest action.

As rurality has come increasingly to be understood as a construct—a phenomenon that is culturally and socially constructed—so power has increasingly become a concept worthy of study in rural research (Cloke & Little, 1997). Yet, because social scientists who study the distribution of power became increasingly discrete in their approach to the power structure of communities, the pictures drawn since the 1960s have not been as helpful for those who need a more holistic and practical picture as the studies done in the 1950s and early 1960s. Wilkinson (1991) discussed the current "scatteration" of themes in rural studies. This is absolutely correct and is probably due to the emphasis on measurement of discrete variables. Consequently, the early holistic community studies of three and four decades ago continue to have merit. Social workers need a *practical* understanding of power in order to be able to talk about empowerment, a popular current approach to practice. Furthermore, "there are important differences between those wishing to allow particular people in particular places to speak for themselves about the power relations in which they are located, and those wishing to incorporate a vision for change" (Cloke & Little, 1997, p. 5).

Social workers belong to the latter group. Thus, they are often more interested in groups that can leverage resources or influence the actions of people in small communities—including, of course, powerful individuals. Social workers want to know how actions that might change the conditions of individuals or groups can be influenced. Consequently, they tend to study power in groups that have the capacity to be influential. Examples of tension among influential groups are common in the literature. For example, conservationists often clash with established business interests (for example, builders or developers) over community development. Sometimes there is the reverse: Powerful and influential people line on the side of conservation, blocking economic development that might open up opportunities for poorer citizens in small towns. Controversies over new schools can pit young middle-class families against influential retirees or influential school boards against powerful developers. As we will see, the more pluralistic the structure of the community, the larger and more diverse the influential groups that can affect any decision. In more elitist communities there are fewer groups or actors, and those tend to have broader spheres of influence.

Practitioners and Small-Town Power Holders

Just as social workers must recognize the potential influence various groups can exert through a variety of means, from voting to forming coalitions, they also must recognize any undue optimism that may result from their own political naivete. Social workers, who are usually deeply committed to the democratic process, can easily miscalculate the influence of the franchise in community change. Although in democratic societies power (in the sense of potential to influence) becomes evident, at least theoretically, in the franchise, actual and particularly long-lasting influence might result, for example, from powerful lobbies who do not necessarily represent majority views.

Many well-developed political science theories have assumed two parallel, equally forceful, systems of power and influence, one based on wealth or command of resources and one on votes. But these assumptions often have proved erroneous. Empirical investigations have concluded that "nothing categorical can be assumed about power [or influence] in any community" (Polsby, 1960, p. 476). Piven and Cloward (1977) supported this conclusion:

> In the 1960s the dominant pluralist tradition was discredited, at least among those on the ideological left who were prodded by outbreaks of defiance among minorities and students to question this perspective. In the critique that emerged it was argued that there were not two systems of power, but that the power rooted in wealth and force overwhelmed the power of the franchise. The pluralists had erred, the critics said, by failing to recognize the manifold ways in which wealth and its concomitants engulfed electoral-representative procedures, effectively barring many people from participation while deluding and entrapping others into predetermined electoral choices. The pluralists had also erred by ignoring the consistent bias toward the interests of elites inherent in presumably neutral governing structures, no matter what the mandate of the electorate. (pp. 2–3)

Piven and Cloward (1982) later examined the historical explanations for this situation, which they saw as a peculiarly American democratic/capitalistic puzzle:

> The great anomaly arises in the United States, for nowhere else did the working class have so little political power, and yet nowhere else were its formal rights so extensive at so early a stage of capitalistic development. This is the puzzle that demands explanation. How was it possible for capital to triumph, and to triumph so fully, in the context of the most fully developed democratic laws in the world?
> The men of property who set out to create a new government following the revolution were as apprehensive as their English counterparts to the threat to property posed by mass enfranchisement. (p. 70)

The answer for the founding fathers, according to Piven and Cloward (1982), was elaborate organizational arrangements in the new representative government: "The wondrous intricacies that resulted are familiar: an elaborate arrangement of checks and balances . . . intended to check what Hamilton called the imprudence of democracy . . . indirect elections . . . and the outright denial of the franchise to women, the unprotected, Blacks and Indians" (p. 72).

Without necessarily embracing a particular ideological position, social workers must at least be familiar with how the power of the franchise has been curbed through the centuries using a range of tactics from old-fashioned coercion and fraud in electoral politics to the more subtle and sophisticated practices of high-cost election procedures to powerful lobbies that in the end can dictate positions and govern many actions among elected leaders.

A most interesting example of the variance between popular sentiment and the power of elected officials was found in the process of impeaching President Clinton. As the polls recorded the popular approval rate of the President, it became increasingly clear that there was a wide discrepancy between the will and decisions of officials and the voice of the citizens recorded by the most credible polls. From a post-1960s analysis what was even more interesting was that elaborate parliamentary maneuvers eventually assured that popular opinion, as recorded in the polls, prevailed.

Wilson (1973) suggested that a group's command of power resources or a group's ability to influence "should be considered in terms of their liquidity, that is, the extent to which they can be deployed or mobilized to exert influence" (p. 17). Some resources can be deployed easily for particular purposes but not for others. For example, during the civil rights struggle, the legal machinery of the National Association for the Advancement of Colored People was (as it still is) an effective resource (Wilson, 1973; Williams, 1987). The same resource might not be as influential in a boycott of products of companies that discriminate. Thus, influence is particularistic; abstract power, or power ability, is affected by perception.

In *Chicano!*, Rosales (1997) discusses the formal and informal defenses used by Mexicans in the early part of the 20th century when abuses to their civil rights were commonly recorded. Informal defenses were important, even if largely unsuccessful, in Texas and California to safeguard the early Mexican colonies (Rosales, 1997, p. 61). No other means were readily available. Rosales points out that "irrespective of these informal efforts at defense, only the organizations or Mexican consulates could muster the necessary resources to sustain successful campaigns that protected civil rights" (p. 61). But in the end, "inability to counter justice abuses such as lynchings sadly demonstrated their lack of influence" (p. 61). They may have had potential but they lacked real influence; this example highlights the difference.

In this sense, people in small communities, including social workers, are at both an advantage and a disadvantage. Often they can readily mobilize to influence particular decisions through town meetings, petitions, and open forums; what they lack in resources is balanced by their ability to mobilize the grassroots. However, the disadvantage is that the influentials are often the same people as the powerful actors.

The viability of the town meeting has become an issue of concern throughout New England. Even though the article excerpted here dates back to 1989, such town meetings continue to be held, and they remain a current expression of what has become the prototype of participatory democracy in the minds of many students of small communities. Some citizens prefer to "do business the old fashioned way," without the use of "Robert's Rules of Order or standard parliamentary procedures" (Bama, 1989, p. 7). Recent local information attests to the fact that school issues and community growth, for example, continue to engage citizens in lively and often heated debate, even though some towns now hire professional managers to carry out day-to-day activities. (A further illustration of the importance of town meetings in Chapter 6 [see excerpt, "When All Politics is Local," p. 228] exemplifies local politics and town convictions.)

Lingeman (1980) described the role of the town meeting in colonial times:

> At the center of the storm of doctrinal controversy and political faction that periodically raged through the towns was the meeting house on the hill—site of the town meeting. It was here that the myriad of individual interests of townspeople were raised and debated; and here that these common concerns were translated into policy and governance. The town meeting spoke for the townspeople as a whole and dealt much more intimately with the urgent concerns of their daily lives . . . than the remote colonial legislatures. (p. 47)

The traditional role of the town meeting has come under scrutiny recently. In its most traditional form, the townspeople elect leaders called selectmen to manage municipal matters. However, the selectmen can do little without first getting authorization from the once-a-year "all town meeting," in which everyone who lives in the town can participate. Unfortunately, many citizens can no longer devote the time required to run affairs of state through direct, participatory democracy. Furthermore, even at the local level affairs of state have become fast moving, complicated, and sometimes cumbersome. (See excerpt, "Use of Ballot," p. 164.)

In a small town, support of or opposition to a particular issue by human services professionals or administrators might have broader consequences than they expected because they will be seen as supporting or opposing the individuals involved in the decision, not just the decision itself. For example, in one small university town, the powerful actors who represent the university's perspective on environmental or developmental issues are the same people who sit on the hospital board, make decisions for United Way allocations, and so forth. Their influence on particular

[Text continues on page 165]

Use of Ballot Changes Town's Way of Doing Business

In Rutland Town on Monday night, 39 people out of a population of 3,300 showed up for the informational town meeting. On Tuesday, Town Meeting Day, 1,206 out of 2,546 voters cast secret ballots, a 47 percent turnout.

In Pittsfield, residents held a traditional town meeting with all business conducted from the floor and with a family-style dinner of baked beans and lasagna, crab meat casserole and a half-dozen varieties of homemade pies. Attendance Tuesday was the highest ever with more than 100 of the town's 396 residents present.

The Pittsfield meeting kept Jim DuWeese, a visitor from Columbus, Ohio, who was here on a ski vacation, entertained all day. It was a meeting of civics lessons, good-natured joking and a display of cooperation among neighbors.

In both towns, slightly fewer than half the registered voters exercised their right to vote. But in most Vermont towns, fewer than 15 percent of the registered voters vote on Town Meeting Day, according to Deputy Secretary of State Paul S. Gillies.

Is the waning interest attributable to the move away from a traditional town meeting and toward the secret ballot? Some say yes and some say no.

Garrison Nelson, a University of Vermont political science teacher and longtime political observer, worries about the future of town meeting and the system of volunteer service that so many towns depend on.

He thinks that along with a decline in the number of towns now having a traditional town meeting has come a decline in participation in local politics. He also believes the attention paid to both substantive and symbolic issues has eroded in the past decade.

Some argue that during the 1980s, as global issues such as the nuclear freeze were introduced into the town meeting debate, the true meaning of town meeting was lost. Nelson isn't sure he agrees with

that; he observes that in 1989, with no global issues up for a vote, the interest in traditional town meeting issues like snow plows and fire trucks has not increased.

"Town meeting has been helplessly corrupted by this time," and its "meaningful effect has been diluted," he says.

Gillies thinks differently. He says interest in town issues and budget remains strong and that the move away from a traditional town meeting was appropriate for some communities, especially ones with growing populations.

When a town adopts the secret ballot, town meeting appears to become "less vital with smaller numbers participating," he says. But the "majority of towns in Vermont are still wedded to the idea of maintaining as much of a traditional town meeting as possible," he says.

Shrewsbury, often considered a bellwether town, did away with some aspects of the traditional town meeting last year after residents argued successfully that many . . . residents could not come to a daytime meeting and, thus, were denied their right to vote.

After much debate, residents voted to elect town officers by secret ballot but conduct all other business from the floor. Although about 75 more people voted for town officers than attended the all-day meeting, Town Moderator Arthur Patten said he did not think the outcome was any different than it would have been with a voice or ballot vote at a traditional meeting.

Patten, who prefers the old-fashioned one-day meeting with all business decided from the floor, said Tuesday's meeting showed why it is important to have people debate issues before voting.

Both the library budget and the budget for the trash-transfer station were increased through amendments introduced from the floor. The trash budget was increased by $2,500, which included $2,000 for a roadside cleanup project and $500 to increase the superintendent's salary. The library budget was increased by $500.

In Waterbury, Town Clerk Edward Finn's advice to Shrewsbury is that things will improve. Waterbury residents voted 13 years ago to elect officers by secret ballot and to conduct all other business from the floor.

Finn, who was among the last officers to be elected by voice vote, says, "Our first year it was terrible and I was against Australian ballot for electing officers. Now I'm convinced it's the way to go."

He says 225 people voted during the business meeting, and 600 voted for officers by secret ballot.

Waterbury's school budget was hashed over for more than three hours, but in the end passed, 123–88. "All the people may not have been happy with the outcome, but most were happy with the manner in which it was done," he says.

In Grafton, residents voted three to one to keep a traditional town meeting. The usual pros and cons of the issue were presented, says Town Clerk Cynthia Gibbs.

But the meeting itself was the best example of the benefits of a traditional town meeting, she says: "One man changed his mind on the issue three times." (pp. 1, 8)

SOURCE: Daley, Y. (1989, March 8). Use of ballot changes town's way of doing business. *Rutland (Vermont) Daily Herald*, pp. 1, 8. Reprinted courtesy of the *Rutland Herald*.

[Text continued from page 163]

issues cannot be divorced from their broader role in the power structure. However, social workers should not become passive or paralyzed. On the contrary, the key to success in small-town political interventions is a heightened awareness of the interconnections of people in Gemeinschaft. Those who make decisions know that the same awareness is required of them if they are to remain influential.

In addition, the amount of leverage a particular group may have on a given issue will depend on the circumstances (Piven & Cloward, 1977). Influence will be determined minimally by how crucial the group's contribution or withholding of it is to others in the community. A group can seldom influence outcomes through withholding noncrucial services, for example; one withholding crucial services can. A strike by teachers is less likely to be influential than one by nurses.

Because influence is particularistic, the narrower the issue the more feasible the concessions vis-à-vis the overall community equilibrium: a group of social workers is more likely to influence county commissioners about the use of specific services by a particularly noninfluential group of citizens (for example, homeless people) than it is to obtain, at once, the use of all public recreational facilities for the same group. Realistically, social change is more likely to be incremental than radical. Particularly in small towns and rural areas, the value base of the population militates against sudden all-encompassing changes. Although more applicable to protest movements than to the influence desired by social workers, effectiveness also depends on a group's (or person's) ability to protect itself from reprisals. It is hardly beneficial to gain influence in one area only to have to make immediate, costly concessions in another.

Leadership

Although power is distinct from influence, and leadership is a corollary of influence, the three are in reality interactive. Leadership, it has been recently observed, is a quality or skill with fairly discrete applicability. The less elitist the community, the more leadership varies from issue to issue: "Increasingly, researchers have moved beyond simple interpretations of leaders as 'born' or a 'special breed.' Leadership is situational and, thus, to a certain degree context-specific and always more complex than monolithic appeal to personal attributes. A variety of theoretical perspectives have been advanced in an attempt to capture this complexity" (Brown & Nylander, 1998, p. 72). Leaders can emerge when more than one person is seeking a particular goal; leadership emerges as a result of the interaction. They can develop their skills through a variety of activities related to their own lives in the community. Leaders emerge in the pursuit of specific goals, as a result of followers motivated by the leader's actions. In the pursuit of goals, leaders and followers are transformed—followers by having to do more than was expected and leaders by having to accommodate the "values, interests and concerns of followers with their own" (Brown & Nylander, 1998, p. 72).

An interestingly different example of the subtle elements of leadership, not in the political sense but in the sense of human responses, is provided by the reflections of Bernice Johnson Reagon, one of the original Freedom Singers in the civil rights movement. Reagon, who had grown up with church music in the little town of Albany, Georgia, reflects:

> I ended up being arrested on the second wave of arrests in Albany. And when we got to jail, Slater King, who was already in jail, said, 'Bernice, is that you?' And I said yes. And he said, 'Sing a song.'
>
> The singing tradition in Albany was congregational. There were no soloists; there were song leaders. If Slater said, 'Bernice, sing a song,' he was not asking for a solo, he was asking me to plant a seed. The minute you start the song, singing the song is created by everybody there. There is almost a musical explosion. (Williams, 1987, p. 177)

In small communities, because the population is smaller and the choices may be less varied, leaders and followers are not found in large numbers. To maintain their interest and stamina, they need a great deal of social support. Where unpaid leadership on community issues is the norm, burn-out can be a serious problem. Social workers who need local leaders to serve as bridges with the community need to be aware of this, since sustaining leader and followers is often one of their main charges.

A common question is whether leadership is a personality characteristic or a learned skill. It is probably a combination of both. Certain traits in individuals are likely to make them enjoy relationships with followers; certain skills can be learned to help them nurture those followers and thus strengthen their leadership. If leadership is in part the ability to mobilize networks of resources and the capacity to maintain those networks, then social workers need to cultivate both, the psychology of leadership (personal traits) and the sociology of it (networks).

Although the concepts of power, influence, and leadership often, at least for study purposes, are considered separately, social workers must consider them complementary in effecting outcomes, particularly in small communities. The most undramatic community intervention has potential for affecting how community decisions are made and for being perceived as impinging, positively or negatively, on the interests of various groups. The development of a cooperative day care center in a small community, for example, might be viewed as affecting the business interests of middle-class day care or nursery school entrepreneurs, who might have had a monopoly on providing such services. On a smaller scale, the decision of a worker, supervisor, or administrator of a child welfare agency to purchase day care from one entrepreneur versus another can represent threat or support for existing community power and leadership groups. These are not dramatic interventions; they are daily occurrences in the field.

On the influence of women leaders, researchers have documented interesting phenomena. Generally women influentials were found in traditionally nurturing or expressive issue areas (health, welfare, human rights, and the environment). Studies by Bell, Hill, and Wright (1961) and Constantini and Clark (1973) documented fixed sex roles in rural communities that determined the lower participation of women in at least the political leadership. Bokemeier and Tait (1980) clarified the distinction between politician and power actor, with the power actor possessing a broader and more varied role in decision making. These researchers documented that the prospect for the increase in women power actors was excellent even though small communities in particular are slow to operationalize changes in social attitudes.

More women have gained access to important positions in the health and welfare arenas and a number of business and political offices have opened up to them. Small communities have significantly assimilated women into the decision-making ranks; women can be found as mayors, councillors, and officers in small towns. Fitchen (1991), for example, found more challenges by women "to long-term officeholders than had generally occurred in the past" and a "loosening up of the solid 'ownership' of certain offices and committee assignments" (p. 182). She also observed that some of the old-time dynasties in small town politics were dissolving and traditional assumptions about leadership were changing. Yet, she still recorded gender-specific roles in small town government. Many female social workers might experience difficulty interacting with power figures who do not share their convictions and commitments to gender equality.

An example of ongoing changes was recorded in a story in *American City and County* (Ward, 1998). In 1996, Pat Owens ran for mayor of Grand Forks, North Dakota, because she wanted to be recognized for work she felt she was already doing. She had been secretary and administrative assistant to the town's previous four mayors, so, in 1996 she ran for the position and won in a landslide. She took on the challenge even though she had to take a pay cut. The story of Pat Owens is reprinted on page 169 to illustrate change in small-town government. While circumscribed by gender roles, women in small towns often use their traditional positions as jumping-off points for breaking barriers.

All community social workers, whether involved in community projects directly or indirectly through the lives of their individual clients, quickly learn that they must be familiar with the power and decision-making structures of the communities in which they function. Inattention to the power ability of community actors can result in damage to the outcome of specific projects and in curtailment of the social worker's capacity to mobilize community resources. For example, in many small communities mental health facilities began to deinstitutionalize. Large homes that were not occupied or were in need of renovation were earmarked for halfway or transitional facilities for mentally ill or disabled citizens. Occupancy of these properties could have benefited many citizens in the small towns. Yet, power actors in these small towns often organized opposition to the moves either because of personal interests (adjacent property values always being a concern) or because they had not been coopted in advance. Mental health administrators often underestimated the scope of their influence.

In small communities, social workers need not be active organizers to come in contact with the powerful, with influentials, and with leaders.

[Text continues on page 172]

The Natural: Grand Forks' Pat Owens

Pat Owens ran for mayor of Grand Forks, N.D., because she decided she wanted to be recognized for work she was already doing. As secretary and administrative assistant to the town's previous four mayors, Owens was the face most of Grand Forks' 52,000 residents associated with City Hall. So, in 1996, Owens ran for the position and won in a landslide. (She had to take a pay cut since the mayor's job is a part-time position.)

It didn't figure to be that difficult. The town is small by most standards and has the small-town reputation that inspires residents to say "Nothing much happens here" and mean it as a good thing. Besides, Owens says, she'd practically been doing the mayor's work for more than 30 years. It was one of those "How tough can it be?" things.

That was in June 1996. In winter, it began to snow seriously; eight blizzards dumped more than 100 inches of snow on Grand Forks and on East Grand Forks, across the state line in Minnesota. Grand Forks, in cooperation with the U.S. Army Corps of Engineers, was in the middle of a flood protection planning process when the realization set in that the plan would be inadequate in the face of a really big flood. (That plan was abandoned, and a new one now is in the works.)

The flood began on April 18, when the Red River, at a record 54-plus feet, poured over the city's dikes. By the next day, most of the city, as well as East Grand Forks, was under water. Huge electrical fires spawned by the flood finished off what the waters didn't destroy.

Prior to the flood, a $17 million cost overrun on Grand Forks' new events center was the worst of Owens' problems. Now, with her town in ruins around her, Owens, a 57-year-old, 5-foot-tall grandmother, did what any grandmother would do: She sympathized, she listened, she cried, she hugged.

Then she did what great leaders do. She made hard decisions (including the controversial decision to evacuate the town), she cajoled, she bullied. "She has won the respect of everybody," said former City Council President Tom Hagness in a newspaper article. "That wasn't an easy thing to do, standing up at that meeting and telling people they should evacuate. But at the end of the meeting, they clapped for her. And those were the people affected."

Her efforts on behalf of her town have made national news. And they have made her American City & County's Municipal Leader of the Year.

A Constant Reassurance

A year and a half after the worst flood in its existence, Grand Forks is on its way to recovery, largely because of the efforts of its mayor. "I've worked disasters for nine years," says Ed Conley, who managed Grand Forks' satellite disaster field office for the Federal Emergency Management Agency (FEMA). "And I've never seen more unsolicited support come in. Pat became such a familiar figure and such a heroic figure. That's one of the reasons Grand Forks got so much in donations. The strength she showed really resonated with people."

And it propelled Owens into the national spotlight. She appeared on "Today" and "Good Morning America" and, along with Julia Roberts, Celine Dion and Madeleine Albright (among others), was listed as one of the Most Fascinating Women of '97 by Ladies Home Journal.

Newspapers gushed. "Pat Owens wears her heart and soul on a flood-dirtied sleeve," read an editorial in the Fargo (N.D.) Forum. "It's a good fit. She's doing a good job in very tough circumstances." The Minneapolis Star Tribune added, "She has been a constant reassurance to her constituency."

Owens, however, is not comfortable being the center of attention. She had, after all, planned on serving out her term in relative anonymity. "I don't know that she likes all the attention," Conley says. "She's a very unpretentious person."

"I would come home and sit down and think, 'My goodness, I just spent the day with [President Clinton,]'" says Owens, whose surprise at the hoopla she helped generate is genuine. "My goodness" peppers her speech, and she retains a sense of wonder that anyone would be interested in her. "My goodness," she says, "do you know I was on 'Good Morning America?'"

Moments later, Owens apologizes, "I'm sorry. I'm not very interesting." According to the people who worked closely with her during what became known as Flood Fight '97, that would depend on the definition of "interesting."

"If I had to sit down and write out a list of the 10 most heroic people I know, Pat would be on it," says Col. Mike Wonsik, the Army Corps of Engineers' St. Paul District Engineer during the flood. "She's a joy to work with. In a community like Grand Forks, which is still a small town trying to become a city, there's a tradition of consensus government. It's tough to be the mayor."

"In every big disaster, someone emerges who just becomes the symbol of the future of the community," Conley says. "She became that person. She had this great empathy and instinctive knowledge of what needed to be done."

Empathy and instinct are fine qualities in a mayor, but they don't pay the bills, and Grand Forks was looking at a huge amount of money to rebuild. Additionally, analysts estimate that the city has lost about 2,000 residents, nearly 4 percent of its population, because of destroyed homes and lost job opportunities.

Getting those people back is a major undertaking. Owens is determined to do just that, and that determination is paying off.

"If she didn't have the optimistic outlook that she's got, I don't know if there'd be a lot of people who would want to come back and try to rebuild this community," said one displaced resident in a Bismarck (N.D.) Tribune story.

Hometown Girl Makes Good

Rebuilding Greater Grand Forks is something of a crusade for Owens, who, with the exception of a year in Greenville, S.C., has lived there all her life. She was born and raised on a farm in East Grand Forks that is still occupied by her 94-year-old father, Willard Guerard. (After refusing to leave his pets, Guerard was helicoptered to safety during the flood.)

A devout Catholic ("Sister Adelaide taught me the ins and outs of business," the mayor says), Owens married at 17. She and her husband, Bobby, recently celebrated their 40th anniversary.

She began her business career waiting tables, then worked as secretary of buildings and grounds for the local school district. A job as a steno clerk in the auditor's office brought her to City Hall initially. Owens moved into the mayor's office in 1964, serving as "secretary" for 16 years ("doing basically the city manager's job," she says) before her title was changed to "assistant to the mayor."

When Owens' predecessor, Mike Polovitz, decided not to seek re-election, he encouraged her to give it a shot. She won with 77 percent of the vote. "I gave up a $47,000 a year job for a $12,000 a year job," she notes, wryly.

Down-home Appeal

The down-home appeal that makes Owens so popular in Grand Forks helped her open the wallets of some of the country's most tight-fisted lawmakers. Making the rounds in Washington, Owens pried loose $171.6 million in Community Development Block Grant money to help Grand Forks rebuild. She also got the federal government to kick in more than $1 billion for buyouts and relocations of homes, businesses and schools; money for farmers who lost livestock; and money for infrastructure repair (including the town's sewer system, which was particularly hard-hit). In fact, North Dakota's Democratic Senator Kent Conrad credited Owens with changing the minds of veteran politicians wary of spending money. Longtime Grand Forks City Councilmember Eliot Glassheim agrees. "We believe that the federal money we got was the result of two things: the spectacular fire that made the national news and Pat Owens," he says. "Her presentation of the situation moved people."

And she's not through with Washington yet. Grand Forks and East Grand Forks are working on a levee project that would help prevent future disasters. The two towns are planning to kick in $52 million for the $300 million-plus project. Owens and East Grand Forks Mayor Lynn Stauss will ask the state to match that. That leaves nearly $200 million that the two mayors are hoping Congress will appropriate through the Water Resources Development Act, now under consideration. The two have done some serious lobbying on behalf of the bill.

It's all paying off for Greater Grand Forks. Slowly, but surely, downtown is coming back. The Grand Forks Herald, which burned to the ground during the flood and still managed to receive a Pulitzer Prize for its coverage of the disaster, has just moved into a spectacular new building. A new Corporate Center is under construction, and the transformation of the old Empire Theater into the Empire Arts Center is complete. Altogether, more than 160 businesses now are open downtown, and, although that's down considerably from the pre-flood 315, it's still reason for optimism.

Helped along by the federal Department of Housing and Urban Development, the Urban Land Institute and Atelier Heamavihio, a Fargo-based urban design consulting firm, the Mayor's Task Force on Business Redevelopment has put together a plan for downtown development. The plan identifies five key elements—greenways, beacons to mark the Red River, town squares for both Grand Forks and East Grand Forks, a corporate/financial district and a cultural district—for the area's new downtown.

Ironically, as the town improves, Owens has less fun being mayor. "It was so much easier being the mayor back then [during the flood]," she told the Associated Press. "There are so many more battles to fight now."

"She's working too hard—15 hour days, seven days a week," Glassheim says. "She doesn't sleep enough. The demands are endless. There are 195 homes in the way of the levee that the Corps of Engineers says have to go. She's caught between what she thinks is good for the city and an informed, determined and vocal minority fighting to protect their homes.

"When she was assistant to the mayor, 15 people would call every day with little problems, and she solved them all," Glassheim says. "Then she would go home and feel good. This division within the city is bothering her."

It is not, however, changing her. Owens still is, as one observer says, "the most accessible mayor I've ever seen, much more accessible than big-city mayors." That may keep her from sleeping as much as she'd like, but it also gives the citizens of Grand Forks a hands-on mayor to lead their rebuilding efforts. For Grand Forks, the trade-off seems like a bargain.

SOURCE: Ward, J. (1998, November). The natural: Grand Forks' Pat Owens. *American City & County.* Reprinted courtesy of *American City & County.*

[Text continued from page 168]

They often will work in agencies whose boards are examples of the power, influence, or leadership structures of their communities. Thus they invariably find themselves persuading, collaborating, coopting, or perhaps opposing community leaders in relation to social services decisions. Social workers might also find themselves initiating community projects. To bring them to fruition, social workers must be able to appraise the presence and position of power actors in the community, whether they be friends, marginal observers, or foes.

Social workers as professionals often find themselves in the position of being "special interests" in small towns. The advent of the social worker as an entrepreneur or private practitioner has resulted in many controversies with vested interests. Contracts with mental health providers for psychotherapy, training contracts in child welfare, or contracts with entrepreneurial groups for foster care all have become areas fraught with the tensions of vested interests. The public sector social worker who is related to an entrepreneurial contractor for the agency is not unusual. Pressure and favoritism in the competitive arena are relatively new phenomena that social workers, administrators, and public service watch groups need to be aware of and avoid. Moral persuasion on behalf of clients or groups will not be convincing if local officials or other power holders know that the professionals have been guilty of surrendering to the pressure of interest groups.

Models of Community Power

Ever since Marx emphasized the maldistribution of resources between the bourgeoisie and the proletariat and documented how the concentration of resources in a few hands affected every other sphere of society—religion, marriage, education, and so on—students of power in society have assumed a definition of power that incorporates control of resources. Weber (1920), pursuing the Marxian idea, defined power as the ability of an individual or group to get things done, to achieve goals, even over the opposition of others. . . . It follows that people have power when they can choose to spend or withhold money, prestige, or other rewards from others" (quoted in Beeghley, 1989, p. 18).

This argument has, of course, very practical implications. It implies that rich people—who can control more resources than middle-class people—have greater power. The fewer the people who control the resources, the more concentrated the power, the more rigid the class stratification. The argument has led to practical models that identify who controls the resources and to important models of power distribution in American communities.

Although not directly concerned with the power structure, many early community studies added lasting observations on the leadership patterns of small towns. *Middletown* (Lynd & Lynd, 1929) and *Middletown in Transition* (Lynd & Lynd, 1937), the two famous studies of Muncie, Indiana, were seminal to the development of community studies in sociology. Although these books have been criticized by more contemporary sociologists as lacking a well-ordered theoretical structure (Bell & Newby, 1972; Madge, 1963), their observations on how power functioned within the structure of the small town were seminal. In *Middletown in Transition*, the Lynds noted the pervasive influence of a single family in the town: "After ten years' absence from the city, one thing struck the returning observer again and again: the increasing large public benefactions and the increasing pervasiveness of power of this wealthy family of manufacturers whose local position . . . is becoming hereditary with the emergence of a second generation of sons" (Lynd & Lynd, 1937, pp. 74–75). Although the Lynds showed that many of the points of control were public spirited, that they revealed the family's willingness to help with local problems, and that leadership and control often would be forced upon the family by circumstances (or public perceptions), it was apparent to the Lynds that the lines of power and leadership were highly concentrated (Bell & Newby, 1972, p. 88). The structure of power in Muncie was clear.

The Lynds also observed the changing nature of the power elite. These observations continue to be valid, although today instead of Eastern capital we might substitute international corporations or conglomerates.

> Every American city has its successful businessmen, but the American success story has been kaleidoscopic in recent years. Local giants, the boys who have grown up with the town and made good, have shrunk in stature as rapid technological changes, the heavy capital demands of nation-wide distribution, and shifts in the strategic centers for low-cost production in a national market have undercut the earlier advantages of location, priority in the field, or energy; and as Eastern capital has forced them out or bought them out and reduced them to the status of salaried men, or retired them outright in favor of imported managements. One can classify American small manufacturing cities into two groups: Those in which the industrial pioneers or their sons still dominate the local business scene, and those in which "new blood" has taken over the leadership; and it is likely that a census would show today a numerical predominance of the second group among cities containing major industries. (Lynd & Lynd, 1937, p. 76)

The term "power structure" was not actually coined and used broadly until 1953, when Floyd Hunter, a political scientist, published *Community Power Structure: A Study of Decision Makers* (Hunter, 1953). Since then, the search for power structures in communities has been on, but the numerous studies of power conducted by sociologists and political scientists have not necessarily contributed much to conceptual clarity. As we have seen, terms like "power," "influence," "leadership," and "decision making" often have been defined imprecisely. Yet what has emerged is a clear demarcation between proponents of two models of how power, influence, and leadership are distributed in communities. These two models, elitism and pluralism, are useful tools of understanding for social workers in the small community.

Elitism

Proponents of *elitism* (Hunter, 1953; Lynd & Lynd, 1929, 1937; Piven & Cloward, 1977; Vidich & Bensman, 1968) suggest that power and influence are highly centralized in communities. For the elitists, power resides in the hands of a few individuals or groups who are directly or indirectly involved in decisions simply because their personal or group interests are so pervasive that it is almost impossible for them to be indifferent to any decision. This was the situation of the X family in *Middletown in Transition* (Lynd & Lynd, 1937). One person interviewed said:

> If I'm out of work I go to the X plant; if I need money I go to the X Bank, and if they don't like me I don't get it; my children go to the X college; when I get sick I go to the X hospital . . . my wife goes downtown to buy clothes at the X department store . . . I get help from X charities; my boy goes to the X YMCA and my girls to the X YWCA; I listen to the Word of God in X subsidized churches . . . and if I am rich enough, I travel via the X airport. (p. 74)

Although the situation in many contemporary small towns is more subtle— the YMCA and YWCA are not likely to bear the name of their main benefactors, the bank may have a more neutral name, and the charities might be only indirectly aided by the X family or families, perhaps through the United Way—chances are that the main actors or leaders in these organizations will be members of a small group of influentials. Old-timers in small towns often readily discern that, although the names of board members of banks, United Way, YMCA, or YWCA might not all be the same, they often are related by marriage, club membership, or other institutional connections. As early as 1935, the Lynds had seen those interconnections: "In view of the tightening of social and economic lines in the growing city, it is not surprising that the type of leisure time organization which dominates today tends, in the main, to erect barriers to keep others out" (Lynd & Lynd, 1937, p. 312).

In 1976, the Center for Program Effectiveness Studies of the University of Virginia undertook a close replication of the second Middletown study. In this third Middletown study, Caplow and Chadwick (1979), using much more sophisticated methodology, found that in the Middletown of the 1970s occupational prestige was still unequal, although the number of people belonging to white collar and professional occupations had increased. They did find an increase in the average level of occupational prestige of the town's population as a whole, explainable by the increase in white-collar occupations in Middletown and the decrease in blue-collar occupations since the 1930s. Although the lack of equalization of occupational prestige indicated the persistence of elitism, other indicators should be considered. Caplow and Chadwick (1979) found that there had been considerable equalization in patterns of daily living. Working class and business people had come closer together on issues of housing quality, marital adjustment, and educational aspirations for their children, issues that are not directly related to the existing distribution of power but do speak in favor of an improved quality of life for all.

Although the new elitism of small communities (particularly in the growing or thriving small town) might be slightly more open (with a larger number of leaders or with a cluster of corporate leaders), even the shrewdest social worker may have difficulty identifying the community power actors. Visually, elitism is often represented pyramidally; the broad base of the pyramid symbolizes the larger participation at the lowest levels of the decision-making structure; the narrower top represents the power or decision-making elite (Figure 1). Today small-town elitism could perhaps be best represented by a truncated pyramid (Figure 2).

Two types of community elites have often been noted in the literature—one based on wealth and another on electoral politics. Many researchers, however, are less inclined to separate the two, because they are often found in close interaction at the upper levels of the pyramid, particularly in small communities. In their study of a small town in New York State, Vidich and Bensman (1968) commented:

> The interlocking, duplication and overlapping of leadership roles tend to channel community policy into relatively few hands, and it results, at the level of the personalities of the leaders, in some degree of community coordination. That is, a wide range of community activities are coordinated simply because a small number of individuals are engaged in a wide range of leadership positions. (p. 258)

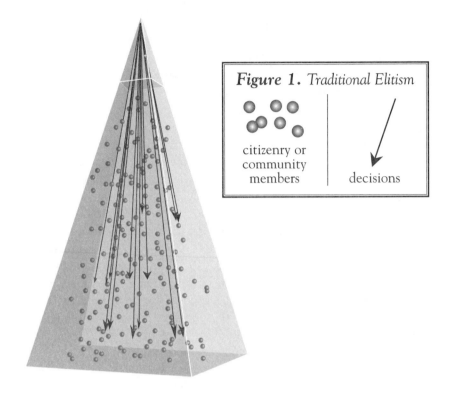

Figure 1. *Traditional Elitism*

citizenry or community members

decisions

The degree of interaction of power actors has been found to be related to the size of the community. Smaller towns tend to have more centralized patterns of decision making. Thus, the smaller the town, "[the fewer] the leaders, who are more often in agreement with each other" (Magill & Clark, 1975, p. 38).

Historically, elitism tended to be associated primarily with Southern small towns because in the colonial model of capitalist social organization, the Southern colonists, who were not Puritans, had supported the town primarily as a form of commercial social organization. In the original colonies, that meant the Southern settlements could more readily establish distances between the classes: "Towns, hubs of commercial activity, markets, ports, seats of cathedrals or universities . . . it was these commercial centers that the London 'adventurers' (capitalists) had in mind when they adjured their 'planters' (settlers) to form towns. Towns were considered the mode of organizing the settlers' labors in order to exploit whatever riches the new land contained" (Lingeman, 1980, p. 16).

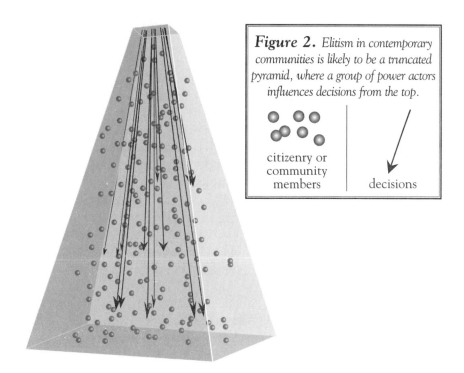

Figure 2. *Elitism in contemporary communities is likely to be a truncated pyramid, where a group of power actors influences decisions from the top.*

citizenry or community members

decisions

The best-known study documenting elitism (Hunter, 1953) was of a Southern town, although Warner's studies of Yankee City (1941, 1942) documented elitist practices in a Northern city. At the same time that many sociologists were documenting class structure, particularly elitist, through the survey method, other observers of Southern society were developing psychological insights into modern social organization. Dollard's *Caste and Class in a Southern Town* (1949); Davis, Gardner, and Gardner's *Deep South* (1941); and Rubin's *Plantation County* (1951) were all Southern examples of this genre. Studies carried out in Midwestern towns also revealed stultifying elitism; among them were *People of Coal Town* (Lantz, 1958), to some extent *Middletown* and *Middletown in Transition* (Lynd & Lynd, 1929, 1937), and of course, Vidich and Bensman's *Small Town in Mass Society: Class, Power and Religion in a Rural Community* (1968).

Although elitism was particularly evident among white settlers in the South, the phenomenon is discernible in small towns of varying racial and socioeconomic composition. A documentary film about small-town politics in the rural South (Stekler & Bell, 1985) depicted power and leadership struggles in Tallulah, a small town in the parish of Madison, Louisiana, that is 75 percent black. The film showed the ascendancy of a black leadership structure not based entirely on money and largely resulting from the struggle of black Americans for the franchise; yet economic ties to powerful interests demonstrably affected the behavior of elected leaders. One elected official, a veterinarian, was viewed by many of the other black citizens as too conciliatory to the white farmers who made up his clientele. The other, a barber who depended more on the support of his black constituency, was viewed as more tied to ideology than to powerful interests. Citizens saw the black leadership structure as not dissimilar from that of white people. In the words of one of the town dwellers interviewed in the film, "The power is split here on two sides of the fence. You've got your white southerners . . . who are your big bosses, the status quo or whatever they call them. On the black side of town, you have a handful of black politicians just running the town. They are all in the status quo and if you don't go with the status quo, you've got to buckle down."

A novel depicting African American social organization among the professional and upper classes is West's *The Wedding* (1995). Some of the novel's descriptions indicate the pervasiveness of class distinctions:

> As the doctor's wife, she was also expected to be immune to temptation. Marriage made sex permissible, desirable, but marriage bound her to one partner, a man whose time of love was contracted by work to some hasty unfinished hour in a bed too late come to and too soon left. The disordered bed of a fever-ridden patient, with her high-pitched cries, her flashing eyes, and her flesh like fire, would not release him to the fevers of the school teacher, who would not die if unattended.
>
> But she was a woman of dignity who would be too faithful to her home and children to let her unused nights diminish the meaning of her days. She deployed her energies a dozen ways, so that her mind wouldn't defile her or her body betray her to the seducers of other men's wives. When she could no longer deny that their relationship was hollow as a reed, she still preferred a public appearance on the arm of the doctor to a private, secret place where love could lie beside her. Her skin would still become flushed with pride at being Mrs. Dr. Coles, and when it did she did not look like a neglected woman. Her trembling was imperceptible. Since she did not look rejected, she supposed she did not feel rejected; she had so much that was more impressive than the thing that no nice woman ever talked about. (p. 154)

Figure 3. *Pluralistic patterns of decision making can connect individuals or groups by areas. Connections can appear at the top of the pyramids, when fewer individuals are influenced, or below the top, when greater numbers participate.*

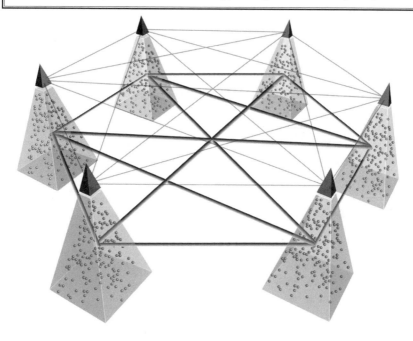

This picture of small-town elitism contrasts with that of larger cities with more decentralized or pluralistic power structures.

Pluralism

Although the philosophic conflicts between elitists and pluralists (Anton, 1963) cannot be justly summarized here, for the pluralists the identification of decision makers is more fluid, changing as the issues change. *Pluralism* can be represented visually by a circular or polygonal design within which a number of small circles or pyramids, or loci of decision making, are found (Figure 3). Thus, the pluralists would not speak of a single-community power structure but of various loci of decisional control:

> The first and perhaps most basic presupposition of the pluralist approach is that nothing can be assumed about power in any community. If any-

thing, there seems to be an unspoken notion among pluralist researchers that at bottom *nobody* dominates in a town so that their first question to a local informant is not likely to be, "Who runs this community?" but rather "Does anyone at all run this community?" (Polsby, 1960, p. 474)

Pluralists object to the sociological hypothesis of a fairly stable and stratified distribution of power. They insist that power is tied to issues and that "issues can be fleeting or persistent, provoking coalitions among interest groups and citizens, ranging in their duration from momentary to semi-permanent" (Polsby, 1960, p. 476). Since Warren defined change as episodic, that is, as attempts at accomplishing different purposes that have a beginning and an end (Warren, 1963), many other professional organizers have focused on episodes of change. Those who speak about episodic change tend to be pluralistic in their assumptions about power, because they believe that each instance of community action has its own particular context (Daley, 1997). Because social workers are primarily concerned with the process of change, understanding power in the abstract is less important to them. To be hopeful about change, it is best to view power as an attribute in flux and as a dimension with potential for change.

The social work literature tends to distinguish between personal and political power. *Personal power* is defined as the ability to control one's destiny and influence the surroundings that affect one's life, *political power* as the ability to alter systems, redistribute resources, open up opportunities and structures, and reorganize society (Dubois & Miley, 1992, p. 217). In order to emphasize the capacity for change, Dubois and Miley emphasize the pluralistic nature of the power structure, a model which is conceptually more malleable.

The current emphasis on empowerment in social work leads us to more pluralistic assumptions. While individuals cannot be empowered in all arenas of activity, they can be in some, and one purpose of social work becomes the realization of those areas where citizens can exercise self-government and control of resources (DiNitto, 1991). But a major objection to the idea that power is only issue-bound can be found in the realization that not all issues become public issues and that individuals or groups can control the issues about which decision making will be public. Can people safely "ignore the possibility . . . that an individual or group in a community participates more vigorously in supporting the nondecision-making process than in participating in actual decisions?" (Bachrach & Baratz, 1962, p. 949). Without disregarding the problems inherent in the pluralist approach to the study of power or overlooking the possible biases of the elitists, the understanding of both perspectives will help social workers ask the right questions. Both perspectives have influenced how people search for sources of influence in communities and work with them to achieve change.

Varieties of Power

Several power structures correspond roughly to points on the elitism–pluralism continuum. Powers (1967a) defined the power structure in small towns as an "identifiable interaction pattern composed of power actors who may relate to each other in a number of different ways" (p. 156). Powers proposed the following patterns of interaction: one-person power structure, tightly knit group, segmented power structure, and power pool or diffused power structure.

- In the *one-person power structure*, power is centered in one individual or family that has dominated the community for generations. Such a person or family might have "lieutenants" who carry out decisions. This type of power structure was more common in the past than currently.
- The *tightly knit group* is closer to the modern elitist community with a truncated but elitist structure.
- The *segmented power structure* refers to divisions of power within an elitist structure. For example, there might be a Democratic and a Republican elite, a Catholic and a Protestant elite, or a labor and a managerial elite.
- The *power pool* or *diffused power structure* is closer to the pluralistic model: "With this more or less loosely-knit group there is some specialization by issue areas. All of the power actors do not act in concert on every issue. For example, only a few will be at the core of issue A. Similarly, three or four may be at the core of issue B. Only one or two may be involved in both" (Powers, 1967a, p. 156). However, Powers (1967a) warns:

> Many communities appear to have a diffused power structure in which the power actors form a loosely-knit structure from which particular individuals are drawn into the core of specific issues—with some overlapping or linkage from one issue to another. This does not mean that all power actors in the "power pool" will always agree. There may be rather well-defined cliques within the pool, with little, if any, overlap. Logically, one could define as a possibility such complete specializa-

tion by issue area that no overlap occurs and thus there are as many separate power groups as there are issue areas. Such a situation has not been found in any community study of social power. For one reason, there is often a common set of resources (capital, credit control, mass media) crucial to nearly every major issue. These resources are often controlled within a community by one individual; that is, there is one newspaper or one bank. As such, there will be some overlap in the individuals involved in different issue areas. (p. 159)

The general opinion among students of small communities is that a power elite probably will be identifiable. Today, this power elite will more likely be a group of influentials who closely interact on many issues, rather than a single family, as was common in the past. The visual representation of a truncated pyramid probably best describes the modern elitist small town (Figure 2).

Communities, Power Distribution, and Policy Decisions

In a philosophical piece discussing the role social scientists can play in policy decision making, Etzioni (1989) suggested that the "me first model" of the social sciences is becoming outdated as people approach the 21st century. He proposed a model of policy development that considers the welfare of the community:

The idea that most people's choices are influenced heavily by their values and emotions provides a beginning. Entire categories of means to ends, whether efficient or not, are judged to be unacceptable and are automatically ruled out. For example, about a third of the people entitled to welfare benefits refuse to apply on the ground that "it's not right." While emotions and values are often depicted as distorting rationality (which they do), they also influence people against using means that may be efficient in the narrow sense but are wrong or hurtful to others. That is, our values influence both our choice of goals and the way we proceed to accomplish them.

The neoclassical model also draws on and contributes to the idea that all moral rights are invested in the individual, who is assumed to be the legitimate decision-maker. Attempts to modify the person's tastes are viewed as inappropriate interventions. For example, most government actions aimed at redirecting the individual are looked upon as coercive. In contemporary terms, neoclassicists are essentially libertarian.

> The most recent philosophical conception of individuals and communities as interdependent attempts to correct radical individualism. It holds that the community has a moral status and rights of its own. While some of its proponents go so far as to neglect individual rights entirely in the name of "the motherland" or some other such cause, a more defensible position is to recognize that both individual rights and duties to the community have the same basic moral standing. For example, the I & we model recognizes both the individual's rights to benefit from the savings of past generations and the obligation to save for future ones; or the individual's right to trial by a jury of peers and the individual's obligation to serve on a jury. (p. A 44)

More recently Etzioni (1998) has again commented on the communitarian significance of all citizens' daily actions. Much earlier Magill and Clark (1975) also offered advice to social workers about influencing policy decisions that affect the welfare of people in communities. The authors conceptualized a continuum drawn according to the socioeconomic characteristics (or level of socioeconomic development) of communities. Centralization and decentralization of power and decision making were identified as corresponding to various points on that continuum. Thus, although elitism and pluralism remained significant theoretical alternatives in the Magill and Clark model, applying those concepts to actual communities involved variables of size and economy.

Because social workers organizing projects cannot always conduct their own power studies, they should consider information derived from previous research:

> If a formal comparative study is impractical, the results of past studies relating socioeconomic characteristics to centralization should be helpful. [Communities] are likely to have more centralized power and decision-making structures if they:
> - are small in population;
> - are economically nondiversified (there are few employers and types of employment);
> - do not have competitive political parties or many voluntary associations;
> - have a city manager (and no mayor or a weak mayor);
> - have nonpartisan elections;
> - have at-large electoral constituencies. (Magill & Clark, 1975, p. 40)

Meenaghan (1976) analyzed more than 80 social science studies in examining the correlation between community characteristics and power structure. Although his methodology was more empirical than that of Magill and Clark, the results were surprisingly similar. Meenaghan (1976) found five variables he associated with power distribution and suggested that community workers attempting to ascertain patterns of community power initially concentrate on these variables:

> The empirical findings show that many of the hypothesized relations between specific variables and types of power structure are not confirmed and should not be stressed in attempts to ascertain patterns of community power. There are, however, variables—region, extent of absentee ownership, number of political and economic groups, degree of competitive-conflict, and instances in which the study focused on public and recurring issues—that were found to be significantly associated with the type of power structure. These are variables on which community workers can rely in initial attempts to determine the patterns of power. (p. 129)

Meenaghan's findings would suggest, for example, that a Southern community is more likely to have an elitist distribution of power than one in another region of the country; that a community with a high degree of competing business interests is more likely to be pluralist; and that a community with a large number of varied political groups is also more likely to be pluralist, whereas locales where business competition is low or where political homogeneity is high would tend to be elitist.

Other investigators do not necessarily agree with Meenaghan. Curtis and Jackson (1977) studied the community forces shaping social stratification in six different American communities. Social rank and displays of social status were common in all communities; they were not necessarily more marked in Southern than in Midwestern or other locations. Changing patterns of population distribution, as well as the effects of central government and court decisions on the life of small towns, have significantly narrowed, but not obliterated, the ability to make generalizations on the power structure based on geography alone.

Another important factor that has recently entered the equation is the postmodern perspective indicating that "to some extent, how 'we look' determines 'what we see.'" (Murdoch & Pratt, 1994, p. 84). If our paradigms do not accommodate the study of the powerless, the powerless will be invisible (Hartman, 1990). Consequently, social workers perhaps should find a variety of ways to look at the rural locality. Current rural studies propose that to do justice in interventions, we need to find a middle way. For Murdoch and Pratt (1994) this middle way "cannot emanate from 'transcendent philosophizing' but needs to be derived from the everyday grain of historically and geographically specific human communities where people are able to discuss issues of local (and possibly wider) importance in a process of 'mutual understanding' " (p. 85).

Social workers who are interested in power distribution as it affects their practice or human services policy decisions might be well advised to look in many corners before settling on one "understanding." Because their object tends to be the action that follows understanding, social workers need to analyze carefully before drawing generalizations.

> The type of power structure that prevails in a community will often influence social work decisions about strategies of intervention. If, for example, power is held by an elite, the intervention might include locating vulnerable points in the power structure, organizing the disenfranchised and powerless, recruiting resources from outside the community, and mobilizing the elite. In communities where the sources of power are pluralistic, intervention might be directed at educating the various leaders about their respective areas of power and at developing and using coalitions. The usefulness of ascertaining the distribution of power before adopting a strategy of intervention makes it desirable to be able to infer the type of power structure from other, more obvious characteristics of the community. (Meenaghan, 1976, p. 126)

Social workers must attempt to anticipate how much support or opposition leadership is likely to offer on a specific issue. They must examine the breadth of the changes sought. "If more fundamental changes are being sought, involving new conceptions of what is important or right, it is hard to avoid dealing with leading members of the power structure as well as with lower-level or more specialized decision makers" (Magill & Clark, 1975, p. 39). The more controversial the policy outcome, the broader the support that will be required to make it materialize.

A public good decision in a small town, for example, will generate more support than a fragile or controversial decision. Consider the public good decision to clean up the water supply. The clean water consumed by group A is also consumed by group B. Theoretically at least, group B has nothing to lose if group A succeeds in implementing a clean water policy. However, even such apparent public good decisions can represent hidden threats. For example, do suppliers of alternative clean water (for example, bottled-water merchants) oppose the policy change? What are the possible gains of the policy versus its costs?

An example of a fragile decision might be the construction of a bypass around a small town. Although such a decision may benefit some interests (such as trucking), it might take away resources from others (such as small downtown businesses). In the social welfare arena, a public good decision particularly in an aging small town might be the establishment of a Senior Center downtown. Most citizen groups would see themselves as being potential beneficiaries of the facility. A more fragile decision would be a halfway house for mentally ill people or a residence for homeless people.

Whether a community is elitist or pluralist, the nature of the change sought will affect the tactics of social workers.

> If the pattern of power is elitist, the worker can examine the probable relationship between the issues relating to change and the interests of the elites. The worker attempts to determine whether the changes will be compatible, neutral, or incompatible with the interests of the elites. So long as these issues are not apt to be perceived by the elites as incompatible with their interests, the worker has justification for inferring that the practice strategy should be collaborative. In this situation, the worker can assume the general role of enabler or facilitator and emphasize the more traditional practice tactics of education, consciousness raising, and joint action. The potential resources for and objects of such tactics might well be select members of the elite, who are disproportionately capable of achieving changes. (Meenaghan, 1976, p. 129)

However, when the nature of the change of policy proposed is incompatible with that of the elites,

> It is essential to identify the resources—actual and potential—of both sides and thus to calculate the probability of engaging in successful conflict. Useful in identifying resources will be state and regional regulatory agencies, public funding requirements, state laws, and the influence and power of state and national organizations. Such extra community resources are especially relevant to conflict strategies in elitist communities, since elites tend to have their disproportionate power precisely because of the resource patterns within the community and the resulting citizen apathy. (Meenaghan, 1976, pp. 129–130)

In pluralist communities, the social worker will need to assess whether the change of policy sought is or is not acceptable to those who are influentials on the specific issue. In terms of a day care policy decision, for example, who constitutes the leadership in that issue area? How do they feel about the proposal? What broader networks might be affected? The worker whose views are compatible with the leadership and interlocking interests who might benefit will engage in collaborative strategies with those leaders. If there is disagreement, the worker may need to undertake conflict-resolving strategies. However, in pluralist communities as in elitist ones, "the more the practitioner moves toward a non-collaborative strategy, the more he/she needs to focus on organizing the sustaining interest groups" (Meenaghan, 1976, p. 130).

Conflictual approaches in small towns are always two-edged. Memories in small communities are long; conflictual relationships often transcend single issues. Although conflict cannot—and perhaps should not—always be avoided, social workers must carefully calculate its consequences. What interest groups favor the policy or change? How broad is their sphere of action in community decisions? What interest groups oppose the change and how broad is *their* sphere of action? The small-community social worker, like a city practitioner, must elicit the necessary information and publicize issues so that individuals, organizations, and groups can assess their interests fully informed; forge coalitions with elements of the community to maximize power resources; educate powerful individuals in relevant specialized areas; and if necessary, negotiate and bargain to resolve any conflict that emerges (Meenaghan, 1976, p. 130). The ways in which education and coalition building are carried out will differ in small communities. At this point in the change process, social workers will test out their informal communication networks as well as their abilities to coopt, directly and indirectly, the influentials.

In Search of Power Actors

Social scientists have proposed a number of ways to identify the power actors or influential members of communities. Powers (1967a) advised that:

> Certain individuals in every social system—family, community, organization, and the like—can and do influence the decisions or actions of others. Often a community social action project fails because key people in the community power structure were not recognized or appropriately involved. The change agent, such as the Extension worker or teacher, who has a basic understanding of social power and who can identify the individual "power actors" in the community, can enhance his chance for success in social action efforts. (p. 153)

Although traditionally each of the most common approaches may have represented the perspectives of particular disciplines or scholars and may have been designed to record a particular type of leadership, multiple approaches are more likely to result in a balanced picture of the power structure of communities.

Every community's power structure is always in a state of transition. The rate of transition, the solidarity or divergence of the power actors, and membership in the power structure may vary considerably not only from one community to another but within a given community over time. Because a community power structure is dynamic, it needs to be studied from various perspectives. Moreover, each participant may hold a different perspective on specific events (Daley, 1997).

Three basic approaches to the identification of power actors in communities have emerged from the literature. They are (1) the reputational, (2) the positional, and (3) the decisional.

The Reputational Approach

In *Community Power Structure*, Floyd Hunter (1953) formulated a technique for identifying the power structure of his Regional City (thought to be Atlanta). Hunter's method, the *reputational approach,* is still useful; it involved asking informants in the city to identify the powerful individuals. His basic assumption was that "reputations for influence are an index of the distribution of influence" (Wolfinger, 1960, p. 634). Informants identified through "reputations" people perceived to be powerful in most situations—power actors rather than influentials (although in highly elitist and in many small communities, the two often overlap). Hunter concluded that a small number of businesspeople and professionals constituted the power elite of Regional City.

The reputational approach is particularly useful in towns and villages where people's actions tend to be more accessible to open community scrutiny. Even informal chains of information or "gossip lines," if used with caution, are useful in telling social workers how community members perceive the distribution of power. Social workers should not disregard obvious sources of information simply because the information cannot be "scientifically" validated. Judiciously evaluated, the opinions of long-time community residents, local newspaper people, and other keen observers in towns and counties across America are useful and important, although perhaps unconventional, sources of information.

The reputational approach should help social workers formulate a list of powerful actors in all fields, some fields, or just the human services field. Small-community social workers need lists in a variety of fields of action because such lists often show the interconnections of influentials, thus helping the practitioner avoid potentially costly errors of tact. Powers (1967b) suggested:

In this approach, most often used by sociologists, a list of community power actors is obtained by asking a number of knowledgeable community residents to name and rank those persons reputed (perceived) to have the most social power. Usually information is sought on several issues (such as health, education, and industrial development) which may have arisen within the last two to five years.

The reputational approach usually involves two major steps. The first step is to interview several knowledgeables (sometimes called a panel), obtaining their perceptions of who are the influential persons in the community. These data are then summarized and at the second step, all the persons who have been named two or more times, for example, are interviewed to obtain their ranking of the persons already named. Each is given the opportunity to add others they perceive to have equal or greater social power than they have. Social scientists have labeled this two-step procedure and variations of it the "snowball" or "cobweb" technique. The study of social power by this reputational technique may identify past, present, or anticipated power. (pp. 239–240)

Although several scholars have criticized Hunter's method, it has continued to be a useful (if not perfect) index of community power, particularly when the cobweb technique is used. The cobweb technique allows new social workers in small towns not only to identify the influentials of the town but also to get to know people, who generally are flattered when interviewed because they have been deemed "influential." Social workers can also use the technique of identification via the reputational method to become known in the community. Local influentials tend to have very strong personal networks. Once a social worker has identified and interviewed one influential, the word is likely to get around and other influentials are likely to make themselves available. Soon the social worker, particularly the novice, will be better known.

The Positional Approach

Another approach often used to identify powerful actors is the study of the civic and business leadership of a town, the *positional approach,* dealing with people like the mayor or bank president who occupy key positions within the town's structure. In the social service arena, policy boards often are positionally constructed. Thus, the United Way and the community mental health boards will have in their ranks the mayor, bank presidents, chamber of commerce leaders, and local corporation executives. Generally, the names of those people in the positional structure who are more than mere figureheads also will appear on reputational lists. However, even leaders who are only figuratively powerful cannot be disregarded because, if not their support, their opposition to community decisions can have serious consequences (Powers, 1967b).

Constructing a positional list of leaders or power actors in a small community is not an insurmountable task, though in large communities where decision making is very diversified, it can be fairly major. Those individuals who have influence because of their positions in the small town will be easily identified; often the list will include not just the individuals themselves but also members of their families (particularly their spouses). Positional actors are often interconnected through family, friendship, school, or religious ties. In identifying positional power actors, social workers will often see that the basic power structure of the town has remained elitist. As we shall see, the most useful conclusions will be drawn when the lists resulting from various approaches are compared.

The Decisional Approach

In the 1960s Robert A. Dahl (1961) and Edward C. Banfield (1961) studied decision making in New Haven and Chicago. They concluded that the structures in both cities were pluralistic. For pluralists, power means participating in decision making. As a result of their studies, Dahl and Banfield developed the *decisional approach* to identifying influentials.

> This [approach], most often used by political scientists, is sometimes referred to as event analysis. Basically, the researcher determines the persons actually involved in several community issues that have occurred recently—or preferably are in process at the time of the research. Persons "involved" are those making public statements, voting to do something, attending meetings, and the like. The major shortcoming of the technique is that it does not search out persons acting "behind the scenes." In addition, the opportunity to observe several community issues covering a wide range of interests is difficult to come by—even for the researcher with time, energy, and money. Furthermore, such a procedure would tend to reveal more implementors of decisions than initiators of decisions. While implementors are important to the ultimate outcome, they do not play the key role of legitimation. (Powers, 1967b, p. 240)

Usually, local newspapers follow town, county, and regional decisions and describe the roles of those involved in those decisions. Using the decisional approach, small-town social workers would study news items, reports, features, and editorials in local newspapers. The major problem of the decisional approach is that some decisions can never be scrutinized: "All forms of political organization have a bias in favor of the exploitation of some kinds of conflict and the suppression of others because *organization is the mobilization of bias*. Some issues are organized into politics while others are organized out" (Schattschneider, 1960, p. 71). In human services, as decisions became more localized the study of power actors and influentials, through the decisional approach became more useful, though more clouded. In following individual decisions about, for example, establishing a halfway house within a particular town, the professional discovers that the decision-making process is both formal and informal.

> Usually viewed as politics, the informal processes actually are individual to individual or group to group inferences, motives, or relationships that affect the outcome of legislation. When attempting to influence legislation, both the formal and informal processes need to be taken into consideration. For example, one group of legislators trying to push through a bill to create public jobs in order to decrease the unemployment rate, may be opposed by another group of legislators who wish to increase a certain defense budget item. These two groups may come together and compromise by creating defense-related jobs, thus enabling both groups to obtain their desired objectives. It is also possible, of course, for this to result in the defeat of both pieces of legislation. (Haynes & Michelson, 1991, pp. 69–70)

What Haynes and Michelson suggested as true for the legislative lobbying process is also true for many community decisions. The social worker in a bird's-eye examination of the process will probably have difficulty identifying the real actors. Minimally, there will be difficulty identifying what went on behind locked doors. Moreover, the actors themselves change as time goes on, or, as Daley suggested in his evaluation of the redesign of children services in a large city, "With few exceptions, representatives of the Governor's office and legislators were less active after the initial meetings. State agency administrators and business members began to send second- or third-level staff representatives. In essence, as time passed the state's top policy makers were more likely to be absent" (Daley, 1997, p. 230).

Be that as it may, the social worker cannot be discouraged and must attempt to use all possible avenues to a comprehensive understanding of the sources of influence. In a small community where numbers are smaller and actors fewer, changes of participants in specific events are likely to be less marked.

Using All Three Approaches

Proponents of pluralism or elitism have favored the three approaches differentially. Pluralists scrutinize single issues to see which power actors or leading groups emerge. They criticize the reputational approach on the grounds that reputed power is not the same as actual power. They also criticize the positional approach because they believe it discloses authority or leadership rather than power. Unlike many sociologists who accept authority as a form of power (Loomis, 1960; Powers, 1967a), political scientists often take pains to distinguish between the two concepts:

> While authority is closely related to power, it is not a form thereof; it is in fact, antithetical to it. In saying this, we reject both the traditional definition of authority as "formal power" and that which conceives it as "institutionalized power."
>
> To regard authority as a form of power is, in the first place, not operationally useful. If authority is "formal power," then one is at a loss to know who has authority at times when the agent who possesses "formal power" is actually powerless. To say that Captain Queeg continued to have authority on the USS *Caine* after he was relieved of his command by the mutineers is to create needless confusion. (Bachrach & Baratz, 1970, pp. 32–33)

On the other hand, the sociologists' notion of authority as formal power can be useful in explaining many of the incongruous mandates issued by outgoing administrators or politicians, who exercise their authority long after they have ceased to have formal power.

Students and new social workers should apply all three approaches to the identification of power actors in their communities, drawing up parallel lists of key actors identified according to each approach—thus constructing a rudimentary barometer of power actors. If a leader's name appears on lists drawn according to the positional, the reputational, and the decisional approaches, the social worker can safely surmise that that particular actor is likely to exert influence in an array of areas. Similarly, if certain names are confined to a single list, those individuals are likely to have a more circumscribed arena of influence. However, as with all rudimentary barometers, it would be unwise to conclude that a person whose name does not appear on any list has no influence.

Figures 4, 5 and 6 illustrate visually how the three approaches can elicit parallel lists of community influentials. Each circle represents one approach and the lists developed using it. When those lists all coincide, the community is probably highly elitist, with only a very clearly identified

Approaches to Identification of Decision Makers
A Rudimentary Barometer

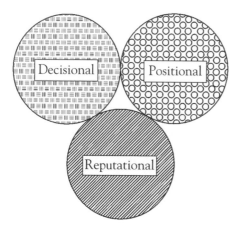

Figure 4. *A dispersed pattern of decision making. When no common actors are identified through the three approaches, the likelihood is that leadership and power are quite dispersed in the community. This situation is more rare in small towns.*

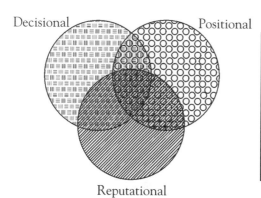

Figure 5. *The degree to which the three approaches render common names of individuals or organizations is an indication of the level of concentration of decision making (and/or power) in a few or many hands.*

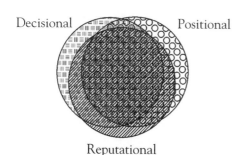

Figure 6. *The high degree of coinciding or common names shown in Figure 6 would indicate a highly selective or elitist community, where decision making is in the hands of a few individuals or groups.*

group of people as leaders, at least in the popular view and perhaps also as in actuality. The larger the area common to the three approaches, the less pluralistic the community. When the lists coincide only in part, the community is moving along the elitist/pluralist continuum.

These graphs provide a visual aid for social workers to develop their own systems for approaching the reality of their communities. The important thing is not how an understanding of the power structure is constructed but the fact that in working toward that understanding, the social worker will learn a great deal about community forces and the people in the community who are active in decision-making, even while becoming known to the members of the community.

Internal and External Influences on Power Actors

Sills (1975) suggested that "all community groups, including those concerned with providing a service or promoting mutual help, are likely to come up against, and have to reckon with, the exercise of power in their locality" (p. 24). For example, groups will confront power actors in carrying out such basic actions as obtaining planning permission or seeking material or human resources. In addition to the locally based power holders, many powerful bodies inside a locality also operate from outside. Warren (1977, 1978), who subscribes to a systemic perception of the community similar to that of Sills or Vidich and Bensman (1968), suggested that:

> Varied studies of status in the macrosystem . . . lend support to the importance of considering local power structures as largely determined by position in the macrosystem and suggest the inadequacy of power structure studies that consider the macrosystem as a largely peripheral issue while concentrating on the internal dynamics of the specific local community. The new manager of the important local branch plant of the national corporation almost immediately finds himself exercising inordinate influence on local situations, not because of any locally generated adulation, but because his position as dictated by the national system gives access to important resources, which can be utilized for positive or negative sanctions vis-à-vis other local actors. . . .
>
> It needs stressing that in virtually every aspect of local community activities, important organization linkages to parts of the macrosystem are operative whether this linkage be through religious denominations, professional associations, company branch subsidiaries, branches of federal and state government, labor unions, or whatever. (Warren, 1978, p. 432)

Warren sees local groups as interconnected with external organizations that must be considered in any power analysis. Strong horizontal and vertical ties exist among community decision makers. Vidich and Bensman (1968) stated that political leaders "not only point up the boundaries of the actual jurisdictions of political units but also indicate the significant linkages and combinations within local government and the political agencies of the wider society" (p. 222).

Whether community members endorse or are critical of the encroachment of external forces, they cannot afford to deny reality. External forces must be assessed for their potential to influence community control. Perhaps it behooves social workers to heed MacKaye's advice: "These forces are neither 'good' nor 'bad' but *so*. And they do not stand still, but flow and spread as we have told. Can we control their flow before it controls us? Can we do it soon enough? . . . What instructions can we issue to our modern day explorer (whether technical or amateur) to guide him in coping with this modern-day invasion?" (1962, p. 209)

One illustration may lend some practical clarity to MacKaye's advice. "Guadalupe's Cohesiveness at Stake" (1998) (see excerpt, p. 197), published in the *Arizona Republic*, discusses a long-standing dispute between the town of Guadalupe, which is located in the middle of the city of Phoenix, and the Yaqui tribe. Yaquis founded Guadalupe around 1910 and it was first known as Yaqui Town, but in the 1930s and 1940s large numbers of Mexican immigrants, many with great affinity to the Yaqui, settled there. Guadalupe is still mostly populated by Yaquis and Hispanics. In 1995 the Pascua Yaqui Tribe bought some acreage in Guadalupe from local doctors who were going to develop the area but decided against it. Thus the conflict began. The Pascua Yaqui tribe asked the Bureau of Indian Affairs to declare the acreage that they had bought a reservation. The mayor of Guadalupe, very concerned about the ramifications of the request, appealed the matter. The illustration not only highlights the sadness of conflict among two groups who, in relation to overall power structures, are not particularly powerful, it also points to the importance of power tensions in relation to the very fabric of a community. External forces, such as decisions of the Bureau of Indian Affairs or the courts, stand to influence very directly the coexistence of individuals within the community. The article illustrates the political issues that can arise in the relationship of small towns to their surrounding communities. It also reflects delicate issues of balance of power among various interests—in this case, those of an Indian nation and those of a small, primarily Indian town.

For those unfamiliar with the many issues in the Southwestern United States that affect Indian nations and tribes, some background might be in order. When the conquistadores invaded Mexico, the Yaquis were able to hold them off and became well known for their war strategies. Around 1617 a Spanish Jesuit, Andres Perez de Ribas, was invited by the Yaquis to tell about Christianity. Many missions were established and Spanish and Yaqui ways became interwoven in culture, art, and religion. In 1907 the Mexican government made another attempt to weaken the Yaquis, deporting several thousand from Northern Sonora, Mexico, to Yucatán. According to Fuentes (1992), Porfirio Diaz, proclaiming himself to be "scientifically" inspired, waged campaigns against the Indian population of Northern Mexico to give their lands to Mexican gentry and U.S. companies (Fuentes, 1992, p. 286). Many thousands of Yaquis had come to what is now Arizona in the 19th century; but the Mexican persecution of the 20th century resulted in the establishment of Yaqui villages in Tucson and near Tempe. Guadalupe is one of those villages. Because the Bureau of Indian Affairs did not recognize Yaqui tribal government until 1982, the extent of their tribal lands has been often disputed.

Sills (1975) constructed a model of community power holders that includes a listing of both externally and locally based powerful actors. Although the exact names of the groups might differ, both local and nonlocal powerful actors can be identified in most U.S. communities. Sills suggested that the local power structure should be seen as comprising externally and locally based organizations, local officials, and political party leaders. Externally based organizations include national or multinational groups that may have local subsidiaries, investment property and contracting companies that conduct business from a distance but can put pressure on local authorities, national newspaper chains that editorially influence local papers, national and state governments that influence local fiscal and administrative decisions, and national and state legislators who might support or oppose local decisions. Locally based organizations include large local firms that sponsor local projects (the community might feel indebted to these firms); small local firms that are prepared to form coalitions to protect themselves and their interests, and other large institutions such as universities, trust funds, or churches that are landowners and that have special tax or other advantages. Local officials and political party leaders are those people who minimally possess one essential tool or resource, that is, the control of both the content and the flow of important information on local matters (Sills, 1975, pp. 24–28).

An excellent illustration of how business operations external to the community affect the life of communities is provided in an article from the *Los Angeles Times*, "Promise of Jobs Brings Diversity to Iowa Farm Town" (see excerpt, p. 199). This is a very positive piece. The influence of out-

[Text continues on page 198]

Guadalupe's Cohesiveness at Stake

Trust issue could rip community apart

Guadalupe was right to appeal the federal Bureau of Indian Affairs' approval of placing 23 acres of the town into trust for the Pasqua Yaqui Tribe. That's a big chunk of a 430-acre town.

Although the land is important, there are other issues to keep in mind as Guadalupe and the Yaquis begin what could become a long legal battle: such things as cohesion, neighborliness and sense of community in a unique corner of the big, urban Valley.

What happens on the acreage, which the Yaqui already own, certainly will affect the town.

For instance, tribal land falls under tribal jurisdiction, according to realty specialist Wayne Sumatakuku of the Phoenix area office of the BIA.

That means that if the 23 acres become Indian trust land, Guadalupe will not be able to collect taxes or building fee revenues. The town could impose no zoning restrictions. It would have no legal control. Guadalupe's Police and Fire departments would have no authority there.

The Yaquis say they need the trust designation so they can apply for federal housing funds that can only be used on tribal trust land. That way, their tribal members can get better homes.

Some worry that once the land is put into trust, the Yaquis could petition the secretary of the Interior to add it to their reservation. That's a move the BIA usually recommends, says Wayne Nordwall, area director for the bureau.

And it's a move that Yaquis say they don't plan to make.

The big fear of many in Guadalupe is that the site, which is close to Interstate 10, U.S. 60 and the new Arizona Mills shopping center, might someday sprout a casino. After all, the Yaquis already operate a casino near Tucson.

That *could* happen. But it's unlikely.

Indian land acquired after 1988 has to meet more stringent requirements to get approval for gaming. Building a casino would require both the Interior Department and Gov. Jan Hull to agree, says Gary Husk, director of the Arizona Department of Gaming, and the governor would have absolute veto power.

At any rate, the Yaquis say they don't want a casino. Husk says that the tribe has always been straightforward with his department and that it has not discussed any plans for a casino. The BIA also says there has been no talk of gaming.

A casino isn't the issue. The issue is, a small town would lose revenue and control over much of its future if it lost this chunk of land.

Guadalupe's appeal of the BIA decision to put the land into tribal trust will be reviewed by the Interior Board of Indian Appeals, a process that could take months.

Perhaps during this appeal, the town and tribe could solve their own problems. If not, depending on the board's decision, it could be appealed by either the tribe or the town to U.S. District Court, a process that could go all the way to the Supreme Court.

Both the town and the tribe are fighting for self-determination. But one of the greatest potential losses could be each side's view of the other.

Yaqui tribal members are part of the town's roots. Yaquis founded Guadalupe at the beginning of the century. They and the Hispanics who came in the 1930s and '40s, helped weave the rich cultural tapestry that is Guadalupe today.

If Guadalupe ultimately loses some [of] its land to the tribe, it will face complex, though not insurmountable, challenges. Cities can, and do, work with tribes that have reservations adjacent.

The tribe's challenges, if it loses its attempt to have the land put into trust, also are daunting. It will have to find another source of funds for housing projects and services to tribal members who need them.

We wonder, does eligibility for federal housing money justify the damage to the cohesiveness of Guadalupe?

The town incorporated in 1975 to preserve its unique community. The development that has since engulfed the town proves that the move was right. But now,

creating trust lands threatens to effectively disincorporate a big part of the town.

Both sides stand to lose something irreplaceable if this becomes a nasty, divisive fight. They *are* the community of Guadalupe. They should be working together.

SOURCE: Guadalupe's cohesiveness at stake. (1998, January 18). *Arizona Republic*, p. 4EV. Reprinted courtesy of the *Arizona Republic*.

[Text continued from page 196]

side networks has brought life back into a small community, whose resources for economic survival were dwindling. The article describes how an Orthodox Jewish firm bought a boarded-up meat packing plant in Postville, Iowa. The opening of that plant attracted a good number of workers from a variety of backgrounds, not only Orthodox Jews, but also Mexicans, Guatemalans, Ukrainians, and Bosnians. The new group brought not only an economic revival to Postville but important changes in the diversity of the town. The mayor comments on the fact that for those who may have wanted a sleepy little town, perhaps the quality of life has deteriorated with such diversity, but for those who wanted economic betterment, the arrival of all these new groups has brought forth a revival. In this case, economic development and heterogeneity appear to have brought prosperity and friendship among diverse groups. Towns like Postville are likely to become examples for the 21st century.

Human services professionals must recognize the influence of both internal and external forces in the small community. In recent years many small towns have been affected, for example, by issues of growth and development. The price of housing in such communities is related to the availability of affordable units. Outside builders and investors are often involved in deciding where and how many units to build. Local firms and landowners often have opposing perspectives because of conflicting interests. Local officials are vulnerable to both internal and external influences. Yuhui (1996) documented similar problems in relation to neighborhood organization in the inner city and Schwirian and Mesch (1993) declared that "under conditions of heterogeneity, effective local action relies on the ability of local systems to engage in coalition formation in order to achieve a successful outcome" (p. 97).

[Text continues on page 200]

Promise of Jobs Brings Diversity to Iowa Farm Town

Locals learn to cope with immigrants

Used to be if you wanted a quickie breakfast, your choices were pretty much limited to doughnuts: one with sticky pink frosting or one smeared with gooey chocolate. Now, you can get a kosher blueberry bagel. Or a loaf of dense, tangy Russian bread. Or even a Mexican pastry.

Diversity has arrived in this tiny farm town, and locals are trying hard to cope.

For 150 years, Postville was all White, all Christian, all Norman Rockwell, an everyone-knows-everyone, live-and-die-here kind of town run by farmers of German and Norwegian stock. Then, a decade ago, an ultra-Orthodox Jew bought a boarded-up meat-packing plant on the edge of town and converted it into a kosher slaughterhouse. Word soon got out that Postville had jobs. Lots of jobs.

The Jews came first—three dozen rabbis trained to kill and inspect kosher meat, plus friends and relatives to help. Then came the others. Mexican, Guatemalan, Ukranian, Nigerian, Bosnian, Czech—dozens, then hundreds, of immigrants swarmed to jobs in the kosher slaughterhouse and in the Iowa Turkey Products plant next door. To locals, it seemed an invasion.

"It was a little scary at first," said Becky Meyer, a lifelong resident.

"You'd see them and you wouldn't really know how to talk to them, how to act around them," high school sophomore Wade Schutte recalled. "It took a while to adjust."

And no wonder. Postville's population is just 1,500, "and that's counting everyone and their dog," locals say. It's isolated too, pinned by endless rolling fields in the northeast corner of a state that's still 95 percent White. Many folks born and raised here until recently had never met a Black person, never met a Jew, never heard a foreign language except in school.

Now they run into rabbis in long black coats and prayer shawls walking down the streets speaking Hebrew. On their way to the pharmacy, they pass a Mexican store decorated with bullfight posters, selling refried beans.

Some locals—raised, no doubt, on the maxim that if they can't say anything nice, they shouldn't say anything at all—purse their lips with unmistakable disgust and refuse to talk about Postville's new look. But many are trying to adjust.

"This is a little town that's 20-some miles from even a McDonald's," reasoned Doug All, a quality inspector at the slaughterhouse, "so we have to get along."

If locals are unsure what to make of the newcomers, the feeling is mutual. Summoned by a sort of international hotline that passes word whenever a friend of a friend of a friend finds work, immigrants come to Postville knowing jobs await them—and knowing precious little else.

"The first time I'd ever heard of Iowa was when we moved here," said 15-year-old Ilya Pakarov of Kazakhstan.

"It's way different from California," said Susy Navarro, who moved from Oakland so her husband could work at the slaughterhouse.

The uneasy melding of cultures in Postville reflects a broader drama playing out across the Midwest and the South. Wherever there are jobs, there are immigrants. And meat-packing plants offer jobs.

But even in the context of rapid demographic change, Postville stands out.

For one thing, it's unusual to see immigrants from so many countries find their way to such a small town. There are so many immigrants from the former Soviet Union that the kosher slaughterhouse posts its safety warnings in Russian—along with English, Hebrew and Spanish.

Experts say it's also rare to see thriving

Jewish communities in rural Iowa, much less ultra-Orthodox communities.

With several dozen Jewish families, virtually all of them adherents to the Lubavich branch of Hasidism and many with six or eight children, Postville "is a very interesting little place," said Mark Grey, an anthropologist at the University of Northern Iowa who has studied the town.

Aaron Rubashkin, who bought the slaughterhouse to supply fresh meat to his kosher store in New York, never explained why he settled on Postville. His son Shalom, who now helps run the plant, can say only that "divine providence" must have guided him.

When the slaughterhouse first opened in 1990, the Rubashkins and the rabbis they hired commuted from large cities with established Jewish populations. But that got wearying. So a few years ago, they committed to Postville. They set up a synagogue. They converted a former hospital into a Jewish school. They bought homes.

The Jews were quickly pegged as snobby because they wouldn't eat in the local pizza joint (it wasn't kosher) or greet their neighbors warmly (among the Lubavich, men don't shake hands with women and women don't shake hands with men). They were thought odd because their little boys all

have such long hair (by tradition, it can't be cut until age 3) and because the women all wear wigs (they cover their natural hair out of modesty).

Plus, there were cultural differences that have nothing to do with religion. These Jews were big-city bustlers, fast talkers who didn't adapt right away to the slower pace of small-town life.

In time, however, many grew to love the measured tempo of Postville. Locals began to relax as well.

The newspaper recruited a Jewish woman to write a regular column explaining Hasidic customs. Kids of all religions started playing together.

Most important, the kosher plant, AgriProcessors, was doing well by Postville's economy. The workers shopped in town, boosting local merchants. They also spurred development in a town that had long been stagnant.

"You could say the quality of life here has deteriorated if you liked a small, sleepy town," Mayor John Hyman said, "but there has been economic betterment."

SOURCE: Simon, S. (1999, January 31). Promise of jobs brings diversity to Iowa farm town. *Arizona Republic.* Copyright, 1999, *Los Angeles Times.* Reprinted by permission.

[Text continued from page 198]

Local and Cosmopolitan Influentials

Social workers need to understand who the influentials and leaders are in small communities to help them assess whether a particular individual, identified as an influential, is likely to be interested in espousing, for example, a local social service cause or project or is more likely to care about an issue outside the local community. Which influentials will be responsive to local problems and concerns and which will not? If leadership energy must be catalyzed around specific events (Daley, 1997; Warren, 1978), which leaders will respond to which projects or issues becomes an important point of understanding. Whom should the local practitioner tap or coopt to help legitimize which causes?

Two types of influentials with different orientations and spheres of influence are effective in the local community: (1) locals and (2) cosmopolitans (Merton, 1949, 1957). These terms do not refer to the regions in which interpersonal influence is exercised but to the types of issues each will espouse. According to Merton (1957), the town or village is essentially the world for local influentials; they are only marginally interested in the outside world; their sphere of action is local issues. The local influential is essentially a very creative local whose scope of interest and activity at most extends to the state. The cosmopolitan, on the other hand, although possibly also an influential in the local community, looks at the outside world with keen interest and regards himself or herself as an active member of a larger society. The state, the nation and the world are the preferred sphere of action.

The two types behave quite differently. The local influential is more thoroughly "adapted to the community" (Merton, 1957, p. 395) and usually is not interested in being influential outside the local community. This person has made a mark in the locality and is interested in staying. Personal contacts legitimize and help local influentials to establish themselves and acquire political, business, and other types of support. Local influentials are truly *gemeinschaftlich* in their style of operation:

> They crowd into those organizations which are largely designed for making contacts, for establishing personal ties. Thus they are found largely in the secret societies (Masons), fraternal organizations (Elks), and local service clubs—the Rotary, Lions, and the Kiwanis. . . . Their participation appears to be less a matter of furthering the nominal objectives of these organizations than of using them as contact centers. (Merton, 1957, pp. 398–399)

Local influentials might become local or county political figures but seldom will run for national office. They are likely to espouse causes that are public and acceptable, like the Red Cross Blood drive or the Kiwanis Pancake Day, but will seldom spearhead a controversial needle exchange project or a campaign to get the local hospital to provide better services to welfare mothers—although a big change in the past decade or so has been the growing number of local influentials interested in fringe issues.

Cosmopolitan influentials also belong to various organizations and espouse causes because their region of influence might also include the local community. However, the nature of those causes and organizations differs from that of local influentials. Cosmopolitan influentials join professional societies and espouse causes where special knowledge and skills are required. They are interested in organizations because of their functions, rather than because of the people they are likely to meet. They want to grow beyond local parameters and act accordingly.

Although neither educational level nor occupational status distinguishes local and cosmopolitan influentials, other characteristics do. Merton (1957) postulated that local influentials are long-time residents of the community. They usually have worked their way up the ladder of influence, generally a slow process. Townspeople know generally the strengths and limitations of local influentials. On the other hand, cosmopolitan influentials usually are outsiders who have arrived in the community with skills, knowledge, and status. They have gained acceptance among the town's influentials quickly, often transferring status from their prior positions into the new community. Cosmopolitan influentials were found in many of the fast-growing small towns of the 1980s. They are the professional or company executives; having taken their place in the power structure of small towns with considerable speed, they are often resented by local influentials.

Understanding local and cosmopolitan influentials is still very important today. The devolution of decision-making to the local level has increased the importance of the local influential. While local leadership has become much more influential in the distribution of governmental resources, many of which still come from the center, the emergence of conglomerates has increased the importance of the cosmopolitan influential. Any local influential must understand the broad global ramifications of decision-making. The cosmopolitan influential whose eyes are on the outside world can provide an important linkage to the local level.

In the past ten years, the social work literature has placed a great deal of importance on "empowerment social work." (Saleebey, 1997; Simon, 1990) According to the authors, empowerment is not giving or returning power to people in a paternalistic way, it is facilitating the capabilities of people to define their own world and make their own decisions within that context. As Colby (1997) has suggested, "The process of [empowerment] is a powerful, non-traditional approach that encourages social workers to view neighbors as full-partnered participants, stake holders, collaborators, and consumers in a community process" (Colby, 1997, pp. 2–3). This situation has increased the role of the local influential. Furthermore, local leaders often emerge from a cadre of local influentials, although they may not necessarily be one and the same.

In his original ideal models of community intervention, Rothman (1974) identified three possible orientations to the power structure. The first was locality development, in which members of the power structure were seen as collaborators in a common venture, because locality development was fundamentally an educationally oriented community intervention. Rothman's second model was social planning policy, in which members of the power structure were seen as employers and sponsors of planning projects. In the third model, social action, the power actors were seen as an external target of action. Rothman himself later stated that the power structure was seen "as oppressors to be coerced or overturned" (Rothman, 1996).

In 1996, Rothman developed a new model, interweaving his three old patterns. Because locality development has tended to be the most fruitful form of intervention in small communities, the interweaving of these three forms of action might be a more useful form of intervention for social workers. In fact, most rural community social workers will find themselves functioning within the locality development model or within a framework that interweaves Rothman's three models. In locality development, the identification of local influentials is essential. In a model that interweaves locality development with policy planning and organization, the identification of both local and cosmopolitan influentials achieves new status.

Many social workers find themselves outsiders in small towns because they either have come from somewhere else or have been outside the community in pursuit of their education. Although social workers might be quickly accepted in the structure of the town, they need to be concerned particularly with local influentials. "The cosmopolitan influential has a following because he knows; the local influential because he understands" (Merton, 1957, p. 403). Merton (1949) believed that the "impersonal welfare worker" could never become a local influential. Nearly 50 years later, social workers continue to be aware of the problems intrinsic to relying only on bureaucratic interactions in small communities. A practice approach that is sensitive to the interconnections of locals and cosmopolitans is still essential. Because partnerships have developed as an essential tool of service, human services professionals in small towns must cultivate relationships with both local and cosmopolitan influentials as they try to connect with clients, leaders, and business and political interests.

Summary

Social scientists have studied power as a separate variable in communities because by understanding how power is distributed, they often have learned about other community characteristics. Likewise, social workers who are interested in community projects or community interventions in small towns must be aware of how decisions are made, who makes them, and how the powerful and influential members of the community often may be intertwined.

The theoretical distinctions between power, influence, and leadership often are obliterated because in small towns power actors, influentials, and leaders are often the same people. Many theorists believe that leadership is more episodic and thus that leaders emerge with each purposeful event. While this is true in more diffuse, pluralistic structures, it is not as common in small towns, where leaders are not as numerous and the same individuals tend to be active in many events. In most modern small communities, although the power distribution is often elitist, what is found is no longer a perfect pyramid—a single individual or family involved in most decisions—but a truncated pyramid with a close-knit group of influentials dominating the decision making. Empowerment social work advises social workers to let the community make its own decisions. This is a useful principle. Yet because rural practice is more likely to be based on a "locality development" model of intervention, members of the power structure and influentials are sought as collaborators, supporters, and educators in many projects.

Social workers attempting to secure legitimacy for their projects or to coopt influentials into their causes need to be able to identify these influentials as local or cosmopolitan. They also need to determine how each type of influentials will react to those causes. Social workers must develop practical lists of reputational, positional, and decisional power actors and decision makers in their small communities. It is often through such exercises that they are able to read the pulse of the town and observe how power, influence, and leadership reveal themselves in the day-to-day life of small communities.

The following story from the *Detroit News* illustrates explicitly some of the points discussed in the chapter on the difference between power and influence. Clarksdale's first black mayor had sought to use his office to empower African American citizens and release them from the grip of poverty. Nevertheless, the 49-year-old politician found that "The ballot isn't enough. We have the right to vote but we don't control the resources." What Henry Espy, the mayor of this Mississippi Delta community found, was precisely what we have discussed: Even though theoretically able to hold power in the sense of achieving positional status, Espy found that the control of resources had very profound meaning. In order to have a practical impact on decisions and on the life of Clarksdale's citizens, Espy discovered that the ability to influence economic decisions was crucial.

Other black politicians, not necessarily in small towns, have similar concerns. "Blacks don't control the financial institutions, the retailing, manufacturing and the major businesses in the service sector that provide the jobs and contribute to the economy of many cities," the article reports. Michael White, mayor of Cleveland, told of the disappointments of black elected officials who are often hindered by lack of economic power. Espy's story brings home the point that, while the franchise does empower people, it does not bring immediate influence.

 ## Black America?

When he became mayor four years ago, Henry Espy had grandiose visions for his dusty rural community in the heart of the Mississippi Delta.

As Clarksdale's first black mayor, he sought to use his office to free many of the town's 18,000 African Americans from the grip of poverty.

Espy had reduced the city's crime rate and mended some of the racial divisions, but 60 percent of the residents still live in poverty.

The 49-year-old politician says simply holding office isn't the cure-all.

"The ballot isn't enough. We have the right to vote but we don't control the resources," said Espy. "We need an economic ballot, an education ballot, a housing ballot. If you give a homeless man a ballot, what in essence have you given him? We are telling our people to go and vote and then sending them back to the same desperate situations."

Many African Americans, like Espy, held high expectations about what blacks in elected office would bring. They believed that as more blacks took office that the clout and influence of African Americans would likewise grow.

Today, there are about 7,600 black elected officials in the United States, but the sobering reality is that there is a sharp difference between holding office and wielding power.

Scholars, politicians and strategists say the political empowerment of African Americans is limited because: Blacks don't control the economic resources in their communities and don't have much influence over how the dollars are directed. Black elected officials don't have a clearly defined agenda for resolving black America's problems. Scholars and political pundits say too many black politicians are playing politics as usual rather than using unconventional methods to solve the black community's extraordinary problems. Black politicians don't have the benefit of a grass-roots social movement like in the '60s to pressure the system to change. And blacks, unlike other special interest groups such as Israeli and Arab interests, the National Rifle Association, and pro-abortion rights and anti-abortion forces, don't have an organized effective lobby with the deep pockets. Although the National Association for the Advancement of Colored People and the National Urban League do actively pressure Congress on behalf of blacks, they are not by definition lobbies because they are nonprofit, nonpartisan and prohibited from making financial contributions to political campaigns.

Despite knowing that government hasn't brought the wholesale changes many had hoped for, blacks still believe it can make a difference in their lives. They continue to have high expectations because government at times has been a partner in their crucial quest for social and economic justice.

Although black elected officials face limitations, they've been able to change policies and practices in education, city halls, police and fire departments and other civil and social service areas. For example, black mayors have been able to integrate city departments, making them much more responsive to community concerns. Black elected school boards have implemented sensitive and relevant curriculums and pushed for more minority teachers.

Such successes may explain why blacks still see government as an effective vehicle through which their concerns can be addressed. According to a Detroit News/Gannett News Service poll of 1,211 African Americans, 71 percent said the Democratic party was effectively representing their interests, putting it only behind the NAACP and the Urban League in meeting the needs of black Americans.

Even today, in the midst of a presidential election, African Americans are pinning their hopes on a change in the White House.

Harold Cruse, a professor of history at the University of Michigan, said African Americans have deluded themselves into thinking that the ballot is a panacea for the communities' ails.

"There's a definite difference between real power and perceived power and black politicians have perceived power," Cruse said. "It's ridiculous to discuss power and influence because we didn't have any (in the '60s) and we don't have any now. At least in the '60s we had leverage—we had the civil rights movement."

Politics of economics

While speaking in Ohio to a group of black mayors recently, Michael White, the 41-year-old mayor of Cleveland, told his peers that being on television, in newspapers and magazines and receiving awards doesn't mean a thing.

"What good is it for you or me to be the mayor if all we do is preside over economic wastelands," White told a group of small-town mayors. "We've got to transform our positions into something meaningful for our people."

Black elected officials are hindered in empowering the black community because African Americans don't wield economic clout, scholars and political leaders maintain.

Blacks don't control the financial institutions, the retail industry, manufacturing and the major businesses in the service sector that provide the jobs and contribute to the economy of many cities. Those institutions are largely in the hands of whites, whose political interests often run counter to those of African Americans.

That difference is crystallized in the failure of the Congressional Black Caucus to force the Reagan and Bush administrations to enact the Humphrey-Hawkins full employment bill—a measure that would create employment opportunities for thousands of unemployed African Americans by reducing the national unemployment rate to 3 percent or less. If the private sector failed to produce enough jobs to get the unemployment rate that low, the government was to create jobs to make up the difference.

Such a policy was contrary to the economic philosophies of the Reagan and Bush administrations. Both presidents abhorred government involvement in the creation of jobs, while relying on the free market to do so.

"The basic agenda of black leadership has been to try to get jobs and Humphrey-Hawkins was their major effort for two decades and it was a failure," said Robert Smith, a professor of political science at San Francisco State University. "It shows how occupying positions of power has not translated into effective power."

John Conyers, the longest serving black in Congress, said he and his colleagues have delivered under difficult circumstances.

"How could we translate political power into social and economic power when we have been under 12 years of conservative anti-black federal authority," said Conyers, a Detroit Democrat who has been in Congress for almost 30 years. "There is no way we can pick the Democratic Party up by the bootstraps and play political judo on the administration, but we can win small victories."

A call for unity

In 1972, black elected officials, scholars and community activists met in Gary, Ind., in an attempt to outline a strategy for political, economic and social empowerment. Twenty years later, Black America still does not have a cohesive agenda.

Rather than harnessing their collective power to improve the lives of African Americans, many black politicians are more caught up in individual agendas, said Ron Walters, chairman of the department of political science at Howard University.

"This business of being elected to represent a district is fine, but black elected officials have to have a wider vision for the good of all blacks," he said. "No one or two of them can do it alone."

"We need far more unity and cohesiveness," said Walters, author of a book on black and presidential politics. "We are in a game that requires power, and power comes in numbers."

Blacks must unite, but that's not going to help them unless they have a solid agenda, said Aldon Morris, a professor of social movements at Northwestern University.

"The unique problems of the African American community, such as the need for jobs and the high proportion of blacks below the poverty line, are the kind of issues that black elected officials need to come together on, sort out, debate and come up with a unified strategy to correct," Morris said.

"I'm not talking about unity based on skin color but one that rises out of analysis and debate."

Donald Tucker, a councilman from Newark, N.J., and a founder of the New Jersey Black Issues Conference, said elected officials must start by setting an achievable agenda on the state level. This can be done by creating local "Black Leadership Roundtables" that meet at a statewide convention.

Walters said he was impressed by the New Jersey Black Issues Conference and impressed with the programs for senior citizens and youth the officials were able to implement.

"You have politicians, community activists and civil rights leaders in a common framework," Walters said. "That level of statewide coordination ought to be present in every state."

Tucker believes you build on the statewide approach to develop a national black political agenda.

"Despite the diversity in officials and their state agendas, you have national issues that can be agreed upon, such as reenactment of the Housing Act to provide low-income and affordable housing, a full employment bill, AIDS research and health care," Tucker said.

Political science professor Smith said that lack of innovation has contributed to lack of African Americans' political progress.

"African American politicians act as though they represent communities that are in the same shape as those represented by white politicians and they don't," Smith said. "They don't use their power to halt the procedures. From time to time, they are rhetorically militant, but in terms of action it has been business as usual.

"Adam Clayton Powell was a protester in Congress," he said. "These guys have come in thinking they can use internal power to get something done for black people and that is clearly not the case."

Congressman Floyd Flake, whose district includes Queens, New York, said too many black politicians were selected by the Democratic or Republican party machines rather than the people.

"In general, their primary agenda and responsibility has not been to other black people, but to the political apparatus that put them there," said Flake, who is a Democrat, but won with nontraditional, church-based support. "many of them are more concerned about keeping their jobs than doing their job for the people."

Others say that present-day black politicians, such as Cleveland's Mayor White, Baltimore's Mayor Kurt Schmoke and Seattle's Mayor Norm Rice, are career politicians replacing lifelong community activists who came from a civil rights background.

"Most of them (black elected officials) have been co-opted—there isn't any question about it," said Ed Vaughn, a former Michigan representative and owner of Vaughn's Bookstore in Detroit. "Sometimes they are voices in the dark and some of them try to keep hope alive, but essentially they are blending in. They're just playing routine politics and falling in line."

'60s strategies for '90s

During the 1960s, black politicians had a unified agenda—one of basic civil rights—and a social movement that applied pressure on the political system.

Today, black politicians don't have the benefit of a grass-roots social movement to pressure for change. The answers to the problems aren't as clear-cut.

Compounding the problem is the influence of lobbies on the political process. Black America, unlike other special interest groups such as the Israeli and Arab interests, the National Rifle Association and the pro-abortion rights and anti-abortion forces, don't have an organized lobby.

Scholars and political pundits say there is a need for mass mobilization and coalition building among blacks and across racial lines.

Bringing together disparate groups as the Black United Front, The Nation of Islam, fraternal groups and grass-roots organizations would give elected officials more clout because it would be clear to the political powers that they are speaking on behalf of a politically active constituency,

said James Turner, professor of African studies and political sociology at Cornell University.

By the same token, the African-American community must demand that black politicians address their concerns and hold them accountable when they don't, said Rufus Browning, professor of political science at San Francisco State University.

"Blacks have not pressured their politicians to be responsive to their needs," said Browning, the author of a book on racial politics in U.S. cities. "Let's face it, black office holders have been protected because we as blacks (are) giving them a break because they struggled so long to get where they are. But that has got to change."

Smith, Browning's colleague at San Francisco State, agrees.

"We need more commitment and criticism from the black electorate. The black electorate has not been as vigilant as it could or should be," Smith said. "We have not fulfilled our responsibility to hold black politicians to the same credibility that we would hold whites to. Black politicians can get by by saying I tried whether they deliver or not. White politicians have to show results."

Besides meeting among themselves, scholars say black politicians have to reach out to other minority groups who share similar goals.

"Black politicians better build coalitions with Latinos and Asians," said Mark Naison, a professor of African American studies and history at Fordham University in New York. "Look what they have done by themselves. What we are dealing with is too powerful for any one group to do by themselves."

William Strickland, a professor of political science at the University of Massachusetts, said African Americans in this new political movement must have an understanding of the political–economic system and how it must be restructured to meet the public interest.

He said it will take a two-prong approach.

"Blacks, women and Hispanics are the base of the Democratic Party. So we have to work out a coalition with them to insist that they be an opposition party," he said.

"Secondly, we have to do what we did during the Vietnam War. Black leadership and others have to reach out to young people who are hurting and whose futures have been indifferently mortgaged by the powers that be and make a concerted effort to educate and form a coalition with them."

SOURCE: Black America? (1992, October 25). *Detroit News*, p. 1A. Reprinted with permission of the *Detroit News*.

CHAPTER 6

Locality and Localism Reconsidered

Casual observation would suggest that, despite modernization, the daily round of life for millions of people is carried out in relatively small, circumscribed, local settings. Modern dwellers draw a manageable radius around their homes, at least as a mental referent, and carry out most daily activity within the radius. The stretch of this radius may vary depending on the region of the country, the nature of the roads, the availability of transportation alternatives, and the socioeconomic status of the individuals. With the exception of the commuting suburbanite, particularly in very large cities, for whom the radius is always expanding, the more urban one's residence, the more one's radius is reduced.

In managing our daily affairs, distances do matter. Distance is time; time is a very finite commodity. Vulnerable people or those who need help, whether in the city or the country, are often bound to the most limited radius. Experience in social work has shown that in helping people resolve daily problems, sophisticated expertise often is much less important than physical proximity. The lonely elderly person or the anxious parent may benefit as much from the ready support of a neighbor as from the sophistication of the remote professional. Perhaps ways should be found to capitalize on localism and reduce its negative consequences—for example, too much attachment to locale may narrow people's horizons and have negative consequences in caring for certain groups.

This chapter draws on the substantive contributions of Roy C. Buck, Professor Emeritus of Sociology, Pennsylvania State University, to a previous book by the author: Martinez-Brawley, E. (1990). *Perspectives on the small community: Humanistic views for practitioners*. Washington, DC: NASW Press.

210

Technological advances, urbanization, and corporate industrialism have encouraged *place release*—conditions of daily life wherein natural or constructed space and environment play limited roles in ordering interpersonal relationships or in contributing to the sense of personal and collective well-being. *Localism*—pride of place or the state of being concerned with locality—sometimes is viewed as an obstacle to intergroup understanding because of its emphasis on boundaries. (Yet as discussed in chapter 5, heterogeneity is not and should not be viewed as antithetical to localism.) Place release has been seen as the mark of a modern cosmopolitan lifestyle. Although thinking exclusively in local terms might be anticosmopolitan and deny the interdependence of the world, the new localism that community workers can support is not of that nature. Furthermore, technology, particularly television and the Web, has radically modified the kind of antiglobal localism that often existed in decades past. Any citizen owning a computer in an industrial country instantly connects to hear the latest news and interact with the world. In fact, retaining local ties has become the bigger challenge.

Ambivalence and even disdain for local ties (often pejoratively labeled "regionalistic") have a long history in literature as well as in the social sciences. For example, Hobbs (1985) discussed how the works of writers often were dismissed by critics and publishers as being "regional" (or "local"):

> While critics of regional literature assert that an author preoccupied with Kentucky (or another rural area) ignores Athens and Rome, its advocates argue that Athens and Rome can only be reached through Kentucky, Nebraska, or Yoknapatawpha. As one partisan puts it, regionalism is not "an ultimate in literature, but . . . a first step. . . ." The coming to close knowledge about the life of a region in which [the writer] lives is a first necessity for sound writing, even as knowledge of oneself—"know thyself "—is also a first necessity. (p. 87)

Little can be universal that is not rooted in a recognizable locale. Certainly, action is always related to one's surroundings. The localism that nourishes communities today and strengthens helping ties is captured in the slogan "Think globally, act locally." The same slogan acknowledges the current importance of local–global relations.

Since early in the 1990s, a different worldwide political phenomenon has contributed to the resurgence of the local and local politics. While not all the activities that have gone with movements of local revitalization have been the kind of efforts the world wants to support—for many have been repressive and cruel—parallel to the resurgence of *locale* as the *home* place, there has been a resurgence of the local as the more important unit of government. Teune (1995) put it as follows:

> The spread of democratic ideas and the emergence of a global system have contributed to a resurgence of the local. One major form of decentralization in the 20th century has been the breakup of empires into nation states, the most recent example being the Soviet Union. The pressures for democratization have led to a new emphasis on local governance below the level of the nation state. The rise of a global political economy provides localities with an alternative to national capitals. Although the patterns of local governance have similar features, the push for democracy will give local politics a greater role in the issues of peace and prosperity than has been true during the long recent period of the rise in authority of nation states. (p. 11)

For many, local government politics have become focal points in political development. In the United States, local government became more important when in the 1990s decentralization became the modus operandi. In other countries, the question of local democracy became critical when governments at the central level began to crumble and local institutions, democratically elected and closer to the people, developed stronger bases. Teune (1995) pointed out the new democratically elected governments in many Latin American countries, Southern Africa, and in many Asian countries. He also highlighted the fact that in Northern Europe, the strongly centralistic provisions of the welfare state began to be decentralized during the 1990s, and that in the United States, the "debate over federalism and the role of government has again gained dominance on the political agenda" (Teune, 1995, p. 12).

Szücs (1995), writing about the welfare state in Sweden, asserted that "since the 1980s, the European social welfare state has been challenged by downsizing, decentralization, and privatization of government services" (p. 105). Szücs (1995) points out that the social welfare state, well represented in Western Europe by the system of Scandinavian countries, particularly Sweden, has been faced with new market-oriented welfare solutions.

> During the 1980s and the early 90s, trends of decentralization and, later, privatization have raised questions about a traditional welfare state in western democracies. . . . The values of a vertically-organized welfare state are assumed to be slowly replaced by images of a more horizontally-organized society, where power and responsibility are more equally distributed to all levels in Swedish society: the state government, the local and regional government, organizations, and individuals themselves. (p. 106)

Interesting assumptions are found in the literature on local government and the move towards localism that emerged not only in the United States but in many European countries. First, it is assumed that decentralization will bring forth efficiency because local structures known to local decision makers make it possible to flatten decision making in a local structure, while this may be very hard in a more vertical structure. The second advantage attributed to local government, though not a necessary corollary, is the possibility of enhanced privatization. A third is that in more horizontal units, individuals have more choice and become responsible for decision-making in more personalistic ways. Such moves are believed to enhance accountability.

Enabling local government to carry out its functions creatively has been a major theme in the writings of political scientists and policy makers in Britain (Flynn, 1991; Hadley, Dale, & Sills, 1984; Hadley & Young, 1990). In the United States entrepreneurial local government has been a theme that politicians picked up from writers during the 1990s (Osborne & Gaebler, 1993). Szücs concludes that the ingrained democratic value preferences of the locals and the democratic culture of a particular locale in Sweden are very important to the success of decentralizing experiments. However, he also concludes that there have been some changes in values at the horizontal level. He attributes the changes to younger and well-educated local leaders who are more in favor of pluralistic, horizontally organized societies, and also to changes in the thinking of local leaders in general. It would appear that local leaders, regardless of age, sex, class, or party affiliation, have become more worldly. In rural areas in the United States, Fitchen (1991) configured a similar trend, emphasizing the new role of women in local government.

The political science literature of the last decade confirms that the rebirth of locality, which was a call to action in the 1980s, became a reality in the 1990s in many countries. Consequently, in reviewing localism at the beginning of the new millennium, it is important to consider at least three aspects of the issue:

1. *Manageability of size and ties to the locale.* This aspect of localism is dear to social workers because here is where most daily activities take place.

2. *Democratization and democratic participation in decision-making.* Bringing decision making to the local level and strengthening horizontal ties has been a political theme of the 1990s. Democratic decision making conquers the imagination of social workers who have been stressing empowerment social work as the new model of practice.

3. *The possible negative aspects of localism.* Just as localism enhances democratic participation and encourages the emergence of local leader-

ship, so it has potential for causing problems associated with the drive for homogeneity, the fear of the different or of the outsider, and the urge to look at the world in only one way.

New local leadership must entertain the possibility that cosmopolitanism and localism may exist in complementary relationship. The challenge will be to embrace a form of localism that enhances pride in community, democratic participation, entrepreneurship, and creativity, but that is not exclusionary, parochial, or negatively nostalgic.

Disparate Understandings of Localism

Students of social work generally are required to take a wide spectrum of social sciences courses, but these are often limited to surveys with only introductory content emphasizing trends, generalizations, macro-demographic summaries, definitions of concepts, and thumbnail sketches of theoretical perspectives. Courses in statistics and research methods dealing with a demographic data sets emphasize drawing judiciously worded conclusions and recommendations for further study. Throughout, students are urged to embrace the value of generalization and be wary of specifics and concreteness.

During the 1980s and 1990s, postmodernists shook many of the ways in which traditional social services curricula were used to train social workers, questioning the low value that had been given to personal experience, narrative data, and often native ways of looking at the world. Unfortunately, by and large the positivistic scientific tradition appears to continue to have a stronghold in the social sciences. Students are still cautioned against the use of personal experiences and observations as valid data. Over time their own homes, neighborhoods, and communities fade into the background and the students take on the abstract, rational, and professionally certified views of instructors, textbooks, academic journals, and professional publications. Particularly in social work, a profession still struggling with its scientific view of self, despite the many changes of the 1990s, publications still do not strongly question our way of building knowledge.

There is an inherent paradox in this approach. Although concrete daily experiences are discarded as too specific and contaminated, scientific scrutiny focuses on small segments of reality. The careful social scientist studies not cosmopolitan or universal experiences but the very specific experiences of particular subjects.

As the 21st century approaches, scholars need to reexamine dispassionately the fears of attachment to locality that plagued the decades between 1940 and 1980. Academics are often antagonistic to local perspectives. In liberal arts or political science courses, students are often not exposed to community in all its local ramifications. Local government may be relegated to a week of lectures in an introductory course or, worse, viewed as a unit to be explored only in high school. Courses in community deal with change rather than locality development or with a radical community action tradition that no longer exists.

Yet many social workers spend significant proportions of their careers employed in small, often quite rural, communities. For them the study of the local community is very useful. Unfortunately, these workers, especially neophytes who have been intellectually and technically nurtured in a university environment, may suffer cultural and intellectual shock and a compelling sense of incompetence as they move into practice. The university environment can be inimical to localism and rural traditions. In small municipalities, towns, counties, or villages, perspectives and specializations neatly compartmentalized for educational purposes tend to blend in the course of daily work.

During a recent visit to Spain, I was asked to lead a training session for social workers newly assigned to serve small communities in a rural province. One of their major concerns was that life in these small communities often was antithetical to what had been described in their courses. They found that, as social workers, they had to approach work matters as personal interactions. For example, a neighbor might check on a particularly belligerent or disliked elderly person as a "favor" to the agreeable new worker. Social workers had been taught that in the bureaucratic world, formal arrangements freed them from personally taxing commitments. Yet the social reality in which these young workers found themselves was different. The social reality of the small community almost anywhere seldom corresponds with the descriptions of community life social workers are offered in professional programs.

Perhaps even more of a problem to young professionals is the stark awareness that they have been so socialized to the language, norms, and values of their profession and age-status cohort that they may have become blind and deaf to the rich, varied, and intricate cultural mosaic that characterizes daily life in the small community. As Edelman (1977) pointed out, "Linguistic reference engenders a 'reality' that is not phenomenologically different from any other reality" (p. 35). The antiprovincial reality created by academic language can become the reality future social workers believe in and the only reality they are open to. If local communities were treated negatively in school, the novice practitioner alone in a small community may perceive it negatively. He or she may have difficulty identifying local strengths and enjoying meaningful contact with local people. Though the professional antiprovincialism of academic language may have served students well during years of formal schooling, ironically that same language is ill-suited to work in small communities where old and young, rich and poor, schooled and unschooled work, play, worship, love, and quarrel in a common but different idiom. The language of community is not just spoken and unspoken; it is made up of lore and custom, tales and imagination. One of the greatest challenges of small community practice is to avoid the common stance that Cloke and Little (1997) have called "self-domination":

> The self dominates, and the other becomes a very poor second, a tolerated periphery marginalized by individualist politics and often painted out in the canvas we use to impose knowledgeable order onto a hugely variegated world. Recognition of the need to give voice to neglected others therefore requires not only a deconstruction of these knowledge-order frameworks, but also a full recognition of the inter-textualities of the self. Our natural tendency is to impose familiarity of language, concept and representation onto other subjects and thus to treat them . . . as 'the other of the same.' The alternative . . . is an openness to new categories, unfamiliar interconnections and unknown language concept and representation. (pp. 5–6)

Drawing from his experiences in Kenya, Chambers (1993) describes a case of rural development that confirms our discussion here. Chambers discusses managing rural development and offers tips to community practitioners:

> Rural management is difficult to observe and difficult to manipulate effectively. Complexity and inaccessibility can combine to discourage the researcher, consultant or senior government servant from exposure to the real feel of the situation and conversely to encourage him to fall back on more abstract thought. This can be dangerous. Abstract thought breeds and nourishes perfectionism. It leads away from reality, from what is feasible, from the accumulated increments of change which can gradually transform performance. It encourages the design and propagation of ideal models which are not only unattainable but also liable to impair rather than improve performance. (p. 16)

Chambers considers it very important in rural development to be real, not to strive at perfectionism but to be informed by what is possible. Local language is often grounded in the pragmatism of the possible. He further recommends that rural development practitioners have a mode of analysis that accepts a wide framework, and provides "simplifications of complex relationships" (p. 17). He encourages practitioners to talk about optimizing, not maximizing, a term that he believes is not grounded in the reality of rural practice. He concludes that in bringing action to the fore, the rural development practitioner must not operate from the bias of the Western world that knowledge is always good. He believes that this premise often generates unthinking demands for information, "demands which misuse administrative capacity and culminate in mounds of unused data" (p. 18). In the view of Chambers, the practitioner needs an opportunity rather than a problem orientation. In summary, he believes that the practitioner's actions must be grounded in the language of the locality and must translate academic or remote demands into the practical language of possibilities.

The "Service Delivery" Mode and Localism

Social work organizations and the professional training of social workers grew significantly during the period of the *eclipse-of-community perspective* (the 1960s and 1970s). The eclipse-of-community perspective offered a favorable climate for methodological and theoretical perspectives centering on bureaucracy, complex organization, and demographic analyses. From this perspective individuals are caught up in rationally organized formal structures and governed by formal procedures over which they have little influence. The impression it gives is that large organizations can exist in isolation from societal and cultural norms. For students after the eclipse-of-community period, understanding complex organization (bureaucracy) and demographic information composed the core of social science knowledge.

Believing that locality and localism were of small import in day-to-day life, human services personnel and agencies were shaped to serve individuals who had been identified by the demographer, who uses numbers and demographic characteristics, rather than the cultural anthropologist, humanist, or even journalist, who would have been more concerned with the cultural fabric of communities. Human services organizations did not ignore community variables completely. Students and social workers did refer to locality and territorial attachments, but merely as referents that explained the settings where clients lived. Community and local ties generally were seen as obstacles rather than assets to service. The emphasis was on the delivery of service and, thus, on the development of comprehensive bureaucratic organizations that could accomplish that delivery.

President Johnson's Great Society was the heyday of the delivery perspective. This is not a criticism of war-on-poverty efforts but a commentary on the prevailing human services ethos. "Delivery system," a euphemism for bureaucracy, entered the jargon of academics and agency workers. Many social workers with benevolent intentions aspired to a desk on the third floor of city hall, equipped with a telephone, a computer printout of known problem areas, and a federal pamphlet outlining guidelines for service. Unfortunately, as soon as a structure for service to clients was in place, mayors or boards of commissioners announced decisively to the press that problems were being met head-on. Typical of bureaucracies is the ambiguity that is created along with a structure for service; the assumption then is that service actually is being provided (Edelman, 1977) and, as social workers have long known, this is not necessarily the case.

Local participation in community development and organization generally remained outside the orthodoxy of service delivery, which was carried out by professionals in vertically organized systems. The public language of politicians and influentials included "community" and "the commonwealth," but these were seldom translated to the local level. For example, although mental health clinics became community-based, care was for the most part provided by professionals who used fairly standardized practices. During the 1960s and 1970s, while access to service improved markedly, in practice social or psychological problems were not dealt with by capitalizing on the unique elements of indigenous local structures and cultural norms. Instead, individuals with problems were named "clients" and "serviced" one by one. The service provider, usually an energetic professional or bureaucratic functionary, often approached the client with "interventions" that relied on introspection and explored primarily psychological dimensions, often removed from the client and disconnected from local resources or realities. Often those interventions did not make use of other community agents; beauticians, bartenders, and clergy always had been part of the helping network of rural communities, but in the more professionalized ethos that dominated practice, their potential often was ignored.

In ethnic communities, too, important caretakers were ignored. Much of the ethnic literature of those days decried this fact. Hispanic communities, for example, often were undervalued by professionals (Badillo Ghali, 1977; Delgado, 1977; Martinez, 1977). In exploring factors that led to the alarming rate of placement of Native American children, Byler (1977), the director of the American Association of American Indian Affairs, observed that "In judging the fitness of a particular family, many social workers, ignorant of Indian cultural values and social norms, make decisions that are totally inappropriate in the context of Indian family life, so that they frequently discover neglect or abandonment when none exists" (p. 1).

In fact, many social workers confused poverty with neglect and ignored one of the best examples of caring in the broad context of community: the collective responsibility assumed by Native American communities for their members. The interventions of the eclipse-of-community era were not only likely to be foreign to the community but often were disdainful of it. Social workers, although describing themselves with a consumer-oriented metaphor—"service provider"—often behaved in a Messianic fashion toward the local community. Thus, the locals were made to devalue their own local wisdom and information.

In a novel about agricultural workers in Cumbria, England, Melvin Bragg (1969) described how a hired hand felt about his own experiential or locality-based wisdom: "In the district he was known for his consistency in all things and his pride lay in keeping that record. Within that tiny locality he was erudite but this knowledge, though different not in kind but only in the material it drew on from that of educated men, he considered as "knowing nothing" whenever faced by a fact or remark outside his experience" (p. 14). The outside expert in the service delivery mode often caused locals to feel they knew nothing even though they had been solving problems for centuries.

Some social workers attempted to scale down and adapt delivery systems in ways that did not ignore local culture, customs, and lore. Some mental health practitioners went out of their way to recognize the influence of local culture on the definitions of mental illness and health (Mazer, 1976; Segal, 1973), but interventions generally continued to rely on knowledge brought into the community. Practitioners feared that the local community would cause harm to their clients. In response, a new specialty in social work, rural social work, was built on the premise of locality-relevant services (Ginsberg, 1976; Martinez-Brawley, 1981; Mermelstein & Sundet, 1978). This specialty, partly a social movement, partly a professional focus, called for a new form of localism. Social workers taking what was then a novel approach deliberately encouraged local collective resourcefulness to solve problems and overcome excesses of power as they impinged on disadvantaged individuals and their collective predicament. Because these strategies often resulted in conflict, they were not always popular with the larger society, nor were they readily embraced by rank and file workers and local public figures.

Throughout the 1980s and early 1990s, a wholly different mood in relation to local matters, more akin to that which rural social workers had espoused, became pervasive in society. We have already discussed how the breakdown of dictatorial political regimes in Europe, Latin America, and Asia contributed to the rebirth of locality, with all its positive and negative consequences. Reflecting on this, Böhn (1995), a Hungarian political scientist, commented:

> A major problem in Europe, and especially central Europe, is border regions dissected by national boundaries. These regions contain ethnically mixed populations. They are now expected to develop as viable democratic politics at the local level. Many have not yet even established their autonomy as legal entities; in most cases, local political parties do not exist there; and the regions have to address the problem of ethnic and language differences. Many of them were closed to their neighbors until the recent democratic transformation. The borders are now open. Although the prosperity of the border regions is dependent on the country of which they are part, they are underdeveloped economically and socially by any standard, certainly a European one. (p. 137)

Issues related to political localism, decision making at the horizontal level, rekindled a number of related issues, both in Europe and the Americas. In Europe, transitions from totalitarian political systems to more autonomous local communities that were becoming more open brought forth great turmoil. Many political and ethnic difficulties persist as citizens iron out the challenges of this new system that gives great importance to the locality.

In the United States in the early 1990s, localism became a fashionable word for agencies combating the financial crunch that was squeezing social services. Conservative leaders for whom localism was a way of diverting funds from social services gave the word a new ring—but unfortunately a negative one among social workers. Now, localism was invested not only with the traditional negative meaning of lack of sophistication, but also with the added dimension of ultraconservatism. Social services providers feared that making use of the broad resources of a local community would simply mean fewer governmental funds. The already dubious intellectual and political tradition of localism was becoming even more complicated. Although the term was becoming one social workers could not ignore, it was not one they could relish.

Richard Margolis (1981), a journalist advocate of the identity-giving aspects of localism but not of its abuses, tried to clarify the matter: "The left's recent romance with localism is understandable and even laudable, given bureaucratic processes and the failure of many public agencies to accomplish much in the face of private power. But there is localism and localism. And there is ample evidence about the fate of social change programs entrusted to the care of the local elites—especially when the local elite was the original obstacle" (p. 33). Margolis put his finger on the dilemma. The new problem with localism was separating its folk-oriented, antibureaucratic, and locality-rooted positive elements from its more negative political components.

Decentralization into locality-based social services, which had become extremely popular in Britain after 1968, crossed the Atlantic. Roger Hadley and Morag McGrath (1980) in *Going Local* captured the concerns of British social workers: "Many of the ideas underlying the present organization and management of the [local welfare authority] services are outdated and inappropriate. [This book] questions the emphasis placed on bureaucratic and professional conceptions of service delivery and the centralized, hierarchic organizations that have been created to apply them" (p. 1). Smaller units operating within the local context and respecting the rich traditions and resources of local communities were viewed as a more effective and efficient way of caring for people. Although localism had a complicated history in the United States, locality and territoriality still were essential elements that could facilitate caring for those in need.

In 1987, Milliken, a former governor of Michigan, wrote about these concerns:

> Teen pregnancy, environmental pollution, the homeless, school dropouts, the financial crisis in health care, AIDS—merely to list some of the major social and economic problems confronting this nation is to raise troubling questions about our ability to solve them. The current absence of creative federal initiatives contributes to a perception of government's incapacity to address intractable domestic policy issues. Moreover, the fiscal constraints imposed by huge budget deficits reinforce the notion that new and innovative federal government programs are [not] feasible.
>
> A more encouraging—and in my view more accurate—picture of government's problem-solving capacity emerges at the state and local level. In jurisdictions throughout the country, imaginative responses to pressing social and economic needs reveal patterns of innovation with valuable lessons for other cities and states as well as the federal government. (p. 13)

Milliken was addressing the complicated interweaving of central and local government decision-making that had spread during the late 1980s. He continued:

> Many innovative government programs involve creative coalition building among public and private agencies that have a common interest in

solving a specific problem. . . . The use of simple technologies to solve complex problems is another hallmark of several creative states and local government initiatives. . . . Another common characteristic of exemplary government programs is a bold leap of imagination that transforms problems into opportunities. (Milliken, 1987, p. 13)

A new era of importance to local government—that of exemplary initiatives—had been launched. Local government was no longer being viewed as backward or inefficient, but rather as having the potential for being creative and efficient.

However, positive lasting returns on programs of human development rooted in the local ethos are always likely to be a long-term proposition. Local programs were soon faced with administrators and politicians who needed to defend budgetary requests with "proof of progress" on a year-to-year basis. Consequently, despite local efforts to support a community orientation, the emphasis on service delivery and client count often made for more bookkeeping that overwhelmed the more personal orientation of local agencies. As Fabricant (1985) suggested, "The drive to increase the productivity of social workers in large public-sector agencies has contributed to the erosion of certain craft elements of practice" (p. 389). In earlier decades, the tasks of the social worker were "to be based not on one model of practice but rather on the different circumstances of individuals and communities. This commitment to differential diagnoses paralleled the industrial artisans' desire to comprehend fully the various component parts of their work" (p. 389). Today, "the functions of social work are becoming increasingly repetitive and mechanistic and opportunities to exercise judgement . . . are becoming limited" (p. 389). Today a premium is placed on getting more from fewer resources; aspects of the social worker's role that do not fit this efficiency drive are suspect.

Because the collection and processing of demographic data have increased, and more data are accessible now through the media, few have patience with the slow processes of structural reform, especially at the level of daily life. All things considered, the eclipse-of-community perspective provided an academically certified rationale for a human services bureaucracy designed to deal with clients not as individual participants in a local setting but as members of categories. Despite renewed emphasis on locality in recent community research, the established social bureaucracy remains operationally and professionally attached to the eclipse-of-community perspective.

It is within this [the formal bureaucratic context] that income maintenance centers have replaced social workers with clerks and that child welfare functions are reorganized primarily into policing and accountability services. Relatedly, quality service is redefined as quality control. This new form of quality emphasizes "getting the statistics in on time" and "moving cases through the process within a time limited schemata." (Fabricant, 1985, p. 393)

Unfortunately, many of the usual models for providing social services have more in common with the assembly line ethos than with the ethos of fostering nonanomic communities in which caring relationships among people will flourish. Budgetary deficits, economic recessions, increasing popular and political disillusionment with service delivery all appear to be forcing social workers to reassess bureaucratic modes and management of service delivery. But even then, a major obstacle to experimentation with alternative approaches is that the present cohort of social work leaders for the most part have been schooled in ways that enhance the role of the expert and diminish that of the lay person. For example, as late as 1979, Perlman was listing among the characteristics of effective neighborhood organizations a full-time paid professional staff, a sophisticated mode of operation, and a number of other prerequisites that did not resound with the language of locale (Homan, 1994).

Moreover, political influentials have borrowed from industry practices heavily imbued with the principles of Frederick Taylor, the famed industrial efficiency expert of the mid-twentieth century. The emphasis of Taylorist structures was on "more limited encounters with citizens, narrow definitions of roles and routinized function" (Fabricant, 1985, p. 392). Technology in the form of e-mail, automated telephone machines, etc., has increased depersonalization in service. Many social agencies have shifted from long-term programs to short-term, crisis-oriented—and cheaper—practice models. Social agencies have been forced to adopt managed care models borrowed from the medical field, which have not proven successful even there. Fabricant and Burghardt (1998) have noted a distinction between "failures of conception and of implementation" (1998, p. 57): "Expenses associated with health care not only are a consequence of implementation and inefficiencies associated with public bureaucracy but also are due to a design that lavishly rewards insurance companies for their 'middle man' role in the exchange between patients and the hospital" (Fabricant & Burghardt, 1998, pp. 57–58).

In spite of strong rhetoric favoring local community and community interventions, social services providers facing constant pressures for productivity look increasingly at the bottom line.

On the positive side, however, empowerment social work became popular in schools of social work during the 1990s and has exercised some influence in the curriculum and in practice settings. Homan (1994), for example, pointedly criticized Perlman's requirements as "less than possible" in many neighborhoods (communities) and listed other, more local, elements of success. Fabricant and Burghardt (1998) asked themselves about the future of social services as part of community building. Their discussion began with a reflection on how professionals interrelate with community, concluding that in spite of their wax and wane through the years, social work has had a rich history in relation to rebuilding communities.

In mentioning settlement house efforts, they caution, however, about the importance of not romanticizing the early work of the settlements, since it was often modest and intolerant of differences. They do recognize that the local emphasis on settlement houses resulted in an emphasis on communal relationships as the cornerstone of an agency's "communal mission" (p. 61). Fabricant and Burghardt (1998) take a balanced position in relation to what they believe social services and community building will become:

> Too often, the problems that plague agencies are exclusively attributed to a scarcity of resources. The centrality of these constraints cannot be minimized. . . . Equally important, however, the agency itself must be accountable as an independent entity that makes decisions regarding the content and structure of social services. To imagine the agency otherwise effectively redefines service as an exclusive creation of external forces. Clearly, service is also an invention of the specific culture, leadership, structure, size and communal integration of the host organization. In fact, it might be argued that now more than ever it is critical for progressive leadership, agencies, and community members to rethink basic understandings of social service. Thinking must be informed by new concepts of social services resonant with recent local experimentation and profound shifts in poor and working class communities. (p. 60)

The Value and Limitations of the Local

Community studies have documented the importance of locality and a collective sense of place in the maintenance of order and well-being. Josiah Royce (1908), an idealist philosopher, saw in *province* and *provincialism* safeguards against "the levelling tendencies of recent civilization" and the rise of "the mob spirit" (p. 54):

> A province shall mean any one part of a national domain, which is geographically and socially sufficiently unified to have a true consciousness of customs, and to possess a sense of its distinction from other parts of the

country. . . . Provincialism [is] first, the tendency of such province to possess its own customs and ideals; secondly, the totality of these customs and ideals themselves; and thirdly, the love and pride which leads the inhabitants of a province to cherish as their own these traditions, beliefs, and aspirations. (p. 55)

Royce warned against the danger of a false provincialism manifesting itself in narrow sectionalism. He also warned against making locally unique values the ideal, because other people's unique values are also ideal for them.

Royce did not see conflict between nation and province. The province provided the essential human scale where the goals and ideals of a nation could be realized:

I should say today that our national unities have grown so vast, our forces of social consolidation have become so paramount, the resulting problems, conflicts, evils, have been so intensified, that we must flee in the pursuit of the ideal to a new realm. It is the realm of the province. There we must flee. I mean, not in the sense of a cowardly and permanent retirement, but in the sense of a search for renewed strength, for a social inspiration, for the salvation of the individual from the overwhelming forces of consolidation. The nation by itself, apart from the influence of the province, is in danger of becoming an incomprehensible monster, in whose presence the individual loses his right, his self-consciousness, and his dignity. (p. 93)

Royce intuitively appreciated the problem of scale. His perspective sounds curiously contemporary at the end of the millennium, when nations throughout the world are struggling to maintain a sense of proportion and a sense of what is global. Immigration and migration of people within nations have become significant topics of discussion once again for social scientists. The issue of inculcating sectarian, regional, or local values in schooling has reached international proportions. Issues of bilingual versus monolingual, secular versus religious, conservative or orthodox versus progressive education resound all over the globe (Lloyd, 1999; Maslen, 1999).

For millions of people, the world, the nation, and the city are too big as referents for giving meaning to the daily round of life. Yet in multiethnic nations people must be distinctly on guard against the divisive consequences of sectionalism. Pluralism and heterogeneity can strengthen regions or localities as long as groups can share in a broader vision rooted in the smaller realities of the day-to-day activities within area boundaries. *Pride of place* gives greater meaning to people's daily experiences, energizing them to participate fully in the communities they know and appreciate. Current movements in the United States to declare English the official language or to enforce the kind of monolingual education that does not foster real learning, for example, are rooted in artificial nationalism. Healthy local cultures can coexist and lend strength to the larger nation. People can feel strong loyalties at the same time to family, locality, ethnic group, profession, nation, and even the globe. It is important to value the local in order to enhance the global.

In an article on the problematic melting pot ideology, Ross (1989) commented:

> My own initial questioning of the melting pot model came not in New York, where I grew up, but as a young field researcher in East Africa in the 1960s, where I was repeatedly told: "Don't mess with ethnicity and tribes; nations are being built." The melting pot model and modernization theory, so prominent at the time, predicted that ethnicity, religion, and other primordial identifications were carry-overs from the past that would, given time, decline in importance. But I saw example after example and turned up systematic data which indicated that Kenyans were not abandoning ethnic identities at all. In fact, the patterns that I found were the opposite of what I had been told to expect. Ethnicity was socially and politically strongest among the better educated individuals, those most attached to city life, those who held better paying jobs. . . .
>
> Many American researchers were coming up with similar results. For example, a prominent study in the late 1960s looking at the rise in support for the idea of black power, which was controversial at the time, found support the greatest among younger, educated blacks, exactly the ones whom the melting pot model predicted would show evidence of declining ethnic loyalty.
>
> I believe that early social science theories erred because they underrated the role of group processes in shaping an individual's identity and self-esteem. The focus on individual but not collective sources of identity is one reason both social scientific and popular images of ethnicity clung to such conceptions as the melting pot, even in the absence of evidence to support them. (p. 1)

Similarly, social science theories underrated the identity-giving aspect of locality and community attachments, be they ethnic, geographic, or both. Government bureaucracy, civic organizations, or social agencies, regardless of their sensitivity and compassion, cannot substitute for the richly nurturing and identity-enhancing social mosaic of day-to-day association.

The concepts introduced in this chapter come alive in the excerpts that follow. The first relates to localism in the sense of local government. The article, from Vermont's *Rutland Herald*, highlights the power of the town meeting, that place where individuals, in the New England tradition, can voice their opinions and become significant.

In his research in an inner-city neighborhood in Chicago, Suttles (1972) emphasized how attachment to locale gave individuals not only identity but a real sense of security. Suttles described how the sentiments and loyalties of primary relationship formed the basis for the social order of the neighborhoods he studied. The student of modern small towns will observe the same phenomenon. Primary ties and local sentiments give real direction, though not always positive, to the daily activities of most people. People live day to day within the intimate confines of a locality. The most universal of all human experiences happen "at home," where one's deepest emotions are revealed.

Contemporary literary critics, reevaluating the work of women from a feminist perspective, have made similar observations in attempting to redefine the "regional" novel. Women have often selected the local or the regional as their theme; the devaluing of the local has often been tied to the devaluing of their work. Writing about Harriet Arnow (1949), Hobbs (1985) stated: "Writing about hill people from her native state of Kentucky, she is alternatively called a 'woman' or a 'regional' writer. While it is generally conceded that the former tag is pejorative, few have considered the assumptions behind the term 'regional.' It is, I suspect, employed as condescendingly as the qualifier 'woman'; a 'regionalist' can be 'good' but only in a limited sphere" (p. 83). Yet the life of a region or locality is generally used as the medium to express basic and universal concerns. It is a healthy pride and appreciation of locality that allows people to be universal in their concerns. This point is beautifully illustrated in an essay by Alice Walker (1983), writing about Zora Neale Hurston, anthropologist, novelist, and folklorist who lived between 1901 and 1960 and whose work is excerpted on page 49:

> Zora was interested in Africa, Haiti, Jamaica, and for a little racial diversity (Indians)—Honduras. She also had a confidence in herself as an individual that few people (anyone?), black or white, understood. This was because Zora grew up in a community of black people who had enormous respect for themselves and for their ability to govern themselves. Her own father had written Eatonville [Florida] town laws. This community affirmed her right to exist, and loved her as an extension of itself. (pp. 85–86)

[Text continues on page 232]

When All Politics Is Local: Small Towns Teach Us That People Will Vote If They Believe They Can Make a Difference

ATHENS—Town Clerk Darlene Wyman, a fit woman in tan overalls and sturdy boots, grabs a shovel and clears the wooden porch of the former one-room schoolhouse in a few quick strokes. Although her usual office hours are 9 a.m. to 1 p.m. Mondays, she's come over on a Saturday afternoon to help Andrew MacIntyre, a strapping 21-year-old who wants to build a snowmobile trail.

Wyman, who has lived in this town of 369 for more than three decades, taught MacIntyre in the parent-run kindergarten (before state regulation did away with it) and later shuttled him along the narrow valley roads when she was Athens' sole school bus driver.

Her knowledge of this tiny Windham County town is evident as soon as MacIntyre describes his proposed route. From memory, she reels off the names of people whose properties he'll cross. Only a friendly disagreement on one parcel spurs her to pull a map from the back room.

It's the last Saturday for voters to register before town meeting, but Wyman doesn't raise the issue until a visitor asks if MacIntyre will attend. The young man says no.

"You haven't signed up yet," Wyman says gently. "Today's your last chance."

MacIntyre doesn't answer. Poring over the map, he refers to one of the property owners. "Eleanor won't be a problem," he says. "She loves me."

He leaves minutes later, still unregistered.

Give him time, Wyman says. He may come around. After all, she didn't start going to town meeting until her children were in school. Now she can't imagine being anywhere else on the first Tuesday in March.

Despite residents like MacIntyre, Athens has consistently high turnouts for its town meetings. The southeastern Vermont community crops up regularly in the work of Frank Bryan, a University of Vermont po-

litical science professor who's been studying town meeting for 30 years.

"They always have some of the highest percentages of registered voters turning out," he says.

About 12 percent of registered voters in towns with traditional town meetings attended them last year, according to Secretary of State Deb Markowitz. The figure for Athens, in contrast, is usually between 25 and 30 percent, and has climbed as high as 57 percent in recent memory.

Bryan expects higher turnout in small towns, where he says people intuitively know an individual vote is more likely to affect the outcome. But he says Athens ranks high even when compared to communities of similar size.

"It's a participatory town," he says. "I'm sure it's not named after Athens, Greece, but that's where democracy began 5,000 years ago, and I think it's remarkable that we still have a little town practicing it."

People in Athens don't make much of the connection to ancient Greece. But they have their own theories about why turnout is high. Some say town meeting is a social event, an opportunity to catch up with neighbors. Others say the community is proud to maintain a distinct identity and local control over issues such as education (it still operates a one-room schoolhouse) and—the perennial hot topic—its miles and miles of dirt roads.

"I love town politics because you can really understand them," says Dorothy Hogan, a former longtime town clerk. "When it gets to the state or national level, I can't follow it."

But many fear this Vermont tradition of local civic participation is in danger. And they don't want to see it go.

"I'm afraid . . . some of the people are getting the sense that it really doesn't matter anymore because the state has set so many regulations," says Harold Noyes, pastor at the Community Christian Church, Athens' only church. "I think a lot of people are getting frustrated. We don't have the authority we used to have."

. . .

Town meeting in Athens starts with a calling of the roll of 183 registered voters. Wyman says it isn't meant to shame people into being present, just to ensure that they're on the checklist. Still, the tradition indicates how much folks here can keep track of one another.

From that point forward, the meeting looks like that of any other small town, where voters decide on the school and town budgets and elect new officers, although here nominations are made from the floor and a candidate's only campaign may be a brief, impromptu speech. This year the hot issue may be whether to change the road commissioner's post from part-time to full-time.

Town meetings have become more efficient since lawyer Stephen Fine took over as moderator seven years ago, says Hogan, who was town clerk and treasurer from 1962 to 1979 and town treasurer from 1980 to 1993. Fine runs meetings by the book, and some locals seem to regret it.

"We didn't break the law or anything," but the meeting used to be much more freewheeling, Hogan says. "It's lost its flavor."

Still, she says, Athens is a place where no one's intimidated about participating. "At our town meetings, you're not embarrassed to stand up and say what you think," she says. "Nobody shuts you up. We're all friends."

That's the essence of town-meeting-style democracy, according to Bryan.

"You don't learn to be a citizen on the Internet or watching TV. You learn by being face to face with your neighbors," he says. "It creates a much more humane civilization."

Towns like Athens steer clear of Australian balloting, the kind of voting used in general elections and in some Vermont towns that have abandoned the traditional meeting. Unless the Australian ballot is legally required, Athens tends to go with a voice vote, then a standing count, and only if there is still confusion, a paper ballot, Wyman says. The Australian ballot is used for union school district votes, and paper for electing officers.

Putting a town's budget votes and elections all on Australian ballot gets more people to vote than traditional town meetings, says Markowitz, the secretary of state. Twenty-five to 30 percent of registered voters usually cast a vote in towns and cities with Australian ballot, she says.

But quantity and quality have to be balanced, Bryan argues. He thinks decisions made by ballot alone are not as good. At a traditional town meeting, policies and budgets are debated and revised, not just voted up or down, so the outcome is likely to be better informed and better representative of residents' views (or at least the views of those who attend), he says.

"Our communities work better the more engagement there is," agrees Frances Moore Lappe of the Center for Living Democracy in Brattleboro. The center, home to the American News Service, focuses on positive models for community problem-solving.

The more people who are involved in an open, inclusive process to make town policy, the less likely it is that opposition will erupt at the end, and the better the policy will be, Lappe says. "The quality of the decision is better and it can be carried through."

In towns that move to Australian ballot for most issues but continue to hold a town meeting, the meeting will be sparsely attended, Bryan says, because there will be less of substance to decide.

While Bryan advocates keeping as many decisions as possible in the town meeting forum, he acknowledges that some people prefer private voting. Disadvantaged groups who might not participate in traditional town meeting are one example. School budget opponents also might prefer going to the polls and voting the budget down to arguing against it in public or taking all day to determine the outcome.

"School budgets survive a whole lot better in a participatory, face-to-face conflict than in a voting booth," Bryan says. [Australian ballot] allows a lot of negativity and a lot of uninformed voting."

. . .

The deciding factor in town meeting turnout, simply put, is political power, Bryan argues.

"If you want democracy to work well, you've got to give real power to the people to make decisions on things that affect their lives," Bryan said. "If there's a real stake in it, they're apt to come out."

Athens moderator Stephen Fine sees that at work in the meeting he runs.

"In a town like Athens, if you add $1,000 to the budget, that's something people will feel. If you add $1,000 in Burlington, nobody feels it," he says. "That probably generates more interest."

Fine says Athens voters closely question any proposed spending, to make sure their hard-earned dollars are being used well, but then usually approve money articles. He thinks there may be more interest, and more people available for a weekday meeting, because the town is poor.

The median adjusted gross income in Athens in 1997 was $17,720, according to the state tax department. The statewide average was $23,576.

Bryan says average income and education, two factors often considered predictors of participation, have no correlation with attendance rates at Vermont town meetings, according to his data from 1,435 town meetings over the past 30 years.

Instead, it is town size, use of Australian ballot, time of the meeting and hot issues that affect participation, Bryan says.

Australian ballot hurts the turnout, as little is left to decide on the floor, and night meetings are less popular than day, he says. Saturday meetings, recently allowed by a change in law, do not draw more voters

than traditional Tuesday meetings, he says, even though they don't conflict with most people's work days.

Bryan says that participation in town meeting is on the decline, but women are becoming a stronger force. In 1969, 41 percent of the people attending a town meeting were women; the number is now 48 percent, he says. Women are also speaking more often and on a broader range of topics.

In Athens, two women ventured into town meeting back in 1915, five years before women won the vote in the United States. "They got the distinct impression that they were not welcome," writes Lora Wyman, a distant relative of the current town clerk, in her 1963 book, "History of Athens, Vermont." But women kept attending, in growing numbers, even before they could vote.

Ironically, fewer Vermonters participate in town meeting than in national elections, even though town meeting is arguably democracy in its most immediate form.

Fifty-nine percent of registered voters in the state voted in the most recent general election, according to Markowitz. She says Vermont consistently ranks among the top 10 states for participation rates in general elections.

The state's voter registration rate is also one of the highest in the nation. It's about 90 percent; of 420,000 to 430,000 eligible Vermont residents, more than 400,000 are registered voters, Markowitz says.

The secretary of state extols the virtues of town meeting democracy. "If you vote for a grader, you get a grader," she says. "We can see the direct results of the power of our vote."

Yet people may know more about presidential candidates than they do about their local listers. Many people get their news from national television networks, rather than the front porch or a local paper.

"We are as a culture suffering from a feeling of placelessness," Markowitz says. "We're losing our roots. People not going to town meeting is one of the many symptoms."

Many Vermonters are trying to promote town meeting, fearing that the tradition may be lost.

Markowitz hopes small towns' traditional meetings won't give way to all-day balloting like that in Montpelier, where she lives. She has turned to the radio waves with public service announcements encouraging attendance.

"I think town meeting makes Vermont Vermont," she says. "I would feel like we were losing some very essential part of who we are if we gave up town meeting for doing everything in the polling booth."

Bryan, the UV professor, points to the town of Jericho as a model for what individual communities can do to increase participation. The town had switched to a Saturday meeting hoping to increase attendance, but it dropped because many families were on vacation during school break.

This year, Jericho will combine all of its annual business in one day: the town meeting in the morning, a luncheon of soup, chili and layer cakes put on by local groups, then the school meeting in the afternoon. Balloting for town officers, school officers and a union school district bond will take place from 7 a.m. to 7 p.m. The town is offering child care, and a local Scout troop will lead the pledge of allegiance.

Still, no one can predict its success.

"I don't know what kind of turnout we'll have," Jericho Town Clerk Debby Fitzgerald says. "It's a coin toss."

Lappe, of the Center for Living Democracy, says the work to make people feel engaged in their communities must be done long before Town Meeting Day.

"We're not so much the quick-fix folks," she says. "Our approach is looking at the whole culture of democracy, that starts in schools, the media and the workplace."

All of those community institutions can help people see that they can play a role in local decision-making, from improving education to addressing parking problems. If people get involved, they'll learn that it's in their self-interest to do so, and that it's fun, Lappe says.

"I think we are all social creatures who get depressed when we feel we're not connected to what's going on [and we are] passive victims of other people's choices," she says.

Too much of the discussion about democracy can make participation sound like a dry duty, like "this is your spinach before you get your dessert of freedom and democracy," Lappe says. Instead, getting involved in town meeting or other civic activities has its own sweet satisfaction. "Engagement is very rewarding and fulfilling."

Bryan advocates keeping power in the hands of the people. Local control makes town meeting meaningful, he says.

To folks in tiny Athens, that rings true. The community is struggling to maintain an elementary school with only 14 students, but so far has been unwilling to ship its students out of town. Many mourn the loss of a popular fire department which used to clean folks' chimneys for free, and often lent the scene of a small fire the air of a social gathering.

The fire department was closed two years ago because it couldn't afford to keep up with regulations. Athens residents wonder what will be next to go.

Harold Noyes, the local pastor, a sometime selectman and a proud member of the former fire department, thinks small towns are being hurt by laws that take away local decision-making. Still, he hopes his neighbors will continue to turn out to run their town the way they see fit.

"I like the sense of town meeting," he says. "I like the fact that we can still call our own shots, in most instances."

SOURCE: Stephenson, H. (1999, February 28). When all politics is local: Small towns teach us that people will vote if they believe they can make a difference. *Rutland (Vermont) Herald*, pp. 1, 8. Reprinted courtesy of the *Rutland Herald*.

[Text continued from page 227]

Hurston returned to Eatonville to do her work:

I didn't go back there so that the home folks could make admiration over me because I had been up North to college and come back with a diploma and a Chevrolet. I knew they were not going to pay either one of these items too much mind. I was just Lucy Hurston's daughter, Zora, and even if I had—to use one of our down-home expressions—had a Kaiser baby . . . I'd still be just Zora to the neighbors. If I had exalted myself to impress the town, somebody would have sent me word in a match-box that I had been up North there and had rubbed the hair off of my head against some college wall, and then come back there with a lot of form and fashion and outside show to the world. But they'd stand flat-footed and tell me that they didn't have me, neither my sham-polish, to study 'bout. And that would have been that. I hurried back to Eatonville because I knew that the town was full of material and that I could get it without hurt, harm or danger. (Hurston, 1990, p. 2)

The rhythms of everyday life are local but they are also universal. The rhythms of everyday life also depend very much on who is the observer, the narrator, the experiencer of those rhythms. Carol Gilligan (1993), writing about the psychological differences between how men and women look at the world, used the following example:

In the second act of The Cherry Orchard, Lopakin, a young merchant, describes his life of hard work and success. Failing to convince Madame Ranevskaya to cut down the cherry orchard to save her estate, he will go in the next act to buy it himself. He is the self-made man who, in purchasing the estate where his father and grandfather were slaves, seeks to eradicate the "awkward, unhappy life" of the past, replacing the cherry orchard with summer cottages where coming generations "will see a new life." In elaborating this developmental vision, he reveals the image of man that underlies and supports his activity: "At times where I can't go to sleep, I think: Lord, thou gavest us immense forests, unbounded fields and the whitest horizons, and leaving in the midst of them we should indeed be giants"—at which point, Madame Ranevskaya interrupts him, saying, "You feel the need for giants—they are good only in fairy tales, anywhere else they only frighten us."

Conceptions of the human life cycle represent attempts to order and make coherent the unfolding experiences and perceptions, the changing wishes and realities of everyday life. But the nature of such conceptions depends in part on the position of the observer. The brief excerpt from

Chekhov's play suggests that when the observer is a woman, the perspective may be of a different sort. Different judgments of the image of man as
giant imply different ideas about human development, different ways of
imaging the human condition, different notions of what is of value in
life. (p. 5)

It is clear that women's fiction and essays are rich in local descriptions; furthermore, they engage the locality in very different ways because
women by and large are concerned with the daily activities centered on
the home, that give meaning to what is close at hand and of more manageable scale.

Much of the current ethnic literature, particularly the Hispanic literature of the Southwest, expresses that concern with the local that enriches
the tie between nations. One of the illustrations at the end of this chapter
provides a regional example of the ties between the small, the local, and
broader concerns; in it Ana Castillo (1994) connects the local Southwestern experience with a broader political context.

The second excerpt illustrates, in beautiful local language and with
the cadences of the Southwest, the high-context interaction of people
living in small-town New Mexico. This introduction to the story that
appeared in Ana Castillo's *So Far From God* (1994) is a masterful piece of
high context. Before Castillo gets Sofia to the house of a friend (*comadre*),
she has established a level of detail and an ambiance of locality that is
unsurpassed.

Human services professionals can learn a great deal from this style.
While the stresses of our times might not permit them to behave in such
leisurely ways, they might better understand that among elderly people,
among very young people, and certainly often among poor people, it is the
richness of the interaction that provides the relief from everyday stresses
and problems.

Communicating in the Local Setting

In *Habits of the Heart* Bellah and his colleagues (1985) discuss traditions
that inspire the lives of many Americans, the different motivations that
move people into action and the different languages citizens speak. The
writers recognize that for everyone there is usually a first language of basic
philosophy and perhaps a number of second languages that reveal subtle-
ties of the users' personalities and social commitments. In the book are
transcriptions of hypothetical dialogues with different individuals, Brian,
Joe, Margaret, and Wayne; though each represents a different American

[Text continues on page 236]

Sofia, Who Would Never Again Let Her Husband Have the Last Word, Announces to the Amazement of Her Familia and Vecinos Her Decision to Run for La Mayor of Tome

It was exactly two days after her fifty-third birthday, while Sofi was putting another load into the washer out in the enclosed back porch, shooing away the moscas and saying to herself things like, "If that Domingo doesn't fix the screen door this week, *I'm* gonna have to do it myself; then I'll throw his butt out for sure; what do I want him for then anyhow?" and things like that, just before the old wringer went out with a big shake and clank (not too surprising considering its age) and she said aloud, "God damn . . . !", quickly pulling out her scapular from inside her white blouse and kissing it to heaven, that she decided she was going to run for la mayor of Tome and make some changes around there. . . .

She called up her comadre, the one who lived down the road, with the ten good acres of bean and chile crops, and asked her to come over. She had big news, she said.

Her comadre, meanwhile, thought that Sofi had called to ask for her Singer back and she didn't want to tell Sofi that after she got her dress for the fiesta at Our Lady of Belen made, she had decided to do her 'jita's new baby's baptismal dress and the silver metallic thread got jammed up somewhere in all that spooling and, well, something happened to the machine, so it wasn't working no more.

The comadre (whose name it is best not to reveal here for this reason as well as some others that we shall soon see) had been after her husband about it. He was pretty good at fixing things, mostly things that were big and wide and not very complicated, like the roof or a viga fence, but he sometimes got something to work again in the house. God knows everything they owned had had its day already, so his efforts came in handy, but truthfully, he was no real handyman. Of course, she could take the old Singer, which as far as she could tell had had its day too, to a repair shop in Albuquerque, but all that meant money that they just wouldn't have until after they were able to harvest the beans and chile.

So she was glad that la comadre Sofi did not mention the Singer when she called. In fact, Sofi seemed a little absentminded about things like that lately, you know? Like she actually forgot to charge the comadre last month for her purchases at the carneceria. For years, the comadre had been buying every week from la Sofi and because times were sometimes a little harder than others and they were comadres and one never knows when she'll need her troca jumped some cold early morning and the compadre down the road never minds too much being woken up to give it a jump, or you might find your comadre's grown daughter with the child's mind wandering down by the acequia barefoot in the snow, so you run to tell her where she is and things like that that happen between neighbors all the time, it all evens out.

So Sofi left such matters as immediate payment for the hamburger for the fried pies and chopped lamb for the green-chile stew go until the end of the month, and once in a while also "forgot" to charge for a week's purchases. But she had never let the charge for the whole month go. So, what favor could the comadre from down the road offer to merit that kind of pardon?

But no, Sofi did not mention the bill. She hadn't asked for her sewing machine back, neither. So the comadre changed her chanclas and put on her black going-out shoes that used to be her Sunday Mass shoes before they got so worn. She didn't know why she was putting them on just to run down to her comadre Sofi's where she had visited a million times, but something in Sofi's voice on el teléfon gave her the impression that the visit was going to be formal.

Maybe it was her business-like tone or maybe it was just the fact that Sofi had never called her on el telefón before. But then, how could she? The comadre had just installed her line when her youngest went to the Army, but before that she had never seen a need for it. Besides, who could afford it? So using el telefón alone made the comadre feel like Sofi must be having an emergency.

The comadre pulled up in front of the house and rapped on the front screen door. Dogs started barking near and far. Then the peacocks that Mr. Charles was mating or breeding, or whatever he called his business, woke up too, and started letting out those strange cat-in-heat sounding calls that they'd been making for weeks. (She didn't know the new neighbor's last name and since she didn't know him hardly at all, she didn't feel right saying just "Charles" to him, even though that was how he had introduced himself to her one afternoon. Just like that. Just like an Anglo to be so forward with a woman!)

The comadre got goosebumps. All the animals around were really going crazy. Then she pressed her nose against the screen and caught a glimpse of La Loca running to her room to hide. Sofi came out from around back where she had been hanging up clothes on the line—soaked and half-washed as they were.

As soon as the comadre got into the house, she asked Sofi what was so important that Sofi had got her away from her quehaceres just to tell her. The comadre wasn't really doing no chores when Sofi called; she just wanted to heighten the drama of the "emergency call" for when she repeated the story later to the other comadres.

"Come on in, comadre," Sofi said, still sounding mysterious and full of importance all of a sudden, like a changed person actually, since the comadre had never known anyone more self-sacrificing and modest than la pobre Sofi. Especially when you considered all those years she had worked to support her four girls without no help from no one and with that . . . *man* having abandoned her just like that when the girls were so small.

You know, la pobre Sofi had never had one moment of fun all those years while she was alone, no birthday or New Year's Eve fiestas, no Christmas posadas. She did not attend one wedding reception, baptismal party, First Holy Communion, Confirmation, or high school graduation fiestas neither. No quinceañeras for none of the girls' fifteenth birthdays. Nada. Well, she hardly had been able to attend even a velorio or a funeral for that matter, although she always tried, out of respect for the *defuncto's* family. But everyone understood. She was alone with four children. What could people expect? . . .

Sofi poured the comadre a cup of coffee from the pot on the stove. With Domingo back, there was coffee made all hours of the day; it was his only addiction, he said. He had to have a cup in his hand all the time—half a cup, grounds, cold, no matter even when he was going to bed.

"Here's my idea," Sofi said, sitting down, with a hand on her comadre's arm, certain that her plan was going to excite her friend as much as it did her. "I have decided to run for mayor!"

La comadre stared at Sofi, not comprehending. "Mayor?" She blinked.

Sofi nodded enthusiastically. "Yes, comadre, mayor of Tome!"

SOURCE: Castillo, A. (1994). Sofia, who would never again let her husband have the last word, announces to the amazement of her familia and vecinos her decision to run for la mayor of Tome. From *So Far from God: A Novel,* by Ana Castillo, pp. 130–137. New York: Penguin Books. Copyright © 1993 by Ana Castillo. Reprinted by permission of W.W. Norton & Company, Inc.

[Text continued from page 233]

tradition, their voices are all familiar to us even as their perspectives differ significantly.

> The arguments that we have suggested would take place among them [Brian, Joe, Margaret and Wayne], if they ever met, would be versions of controversies that regularly arise in public and private moral discourse in the United States. One of the reasons for these differences is that they draw from different traditions. . . . Yet beneath the sharp disagreements, there is more than a little consensus about the relationship between the individual and society, between private and public good. This is because, in spite of their differences, they all to some degree share a common moral vocabulary, which we propose to call the "first language" of American individualism in contrast to alternative "second languages" which most of us also have. (Bellah et al., 1985, p. 20)

What is important about this statement is that it introduces us to the awareness of the many languages that we all speak, languages that are not necessarily foreign in etymology, history, or vocabulary, but that convey different styles of conversation, different stories, different narratives.

Many authors have discussed the high or low values that are ascribed to various forms of communication. Unfortunately, in the formal setting of government, educational, or other institutions, "we learn to ascribe a high degree of formality and rationality to the utterances of educated people, especially if they express themselves in the conventional speech of the upper middle class, and to derogate the conventional speech of the working class and the poor as imprecise, sloppy and impoverished" (Edelman, 1977, p. 114). Social workers are acculturated to the language not only of academic institutions but also of bureaucracy. This latter language is rigid and fragmented; it calls attention to roles, skills, and competencies, and serves to control people's performances.

The language of bureaucracy is not rich in description and storytelling; it is immersed in categories and codes that shortchange the human elements of an interaction. There is distance between the local language of people with a high investment in everyday creative activities (farming, painting, baking, building, selling, rearing children) and the language of the bureaucrats who are judged by their identification with the norms of a complex organization. There is similarly distance between the language of, for example, local papers and that of the national press. People in small towns prefer the local press not because they are not interested in more global issues but because the language of the national press often lacks the story-telling intimacy they seek. It is not surprising that social workers and locals often fail to communicate.

In *Beyond Culture*, Hall (1981) advanced a view of communication and intergroup relations that, translated into practice, could help increase social workers' competence in working with people in their immediate community. His is a theory that engenders respect for local differences. Hall differentiated between *high-* and *low-*context linguistic style: "A high-context communication or message is one in which most information is either in the physical context or internalized in the person, while very little is in the coded, explicit, transmitted part of the message. A low-context communication is just the opposite, i.e., the mass of the information is vested in the explicit code" (p. 91).

As an example of high-context communication, a client in a basic needs program, who needed to have a grocery order filled, told the student working in the program that his former social worker always took his order to X rather than Y food bank. Only after many months did the student discovered that X bank was much more generous (cans were larger, frozen items more appealing). The client never explicitly mentioned to the student the disadvantages of Y food bank, even though the student would have been responsive.

High-context people are likely to be locals; low-context people are likely to be cosmopolitans:

> One of the reasons most bureaucrats are so difficult to deal with is that they write for each other and are insensitive to the contexting needs of the public. The written regulations are usually highly technical on the one hand, while providing little information on the other. That is, they are a mixture of different codes or else there is incongruity between the code and the people to whom it is addressed. Modern management methods, for which management consultants are highly responsible, are less successful than they should be, because in an attempt to make everything explicit (low contexting again) they frequently fail in their recommendations to take into account what people already know. This is a common fault of the consultant, because few consultants take the time (and few clients will pay for the time) to become completely contexted in the many complexities of the business. (Hall, 1981, p. 93)

Low-context younger professionals face many problems in working with high-context clients in hills and valleys as well as inner-city neighborhoods. They may assume the clients are nonverbal. However, the issue is not so much the client's inability to communicate as the social worker's underdeveloped skill in receiving high-context messages. These combine body and verbal language into an idiom shaped and colored by the immediate sociocultural environment, with unstated references to common experiences that constitute the cultural bases of interaction.

High-context people are event-centered. When asked a question, rather than provide specific answers, high-context people tell stories. In a study of farm families (Martinez-Brawley & Blundall, 1989), the interviewer asked a farmer about the personal characteristics he would like to see in a social worker. With much gesticulation and relish, the farmer began telling about a father and son team of photographers who many years before had visited the area and photographed his farm. The farmer pointed out how the younger photographer, evidently low-context, was unable to get the farmer to buy the photograph, whereas the older photographer, who was high-context, got the farmer to buy two copies. The summarizing statement was that the older photographer had been "a peach of a guy." Here the story ended. The interviewers were left to surmise that the qualities of the peach of a guy the farmer had found so irresistible were the ones he would want to see in a social worker.

Low-context, information-centered interviewers looking for specific answers may become impatient with high-context respondents. Their impatience, despite attempts to cover it, is readily apparent to high-context people who are skilled at reading nonverbal signs. Lack of information, a problem for low-context professionals, is caused not by the absence of information but by the interviewer's lack of skill in entering the high-context linguistic world of the respondents. Often as a result of their education the knowledge of professionals is not grounded in the eventful lives of real people. People are cataloged in the certified low-context language of academic studies or agency practice.

The classroom is not a high-context environment. Therefore it is difficult to introduce cultural analysis of localism and its rich high-context language in ways that elicit serious student response. Students can be introduced to the "real world" of social work through internships and field experience in small communities. However, the agencies to which students are assigned often are staffed by professionals who themselves view negatively the more informal ways in which the small community functions. Thus even in small-community agencies, students often have little opportunity to work outside bureaucratic parameters. One student, analyzing her small-town-agency experience, wrote:

> Once this summer, I was asked by "Jane" (the student's supervisor) to take a woman to the grocery store. I was curious about the woman because Jane did not like her at all, so I was glad to do it. After I brought the woman

back, she invited me in. Although I should have gone back to the office and worked on records, I decided to go in. I figured out that the woman not only wanted to talk to someone but probably also felt it was polite to invite me in after I had done her a favor. In talking to her, I found out a little more about her life (I stayed on two hours!) and although her case was closed after that, I was glad that I had visited with this woman.

There were many times when I spent hours at someone's house talking to them. I knew this would have been considered inefficient, but I felt people trusted me much more after I had put time into finding out about their lives beyond our worker/client relationship.

Extended residence in a small community under the watchful eye of an instructor sympathetic to the community might be an effective way to learn the intricate details of the community structure and system of communication. A group practicum in the community has the added advantage of letting students together see at close range both the work of agencies and the real life of the community. Thus, students have the opportunity to learn how clients adapt to life between two cultures: the small community of daily contact and the scheduled contact with agency personnel. Removed from the low-context setting of a university campus, the class faces practical problems of sufficient magnitude to guarantee major behavior changes and intellectual and linguistic reorientation.

Working together on joint projects allows high- and low-context people to discover ways of understanding each other's culture. For example, in one class future social workers were asked to immerse themselves in a joint undertaking with a community group. The class organized an award presentation for a group of 200 senior citizens from the small towns of a relatively rural county. Students told of how day-to-day problems were solved. One widow who needed a ride never asked for one; instead, she recounted how life was different when her husband was alive and her daughter lived nearby. Many elderly people brought crafts to display during a luncheon event. The elderly people, who were eager to sell them, mentioned how their friends and neighbors often sought their useful items. All communication was couched in high-context stories.

Formally trained social workers often face problems similar to those of students in working productively with their clients. Hall (1981) makes a case for intercultural experiences as a way to bridge the gap between these professionals and high-context individuals. Students often must be reminded that intercultural experiences do not always require travel to distant lands. There is sufficient cultural variation within the bounds of any city, county, or state to observe and participate in microcultural systems often excitingly different from one's own.

Used properly, intercultural experiences can be a tremendous eye-opener, providing a view of self seldom seen under normal conditions at home. Controlled and directed, they can help people learn how the cultural context affects one's behavior in space—for example, elevators or other close places; in time—for example, people's sense of punctuality; in relation to sharing—for instance, communal meals and sleeping quarters. Intercultural experiences are a magnificent way of becoming cognizant of "culture," one's own as well as that of others, as a dimension of daily patterns of interaction. Culture orders personalities; the cultural context has a profound effect on how people look at things, behave politically, make decisions, order priorities, organize their lives, and think (Hall, 1981).

Empowerment, properly understood, means developing an ear and an appreciation for high context as well as low. When social workers talk about empowering citizens, one of their major tasks at hand is to learn how to converse with others in a language that is genuine and meaningful to them. One of the very enriching things that social workers can do is to read a great deal of local literature. Much of it is deeply imbued with high-context description.

Smaller cities, towns, villages, and the rural hinterland have attracted people from major metropolitan centers. A strong motivating factor pulling people toward small settings for residence and work is the lure of scaled-down civic and municipal infrastructure and the hope of a less hectic lifestyle closer to nature. Many people who do not choose to leave the city make a renewed effort to revive urban space into more supportive and satisfying neighborhoods or communities. People in both city and countryside are experimenting with ways to recover a scaled-down yet enlivened and enriched lifestyle. Sense of place is an important factor in these efforts. The significance of place and the need for roots are increasingly appreciated as contributing to civic order and personal stability. The significance of place and cultural roots has motivated important and creative business ventures that help keep a locality alive.

The significance of place has led to the recognition of the significance of rusticity, remoteness, and living in areas that up to now may have remained unrecognized. Ching and Creed (1997) noted:

> Essential secrets of power often lurk in the last *place* where you would think to look. Finding them is inevitably difficult, but the value of seeking lies in the possibilities for self-determination that these secrets promise. We thus propose looking in the places that are culturally the most remote: In the sticks, in the middle of nowhere, in the backwaters of this country and many others, in a word, in the countryside. While the forces

of (post) modernity insistently direct our attention to city life, no degree of "development" can obliterate the continuing economic importance and cultural distinctiveness of the countryside, where food is produced and human life sustained. (p. 1)

The good life, regardless of one's station, is being redefined as life together in settings where one is known as a person with a name and a definite community status. A renewed sense of social responsibility and interdependency has brought a corresponding decline in the pursuit of individualism and self-sufficiency. Even the current cult of electronic communication aims at making people more "connected."

The Professional's Predicament

Human services professionals in small communities face the daily task of translating vertically generated policies and programs into specific action geared to the civic and sociocultural style of the community. Professional workers burdened with this responsibility need out of sheer necessity to be informed, "worldly" locals. Thinking globally or nationally, they must act locally in appropriate ways. The contradictory demands of high-context locals and low-context policies are likely to be major sources of job anxiety and personal discontent, especially for younger workers. Supervisors in the vertical system rarely see clients or work with locals on a continuing basis; instead, they "see" social problems, described in impersonal low-context terms. Bureaucrats and politicians formulate policies and administrative regulations in the abstract—for theoretical, not real, communities. The local worker sees people in all their concrete manifestations, embedded in a high-context sociocultural milieu. Because the responsibility for program adaptation and integration falls on the shoulders of the horizontally situated (the local) worker, that worker needs to reconceptualize the local context in a more positive manner in order to survive. Officials in the central offices of bureaucracies may speak cavalierly about the need to adapt and the great opportunity local workers have to be innovative in shaping programs (be they federal, state or county) to meet local needs. However, they seldom provide helpful perspectives on making these adjustments.

Because new workers in social services bureaucracies often begin work in the local community, the local community should become a major focus in courses of study. Generally, this has not been the case. Educators often teach community to prospective professionals as if they were immediately to hold upper echelon staff positions in state capitals. Of course, professionals should know the big picture; career advancement often means moving from the horizontal to the vertical system. Nonetheless, the local community is the locus of program activity and it is in the local community that the new worker begins.

What, then, is required for human services professionals to be successful in the local context?

To begin with, they must shed any preconceived notions of "good" and "bad" communities. Community in and of itself is a positive force for those who find in it support for their daily existence. There are no ideal communities comprising only supportive people, or open-minded people, or generous people, or benevolent people. Real communities will exhibit both positive and negative characteristics. It is how workers deal with those attributes that matters.

In addition, social workers must realize that it is "in community" where real-life encounters occur. In community, helping is not an abstract activity reduced to systematic entries in books where not even the names of those helped appear. Helping in the local context is making sense of the tortuous lives of neighbors. Helping in community is using the resources of neighbors to support other neighbors. The small-town worker who is uncomfortable with this intimate way of relating, preferring more bureaucratic encounters, will be dissatisfied and will not become a positive force in the helping networks of the community.

Radio Days: Helping in the Local Context

The events in small towns tell wonderful stories that reveal local spirit. Every town has a tradition and in it many stories of individuals and families are inscribed. One of the many interesting stories I discovered while doing the research for this book was that of a small radio station in Perryville, Missouri.

Small local radio stations used to keep the pulse of towns nationwide. However, with consolidation in the radio business and in the retail businesses that used to support radio advertising, small stations have become relics whose preservation requires much effort:

> Often lost in the flurry of reportage on multimillion- and billion-dollar broadcast mergers, the light of small stations is a mirror on small-town economics and values. The stations, along with the Main Street merchants, are among the first to feel the effects from the arrival of that

[Text continues on page 244]

No Ivory Tower: Rise of the Street-level Think Tank

OAKLAND, CALIF.—If you think researchers wear white lab coats, meet Rosalia Chavez, who dons T-shirt, jeans, and platform sneakers to interview city officials about why the schoolyards here are sometimes as menacing as the mean streets of the city itself.

If you think researchers work in an ivory tower and rarely intersect with daily life, meet Anne Brisano. She has figured out why a large industrial park with more than 5,000 jobs hasn't helped her low-income neighborhood in St. Paul, Minn., lower its high unemployment rate.

Both are examples of an expanding network of street-level researchers around the United States. They are generating community-based research and finding solutions to local problems that traditional research institutions haven't provided.

"Quietly, with no one really noticing, there is a system emerging that can be responsive to these intensely local problems. It's not speculative stuff, it's urgent," says Richard Sclove of the Loka Institute. Loka is a nonprofit organization in Amherst, Mass., that studies this growing sector of local, socially oriented, applied research.

The US has a formidable research-and-development infrastructure already in place. It spends nearly $200 billion per year in combined federal and private funding. Yet with the cold war over, many critics feel the research community should more rapidly shift its focus to social issues.

While the fastest-growing sector of government-supported research is health, some 53 percent of federal funding remains devoted to defense-related issues, according to Al Teich, director of science policy at the American Association for the Advancement of Science in Washington. Within that research world, community-based activities are a drop in the bucket. Loka, in a report released this week, estimates that 50 to 60

centers across the country are spending about $10 million on neighborhood issues.

But many analysts regard it as an increasingly important vehicle for solving seemingly intractable local problems that often fly beneath the radar of the more established research industry.

"It's a fundamentally important approach," says Anne Petersen, senior vice president for the W.K. Kellogg Foundation in Battle Creek, Mich., and former deputy director of the National Science Foundation. "In the post-cold-war era, we've talked about the need to turn our attention to social issues. . . . The community-based research organization is one effective route for that."

Teen researchers

Rosalia Chavez knows little about the cold war, but as a teen about to enter her junior year in an Oakland, Calif., high school, she knows firsthand what's wrong with the troubled school system. "The security patrol at our school isn't working. They get high and get into fights with the kids," she says.

Rosalia is one of 15 high school students from across the city working this summer with Pueblo, a neighborhood organization attempting to improve school safety. They are researching the school budget and looking for ways to train the security staff. The Pueblo project is typical of community research in that it starts with a need, or problem, identified by neighborhood residents themselves. And then it involves people directly affected by the issue.

In Florida, the Jacksonville Community Council surveys the school board, the mayor's office, and local residents each year to determine what problems need addressing. "Is it timely? That's a key question for us," says executive director Lois Chepenik. Research in 1994 about basic city services—

police, fire, garbage—found inequities that led to an "equity index" solution. That has been used in recent years to make the distribution of basic city services more equitable to all of Jacksonville's neighborhoods.

Search for practical solutions

Most community research organizations are born of a spirit of local activism and have their own political orientation. The Center for Neighborhood Technology in Chicago, for instance, does work related to the environment, based on the premise: "Environmental improvement, done right, pays off. It's not a cost," says Scott Bernstein, founder of the organization.

In St. Paul, the focus is economic development. When several major employers left the area in the 1960s and 1970s, a new industrial park was built and sagging employment seemed to have found its answer. But unemployment levels failed to drop, and the community couldn't figure out why. The Riverview Economic Development Association, a neighborhood group, conducted three months of research, talking to employers of the industrial park as well as others. They determined that most entry-

level jobs in the area required a high school degree and most job-seekers didn't have one. The group went to the School Department and persuaded it to open a high school equivalency program.

The Riverview project was backstopped by a consortium of local universities called Neighborhood Planning for Community Revitalization, which reviews research proposals and helps neighborhood groups decide which are likely to have impact. It then helps construct the research methodology and offers guidance throughout the process as well as synthesizing the results.

That kind of backstopping by either local universities or larger organizations is typical of how many community organizations work. Loka is working to stitch them into a network that can share knowledge and practices. "It's obvious it's growing now and it's hit a sort of critical mass," says Sclove.

SOURCE: Van Slambroück, P. (1998, July 24). No ivory tower: Rise of the street-level think tank. *Christian Science Monitor*, p. 1. Reprinted courtesy of the *Christian Science Monitor.*

[Text continued from page 242]

economic Tyrannosaurus rex, Wal-Mart Stores, Inc., which does not advertise on radio. Declining local economies, and shrinking and aging populations—signatures of thousands of isolated small towns across the nation—usually cause big problems in the local radio studio.

"This is like the other radio business," said Tom Buono, president of Chantilly, Va.-based radio consultancy BIA Cos. "I've seen small-market radio be very profitable and others that are just knocking their heads against the wall. . . . The smaller they get, generally, the more difficult it is for them to make a margin." There are at least 300 stations—most of them from small markets—that have recently "gone dark," the broadcast term for off the air, according to BIA. The numbers underscore the challenge of profiting in the delicate ecosystems of small communities, many of which missed the economic revival of the '90s—as well as the '80s, and maybe the '70s. (Jones, 1997, p. 1)

An article in the *Chicago Tribune*, "Small Stations Struggle to Find Their Radio Days," called attention to the heroic struggle of a local radio station as its owner attempted to survive the devastating rise of the mighty Mississippi over the Missouri towns of Perryville, Ste. Genevieve, and Chester. Elmo Donze, owner and manager of KSGM-AM radio station, was contacted to help fill in the blank spaces in the *Tribune* article. He was not only an excellent and generous storyteller but the details he offered to fill the gaps showed incredible determination and the dreams of a man who truly represented "radio days."

Elmo Donze was born, as he told me, above the radio station his father had built in Perryville to serve the surrounding communities. Donze grew up with radio in his blood. The daily round of births and deaths, high-school sports, county fairs and 4-H dinners, auctions and markets, was all part of Donze's natural broadcasting rhythms until the flood of 1993, probably the greatest Mississippi River flood on record, passed the town of Perryville in July. The crest of over 47 feet completely flooded KSGM's 32 acres of property; the area eventually became a federal wetland.

"The community has never experienced a catastrophe the likes of the flood of 1993. And perhaps there has never been a more determined effort put forth by its citizens than the one . . . to prevent further tragedy," commented a story in the *Ste. Genevieve/Perryville Sun Times* (Schwent, 1993, p. 1). The determination of local citizens to beat the river was implacable. The threat of extraordinary forces highlights the resilience of small towns.

With the flood, the radio station lost not only its power, land, and buildings, but also its capacity to transmit. Although the towers didn't fall at the time of the flood, they were eventually torn down because the Federal Aviation Authority could not permit them to remain standing without proper illumination.

Donze faced not only having to move his radio station to new quarters, but also re-erecting the towers and rebuilding the spirit of his organization, all within a specified time if he wanted to keep his license.

With tenacity, or even some might say adamancy, he rebuilt his family-owned KSGM and continued to transmit to the surrounding communities. When I called him, early in January 1999, KSGM-AM, still awaiting final licensing, had just transmitted the news on the first new babies born in 1999 in the three small towns that are the station's main audience.

Local news is an important tool for understanding small communities.

Local radios and local newspapers can fill a tremendous gap in disseminating those news. They speak the language of local citizens and narrate their stories in "high-context" voices. KSGM appears to have survived the oscillations of fate. In small towns, the pendulum continues to swing from good days to bad days, but a surviving balance is maintained.

Local Community Research

Recent approaches to research in local communities suggest such a hands-on, practical, approach to solving the problems of real communities:

> This increased interest [in community development] may reflect a cycle of concern for community-level social organization that is played out in the frame of economic uncertainty, persistent ethnic segregation, increasingly divergent sensors of the common good, and the new communitarian and post-modern sensibilities, as well as the tendency to develop new forms of quasi-community social relations made possible by technical advances. (Harrison, 1995, p. 561)

A final illustration in this chapter makes the case for applied, local research (Van Slambroück, 1998). While social scientists have been concerned by and large with global issues and have limited their investigations to those that would permit broad generalizations, the trend in the past 10 years has been to return to local research, particularly on community improvement, with the help of federal and foundation grants directed particularly to local social problems that pivot on youth and families. The illustration comments on precisely that thrust. It points out how the federal government and foundations are attempting to validate local researchers to carry out investigations that render practical outcomes for community improvement. When we talk about local researchers, as this illustration shows, we are talking about people who are looking carefully at a local environment and formulating solutions to daily problems.

Human services professionals must also be aware that local attachments translate into relationships not with abstractions but with real people—people with names, faces, and idiosyncrasies. Those unique individuals will in turn relate in the same way to the worker. Small-town relationships are personal. Because workers will not be anonymous faces but known members of the group, people will be interested in their activities, thoughts, and feelings. For those not used to this degree of personalism, the "gossip lines" (Norris, 1993) may curtail freedom in painful ways. Only those workers who are willing to exchange anomie for a measure of scrutiny find the local community satisfying.

And ultimately, workers in local settings must be prepared to change their ways of understanding the world. Local information will be provided in high-context language. The story, the anecdote, the bit of news all will convey important information whose meaning a worker must decipher. Listening to someone tell a lengthy anecdote is not a waste of time but a way of discovering the ethos of the locality. In a wonderful quote from Mary Pellaver, Norris (1993, p. 69) tells us that "if there is anything worth calling theology, it is listening to people's stories, listening to them and cherishing them."

Social workers must recognize that local attachments are alive because people live their daily existences within the boundaries of locale. Attachment to locale should be viewed neither as exclusively positive nor as exclusively negative. Local attachments will be both healthy and unhealthy; the important common denominator is that people want to feel significant in affecting local events. Even those locals who recognize the interrelatedness and interdependence of the world usually can act only locally. The challenge for social workers is to not succumb to any local inertia that may exist. A positive way of counteracting negative localism is to facilitate actions that, although local, highlight the global aspects of human existence and transform even local animosities into global concerns.

Summary

This chapter has provided a way of reconceptualizing our understanding of localism. Localism has a political dimension; it denotes the interaction of national with state and local government. It involves decision-making as close to the citizens as possible; in the new terminology, given the global push to bring democracy closer to the citizens, it has experienced a rebirth.

Localism also means attachment to locale. People by and large grow up in environments that are within a manageable radius of where they live. This is understandable, given that transportation and other resources limit anyone's scope of interaction. While the emergence of electronic communication (radio, television, telephones, e-mail, the Internet) has helped to expand the radius of interaction of individuals, placelessness is still not desirable. Mental health requires connectedness to lend significance to locality.

In this chapter we have also discussed the various languages espoused by citizens in general and social workers in particular. Those who work in communities, especially rural communities, speak a language that is different from the language of bureaucracy. The language of the local is high-context, rich in stories and narratives, often colorfully descriptive, and time-consuming. The language of bureaucracy is more impersonal, detached from the day-to-day routine of people's lives, and low in context. In order for social workers to handle both the pressures of the low-context environment, of the bureaucracies for which they tend to work, and the demands of the high-context environment of locality, many bridges must be built. Social workers are well advised to become cognizant and familiar with the high-context narrative of local citizens. The wisdom that the local worker will gain from listening to local stories can best be described in an American Indian story told by Silko (1983):

> All Pueblo tribes have stories about such a person—a young child, an orphan. Someone has taken the child and has given it a place by the fire to sleep. The child's clothes are whatever the people no longer want. The child empties the ashes and gathers wood. The child is always quiet, sitting in its place tending the fire. They pay little attention to the child as they complain and tell stories about one another. The child listens although it has nothing to gain or lose in anything they say. The child simply listens. Some years go by and great danger stalks the village—in some versions of the story it is a drought and great famine, other times it is a monster in the form of a giant bear. And when all the others have failed and even the priests doubt the prayers, this child, still wearing old clothes, goes out. The child confronts the danger and the village is saved. Among the Pueblo people the child's reliability as a narrator is believed to be perfect. (p. 21)

Local narrative empowers the narrators to carry out the tasks needed for healthy living; it also empowers the worker to function successfully in the local context.

CHAPTER 7

The Community and
Social Work Practice

Human services professionals in traditional community-oriented positions and generalist social workers need to view the small community in a more positive way. Social workers often have relegated thinking about the community dimensions of practice to those who specialize in community organization or community work. Yet community variables affect all fields of social work: case management, gerontology, child welfare, advocacy, and psychotherapy. It is not that community dimensions provide a panacea that solves all social ills; however, particularly in small, local settings the community milieu, if better understood and appreciated, can become a major asset in practice.

Most of the ideas that follow were proposed in my book, *Perspectives on the Small Community*; on reviewing this chapter for the new millennium, my conclusion is that they still apply. State legislatures have attempted to focus the sights of human services and social development practitioners on the small town through initiatives like the Center for Rural Pennsylvania, which supports economic, social, and cultural development. The journal *Human Services in the Rural Environment* and the Rural Social Work Caucus have worked through the decades to highlight the rewards and complexities of small town practice. The Rural Sociological Society devoted its 1995 Rural Studies Series volume, *Investing in People*, to the "human capital needs of rural America," fearing that the economic woes resulting from the transformation of the labor force would drastically affect the quality of life of poor and working people in rural America (Beaulieu & Mulkey, 1995). International conferences in Australia (at James Cook University in 1994) and in Canada (at Malaspina University College in British Columbia in 2000), among others, focus on the human service needs of rural communities in the "global millennium."

In spite of all these efforts, social workers have remained reluctant to accept the challenges of non-urban practice. In states like Arizona with large nonurban land areas, administrators in basic services have become deeply concerned about securing trained social workers to work in child welfare and other essential services in rural areas. The Arizona Department of Economic Security funded a training grant with Arizona State University (1995–2001) just to address this need. In all instances, even when specialized skills, such as in child welfare, are called for, what is needed in rural areas are strong community-oriented practitioners who can capitalize on local resources.

Moving toward Practice in Community

In the past, most practitioners and academicians have felt more at ease emphasizing vertical over horizontal ties, national over local organizations, and vertical or external over horizontal or communal relationships. Because social work practice relates to current major social problems, social workers have historically sought solutions from central systems, among them the federal or state government and the national plans of voluntary organizations. In general, the nature of the problems social workers confront in designing systems to serve needy people have prompted centralistic and large-scale solutions. For example, during the Depression, the federal government had to actively undertake large scale programs of relief. In addressing the enormous differential of opportunities for minority people, the federal government intervened through standardized legislative and administrative measures that were by their very nature not local. These historical experiences sometimes led to the assumption that central solutions were always best.

Generally, central bureaucratic solutions are more standardized than *gemeinschaftlich* or local responses, which tend to be more personal. On the other hand, bureaucratic responses are, at least in theory, less nepotistic and have fewer strings attached. Nevertheless, no one level of organization, whether central or local, has a monopoly on positive or negative attributes. Not all central solutions are universal and egalitarian; nor are all local efforts fraught with difficulties or nepotism or punitive of particular groups. Yet with the centralist policies often come centralist administrative practices. These curtail the autonomy of social workers and other practitioners to respond to local needs in ways that are sensitive to unique local environments. Even when practitioners themselves understand the small community and want to relate to it differently, bureaucratic demands may prevent them from doing so.

Efforts at decentralization started during the Nixon administration, continued during the Reagan era and were furthered during the Clinton administration, not only because of welfare reforms that devolved decision making to the states, but also because of Vice President Gore's "reinventing government" campaign. This followed the thinking of Osborne and Gaebler (1993) in their very popular *Reinventing Government: How the Entrepreneurial Spirit is Transforming the Public Sector*. Gore's campaign moved administrators, politicians, and social workers to examine carefully the creative and entrepreneurial spirit of locality and local solutions. As Johnson (1998) suggested, "Driven by funding from major philanthropic foundations and also by recent changes in federal entitlement legislation, these efforts at system reform are designed to make services for vulnerable populations more effective, accessible, integrated, and comprehensive in the context of the local community" (p. 37). However, even in designing local solutions, people today often duplicate the centralist ethos; many government efforts in large states have taken on the characteristics once criticized in the federal bureaucracy.

What Hadley and Hatch (1981) wrote in discussing the origins of centralist policies about British social services also applies to the American situation:

> For some historians centralist policies are simply the corollary of collectivism, and collectivism is the product of industrialization. Clearly the major economic, social and political changes that were taking place in the nineteenth century posed new problems which neither the old paternalism nor the new individualism could cope with. Rapid increases in population, urbanization and the shift from an agricultural economy to an industrial economy greatly inflated the problems of unemployment, poverty, public health, law and order, and led to important shifts in power within the country towards the new middle and working classes. The development of organized public action (or collectivism) to deal with such problems has been a common response in the history of all western countries as they have gone through the phase of industrialization.
>
> But the history of other industrializing countries by no means bears out the second part of the thesis, to show that collectivism necessarily leads to centralism. In Belgium, Holland and Germany, for example, substantial public funds are devoted to the provision of social services, but within the framework in which independent voluntary organizations play a large role, and in which central control and direction is much less developed. (p. 6)

In the United States, central government measures have been essential to the development of a welfare system. In social security, public assistance, and mental health, for example, standardization and strong central government involvement have been seminal. Yet these positive and re-form-oriented central policies often have been accompanied by an attitude that equated central with high status and advanced thinking and local with lower status and lower creativity. Because of this misconception, local areas often have been drained of the people who could have energized them: "By concentrating power in the center and by implication attracting the best politicians and administrators to work in national government [or other central bureaucracies], a climate is created in which *ipso facto* those involved in local government are regarded as second rate. This neatly provides those at the center with the grounds for recommending still more centralization" (Hadley & Hatch, 1981, p. 16).

After many years of strong centralistic practices both in Europe and the United States, the situation took a slight shift in the 1970s, when political explanations contended that national governments were experiencing an overload that led to "dumping problems on local governments" (Teune, 1995, p. 20). Since the late 1970s, "In the United States, there have been episodic efforts to readjust federal-state relations, variously called 'new' federalisms. Relations between the central government and lower-level tiers of government, as a consequence of the fast-changing global developments, now require almost continual adjustment" (Teune, 1995, p. 20).

Just as governmental relations experienced changes in the balance between the central and the local through the decades, so did human services thinking. However, given the history of social welfare measures, it has been difficult for social workers to take an entirely new look at the local community in the midst of societal ambivalence. Though caring for people has always been very local and community-based, social workers have often been hard-pressed to recognize that their caring had any context other than a central bureaucracy. All human services practitioners are at a pivotal point for energizing local resources through the concept of helping. Local leadership can be developed and new strengths and human capacities unearthed to create a new chain of events. Speaking about the new interest in community-based practice as a form of direct practice, Johnson (1998) suggested: "Behind this interest in community-based practice is the need to make direct services more effective, accessible, integrated, and comprehensive in the context of the local community where services occur. In effect, these cutting-edge foundation initiatives are pushing direct service agencies to develop a community-based approach to service delivery" (p. 38).

There is no question that community-oriented, or as it is sometimes called, community-based, practice is not a new discovery, but it has certainly come back into fashion since *Perspectives on the Small Community* was published in 1990. The input of both foundations and for-profit companies, who enter the philanthropic arena as a form of public relations, has been tremendous. Most private funders want to involve citizens not just because they are the recipients of services but because it is with them that their philanthropic efforts must register. This is not to deny the merit of private funding (whether from nonprofit or for-profit organizations); it has been extremely valuable. The special merit of the focus on community from various foundations, however, is that it has made community-oriented practice a term that is current and meaningful to practitioners as we move into the new millennium.

Returning to our main theme, the tension between local and nonlocal cultures has affected all forms of practice from the most micro to the most macro. The emphasis on objectivity—which sometimes borders on depersonalization—and on anonymity—which often results in unrealistic demands for confidentiality—that is characteristic of a nonlocal ethos reflects common attitudes that are detrimental to local community involvement. Nearly two decades ago, for example, Moore-Kirkland and Vice-Irey (1981) said of anonymity and confidentiality:

> To define confidentiality only in relation to the one on one psychotherapeutic process between worker and client places unnecessary limits on social workers. The definition of confidentiality must deal with people in their social environments—the very relationship that social work claims as its unique focus. Social workers cannot view individuals in their relationship to workers apart from the social context. The issue of confidentiality within the social context is especially acute in rural environments. In small towns and communities, social workers and clients must function not only in therapeutic sessions but also in daily interactions within circumscribed social systems. (p. 319)

Most social workers are used to accomplishing their aims within the confines of agencies. Professional standards use the agency or organization, not the local community, as the frame of reference. The problems inherent in this approach are apparent in small communities, where the more intimate scale of living makes it difficult not to redefine certain standards. During the early 1990s, as an NASW Commission worked on a new *Code of Ethics* for professional social workers, there was much discussion of how the new code could limit, perhaps in unrealistic ways, the abilities of rural practitioners to work within a community orientation. Having been part of the group that discussed this with the NASW Commission, I can attest to the effort put into modifying statements on such topics as "dual relationships" and how they could affect rural social workers. The original paragraphs, later clarified by the commission, would have presented serious problems of interpretation in rural areas where, as Moore-Kirkland and Vice-Trey had suggested in 1981, clients and workers play many roles without necessarily engaging in dual relationships.

The *Code of Ethics* (NASW, 1996, 1999) attempted to provide greater sensitivity for the uniquely complex situations confronting social workers in Gemeinschaft than had been the case in the past. Reamer (1998) clarifies this:

> Social workers also should recognize that some dual and multiple relationships are more avoidable than others. For example, they can easily avoid planned social encounters with their clients, such as spending together a day at the beach or going out to dinner. In contrast, it may be difficult for social workers to avoid dual or multiple relationships in small or rural communities where, for example, a former client may marry her social worker's closest friend in town, a current client is elected to the local court in which the social worker's spouse often practices, or a social worker and her client are both appointed to the board of their community church. In such circumstances, according to Standard 1.06 (6c), social workers must "take steps to protect clients and are responsible for setting clear, appropriate, and culturally sensitive boundaries." At a minimum, social workers should discuss the boundary issues frankly with their clients; in addition, they should consult colleagues and supervisors to discuss the most appropriate ways to handle boundary issues that have emerged. (pp. 53–54).

Professional commitments to anonymity and definitions of confidentiality all require modification in the less bureaucratic context of small towns. Small-town practitioners, more so than others, must practice from a strength perspective. The community itself is part of their strength. The basic theme of this book has been to help social workers recognize that strength. Saleebey (1997) defined as one of the basic principles of the strength perspective the concept of environmental resources.

> In communities that seem to exemplify individual and group resilience, there is awareness, recognition and use of the assets of most members of the community. . . . Informal systems of individuals, families, and groups, social circuits of peers, and inter-generational mentoring work to assist, support, instruct and include all members of a community. . . . In inclusive communities, there are many opportunities for involvement, to make contributions to the moral and civic life of the whole, to become, in

other words, a citizen in place. No matter how harsh an environment, how it may test the mettle of its inhabitants, it can also be understood as a potentially lush topography of resources and possibilities. (p. 15)

Gemeinschaftlich environments present the ideal topography for practice from a strength perspective. Furthermore, the vaunted resiliency of individuals who have lived in remote locations and become acclimated to "the school of make-do" adds to the inner resources of each rural citizen. The resiliency of rural individuals was well illustrated by Fitchen (1991) when she spoke about dairy farmers and their response to the farm crisis. Speaking about independence and "making it on your own," Fitchen told of how many families in financial trouble coped. Most of them increased their working hours, tightened their working conditions, and made their families do with less during the crisis. Even farmers who had already a heavy workload often increased their milking herd in an effort to survive: "The last thing I wanted to do was increase the number of milking cows because it was all the hired men and I could do to keep up with the ones we had. But it was the only way that I could generate enough cash to keep the creditors from my door. So, we added ten more to the milking herd and we're working harder now than ever before" (Fitchen, 1991, p. 30).

Working harder, making do, not relating to need in negative ways but trying to find creative solutions are classic examples of rural resiliency. The business leader and philosopher Charles Handy, author of both *The Age of Unreason* (1989) and *The Age of Paradox* (1994), suggested in *Beyond Certainty* (1996) that in a changing world we must never be so preoccupied with efficiency that we lose sight of the means we use to achieve our ends:

> To say that profit is a means to other ends and is not an end in itself is not a semantic quibble, it is a serious moral point. In everyday life, those who make the means into ends in themselves are usually called neurotic or obsessive, like the great aunt of mine who was meticulous about how we dressed and adorned for church each Sunday, the way we knelt and the prayer book we carried, but seemed not to understand or be interested in the theology of it all, the content of the preaching or the praying. In ethics, to mistake the means for the ends is to be turned in on oneself, one of the greatest sins, said Saint Augustine. (p. 62)

In "Victors or Victims?" Goldstein (1997) refers to the use of language in the helping relationship. In his view there are multiple interpretations of reality and the interpretations that people, both practitioners and clients, assign to their reality determine their attitudes toward it. He further stresses how the language we use conveys images and how the language of the "folk" can open the door to a myriad of possible interpretations. As we have seen, to use the high-context language of the folk is to affirm strength instead of weakness, to see peculiarities rather than deviations, quirks instead of pathology. The *gemeinschaftlich* environment of the small town presents an incomparable scenario for this kind of reflection. Yet the complexity of current cases and the litigious nature of our society have in many instances hardened the professional belief that bureaucratic language must be spoken and bureaucratic rules must be rigidly followed—because they are there to protect the professional. Unfortunately, a common current admonition to professionals of all kinds is to "practice defensively" at both the personal and agency levels.

Without underestimating the value of defensive practice given the realities of our times, what is important here is to point out to those who will practice in more *gemeinschaftlich* environments that the perils of litigation are often fueled by our own thinking. Tannen (1998), a communications expert, says that in modern society we are often victims of our own habit of looking at the world in dual opposites. For example, when we compare two cultures, she says, we tend to see one as positive and one as negative. But if we can compare three, we are more likely to think about each of them on its own terms (Tannen, 1998, p. 285). As a goal, she recommends that we catch ourselves when talking about *both* sides of an issue and talk instead about *all* sides of the issue. After asking what went wrong in a particular situation, Tannen suggests, we should ask what went right as well.

A danger for novice practitioners is to view our adversary system as a system that supports the search for justice. Tannen says that in our system of law, "justice lies in having advocates of the two sides making their best case. If no one will advocate for one of the sides, there can be no justice" (Tannen, 1998, p. 152). She adds:

> Nothing is more partisan than our legal system in which facts are uncovered and revealed by lawyers who are advocates for the two parties to the dispute. How else could it be? In the German and French systems, fact-gathering is controlled by a judge, not by attorneys. The judge does most of the questioning of witnesses, and the judge's goal is to determine what happened, as nearly as possible. Such a system surely has its own liabilities, but it provides some illuminating contrasts to the goal of attorneys in the adversary system: to manipulate facts to the advantage of their side. (pp. 132–133)

What human services professionals must keep in mind is that our enormous efforts at practicing defensively are not necessarily efforts at bringing about justice. The most creative possibilities for practice, not only in small communities but in all communities, lie beyond defensive practices in recognizing the resources that people bring to their social encounters.

The tenets of community-*oriented* practice, a term that appeared in the United Kingdom in the late 1970s and early 1980s, have since been translated in the United States into an approach called community-*based* practice. While the principles of working "in community" from a strength perspective, showing a deep respect for the resourcefulness of community members, and understanding the resiliency of the people we serve are probably similar in both approaches, Johnson's (1998) operational definition probably best captures what practitioners have been doing in the 1990s:

> [Community-based practice is] a direct service strategy implemented in the context of the local community (geographic area, neighborhood, etc.). It is the integration of direct services with skills traditionally associated with community organization and community development. This integration of selected macro skills with direct practice adds the "community component to direct practice work—hence, the name community-based practice." (p. 41)

This definition as well as Weil's statement that "community practice is the term that encompasses . . . processes of work with individuals, task groups, organizations, and communities to produce positive social outcomes in community life" (1994, pp. xxx–xxi) are closest to the operating principles suggested in this chapter for the practice of social work in small towns. The one additional element that becomes essential in the *Gemeinshaftlich* context is an emphasis more on community or locality development than on traditional community organizing techniques. The social worker in a small town must create, invent, and "make do." Only through inventiveness and creativity will he or she gain respect from the locals. Furthermore, as Miller (1997) said:

> With the diffusion of information through new and accessible technologies, knowledge-sharing institutions are changing the power of relationships among collectives at all levels. Those at the summit of political power must operate more transparently; those at the base are sharing skills and information in unprecedented quantities. Their needs call more for institutions in the business of exchanging information. The role of the outside development organization [or of the social worker] has been transformed from "change agent" to "exchange agent." (pp. 26–27).

Here social workers would be well advised to remember the admonitions of Goldstein (1997):

You can't say that the strengths/resilience perspective is "better than," "more effective than," "works better than" other practice models. Comparison is pointless. The perspective, however, by its very nature naturally embraces and operationalizes the essential enduring precepts of social work: Self-determination, starting where the client is, the importance of relationship, and so on. The perspective does not abstract, objectify, or theorize the client's circumstances; it uses the client's language, idiom, and narrative; it strives to understand and be sympathetic to the client's real-life ordeal as it is *experienced*: It not only gives credibility to subjective understanding but strives to refine this way of making sense and finding meaning through the development of reflective thinking. (p. 35)

Locals and Professionals in Community-Oriented Practice

Practice in local settings requires greater involvement of the locals. This usually means that nonprofessionals must be relied upon to provide significant and meaningful services. The bureaucratic ethos has often frowned on the use of the outsider (that is, the person not in the bureaucracy) because of issues of responsibility already discussed. Yet local community practice by its very nature requires partnerships with the grassroots. With regard to the use of laypeople in the context of community, Hadley and McGrath (1980) commented: "The compartmentalism and rigidity of the bureaucratic structure reinforces the emphasis on qualifications and narrow interpretation of professionalism held by many social workers. It encourages a view in which care is seen as the prerogative of the professional, in which the unqualified should be relegated wherever possible to routine tasks and in which volunteers should be confined to marginal, dogsbody roles" (p. 7).

Particularly in small towns, a different kind of practice has always been required, although this practice has not been systematically taught or regarded as bona fide in many circles. In this practice members of the community provide care to each other, in mutually supporting relationships, and social workers and other human services personnel also provide care, in partnership with friends, neighbors, and volunteers. In this practice confidentiality must be reinterpreted to suit the context, the use of nonprofessional helpers in many tasks and greater reliance on neighbors and churches. These principles constitute the basis of community-oriented social work and of the way of working we are now labeling community-based practice.

The case for community social work as stated by the 1980 Barclay Working Party, which was set up in Britain by the Secretary of State for Social Services to study the role and tasks of social workers, "rests upon our understanding of the nature of community and the meaning of social care" (National Institute for Social Work, 1982, p. 199). The Working Party's report defined *community* as "a network, or informal relationships between people connected with each other by kinship, common interest, geographical proximity, friendship, occupation, or the giving and receiving of services—or various combinations of these" (p. 199). The Working Party defined *social care* as "the sum of helping (and when need be, controlling) resources available to people in adversity, whether provided informally by community networks or formally by the public services" (p. 199) or, in the case of the United States, whether provided by formal services—public, voluntary, or private—or by informal networks of kin and friends.

The Working Party suggested that community social work was not a specific technique or method but rather depended on "an attitude of mind in all social workers, from the director of the department or agency to front-line workers, which regards members of the public as partners in the provision of social care" (National Institute for Social Work, 1982, p. 198). Community-oriented social work depends on an attitude of mind that sees community as a potentially nourishing source of support and identity to its members. The notion that community nourishes its members is not common. It probably is not an idea that is in the forefront of consciousness when social workers help clients make decisions. Although community-oriented social work is important, there is no single recipe that those who use and provide social care should follow. "Each statutory and voluntary agency must consider the geographical area and the nature of the people and the communities it serves before deciding upon the particular forms and combinations of community social work it wishes to develop" (National Institute for Social Work, 1982, p. 198).

Abrams (1980), generally a critic of the model, suggested that community-oriented social work can develop in four possible ways, ways that describe the types of relationships that emerge between the formal system of agencies and organized services and the informal system of kin, neighbors, and friends caring for each other "in community." The four alternatives are (1) domination, (2) appropriation, (3) incorporation, and (4) coexistence. These provide an excellent framework for analyzing how partnership with community-based organizations often proceeds.

Abrams (1980) sees *domination* existing when the governmental or voluntary agencies "merely impose their own preferred hierarchies and control on local systems" (p. 20). The formal system tends to dominate in most projects where both formal and informal operate. For example, in one "friendly neighbor" scheme in a rural village, local citizens operated a telephone line to arrange for rides for elderly citizens when they needed them and friendly visits to people who were lonely. Through the telephone, local citizens also answered questions and provided neighbor-to-neighbor advice. At one point, the informal group contacted the social workers at a government agency to secure a few answering machines for some of the neighbors' houses to help them refer calls from one neighbor to another when one of the neighbors was unavailable to take a call. The formal system with its resources came to the rescue, but with the answering machines came a number of suggestions on how to operate the system "more efficiently." To illustrate, "off-times" for answering the line were suggested, even though the point of the scheme had been to provide ready, immediate responses to people in need, regardless of time. The group was encouraged by the social worker to organize formally and elect officers, although it had been operating on the basis of collective responsibility. Many other suggestions from the formal system were practical and increased efficiency, but the price paid by the informal group was that the formal system imposed its structure and consequent tendency toward professionalization.

Appropriation occurs when boundaries are drawn so that they redefine previous perceptions of the formal and informal systems (Abrams, 1980, p. 20). The informal becomes an extended part of the formal. "The advantages of appropriation are the advantages of bureaucratic tidying up and control. Unfortunately . . . the administrative gain is in practice usually the informal sector's loss" (p. 20). This situation is common when innovative services that were started as lay community efforts seek funding, for example, from United Way. In many small towns, women's centers that emerged as places where neighbors helped each other informally and outside the organized service structure had, out of necessity, to become formal organizations when they tried to get support from organized community funding efforts.

Incorporation occurs when the formal system makes significant efforts to respect the "untidiness" of the informal system and actually tries to incorporate some informality into its own formal structure. For example, during crises, communities may respond informally to a given threat and the formal system then tries to follow up on those responses. The formal system often realizes that to succeed it must limit its bureaucratization. For instance, during the farm crisis of the 1980s, in some Midwestern states support groups that had begun as informal neighborly gatherings were incorporated into mental health services. It became apparent to the system that the "untidiness" and integrity of the informal efforts had to be respected even if their approaches were unorthodox (Blundall, 1987). One social work student who had worked in a basic needs project that had started as an informal effort by a local group but had been incorporated into a voluntary counseling service described the methods that she had had to use:

> Some of the things that . . . I did seemed to me to be unorthodox at first. I could not really explain them from a social work perspective but, when I thought about my experiences in a project I did with real citizens in the community and when I thought of the ways in which Bell and Newby . . . described primary relationships in community, I felt justified in what I did. I often exaggerated certain client characteristics or understated others to get help from specific groups. If I needed help from a church, my clients' religious merits would be emphasized while their "spiritual" shortcomings were deemphasized. . . . At first, I was concerned that what I was doing was not technically quite right; but then, I thought about my ways as using what I knew about *gemeinschaftlich* relationships in community to help my clients.

The most viable and potentially successful alternative for a healthy orientation to the community is *coexistence*. According to Abrams (1980),

> What I have in mind is sufficient strengthening of the informal sector to enable it to deal intimately but on equal terms with agencies in the formal system. Co-existence would differ from incorporation not only in the extent in which informal and formal social care were closely meshed together but in the fact that in a relationship of co-existence, the values, norms and relationships of the informal sector would be brought forward and sustained as a basis for social policy in their own right and not as remade to suit the administrative or other purposes of the formal system. This means that instead of patronizing or colonizing the local community, the existing statutory and voluntary agencies are going to have to learn to live with it as an equal. . . . Some serious surrender of powers is unavoidable if one really wants any significant measure of social care to be provided within neighborhood social networks. (p. 23)

The Abrams model of coexistence implies the need for a fuller understanding of community. To achieve community-oriented practice, social workers must correct their neglect of community by nurturing a more sympathetic view of the forces that make up communities, particularly small ones. They must understand how *gemeinschaftlich* relationships, values, and norms influence (whether in support or contradiction) practice principles and behaviors.

Relationships, Values, and Norms and Practice Behaviors

If one views community as "an alternative to emphases on individualism, self-sufficiency and mass society ordered by comprehensive legal, rational authority" (personal communication with R. Buck, professor at the Pennsylvania State University, October 20, 1982), then relationships in community will emphasize local ties, will be personalized, will be based on affect, and will be more public than anonymous or confidential. Social workers need to appreciate the effects of local ties, community values, anonymity, confidentiality, and accountability on their practice behaviors.

Local Ties

The few human services professionals who are perceived by their colleagues as too attached to local ties often are viewed with considerable condescension. One social work student who worked in a basic needs program in a small town commented in her diary:

> I noticed, among some of the more "esteemed and established" social workers who led the traditional agencies in [Town X], an attitude that was quite condescending. Many of them felt sorry for my clients not only because they were poor and couldn't get out of poverty, but also because they seemed destined to spend their entire lives in [Town X] or the closest neighboring communities. At the time, this condescension made me feel edgy but I couldn't place why. Talking about "pride of place" in class helped me understand better why this discussion of pity made me angry beyond the obvious "looking down on the poor" it implied.

An additional component of such condescension is the assumption that highly "specialized" workers are "more advanced," "better skilled," or some other similar descriptor. While they may be, they are not necessarily so since social workers, whether generalist or specialist, typically hold MSW degrees. But bureaucratic organization demands "functional specificity"; thus the more specialized the function, the higher the recognition given to it by the bureaucracy. Work "in community," on the other hand, demands generalist skills. Community-oriented practice is more a philosophy than a specialization.

Social workers practicing with ethnic groups often experience feelings similar to those the student recorded in her diary. Coexistence in community requires that the professional place high value on the experience. The local community and its citizens must be viewed as a source of improvement of the quality of life. Sadly, the student's example makes it apparent that some social workers in Town X could not see any strengths in those clients' local relationships or never thought the clients might actually be attached to their communities in positive ways.

In America's mobile society and in social work culture, attachment to locality is often seen as a red flag warning of lack of independence. Clearly, the student faced an inner struggle to reach the conclusion that "living in [Town X] for all one's life would not be the worst a person could experience." Generally, a strong attachment to locality is viewed as a forgivable trait among elderly people because many locality-based networks can help make appropriate living arrangements for people who can no longer manage independently. Although it is important that attachment to locality should be recognized, it should also be recognized as a positive force for strength with young clients, mothers, children—and everyone else.

Attachment to locality and the intertwined local relationships among individuals become apparent, for example, when clients who have housing difficulties refuse to move "alone" even to nearby communities. Social workers often surmise that there must be an unhealthy dependence among neighbors or families to be overcome. Yet for people with limited resources, the value of proximity to their communal networks of support is incalculable. What surprises workers even more is that the people in those networks often appear to be highly needy individuals themselves. In this context, it is essential to understand the nature of networks in communities and to apply a strength perspective. Johnson (1983) noted that "community networks are not developed; they emerge" and that "networks seem to emerge around an exchange or reciprocity in terms of limited resources" (p. 28). Real networks of support are likely to increase in importance as resources decrease. The older, the less mobile, the poorer the client, the greater the importance of his or her local networks. They are sources of support, of mutual legitimacy, of common language and culture. The following example illustrates a network.

Four only distantly related families always moved as a block. They lived in rented trailers but always moved together, even if only one family was dissatisfied or was experiencing problems with housing arrangements. Although the relationship among the four related families on the surface may have appeared as too dependent and limiting of their individual possibilities, they derived great support from their tight network. While it could have been argued that their network limited their individual opportunities, the four families represented to each other a supportive community.

The social worker who practices with an orientation to the community needs to be not only particularly sensitive to natural networks among people but also willing to surrender a great deal of control to enhance those networks. If professionalism acts to control, impose structures, and formalize them, it can become destructive to natural networks (Sarason & Lorentz, 1979). In *domination* and *appropriation*, professionals may destroy networks because professionalism does not always recognize the autochthonous language and culture of a community. Inability to appreciate the different ways in which ordinary people secure support can be potentially dangerous for human services professionals. However, the community-oriented practitioner can be supportive of networks once he or she has learned to appreciate them; it is through coexistence that the professional accommodates the informal system.

The practitioner will sometimes serendipitously facilitate the development of effective informal networks. One related:

> The agency had what was called a "budgeting class" which was supposedly devised to teach poor people in the small town how to budget their money. I was annoyed and politically opposed to the class because, although it was open to anyone who wanted to come, I knew that those who came were likely to be our poor clients who were probably being "encouraged to come" by various agencies. Surprisingly, I soon began to discover that a steady group came of their own volition. Many were not even clients. The class was clearly an excuse for people to get together; discuss money matters and network.

In this case, the agency running the budgeting class was serendipitously but successfully strengthening a network. As long as no one was upset about whether the clients learned a prescribed curriculum, the effort was an effective though indirect way of strengthening community. Social workers must recognize and be positive about what they are doing. Operating from a strength perspective, the serendipitous results in this case would need to be supported and preserved even if the funding source questions the outcome. The community-oriented worker needs to articulate goals and objectives for funding sources that permit validation and appreciation of serendipitous results.

Another important but seldom used way to strengthen natural community ties is for the formal sector to provide financial support to people who help each other. Wenger (1984) found that although neighbors are often prepared to support old people with day-to-day help in their homes (for example, cooking extra for them or taking them shopping), they often are unable to do so because of cost. Unfortunately, few agencies are willing to provide even the smallest financial help to those neighbors because they are concerned about accountability and legal risks. Yet in many small communities it could be possible to redefine accountability in ways that do not preclude more flexible arrangements among people. Wenger (1984) suggested that although in government agencies accountability may be rigidly defined, in the voluntary sector, particularly in working with elderly people, there are many opportunities to redefine accountability, giving more weight to negotiating informal arrangements and stressing creativity in the use of funds to support those arrangements.

The move toward localism—locality-based government, locality-based social services, community-oriented or community-based social services—attempts to facilitate the creation of flexible opportunities for democratizing government and taking care of people. The strength-oriented perspective that followed as a consequence of this community orientation would also facilitate the care of people. Yet actual social workers in the context of community are finding themselves unable to be flexible in using the resources allotted to them. It is sad that what was created to increase flexibility has become much less flexible than anticipated. Wenger's proposals for achieving accountability are no longer possible in many practice settings. Workers have the responsibility and the challenge to continue to interpret the need for good judgment, local decision making, and flexibility in the use of resources. This does not mean that community-oriented social work gives license to operate in haphazard ways but that it recognizes that without flexibility there can be no tailoring to locality.

Other concerns in community-oriented practice pivot on insider/outsider considerations. We have alluded to the difficulties professionals encounter in local settings when they are perceived as outsiders. In many small towns, the person who has lived in the town since birth is respected as an authority by other locals. Yet this same person might be treated with little deference by the professional who does not understand the town's history. This difference might inhibit communication. Locals may be clients, but they are also volunteers, friendly neighbors, or board members. Community-oriented social workers need to know a great deal about the unique claims of these residents to legitimacy, not only because they are part of the town's power structure but because they are part of the community's fiber. People in small towns often judge outsiders, including service providers, by their decorum, their observance of the community's conventions. Thus, adherence to local norms will be demanded of the community-oriented social worker, perhaps even more strongly than of the locals. Insiders will feel that they can criticize the outsider or other locals more readily than the outsider/professional can. The social worker will be closely scrutinized and tested for allegiance to the locality. Allegiance to the local community does not necessarily mean traditionalism; if the community is very unconventional, then allegiance to unconventional mores may be tested.

Finally, community-oriented practice clearly differs from traditional community organization in many ways. In this book I have preferred to use the term "community work" to encompass the three traditional approaches to work in the community identified by Rothman (1974, 1996), Jacobsen (1980, 1988), and many others: (1) locality or community development, (2) social planning, and (3) social action.

Locality or community development is "'a process designed to create conditions of economic and social progress for the whole community with its active participation and the fullest possible reliance on the community's initiative' [according to the United Nations]. Community development practitioners tend to assume that social change can best be pursued through broad participation of a wide range of people at the local level" (Jacobsen, 1988, p. 313).

Social planning usually addresses specific issues or problems of the community. Goals are often more important than process for the social planner. Planning seems to be an essentially future-oriented approach to community problems. Representatives of the community usually act as advisors.

The overriding goals of *social action* have been basic changes in community institutions. The social action practitioner tends to see the community as structured through power and privilege; it is that very structure that the social action practitioner targets (Jacobsen, 1988).

Of the three traditional models, locality development is most closely connected to community-oriented work. Locality development is even more important for small communities, not only because building the economy and the culture is a necessity but also because in locality development, powerful and non-powerful locals are viewed as important collaborators of the practitioner. In social action, powerful actors often are viewed as part of the existing structure and thus a target for action; the social action model tends to be adversarial. The community-oriented model is coalition-building. This is not to say that the power structure might not need to be addressed; however, change in the community-based model, in small communities in particular, needs to be the collaborative endeavor of many inside forces. Even if the insiders wish to change the power structure, efforts of the outsider will not be viewed kindly. Outsiders often will be accused of polarizing, of "meddling."

Community-oriented social workers must be particularly sensitive to the language and needs of locals—whether or not the locals are decision makers—because locals legitimize the social worker in the community. Discussing the contrast between the language of professionals and the language of clients, Goldstein (1997) says:

> We are the inheritors of abstractions and concepts—a professional language comprising value-laden metaphors and idioms. It is the language that has far more to do with philosophic assumptions about the human state, about the ideologies of professionalism, and, not the least, the politics of practice than with some objective and rational hypothesis. The rhetoric of the two perspectives inevitably dictates (at least in broad terms) the professional's role *vis-à-vis* that of the client's. In so doing, unavoidable ethical questions come forward about the allocation of power and authority (and a matter of self-determination) in the helping experience. As happens with a medical–scientific approach to practice, the weight of influence is set by the expertise of the practitioner. (p. 26)

It is very important to understand how the language frame of reference makes a difference in our communications in the local setting. Particularly in small communities, the language of the local will be different from that of the outsider or the cosmopolitan not only because of its context but also because of the philosophic framework and referents used. The term "referent" here denotes the constructs, the multiple variables, that make up our mental and real frames of reference in everyday interactions. A story told by Trimble (1999) in an article about the spirit of the Western United States illustrates this:

> "Try to find Gold Tooth, Arizona," Tony Hillerman says. "It's a great exercise in understanding the West."
>
> When Hillerman, a best-selling mystery writer, tried to find the deserted Navajo settlement using his trusted AAA Guide to Indian Country Map, he couldn't. He went back to Tuba City and asked a Navajo woman for directions. She didn't say, "Turn left where the windmill used to be" (my favorite from my own travels). But she came close: "Go up that big hill past Moenkopi Wash and look for tracks where people have been turning off the pavement." (p. 1)

This story illustrates in amusing but yet very real fashion the referents that locals use. The geography of places, the mental maps that people carry are determined by experiences. Regardless of where people live, people often navigate the geography of their locality by mental maps. Those maps depend on people's ages and their relationship to the locality. That sort of generational local geography exists in most communities but it is particularly tale-telling in small towns. The hidden meaning of the referents people use in navigating the locality will tell a great deal, about both clients and social workers. One young social worker who worked with elderly people in a small town that was changing rapidly told me, how clients directed her to their houses by landmarks that no longer existed. "I live upstairs from the cinema," an elderly client would say, though the cinema was no longer there. Although the social worker thought it was the peculiar way of elderly people, this mapping process, part of people's system of referents, tested her wits as well as her ability. She eventually learned to rely on other locals to decipher or elaborate on the directions.

The situations newcomers face in a small town are illustrated in an excerpt from the *Centre Daily Times* of Pennsylvania (see p. 269). The excerpt is a highly practical display of the shock of change from the perspective of landscape, guidelines, and landmarks that orient individuals to the structure of their town. One of the acid tests of newcomers in small towns is their ability to find places whose location is supposed to be common knowledge. This test also applies to new social workers who need to navigate small towns based on directions from their clients. New social workers often search in vain for nonexistent landmarks or addresses. Perhaps the problem is not so much the directions but the different frames of reference used by old-timers and social workers, who usually are not only younger but also newcomers. The article by Bill Welch (1986), "Your View of Town May Depend on Your Age," discusses this problem. Perhaps human services professionals—like other newcomers—should first identify a common navigation map with those who provide directions before setting out to find small-town hideouts.

Understanding local community mores, attachments, language and referents fully is an important element of community-oriented practice. The way in which the worker conceptualizes and appreciates those elements of local culture will affect his or her understanding of events and situations, determine his or her views and behavior toward local people, and influence his or her ways of serving people.

Ethical Considerations

One of the major concerns of social workers used to functioning in fairly large and anonymous agency settings is the difficulty of maintaining anonymity or confidentiality in the small town. Anonymity and confidentiality are closely intertwined in the small community.

[Text continues on page 270]

Your View of Town May Depend on Your Age

We all navigate by "mental maps," visualizing where we are, want to go, have been. Your age will determine many of the landmarks on your mental map.

This sort of generational geography no doubt occurs in most communities, but I specially notice it in State College, which has been undergoing rapid change for the last quarter of a century.

If my 17-year-old daughter were to give you directions on how to walk from the Pugh Street parking garage to the Fraser Street parking garage two blocks away, it might go something like this:

"Go up Calder Way, past Rapid Transit and Harvard Square, make a left at the Fraser Street Mini-Mall, and you'll see it."

If her father were to give the same directions, they'd sound like this:

"Go up Calder alley, past Metzger's and the Nittany Theatre, make a left at the CDT building and go up to the old Scurotino market. You can't miss it." Or, if I was talking to a fellow survivor of the Sixties, I might mention Peoples Nation, which briefly flowered in the Metzger's space. The name came from scraping the appropriate letters off the Peoples National Bank sign on the window, the only reminder that the bank had occupied the space for a short time. Peoples Nation was a sort of voo-doo version of "Hair," an indoor Art Festival with lots of incense, black lights, cigarette papers and underground comics. It soon withered and we radicals went back to buying New Directions paperbacks at Nittany News.

An earlier generation than mine might use the Pastime Theatre and the borough power station as landmarks. (Both stood on the south side of the 100 block of Wester Calder Way.)

And for the generation that still remembers, the early years of this century, when a long automobile ride was one from the corner of College and Atherton all the way out to Buckhout Street—a trip Ethel Wahl once told me she made shortly after coming to town in 1907—the presence of parking garages must seem fantastic.

Generational geography has a corollary in our town's hidden geography: those place names that everyone of a certain age knows, but that are not written down anywhere, that go unproclaimed by signs. Here are a few; long-time residents will have many more to offer:

Catholic Hill: The steep hill on South Fraser Street south of the Fairmount Avenue intersection. The name comes from Our Lady of Victory Catholic Church which once stood at that intersection. The hill long was considered the most challenging street for winter sledding, although College Heights kids liked Ski Hill, a more gradual, unpaved slope that ran down to the Bellefonte Central Railroad tracks, below Sunset Park.

Mudville: More properly know as Lytle's Addition, this area today is bounded by South Atherton Street, Westerly Parkway, South Allen Street and West Hamilton Avenue. ("Addition" meant that the area had been annexed to the borough.) Nadine Kofman's home town.

The College Township Island: This was a small piece of land belonging to College Township that, thanks to several "additions" to State College Borough, became completely cut off from the township. The "island" was located around the 700 block of South Atherton Street, about where the Pizza Hut now stands. The island ultimately was annexed to the borough, some time in the 1960s.

Windcrest: This was a trailer park that sprang up immediately after World War II to provide housing for returning student veterans and their families. Located on the slope now occupied by Penn State's South Halls, along East College Avenue, Windcrest had more mud than Mudville. . . .

While we're on the subject of geography, here's a quick quiz to test your State College knowledge:

Where is the highest point of land in the borough?

Want some clues? All right, it's not Catholic Hill.

How about College Heights, Ridge Avenue, Hillcrest Avenue?

The borough's high point is near the Nittany Lion Inn, at the corner of West Park Avenue and North Atherton Street.

That no doubt explains what [*sic*] that intersection is so often piled high with traffic. . . .

SOURCE: Welch, B. (1986, October 4). Your view of town may depend on your age. *Centre Daily Times*, p. B4. Reprinted courtesy of the *Centre Daily Times* and the author.

[Text continued from page 268]

Anonymity

Anonymity refers to the state or situation of being without a name. A client in a large city may occasionally meet an agency worker on the streets or in the market, but relationships generally can remain anonymous, not because people do not recognize one another, but because when they do, people and names will seldom be put together in a way that is meaningful to anyone else. In the small community, faces and names are always put together in meaningful ways. People often move to small communities precisely because they do not want to remain anonymous. They enjoy doing business in highly personalized ways. They value being recognized and treated as people with names at the grocery store, the school, or the playground. Liked or disliked, small-town dwellers are seldom anonymous.

However, it is impossible for a person seen in the small-town agency to remain anonymous. The secretary who greets the client at a social agency will recognize individuals and attach the act of coming to the agency to a known person, not an anonymous case; other people in the waiting room will also know the person has been there. Even before the confidentiality of the professional contact becomes a concern, lack of anonymity can thus be a worry for the client. The use of the Internet at least for informational purposes has caused some of the more acute contradictions in relation to anonymity at the end of this century. Individuals can readily access basic information on social problems or social issues without being seen, thus being anonymous at least at the start. This, however, has not remedied the root problem of stigmatization among those who use social services in communities where people know each other, but it can provide some comfort to individuals who, even in small communities, value anonymity while they take first steps toward help.

Perhaps the more significant issue to be analyzed is whether anonymity really has value for clients and practitioners in small communities. People who grew up in small towns generally value personalization, or at least are more used to handling highly personalized community encounters than are social workers. For elderly people, the lack of anonymity of the small community is usually an asset; it can be transformed into a major component of care. Consider, for example, Stella Jones, 89, who always gets her hair done on Mondays. She did not show up at the hairdresser's one Monday—everyone noticed. Social workers who care for elderly people try to develop networks of community support and channel their knowledge of the lives of elderly people into appropriate action. What social workers want in these situations is a response from the network, whether it be calling Stella Jones, visiting her, or calling the social worker. Of course, it might well be that Stella Jones never wanted to be missed in such a highly personal way, but the fact that she still lives in the community makes it unlikely. It is possible that she counts on people checking up on her, that she values and enjoys the attention. If so, the lack of anonymity is serving her well.

Mutual help organizations often rely on lack of anonymity, at least among their members. Powell (1987) analyzed the possible activities of habit-disturbance organizations (such as Alcoholics Anonymous), general-purpose organizations (for example, those for grief or mental illness recovery), lifestyle organizations (for example, those for breast-feeding mothers), and organizations for significant others (for example, those for parents of mentally ill people). They all based their support on the assumption that acknowledging conditions is a first step in recovery, that others endure similar predicaments, that it is easier to undertake challenging tasks with others, and that supporting family members with their concerns is beneficial. In small communities mutual help organizations encounter special problems, including lack of distance from the community at large. It is the challenge of the human services professional, community members, and volunteers to deal with these issues at the outset and to turn lack of anonymity into an asset for participants.

While in working with elderly clients, social workers have been willing to put lack of anonymity to good use, their behavior can be quite different in other areas of practice. Social workers often do not know how to handle comments from people who have noticed that children are no longer living at home or that an alcoholic person is once again drinking. Social workers and the social services system have been able to make lack of anonymity positive in certain situations but not in others, perhaps because of the stigma attached to particular services (such as child welfare).

The challenge of community-oriented social work is not to control what people notice—it cannot be done—but to see how public knowledge can be used in helpful ways.

Social workers who deal with public knowledge of issues can afford to be more relaxed about confidentiality. In small communities, clients themselves often reveal problems to friends and neighbors. For example, where a person with acquired immune deficiency syndrome (AIDS) had disclosed positive test results to a roommate and to a local volunteer fire department, a judge stated that "once the condition has been disclosed, there is no longer any reason for the (confidentiality) privilege" (Schwartz, 1989, p. 224).

One social worker who works in a mental health center in a Midwestern state told a story in which "what everybody knows" was used to help save lives during the farm crisis of the 1980s. A small-town veterinarian noticed during his rounds that many of the farmers with whom he was interacting were depressed because of the stresses they were experiencing. As a result, he formed a group of people who cared about their neighbors and were willing to become "active listeners" as they went about their daily rounds. The vet consulted the local mental health agency for pointers on how to listen, but other than that, the group of approximately 12 people was never formalized.

One day, the vet went into the feed store and noticed that the manager was looking glum. He chatted with the manager, who "joked" about pulling in front of a tractor or taking all his heart medication at once. Not knowing exactly what was happening, the "active listener," as a neighbor, called the manager's wife. Later that day, the feed store manager entered the local mental health center for treatment for depression. His wife had convinced him to go.

This story exemplifies the need for good communication partnership between professionals and nonprofessionals. Dubois and Miley (1992) point out that this relationship has often been rocky; professionals tend to be skeptical of the lack of educational credentials of nonprofessionals, who generally address problems in a very different and more emotional way. Also, professionals often try to exert control over the behavior of lay persons. Yet though nonprofessionals approach helping in a different way, that is precisely their value. They are less curtailed by anonymity and confidentiality issues and can often intervene in situations where the professional cannot or may not want to. Practice in small communities requires strong collaboration of the two sectors.

The notion of the partnership of all community members in caring for each other transforms lack of anonymity into privileged knowledge. What is important is to help the community use this knowledge for positive action. Many public service campaigns are predicated on this same principle. For example, campaigns against drunk driving rely on the fact that people know when someone has had too much to drink. Not allowing that person to drive is not an indictment of the individual's character but an act of community responsibility.

An important element of community-oriented services is reciprocity (Martinez-Brawley & Blundall, 1989). If the social worker is successful in helping people see that their care for others might one day result in care for themselves, stigmatization may be reduced.

Partnerships must rely on the capacity of all partners to bring strengths (resources) to the table, albeit of different kinds. The frequent differences in community status that become apparent between practitioner and client, because generally the clients of social work are poor and marginalized persons, do not change the centrality of caring relationships. For many, too, the terminology of social work practice, with its emphasis on client and worker, or client and therapist, stresses inequality. In a study of community-oriented social work in Britain, Harrison (1989) found that many community-oriented social workers had trouble with the term "client." They did not "want the people with whom they worked to be dependent objects of their interventive efforts" (p. 74). "Clientizing" people was a process they were trying to avoid. "The needs for interdependence and assistance are so great that a concept of clienthood to distinguish a troubled minority may be obsolete" (p. 74).

But while names (whether clients, customers, or consumers) are important, attitudes are even more so; in the absence of a better and more consensual term to supplant "clients"—which at least implies a level of consumer choice—we might find ourselves retaining the name but modifying the attitude, which is what community oriented practice requires the professional to do. Community-oriented trends in practice are appropriate to a postindustrial society in which individuals face complex and rapid changes with broad consequences.

Proponents of the empowerment approach in social work practice recognize that consulting with clients as partners offers a new challenge. "The partnership approach . . . challenges the practitioner to examine the bias inherent in the traditional notions about client worker relationships" (Dubois & Miley, 1992, p. 91). Maluccio (1979), comparing the perceptions of clients and social workers, stated that while workers often looked at the clients as reactive participants in interactions with the environment, clients viewed themselves as capable of autonomous functioning, change, and growth. While there may be exceptions, strengths-based or empowerment-oriented social work, looking at this reality, has proposed principles that help workers function accordingly.

Community-oriented social work preceded in many ways the current empowerment thrust simply by stressing the importance of the contributions of all people to the resolution of the problems of living. The terms "community-oriented" or "community-based" have absorbed the "empowerment" dimension in very natural ways. Because workers in small communities have always been confronted with a shortage of professional resources, empowerment social work had to be applied in small communities before the label made its appearance in practice language. More than 10 years ago, Johnson (1989), coming from a background of rural practice, made clear that enabling or enhancing maturation, interaction, action, and learning were all means of building relationships.

In a study of farm families' perceptions of the personal social services during the farm crisis of the 1980s, it was found that, despite concerns about the family's reputation in the community, they wanted social workers to visit with them, just to talk about what preoccupied them and to discuss their options, long before any services were required (Martinez-Brawley & Blundall, 1989). Those families were instinctively suggesting the community-based prevention efforts that must be part of community-oriented social work. Those same families were much more willing to participate in services if they viewed them as something in which recipients and providers shared jointly. Without using the term empowerment, the families interviewed viewed equality, mutuality, reciprocity and an emphasis on the commonalities of problems, as essential to the types of interventions they could use and support.

One family, referring to the lack of anonymity in small communities, commented that it was impossible for people not to know what was going on. The family suggested that it might be best for family and social workers to confront those situations directly, so that they might be able to help instead of gossip (Martinez-Brawley & Blundall, 1989). The first step in dealing with concerns about anonymity is to confront them and analyze their importance. Is the lack of anonymity a problem? If so, can it be transformed into an asset for both individuals and communities? If not, what can realistically be done about it? How important is anonymity to the people involved in the transaction? Answers to these concrete questions might form the basis for decisions. Because the questions are asked in context, the answers will be different in each situation.

Notions of empowerment and resiliency have become pivotal in social work practice in the past decade. Community-oriented social work was always based on the ideas that people could regenerate their strength, that individuals and groups were not fragile, and that under the most stressful situations individuals and the communities, properly aided, could bring forth strength to help them resolve their own problems. Saleebey (1997) has pointed out that "community and individual and group resiliency are inextricably bound together" (p. 200). With this in mind, the principle of anonymity takes on very different dimensions. Perhaps it is not anonymity that individuals want in the intimacy of their relationships, but the trust that others will be respectful of their strength as well as their liabilities.

Confidentiality

Another major concern of social workers considering a more community-oriented practice in small towns is safeguarding confidentiality. *Confidentiality* means that a social worker or therapist who receives information from a patient or client will not reveal it to others except under certain circumstances, and then only for the purpose of helping the client (Reynolds, 1976). Confidentiality, the right to privacy, implies that persons must give explicit consent before such information is divulged in any way. But rarely is confidentiality absolute; it is always governed by prevalent practices, state law, and specific circumstances.

The *Code of Ethics* (NASW, 1996, 1999) says that the social worker's primary responsibility is to the client and that the social worker should hold in confidence all information obtained while rendering professional services. Yet it also acknowledges that social workers must share with others confidences revealed by clients, without their consent, when there are compelling professional reasons. In 1976 in *Tarasoff v. Regents of the University of California* (17 C.3d 425, 1976), the California court stated that "the right to privacy ends where the public peril begins" (Schwartz, 1989, p. 225). In child welfare cases, the privilege of protecting confidential communications must yield to the duty of the courts to protect the welfare of the child. Where reporting to central registries on certain situations is mandated, social workers also must disclose information. The matter of confidentiality is highly complex and situation specific.

Unfortunately, discussions of confidentiality that portray communication as "a simple dyadic exchange in which the worker guarantees the privacy of the client" (Moore-Kirkland & Vice-Irey, 1981, p. 319) have been common in social work classes and even in the early literature. Yet, "To define confidentiality only in relation to the one-to-one psychotherapeutic process between worker and client places unnecessary limits on social workers. The definition of confidentiality must deal with people in their social environments—the very relationship that social work claims as its unique focus. Social workers cannot view individuals—including individuals in their relationship to workers—apart from the social context" (Moore-Kirkland & Vice-Irey, 1981, p. 319).

The problems of the traditional dyadic interpretation of confidentiality have become apparent in the dilemmas experienced by social workers who treat elderly people or people with AIDS. Fortunately, the NASW *Code of Ethics* was formulated with more understanding. On confidentiality, for example, it states, "Social workers should protect the confidentiality of all information obtained in the course of professional service, except for compelling professional reasons. The general expectation that social workers will keep information confidential does not apply when disclosure is necessary to prevent serious, foreseeable, and imminent harm to a client or other identifiable person" (NASW, 1996, p. 1.07-C). In small communities, not only must confidentiality be limited to protect the well-being of others, social workers often find that what they believed to be confidential was in fact public information. Social workers treating alcoholism may believe they are the only persons knowing about a client's alcoholism, only to be surprised when others in the community inquire about the stage of treatment or the well-being of the client. The social worker must behave in a professional way yet without alienating community members who might give the client ongoing support.

The lack of anonymity in the small community social context thus requires a reexamination of confidentiality. Threats to confidentiality are generally thought to be external, such as computer systems or even written records that social workers or agencies may not know how to protect. Legal concerns about records being subpoenaed and about privileged communication often constitute the crux of decisions about confidentiality.

The concerns of practitioners in small communities are more basic. They relate to what is truly private and what becomes public information naturally in small towns.

Consider a social work client, Mr. M, whose family has lived in a small town for three generations. His wife's family has lived there even longer. Mr. M's alcoholism is common knowledge in the community, which began to observe the disintegration of Mr. M and his family long before he was sent to a treatment center out of the county. The neighbors sheltered Mr. M's wife when her husband became violent and have occasionally provided financial assistance for the family. Church members and school teachers cluck with concern over the plight of the children and are already predicting that the 12-year-old son, always a problem in school, will turn out just like Dad. No one can understand—yet everyone speculates—why Mr. M, whose parents are pillars of the community, has turned out this way, though they know that he and his father get along poorly. Mr. M's neighbors, work associates and children's teachers all know of his hospitalization and will view his return to the community from the perspective of their own relationship with the family, their own understanding of alcoholism, and their own opinion about the prognosis. These expectations will shape the community's behavior toward Mr. M and toward each family member. These expectations are an integral part of the social context with which Mr. M and his family must cope. His return home is thus a social event, not a private affair, and the question is not whether the community knows about the problem but what blend of information and misinformation has evolved. Speculation will fill in the gaps. (Moore-Kirkland & Vice-Irey, 1981, p. 320)

Confidentiality in such instances must be examined in relation to what the client, the agency, the social worker, and even the community are trying to achieve. How will withholding or correcting information affect the well-being of clients? What are the clients' views and preferences? Have they had an opportunity to assess the realistic limits of confidentiality in their case? Are they being presented with all the alternative scenarios, or are they just given the one in which the agency battles to protect information that the community probably already has?

There are cases in which confidentiality might be more important to the agency or social worker than the client. There are others when, although the social worker might assume that certain information is confidential, the client behaves otherwise. For example, one chronic alcoholic periodically spent time in a state hospital. During a ride back to his native small town upon discharge from the hospital, the well-meaning social worker who was driving, assuming the client wanted an inconspicuous return, asked him where he wanted to be dropped off. Going to his home necessitated a ride the entire length of Main Street and she was driving a clearly marked state vehicle. She was surprised when the client wanted to be taken all the way home, regardless of the route. She was further surprised when the client rolled down the window and greeted all the passersby on Main Street.

Obviously, the strength of that particular client's network did not depend on his keeping his hospitalization secret. The client was direct, resilient, or empowered enough not to have to rely on secrecy. The social worker would have to reexamine his or her confidentiality concerns to concentrate on helping the client and community use their knowledge for positive ends and mutual support.

Speck and Attneave (1971) suggested that perpetuating the existence of "secret" information among networks of people often leads to pathological social relationships. Secrets, alliances, and collusions might need to be opened up to scrutiny before change can occur in those networks. Sometimes, helping people reveal "false" secrets can have positive consequences. Natural helping groups often do just that as part of the recovery process. Again, empowerment social work recognizes that clients are often more open than workers have expect them to be.

Social workers in small communities where the networks are strong may sometimes need to manage information to help make potentially harmful alliances beneficial. Confidentiality must be examined in relation to the social worker's roles of manager, advocate, mobilizer, or resource and friendly neighbor. Although professionals need standards based on general moral values and specific principles to guide their behavior in relation to confidentiality, "there will be no single, definitive answer to tell the confused practitioner what to do" (Wilson, 1982, p. 338). Each instance must be considered in its unique social and statutory context, which has an added dimension in working with the community. Social workers will not only need to be cautious about the effects of revealing (or not revealing information), but also conscious of their role as interpreter of the client's situation to a community that already has information, both relevant and irrelevant.

Social workers must also be mindful that trust is another aspect of their relationship with both clients and community (Johnson, 1983). A minister in a small town once called a social worker to ask where to complain about the "offensive" behavior of a child welfare worker. Recognizing that a teenager's problems required more than his guidance, he had convinced her to seek the agency's specialized counseling. Meeting the agency social worker in the market later, he had asked her whether the young woman had gone to the agency. He was curtly told that agency information was confidential. The minister felt that his helpful efforts had been rebuffed; he had only been concerned about the young woman's well-being. The social worker, taking refuge behind the shield of confidentiality, had not addressed skillfully the real issue of how to appreciate community support without divulging confidential information.

Even if the social worker had been skillful at the informal level, she still would have faced a confidentiality dilemma: deciding how much she could tell the minister. In this case, the client had already disclosed her troubles to the minister. A review of how pertinent state laws have been interpreted, consultation with the client, examination of agency practices, and legal counsel can all provide guidance in reaching satisfactory decisions. What is often ignored is the social context in which the interactions occur and the consequences to clients of sharing or not sharing information.

Levy (1976) said that "The social worker has the ethical responsibility to make provision for the consequences that his own professional acts may generate and to determine a priority ordering of the alternatives at his disposal and of the values affecting them that may be in conflict with one another" (p. 88). The values of the community and the values of the social worker can sometimes conflict. This is where Levy's principle of ethical responsibility can provide guidance. Perhaps the offense to the minister might have been alleviated had the social worker honestly told him that she was faced with a dilemma. She needed to draw on the collective wisdom of the agency or consult with the client to determine how much she could tell the minister.

The case also illustrates the need to prevent potentially embarrassing situations when working in small communities; the social worker might discuss the sharing of information with the client at the beginning. Particularly with referrals from other community members, the social worker's dual responsibility to the client and to the referring source must be clarified immediately. In small communities, particularly for groups that might profit from communal responses (for example, the elderly or children), the client should have a chance early on to reflect on what types of information must remain confidential at all costs, what may be shared, what must by law be shared, and what is already essentially public.

Such honest discussions not only solve practical problems but help establish trust among social worker, client, and community. Essentially, the social worker is not boxed into behaving in a particular way. As Hall (1952) said, it is impossible to reduce conduct in all situations to simple rules. What social workers must do is to consider the alternatives available. In community practice, they must consider their alternatives in the light not only of the law but also of their professional responsibility to community networks of support.

Today, fear of litigation often clouds common sense and judgment. Yet, given the numbers of people served, cases against agencies or social workers are relatively few and usually relate to sexual impropriety or incorrect treatment rather than breaches of confidentiality. For agencies, child protection cases are the most worrisome cases (NASW, 1989). The stress of rural practice comes not so much because the social worker, particularly the new social worker, worries about divulging confidential information given by the client in a formal office setting, but because the social worker does not know how to handle immediate judgment calls.

Consider the friendly neighbor who stops the social worker who has been visiting an elderly lady down the street. The neighbor wants to know what is wrong and how to help. The practice dilemma is how to capitalize on a positive community response without violating a person's right to privacy.

Consider also the common situation of the return to a small community of a patient from a psychiatric hospital. Let's suppose that the patient had previously been gloomy, moody, and even aggressive toward community members. A negative atmosphere will make adjustment difficult or impossible. How does the social worker create a more favorable atmosphere in the community when the patient returns? Some social workers would want to energize supporting community networks. Others might opt to work to strengthen the patient's coping capabilities. The challenge for a community-oriented social worker would be how to help both patient and community to develop mutually supportive networks without damaging confidentiality. Furthermore, the social worker (perhaps unlike the psychiatrist or psychologist) also has an ethical responsibility to correct misinformation in the social environment that might adversely affect the client (Moore-Kirkland & Vice-Irey, 1981). The social worker in a small community has unique challenges.

Unfortunately, the recent tendency among professionals has been to ignore the duality of the social worker's ethical responsibility. Yet if social workers practicing community-oriented social work are to recognize the strengths of the communal system, they must consider the duality of their responsibility as they negotiate confidentiality agreements with clients. Levy (1976) said that social workers must use client confidences for them, not against them. Although there are risks in assessing the long-term consequences of any action, social workers must secure permission from clients as needed to operate with good judgment. The courts have been helpful in this respect: "To constitute a waiver, there must be a clear relinquishment of a known right. . . . No particular form (or indeed any form at all) is necessary in drafting a release; all that is required is an expression of present intention to renounce a claim or discharge an obligation. . . . However, obtaining a written release is the safest practice because it helps forgetful clients recollect that they authorized such release" (Schwartz, 1989, p. 224).

For effective community-oriented work in small towns, it is essential that social workers be aware of the parameters within which they may exercise discretion in using information for the benefit of the client. Agencies need to discuss their policies in light of local community strengths; they must be guided by the experiences of social workers and clients in that community. Clients must be made aware of the potential benefits stemming from community networks as well as the drawbacks of public knowledge of private concerns.

Moore-Kirkland and Vice-Irey (1981) challenged the profession to examine the concept of confidentiality in a more realistic way to serve those who practice in small communities. Their challenge is doubly important to social workers who practice with a community orientation. Although laws that govern the behavior of social workers are sometimes clear, in the fields most amenable to a community orientation (for example, work with elderly people and child welfare) decisions still require careful judgment. After the publication of the original *Code of Ethics* in 1996, NASW published a brief volume, *Current Controversies in Social Work Ethics: Case Examples* (1998). It clearly indicates that the NASW *Code of Ethics* "often does not address ethics problems on a level of specificity that is truly satisfying to someone in the mist of an conundrum" (NASW, 1998, p. 1). The array of actual situations, although disguised and altered, is intended to expand the thinking of social workers. The *Code of Ethics* is an important tool for social workers in ethical decision making; the handbook of examples illustrates the range of possible ethical dilemmas, with references to the Code for social workers struggling with specific cases.

Accountability

Community-oriented social work services must use all the resources, formal and informal, that are available in the small community. However, the closer social workers get to adapting their ways of caring to the patterns of the informal system, the more they encounter problems of accountability. *Accountability* is not only the concern of the formal sector—whether public, voluntary, or for-profit—but also a genuine preoccupation of the informal sector, although the mechanisms through which social workers account for what they are doing may differ from sector to sector.

In the public sector, accountability is generally seen as a bureaucratic process through which the public learns of what elected officials and public employees do and monitors the use of tax moneys. It has also been construed as the way in which elected officials monitor what public employees are doing to account to the electorate. In the private sector accountability refers to how organizations justify to their sponsors how they are using their resources to carry out their mission. Despite the mystique that often surrounds the concept, social workers, whether in rural or urban areas, in the public or the private sector, at home or in business, must often justify how they have used resources because resources are finite and priorities must be set.

For Carter (1983), accountability measures fall into two categories: efficiency and effectiveness. *Efficiency* refers to output or outcomes in relation to resources, for example, the number of clients served by each social worker. *Effectiveness* refers to the achievement of goals, for example, the number of elderly people who were in danger of becoming institutionalized who are still at home a year after the start of a home-help program. Efficiency stresses how much one gets for his or her money; effectiveness stresses how well the job is done.

One of the concerns of service managers and social services providers in small communities and rural areas is that the size of the population makes criteria of efficiency inappropriate. Most small communities cannot afford certain services because the number of people served, as a sole criterion, does not justify the expense.

Community-oriented approaches can address this problem. They can make use of resources that already exist in the community. The dilemma here is to reconcile funding sources, which are generally specific, and service needs, which may be more generic. Although in the past decade more resources for community-based services have become available, small communities still face efficiency criteria. Expected outcomes must be carefully defined at the outset.

Also, when voluntary activities in small communities need support from the formal sector to keep going, social workers find themselves unable to help because such indirect support does not meet efficiency criteria for funded programs. Resources—whether time or money—often need to be spent not on the client who is being cared for by the network, but on the network itself. Natural networks, like people, can become exhausted. For example, research with elderly people shows that rewarding caring behavior from kin and friends is important, perhaps even essential, to maintaining networks of support. Yet because kin and friends are seldom defined as the "client," social workers often cannot spend time with them. Social workers doing community-oriented work need to be active in ensuring the care of social support networks. These cannot be readily mobilized, whether for direct practice or social development, unless they are assiduously cultivated (Brown & Nylander, 1998; Youmans, 1990).

The type of accountability that gives social workers the opportunity to exercise discretion in the use of funds—even small amounts—is creative but hard to secure. Yet this may be necessary to strengthen the informal sector. For example, a researcher visiting a small town in an agricultural county needed to talk with people who were carers but not necessarily participants in any organized form of voluntary organization—true natural carers: the neighbor who visited elderly people who lived alone, or the one who cooked for a neighbor when he or she was not well. Almost everyone knew who these carers were, but three neighbors were identified by the local social worker as particularly important to the village's caring scheme.

Because these three neighbors were themselves elderly and not mobile, they did not participate in any organized efforts. Yet each visited or kept an eye on a neighbor, and one had routinely cooked for an even more elderly friend next door once a week for many years. The social worker had tried to reward these elderly people. What she thought they would enjoy most was an occasional meal out with her. Yet she had no discretionary funds. When she found that the visiting researcher searching for conversation was willing to invite them to lunch, she was delighted.

Nourishing these informal carers on a regular basis through such informal interactions as lunch should not have been left either to the personal resources of the social worker or to the serendipitous arrival of a researcher. Discretionary funds in this instance would have made for justifiably effective community-oriented social work. Fortunately, some philanthropic foundations, having discovered the importance of the informal sector, are beginning to offer more open ways of supporting it.

Social services providers often rely on formalized ways of helping people because these give them more control and reduce liability; they can standardize the menu of centrally prepared Meals on Wheels programs but cannot similarly control what natural carers cook for their neighbors. Yet the interaction of a neighbor-to-neighbor cooking arrangement can enhance the quality of life of an elderly person more than the well-balanced but somewhat antiseptic meal delivered by strangers.

In this respect, our society is again fraught with contradiction. We want to support a community orientation and encourage exchange among the folk but fear litigation. Social services providers need to weigh many factors in choosing solutions. If their goal is to encourage ongoing interaction for the elderly person rather than controlling diet, the less formal arrangement might be more efficient and effective, provided they can justify their decision.

Once goals are set, it is easier to establish relationships among the various factors, including community factors, that may have gone into achieving those goals. To be accountable, social workers must be able to explain and justify their actions (Doel & Shardlow, 1996). "The accountability measure employed varies according to where an individual is located in the decision-making process. The closer a staff member is to the actual delivery of services to clients, the more likely he/she is to use effectiveness as a criteria" (Carter, 1983, p. 20).

Unfortunately, however, administrators, constrained by policymakers, tend to emphasize efficiency over effectiveness. A review of "efficiency and effectiveness criteria used at the state level illustrates that effectiveness measures are not often assigned much importance" (Carter, 1983, p. 20). In analyzing how policymakers assess accountability, Carter (1983) found that cost measures (that is, the number of clients served) were systematically collected and used, but other effectiveness measures were gathered only on a special one-time basis.

Historically, social programs have been affected by an "ethic of intrinsic goodness"—the assumption that the more it costs, the better it is—which focuses on the largesse of the giving rather than on the outcomes achieved. This arose from the philanthropic origins of social services and expresses the symbolic commitment of society to do good (Benton, 1981; Specht & Courtney, 1994). "As a result, the extent of the society's commitment has traditionally been measured in the size of the investment in programs to meet the economic and social needs of deserving individuals, families and communities. That is, the more we would spend on social programs, the better" (Benton, 1981, p. 1). The ethic of intrinsic goodness may have been just one factor preventing the full use of a variety of effectiveness measures; but the public seldom spent enough on social programs consistently over the long term to conclude that resources have been spent on ineffective programs, despite the negative view of social programs politicians often expressed in the early 1970s (Brawley & Martinez-Brawley, 1988).

Many other factors prevented the full use of effectiveness measures, among them the state of the art in program evaluation and the reluctance of social workers to use those measures. During the Nixon years, when the "accountability crisis" reached its peak (Newman & Turem, 1974), the state of the art in program evaluation could rarely show tangible evidence of effectiveness. When Ronald Reagan campaigned on a platform of reduced social programs, it became absolutely essential for social initiatives to show that they were being efficient and effective (Ginsberg, 1998, p. 33).

Although program evaluation, like accountability, has been surrounded by an aura of mystique, and although social workers have associated program evaluation with complicated measures, charts, and figures, it can be simple. It traditionally has used, among others, goal attainment indicators, which social workers can follow. Used continuously, these can provide policymakers with ongoing information on program effectiveness.

One of the advantages of program evaluation is that descriptive information on community networks, for example, how those networks are caring for people, can be incorporated into the evaluation. Unique approaches that defy rigid efficiency measures can be documented through the program evaluation approach. The challenge is to find evaluators who are willing to use assessments and arrive at holistic judgments, rather than rely on standardized measures, which tend to be easier, cheaper to apply, and faster to document.

To document community-oriented approaches to caring for people in small towns, it is essential to use the program evaluation methodology flexibly, ensuring that it includes effectiveness as well as efficiency measures of accountability. Used routinely, it can provide policymakers with a history of consistent information on community-oriented efforts. The information can also be used to secure the cooperation and support of the community for what the agency is doing (Brawley, 1985/1986).

Program administrators in small towns must stress the importance of their effectiveness measures when their programs are reviewed. As long as they comply with efficiency measures that are inappropriate to their organizations, they reinforce policymakers' reliance on those measures to the exclusion of others. Bureaucracies tend to emphasize mechanistic forms of accountability that often are inappropriate to the more flexible conditions of the small community (Aldridge, Macy, & Walz, 1982). One major advantage of decentralizing administrative structures has been to stress the usefulness of certain measures of accountability in certain environments and their lack of usefulness in others. In the 1990s, the U.S. Congress emphasized the devolution of decision-making to localities (Ginsberg, 1998, p. 121). Although there have been inherent contradictions in the conservative trends—entrepreneurship and creativity are to be encouraged, while fast profits based on high outputs are to be maintained—opportunities for creative endeavors have opened up. It is possible to capitalize on the principles of devolution to show how accountability must reflect local conditions and local outcomes.

In her research on business organizations, Woodward (1965) classified firms into mass production and small batch firms, showing how organizational structures and approaches differed for the two types. Woodward and other contingency theorists "make clear that an effective organization can run the gamut from traditional bureaucracy to a highly organic, constantly changing structure" (Lewis & Lewis, 1983, p. 83). Contingency theories minimally can offer social workers a means of designing ways of functioning and measures of accountability that are appropriate for their own organization.

If human service professionals were to use contingency theories to determine the best way to structure the work of their programs or agencies,
they would, as a first step, identify the most salient characteristics of their
services and settings. Following Woodward's example they would need to
ask whether their agencies were in fact mass production firms or small
batch firms. Human service workers who viewed themselves as technicians offering consistent services to a wide range of clients might be able
to use mechanistic organizational structures, but such designs would be
inappropriate for professionals attempting to deliver multifaceted services
based on community. (Lewis & Lewis, 1983, p. 83)

Weinbach (1990) discussed the relationship between the prolifera-
tion of bureaucratic activities and the degree of hostility from outside forces
that some organizations face. The more hostile the environment in which
an organization functions, the more rigid and bureaucratic its procedures
become. Community-oriented approaches can help decrease the level of
outside hostility, and thus decrease the perceived need for bureaucratic
forms of accountability designed solely to protect the organization.

A business or corporation exists to make a profit. Consequently, it is
"efficiency driven." Any activity that will reduce the cost of production of a product has the potential to increase profit. . . . If after a
reasonable time, efficiency methods cannot generate a profit, the product will be dropped. . . .The decision is purely an economic one. . . .
Sentiment and concerns over fairness rarely enter into the decision to
drop a product or division. They may play a role only in treatment of
employees who are displaced, require retraining, or are otherwise negatively affected by the decision. In contrast, a social agency and the
managers who must make decisions within it must attempt to balance
efficiency and equity. A social agency cannot ignore efficiency. It must
pay utility bills, salaries and address the other expenses incurred. But it
must also meet professional obligations to client service and cannot
afford to develop a reputation for being overly preoccupied with efficiency. (Weinbach, 1990, pp. 31–32)

Certainly, in orienting services to the community, effectiveness, responsibility, and ethics should dictate more than efficiency. The more community-oriented services are, the more those services involve local networks
of support and the more constituents will rise to their defense. Participants who feel empowered will defend social programs more than those
who feel marginalized by the programs. One of the pleasures of working in
small communities is that constituent support can be quickly translated

into pressure on policymakers. The persuasiveness of a supportive community is often the most powerful argument in resolving conflicts about social services.

Indicators of Community-Oriented Social Work

Community-oriented social work is predicated on the interweaving of formal and informal systems of care—on the notion that caring for people is a task common to professionals and lay people in their roles as friends and neighbors. Thus it necessitates a truly cooperative, egalitarian relationship among all the caring systems in the community. Community-oriented social work thus presupposes a power shift in the professional relationship.

Community-oriented social work has always been based on strengths. It presupposes that the professional is open to different ways of accomplishing goals, although often constricted by standards and particular techniques of helping. The lay person is not so constricted. From the interweaving of different ways of doing, community-based approaches emerge. For example, the accountability of the professional has been to the agency and to the profession; the accountability of the community member has been to a code or norms that govern community interactions. In community-oriented social work, these two ways must negotiate with each other to achieve harmony.

Community-oriented social work emphasizes an egalitarian environment in which local people help plan and provide services. Such an environment inexorably opens professionals and agencies to closer public scrutiny and even to criticism from citizens; yet it also opens them to the possibility of attaining support they never had before. Social workers need to be prepared to handle these situations.

Community-oriented services are as much an attitude as a collection of techniques. They necessitate "a shift from the dichotomous separation of macro and micro orientations toward an integration of these skills" (Johnson, 1998, p. 41). As Soifer (1998) noted, organizing in small communities is about building relationships. Because communities and people vary, community-oriented social services will have unique aspects in each local community.

However, community-oriented social work and a greater reliance on community networks do not deny the importance of the professional. Community-oriented service means only that the professional will perform a different, though equally necessary, role in direct care. Even in the most caring community, "often people will feel inhibited from helping where an offer of help might be construed as a slur" (Wenger, 1984, p. 93). Professionals still will have responsibilities beyond the boundaries of communal interactions. Community-oriented social workers simply rely more on the help of natural caregivers.

Community-based social work can generate new concerns. Because women often are the caregivers, they are likely to be the most active participants in community-based efforts. The new community care patterns can also bring with them a kind of "enforced altruism" (Davis & Ellis, 1995). Gender patterns of care may be a major issue in the future of community care:

> The current debates on community care, and the policies and social work practices emerging in local authorities, have a particular impact on the gendered world of caring, relating to the roles and responsibilities which individuals assume as family members.
>
> . . .
>
> [W]hat families can and do offer their members is negotiated as part of a complex interaction of duty, obligation and responsibility where choices are constrained by economic, social and cultural factors. Within this context "rights, duties and obligations work differently for women and men in practice." (Davis & Ellis, 1995, p. 145)

Davis and Ellis (1995) believe that in caring *about* other members of the family or other community members, women often take on the additional responsibilities of caring *for*. The distinction between caring *for* and caring *about* is useful. The dilemma arises when authorities responsible for providing support to those who need help do not understand the distinction and view care provided by natural networks as free. This enforced altruism worries social workers who practice community-based care.

The role of women in other aspects of community decision-making is also affected. While on the one hand care-giving opens avenues for community leadership (Martinez-Brawley & Zorita, 1995), on the other it represents an additional burden on women. These topics will require a great deal more exploration as we embark upon the new millennium.

Community-oriented social work presupposes a great deal of knowledge of the community and its people. It also requires considerable diplomacy, the ability to interpret events in the language not only of the agency but also the policymaker, the politician, and the local citizen.

Community-oriented services focus on strengths, incorporate the full richness and diversity of the citizenry, and move beyond traditional reliance on bureaucracy. This kind of social work moves practice beyond how we have served for the past hundred years into new ways of caring.

Not everything that will be done in the name of community will be positive. The social worker will continue to provide safeguards for those who need to be cared for within the community without requiring that they further limit their autonomy or their options. The role of the social worker will be to respect the ethos of serving with integrity while empowering citizens to join in the very mixed economy of caring that communities, both small and global, will face.

References

Abrams, P. (1980). Social change, social networks and neighborhood care. *Social Work Service, 22,* 12–23.

Agee, J. (1997). *South of resurrection.* New York: Penguin Books.

Aldridge, M., Macy, H., & Walz, T. (1982). *Beyond management: Humanizing the administrative process.* Iowa City: University of Iowa School of Social Work.

Alinsky, S. D. (1971). *Rules for radicals.* New York: Random House.

Allemand, E. L. (1976). The ideal for the nation: Josiah Royce's view of community. *Intellect, 105,* 47–48.

Amparano, J., & Shaffer, M. (1997, April 13). When cultures collide. *Arizona Republic,* pp. A1–A11.

Anderson, S. (1919). *Winesburg, Ohio.* New York: Viking.

Anton, T. J. (1963). Power, pluralism and local politics. *Administrative Science Quarterly, 7,* 448–457.

Arensberg, C. M. (1955). American communities. *American Anthropologist, 57,* 1143–1162.

Arnow, H. (1949). *Hunter's horn.* New York: Macmillan.

Bachrach, P., & Baratz, M. (1962). The two faces of power. *American Political Science Review, 57,* 947–952.

Bachrach, P., & Baratz, M. (1970). *Power and poverty: Theory and practice.* New York: Oxford University Press.

Badillo Ghali, S. (1977). Cultural sensitivity and the Puerto Rican client. *Social Casework, 58,* 459–461.

Bama, E. (1989, March 8). Business (and pleasure) the old-fashioned way. *Rutland (Vermont) Herald,* p. 7.

Banfield, E. C. (1961). *Political influence.* New York: Free Press.

Barbieri, S. (1996, January 26). Gay in a small town. *St. Paul Pioneer Press,* p. 1A.

Beard, B. (1999, January 17). "Humble" health clinic gets new space. *Arizona Republic,* pp. EV1–EV2.

Beaulieu, L. J., & Mulkey, D. (Eds.). (1995). *Investing in people: The human capital needs of rural America.* Boulder, CO: Westview Press.

Beeghley, L. (1989). *The structure of social stratification*. Needham Heights, MA: Allyn & Bacon.

Bell, W., Hill, R. J., & Wright, C. R. (1961). *Public leadership*. San Francisco: Chandler.

Bell, C., & Newby, H. (1972). *Community studies: An introduction to the sociology of the local community*. New York: Praeger.

Bellah, R., Madsen, R., Sullivan, W. M., Swindler, A., & Tipton, S. M. (1985). *Habits of the heart: Individualism and commitment in American life*. New York: Harper & Row.

Bender, T. (1978). *Community and social change in America*. New Brunswick, NJ: Rutgers University Press.

Benson, E. F. (1977). *Make way for Lucia*. New York: Crowell.

Benton, W. (1981, August). Keynote address to the International Council on Social Welfare, Toronto, Ontario, Canada.

Berger, B. M. (1981). *The survival of a counterculture. Ideological work and everyday life among rural communards*. Berkeley: University of California Press.

Black America? (1992, October 25). *Detroit News*, 1A.

Blundall, J. (1987). *Dealing with the human pain of the rural condition* [Mimeograph]. Spencer, IA: Northwest Iowa Community Mental Health Center.

Böhn, A. (1995). Local politics in border regions in central Europe. *Annals of the American Academy of Political and Social Science, 540*, 137–144.

Bokemeier, J. L., & Tait, J. L. (1980). Women as power actors: A comparative study of rural communities. *Rural Sociology, 45*, 238–255.

Bragg, M. (1969). *The hired man*. New York: Knopf.

Brawley, E. (1985/1986). The mass media: A vital adjunct to the new community and administrative practice. *Administration in Social Work, 9*, 63–73.

Brawley, E. A., & Martinez-Brawley, E. E. (1988). Social programme evaluation in the U.S.A.: Trends and issues. *British Journal of Social Work, 18*, 391–413.

Brown, R. B., & Nylander, A. B. (1998). Community leadership structure: Differences between rural community leaders' and residents' informational networks. *Journal of the Community Development Society, 29*(1), 71–89.

Bryson, B. (1990). *The lost continent: Travels in small town America*. London: Abacus.

Bryson, B. (1998, June). Orkney: Ancient North Sea haven. *National Geographic, 193*, 49–59.

Buck, R. C. (1980, January). Being Amish: Some notes on childhood socialization and acculturation among the Old Order Amish. *Children in Contemporary Society, 32–37*.

Burnett, K. (1996). Once an incomer, always an incomer? In P. Chapman & S. Lloyd (Eds.), *Women and access in rural areas*. Aldershot, England: Avebury.

Byler, W. (1977). The destruction of American Indian families. In S. Unger (Ed.), *The destruction of American Indian families* (pp. 1–11). New York: Association of American Indian Affairs.

Caplow, T., & Chadwick, B. (1979). Inequality and life-styles in Middletown, 1920–1978. *Social Science Quarterly, 60*, 367–386.

Carter, R. K. (1983). *The accountable agency*. Beverly Hills, CA: Sage Publications.

Castillo, A. (1994). *So far from God*. New York: Plume, Penguin Group.

Castle, E. N. (1995). *The changing American countryside: Rural people and places*. Lawrence: University Press of Kansas.

Chambers, R. (1993). *Challenging the professions: Frontiers for rural development*. London: Intermediate Technology Publications.

Chapman, P., & Lloyd, S. (1996). *Women and access in rural areas*. Aldershot, England: Avebury.

Cheers, B. (1996). Global change and rural people. *Centre for Development Studies* [Monograph Series No. 2]. Perth, Western Australia: Edith Cowan University.

Cheers, B. (1999). *Welfare bushed: Social care in rural Australia*. Aldershot, England: Avebury.

Ching, B., & Creed, G. W. (1997). *Knowing your place: Rural identity and cultural hierarchy*. New York: Routledge.

Christie, A. (1950). *A murder is announced*. New York: Dodd, Mead.

Christie, A. (1963). *The mirror crack'd*. New York: Dodd, Mead.

Cisneros, S. (1984). *The house on Mango Street*. New York: Vintage Books.

Clark, D. C. (1973). The concept of community: A reexamination. *Sociological Review, 21*, 397–416.

Clinton, H. R. (1996). *It takes a village: And other lessons children teach us*. New York: Simon & Schuster.

Cloke, P., & Little, J. (Eds.). (1997). *Contested countryside cultures: Otherness, marginalization and rurality*. London: Routledge.

Colby, I. C. (1997). Transforming human services organizations through empowerment of neighbors. *Journal of Community Practice, 4*(2), 1–12.

Conklin, C. (1980). Rural community care givers. *Social Work, 25*, 495–496.

Constantini, E., & Clark, K. H. (1973). Women as politicians: The social background, personality and political careers of female party leaders. *Journal of Social Issues, 28*, 217–236.

Curtis, R. F., & Jackson E. F. (1977). *Inequality in American communities*. New York: Academic Press.

Dahl, R. A. (1961). *Who governs? Democracy and power in an American city*. New Haven: Yale University Press.

Daley, J. M. (1997). The episode of purposive change: Field testing a practice model. *Journal of the Community Development Society, 28*(2), 225–241.

Daley, Y. (1989, March 8). Use of ballot changes town's way of doing business. *Rutland (Vermont) Herald*, pp. 1, 8.

Darley, G. (1978). *Villages of vision*. London: Granada.

Davis, A., Gardner, B. B., & Gardner, M. R. (1941). *Deep south: A social anthropological study of caste and class*. Chicago: University of Chicago Press.

Davis, A., & Ellis, K. (1995). Enforced altruism in community care. In R. Hugman and D. Smith (Eds.), *Ethical issues in social work* (pp. 136–154). London: Routledge.

Davis, P. (1982). *Hometown: A contemporary American chronicle*. New York: Simon & Schuster.

Dean, L. R. (1967). *Five towns: A comparative community study*. New York: Random House.

Deener, B. (1996, June 26). A question of judgment. *Dallas Morning News*, p. 1D.

Delafield, E. M. (1931). *Diary of a provincial lady*. New York: Harper & Brothers.

Delgado, M. (1977). Puerto Rican spiritualism and the social work profession. *Social Casework, 58*, 451–458.

De Tocqueville, A. (1899). *Democracy in America*. New York: D. Appleton & Co.

Dewey, J. (1930). *Individualism old and new*. New York: Capricorn Books.

DiNitto, D. M. (1991). *Social welfare: Politics and public policy*. Englewood Cliffs, NJ: Prentice Hall.

Doel, M., & Shardlow, S. (1996). *Social work in a changing world: An international perspective on practice learning*. Aldershot, England: Arena.

Dollard, J. (1949). *Caste and class in a southern town* (2nd ed.). New York: Harper.

Donahue, P. (1982, November 30). [TV interview with "Tough Love" member].

Dubois, B., & Miley, K. (1992). *Social work: An empowering profession*. Boston: Allyn & Bacon.

Edelman, J. M. (1977). *Political language: Words that succeed and policies that fail*. New York: Academic Press.

Etzioni, A. (1989, February 1). The "me first" model in the social sciences is too narrow [Editorial]. *Chronicle of Higher Education*, p. A44.

Etzioni, A. (1998). *The essential communitarian reader*. Lanham, MD: Rowan & Littlefield.

Fabricant, M. (1985). The industrialization of social work practice. *Social Work, 30*, 389–395.

Fabricant, M., & Burghardt, S. (1998). Rising from the ashes of cutback, political warfare and degraded services: Strategic considerations for community building: An editorial essay. *Journal of Community Practice, 5*(4), 53–65.

Fenby, B. L. (1978). Social work in a rural setting. *Social Work, 23*, 162–163.

Fitchen, J. M. (1991). *Endangered spaces, enduring places: Change, identity, and survival in rural America*. Boulder, CO: Westview Press.

Fitzgerald, F. (1986a, September 22). Rajneeshpuram, Part 1. *New Yorker, 62*, 46–60.

Fitzgerald, F. (1986b, September 29). Rajneeshpuram, Part 2. *New Yorker, 62*, 83ff.

Fitzgerald, P. (1997). *The bookshop*. New York: Houghton Mifflin.

Flynn, N. (1991). *Public sector management*. Hemel Hempstead, England: Harvester Wheatsheaf.

Frankenberg, R. (1957). *Village on the border*. London: Cohen and West.

Frankenburgh, R. (1966). *Communities in Britain: Social life in town and country*. Baltimore: Penguin Books.

Freeman, J. (1973). The origins of the women's liberation movement. In J. Huber (Ed.), *Changing women in a changing society* (pp. 30–49). Chicago: University of Chicago Press.

Freeman, L. C., Fararo, T. J., Bloomberg, W., & Sunshine, H. (1968). Locating leaders in local communities: A comparison of some alternative approaches. In W. D. Hawley & F. M. Wirt (Eds.), *The search for community power* (pp.189–199). Englewood Cliffs, NJ: Prentice Hall.

Freilich, M. (1963). Toward an operational definition of community. *Rural Sociology, 28,* 117–127.

Fuentes, C. (1992). *The buried mirror: Reflections on Spain and the New World.* New York: Houghton Mifflin.

Fuguitt, G. (1995). Population change in nonmetropolitan America. In E. N. Castle (Ed.), *The changing American countryside* (pp. 77–102). Lawrence, KS: University Press of Kansas.

George, A. J. (Ed.). (1904). *Complete poetical works of William Wordsworth.* New York: Houghton Mifflin.

Gergen, K. J. (1994). *Realities and relationships: Soundings in social construction.* Cambridge, MA: Harvard University Press.

Gilligan, C. (1993). *In a different voice: Psychological theory and women's development.* Cambridge, MA: Harvard University Press.

Ginsberg, L. (Ed). (1976). *Social work in rural communities: A book of readings.* New York: Council on Social Work Education.

Ginsberg, L. (1998). *Conservative social welfare policy: A description and analysis.* Chicago: Nelson-Hall.

Glass, R. (1966). Conflict in cities. In A. DeReuck & J. Knight (Eds.), *Conflict in society* (p. 148ff). London: Little and Churchill.

Goist, P. D. (1977). *From Main Street to State Street: Town, city, and community in America.* New York: Kennikat.

Goldstein, H. (1997). Victors or victims? In D. Saleebey (Ed.), *The strengths perspective in social work practice* (2nd ed., pp. 21–35). New York: Longman.

Goode, W. J. (1957). Community within a community: The professions. *American Sociological Review, 22,* 194–200.

Grado, G., & De Isasi, C. (1998, February 9). Police, Hispanics have different views on community acceptance. *[Phoenix] Tribune,* pp. A1–A4.

Greenwood, E. (1961). The practice of science and the science of practice. In W. G. Bennis, K. D. Benne, & R. Chin (Eds.), *The planning of chance: Readings in the applied behavioral sciences* (pp. 73–82). New York: Rinehart & Winston.

Guadalupe's cohesiveness at stake. (1998, January 18). *Arizona Republic,* p. EV4.

Guba, E. G., & Lincoln, Y. S. (1994). Competing paradigms in qualitative research. In N. K. Denzin & Y. S. Lincoln (Eds.), *Handbook of qualitative research* (pp. 105–118). Thousand Oaks, CA: Sage Publications.

Hadley, R., Dale, P., & Sills, P. (1984). *Decentralizing social service: A model for change.* London: Bedford Square Press.

Hadley, R., & Hatch, S. (1981). *Social welfare and the failure of the state.* London: Allen & Unwin.

Hadley, R., & McGrath, M. (1980). *Going local: Neighborhood social services.* London: Bedford Square Press.

Hadley, R., & Young, K. (1990). *Creating a responsive public service*. London: Harvester Wheatsheaf.

Hall, E. T. (1981). *Beyond culture*. Garden City, NY: Anchor Books.

Hall, L. K. (1952). Group workers and professional ethics. *The Group, 15*, 3–8.

Handy, C. B. (1989). *The age of unreason*. London: Business Books Ltd.

Handy, C. B. (1994). *The age of paradox*. Boston: Harvard Business School Press.

Handy, C. B. (1996). *Beyond certainty: The changing worlds of organizations*. Boston: Harvard Business School Press.

Harowitz, C. (1993).The new anti-Semitism. *New York, 26*(2), 20–22.

Harrison, W. D. (1989). Social work and the search for postindustrial community. *Social Work, 34*, 73–75.

Harrison, W. D. (1995). Community development. In R. L. Edwards (Ed.-in-Chief), *Encyclopedia of social work* (19th ed., pp. 555–562). Washington, DC: NASW Press.

Hartman, A. (1990). Many ways of knowing. *Social Work, 35*(1), 3–4.

Hartman, A. (1994). *Reflection & controversy: Essays on social work*. Washington, DC: NASW Press.

Haynes, K. S., & Mickelson, J. S. (1991). *Affecting change: Social workers in the political arena* (2nd ed.). New York: Longman.

Herriot, J. (1985). *All creatures great and small*. New York: St. Martin's Press.

Herzberg, M. (1985, January 25). *Prayer for Christian unity*. Sermon presented at the Remsen Lutheran Church, Remsen, Iowa.

Hill, A. (with H. Lapham) (Eds.). (1998). *An historical and anecdotal walking tour of the small (but fascinating) village of Occidental, California* (5th ed.). Occidental, CA: Mark Wiley of Wild Oak.

Hinchey, F. (1998, December 20). Thousands turn out to honor Glenns in hometown. *Columbus [Ohio] Dispatch*, p. 6B.

Hobbs, G. (1985). Harriet Arnow's Kentucky novels: Beyond local color. In E. Toth (Ed.), *Regionalism and the female imagination* (pp. 83–91). New York: Human Sciences Press.

Hobbs, D. (1995). Social organization in the countryside. In E. N. Castle (Ed.), *The changing American countryside: Rural people and places* (pp. 369–396). Lawrence, KS: University Press of Kansas.

Hölbling, W. (1995). Main Street Lake Wobegon and halfway back: The Midwest small town as a literary place in twentieth century United States literature. In H. Berten & T. D'Haen (Eds.), *The small town in America: A multidisciplinary revisit* (pp. 97–108). Amsterdam: Amerika Instituut.

Homan, M. S. (1994). *Promoting community change: Making it happen in the real world*. Pacific Grove, CA: Brooks/Cole.

Howarth, W. (1995). Land and word: American pastoral. In E. N. Castle (Ed.), *The changing American countryside: Rural people and places* (pp. 13–35). Lawrence, KS: University Press of Kansas.

Howe, D. (1994). Modernity, postmodernity and social work. *British Journal of Social Work, 24*, 513–532.

Hunter, F. (1953). *Community power structure: A study of decision makers*. Chapel Hill: University of North Carolina Press.

Hurston, Z. N. (1935). *Mules and men*. Philadelphia: J. B. Lippincott.

Hurston, Z. N. (1990). *Mules and men* [first Perennial Library edition]. New York: Harper & Row.

Hyman, D., Gamm, L., & Shingler, J. (1995). Paradigm gridlock and the two faces of technology. In J. Lionel, J. Beaulieu, & D. Mulky (Eds.), *Investing in people: The human capital needs of rural America*. Boulder, CO: Westview Press.

Ingley, K. (1997, May 14). Dairy farmer refuses to yield to subdivisions. *Arizona Republic*, p. A1.

Jacobsen, M. G. (1980). Rural communities and community development. In H. W. Johnson (Ed.), *Rural human services* (pp. 196–202). Itasca, IL: Peacock.

Jacobsen, M. G. (1988). Working with communities. In H. W. Johnson (Ed.), *The social service: An introduction* (pp. 308–323). Itasca, IL: Peacock.

Jennings, D. (1995, January 22). A country comeback: Rural Texas counties rebounding from years of population loss. *Dallas Morning News*, p. 1A.

Johnson, A. K. (1998). The revitalization of community practice: Characteristics, competencies, and curricula for community-based services. *Journal of Community Practice, 5*(3), 37–62.

Johnson, L. (1989). *Social work practice: A generalist approach* (3rd ed.). Boston: Allyn & Bacon.

Johnson, L. C. (1983). Networking: A means of maximizing resources. *Human Services in the Rural Environment, 8,* 27–31.

Jones, G. (1980). Nature makes no leaps. In H. Roger & M. McGrath (Eds.), *Going local: Neighborhood social services* (pp. 16–28). London: Bedford Square Press.

Jones, T. (1997, January 26). Small stations struggle to find their radio days: High school sports, morning devotionals don't bring in big advertising dollars. *Chicago Tribune*, p. 1.

Kanter, R. M. (1972). *Commitment and community: Communes and utopians in sociological perspective*. Cambridge: Harvard University Press.

Keillor, G. (1985). *Lake Wobegon days*. New York: Viking.

Keillor, G. (1997). *Wobegon boy*. New York: Penguin Books.

Keyes, R. (1973). *We, the lonely people: Searching for community*. New York: Harper & Row.

Kraybill, D. B., & Nolt, S. M. (1995). *Amish enterprise: From plows to profits*. Baltimore: Johns Hopkins University Press.

Kuhn, T. S. (1962). *The structure of scientific revolutions*. Chicago: University of Chicago Press.

Lantz, H. R. (1958). *People of coal town*. New York: Columbia University Press.

Larson, O. (1978). Values and beliefs of rural people. In T. Ford (Ed.), *Rural U.S.A.: Persistence and change* (pp. 91–112). Ames: Iowa State University Press.

Letts, B. (1995). *Where the heart is: A novel*. New York: Warner Books.

Levenberg, S. (1976). Building consultative relationships with rural fundamentalist clergy. *Professional Psychology, 7,* 553–558.

Levy, C. S. (1976). *Social work ethics*. New York: Human Services Press.

Lewis, S. (1920). *Main street*. New York: Harcourt Brace.

Lewis, J. A., & Lewis, M. D. (1983). *Management of human service programs*. Monterey, CA: Brooks/Cole.

Lingeman, R. (1980). *Small town in America: A narrative history, 1620–the present*. New York: Putnam.

Lloyd, M. (1999, February 19). Hindu nationalists campaign to remake education in India: Ruling party and its allies enlist academics to revise the canon. *Chronicle of Higher Education*, A56–A57.

Logsdon, G. (1986). Amish economics. *Whole Earth Review, 50*, 74–82.

Long, K. (1987, November 20). Clubs: Small communities in the big city. *Atlanta Constitution*, p. 38.

Loomis, C. P. (1960). *Social systems*. Princeton, NJ: D. Van Nostrand.

Lynd, R. S., & Lynd, H. M. (1929). *Middletown*. New York: Harcourt Brace.

Lynd, R. S., & Lynd, H. M. (1937). *Middletown in transition: A study in cultural conflicts*. New York: Harcourt Brace.

Macdonald, F. J. (1983). *Crowdie and cream: Memoirs of a Hebridean childhood*. London: Futura.

MacIntyre, A. (1984). *After virtue*. Notre Dame, IN: University of Notre Dame Press.

MacIver, R. M. (1924). *Community*. New York: Macmillan.

MacKaye, B. (1962). *The new exploration: A philosophy of regional planning*. Urbana: University of Illinois Press.

Madge, J. (1963). *The origins of scientific sociology*. London: Tavistock.

Magill, R. S., & Clark, T. N. (1975). Community power and decision making: Recent research and its policy implications. *Social Service Review, 49*, 33–45.

Maluccio, A. N. (1979). *Learning from clients: Interpersonal helping as viewed by clients and social workers*. New York: Free Press.

Margolis, R. J. (1980). At the crossroads: An inquiry into rural post offices and the communities they serve (Report No. 052–062–00034–9). Washington, DC: U.S. Government Printing Office.

Margolis, R. J. (1981). The limits of localism. *Working Papers for a New Society, 8*, 32–39.

Marquand, J. P. (1949). *The point of no return*. Boston: Little Brown.

Martinez, C. (1977). Curanderos: Clinical aspects. *Journal of Operational Psychiatry, 8*, 35–38.

Martinez-Brawley, E. E. (1981). Rural social and community work as political movements in the United States and United Kingdom. *Community Development Journal, 16*(3), 201–211.

Martinez-Brawley, E. E. (1986a). Community-oriented social work in a rural and remote Hebridean patch. *International Social Work, 29*, 349–372.

Martinez-Brawley, E. E. (1986b). Rural social welfare: Views from the French Pyrenees. *Human Services in the Rural Environment, 10*, 20–22.

Martinez-Brawley, E. E. (1990). *Perspectives on the small community: Humanistic views for practitioners*. Washington, DC: NASW Press.

Martinez-Brawley, E. E. (1991). Social services in Spain: The case of rural Catalonia. *International Social Work, 34,* 265–286.

Martinez-Brawley, E. E. (1995). Community. In R. L. Edwards (Ed.-in-chief), *Encyclopedia of social work* (19th ed., pp. 539–548). Washington, DC: NASW Press.

Martinez-Brawley, E. E., & Blundall, J. (1989). Farm families preferences toward the personal social services. *Social Work, 34,* 513–522.

Martinez-Brawley, E. E., & Zorita, P. (1995). *Feminist practice in the 21st century.* Washington, DC: NASW Press.

Maslen, G. (1999, February 19). Aborigines blast Australia for slashing student-aid program. *Chronicle of Higher Education,* A57–A59.

Masters, E. L. (1915). *Spoon river anthology.* New York: Macmillan.

Mayes, F. (1997). *Under the Tuscan sun: At home in Italy.* New York: Broadway Books.

Mayle, P. (1994). *Hotel Pastis: A novel of Provence.* New York: Vintage Books.

Mazer, M. (1976). *People and predicaments.* Cambridge: Harvard University Press.

Meenaghan, T. M. (1976). Clues to community power structures. *Social Work, 21,* 126–130.

Mermelstein, J., & Sundet, P. (1978, March). *Education for social work practice in the rural context.* Keynote address given at the Conference on Educating for Social Practice in Rural Areas, Fresno, CA.

Merton R. K. (1949). *Sociological analysis.* New York: Harcourt, Brace.

Merton, R. K. (1957). *Social theory and social structure.* Glencoe, IL: Free Press.

Miller, G. D. (1997). Knowledge-sharing institutions: A movement to transform change agents into exchange agents. In E. Shragge (Ed.), *Community economic development: In search of empowerment* (pp. 19–28). Montreal: Black Rose Books.

Milliken, W. G. (1987, October 15). Creativity in government [Editorial]. *Christian Science Monitor, 79,* 13.

Mitchell, W. J. (1995). *City of Bits.* Cambridge, MA: MIT Press.

Mohan, R. P. (1972). A structural functional analysis of defense and non-violence. *Revista internacional de Sociologia, 30* (1/2), 113–122.

Moore-Kirkland, J., & Vice-Irey, K. (1981). A reappraisal of confidentiality. *Social Work, 26,* 319–322.

Morganthauw, T. (1981, July 6). Our town boom. *Newsweek,* 26–37.

Mortimer, J. (1984). *Paradise postponed.* New York: Viking Penguin.

Murdoch, J., & Pratt, A. C. (1994). Rural studies of power and the power of rural studies: A reply to Philo. *Journal of Rural Studies, 10*(1), 83–87.

Murdoch, J., & Pratt, A. C. (1997). From the power of topography to the topography of power. In P. J. Cloke & J. Little (Eds.), *Contested countryside cultures: Otherness, marginalisation and rurality.* London & New York: Routledge.

National Association of Social Workers. (1989). *Malpractice claims against social workers.* Silver Spring, MD: Author.

National Association of Social Workers. (1996). *Code of ethics.* Washington, DC: Author.

National Association of Social Workers. (1998). *Current controversies in social work ethics: Case examples.* Washington, DC: Author.

National Association of Social Workers. (1999). *Code of ethics of the National Association of Social Workers* [revised]. Washington, DC: Author.

National Institute for Social Work. (1982). *Social workers: Their roles and tasks* [Barclay Report]. London: Bedford Square Press.

A new south lures blacks from north. (1996, August 1). *Chicago Tribune.*

Newton, J. (1997, September 14). L.A. mayor offers plan to empower communities. *Los Angeles Times*, pp. A16–A17.

Newman, E., & Turem, J. (1974). The crisis of accountability. *Social Work, 19,* 5–16.

Nisbet, R. (1953). *The quest for community.* New York: Oxford University Press.

Noddings, N. (1984). *Caring, a feminine approach to ethics and moral education.* Berkeley, CA: University of California Press.

Norris, K. (1993). *Dakota: A spiritual geography.* New York: Houghton Mifflin, pp. 69–76.

Norris, K. (1996). *The cloister walk.* New York: Riverhead Books.

Osborne, D., & Gaebler, T. (1993). *Reinventing government: How the entrepreneurial spirit is transforming the public sector.* New York: Plume.

Ostendorf, D. (1987). The church and the covenant of the land. In K. Schmidt (Ed.), *Renew the spirit of my people* (pp. 2–10). Des Moines, IA: Prariefire.

Overholser, G. (1995, September 10). Ruby Ridge: Getting the whole story. *Washington Post*, p. C6.

Owen, H. (1997). *The measured man.* New York: HarperCollins.

Pahl, R. (1966). The rural–urban continuum. *Sociologia Ruralis, 6,* 299–329.

Parade. (1994, May 1). No title, p. 20. New York: Parade Publications.

Parker, K. (1998, November 3). Secret of living in small towns: Everything you do matters. *Arizona Republic*, p. B7.

Parks, T. (1993). *Italian neighbors or, a lapsed Anglo–Saxon in Verona.* New York: Fawcett Columbine.

Payne, M. (1991). *Modern social work theory: A critical introduction.* Chicago: Lyceum Books.

Pearson, T. R. (1985). *A short history of a small place.* New York: Ballantine Books.

Pearson, T. R. (1987). *Off for the sweet hereafter.* New York: Ballantine Books.

Pelly-Effrat, M. (Ed.). (1974). *The community: Approaches and applications.* New York: Free Press.

Petersen, W. (1968). The ideological origins of Britain's new towns. *Journal of the American Institute of Planners, 34,* 160–170.

Piven, F. F., & Cloward, R. A. (1977). *Poor people's movements: Why they succeed, how they fail.* New York: Random House.

Piven, F. F., & Cloward, R. A. (1982). *The new class war: Reagan's attack on the welfare state and its consequences.* New York: Pantheon Books.

Polsby, N. W. (1960). How to study community power: The pluralist alternative. *Journal of Politics, 22,* 474–484.

Ponce, M. H. (1993). *Hoyt Street: Memories of a Chicana childhood.* New York: Anchor Books Doubleday.

Powell, T. J. (1987). *Self-help organizations and professional practice.* Silver Spring, MD: National Association of Social Workers.

Powers, R. C. (1967a). Power actors and social change, Part 1. *Journal of Cooperative Extension, 5,* 153–163.

Powers, R. C. (1967b). Power actors and social change, Part 2. *Journal of Cooperative Extension, 5,* 238–273.

Preciado, P. M. (1996). *El Milagro and other stories.* Tucson: University of Arizona Press.

Raban, J. (1997). *Bad land: An American romance.* New York: Vintage.

Reamer, F. G. (1998). *Ethical standards in social work: A critical review of the NASW Code of Ethics.* Washington, DC: NASW Press.

Redfield, R. (1941). *The folk culture of the Yucatan.* Chicago: University of Chicago Press.

Redford, R. (Director). (1998). *The horse whisperer.* Touchstone Pictures.

Reese, M., & Malamud, P. (1981, July 6). Our town in 1981. *Newsweek,* p. 28.

Reynolds, M. (1976). Threats to confidentiality. *Social Work, 21,* 108–113.

Riesman, D. (1955). Some informal notes on American churches and sects. *Confluence, 4,* 127–159.

Rivera, F. G., & Erlich, J. L. (1981). Neo-Gemeinschaft minority communities: Implications for community organization in the United States. *Community Development Journal, 3,* 189–200.

Roberts, L. (1996, August 4). Valley of the shun: Newcomers isolated by neighborly ways. *The Arizona Republic,* pp. H1–H2.

Rosales, F. A. (1997). *Chicano! The history of the Mexican American civil rights movement.* Houston, TX: Arte Public Press University of Houston.

Rose, J. (1997, August 31). Last resort? *Yakima [Washington] Herald-Republic,* p. A1.

Rosenberg, H. (1996, May 18). "Ruby Ridge": A tragedy or an inevitable end? *Los Angeles Times,* p. F1.

Rosenblum, N. L. (1998). *Membership and morals: The personal use of pluralism in America.* Princeton, NJ: Princeton University Press.

Rosenau, P. M. (1992). *Post-modernism and the social sciences.* Princeton, NJ: Princeton University Press.

Ross, M. G. (1955). *Community organization: Theory and principles.* New York: Harper & Brothers.

Ross, M. H. (1989). The demise of the melting pot model. *Bryn Mawr Alumnae Bulletin,* Spring, 1–3.

Roszak, T. (1978). *Person/planet: The creative disintegration of industrial society.* Garden City, NY: Anchor Press/Doubleday.

Rothman, J. (1974). *Planning and organizing for social change: Action principles from social science research.* New York: Columbia University Press.

Rothman, J. (1996). The interweaving of community intervention approaches. *Journal of Community Practice, 3* (3/4), pp. 69–99.

Royce, J. (1908). *Race questions, provincialism and other problems.* New York: Macmillan.

Royce, J. (1916). *The hope of the great community.* New York: Macmillan.

Rubin, M. (1951). *Plantation County*. Chapel Hill, NC: University of North Carolina.

Saleebey, D. (Ed.). (1997). *The strengths perspective in social work practice* (2nd ed.). New York: Longmore.

Santino, J. (1989). *Miles of smiles, years of struggle: Stories of black Pullman porters*. Urbana: University of Illinois Press.

Sarason, S. B., & Lorentz, E. (1979). *The challenge of the resource exchange network*. San Francisco: Jossey-Bass.

Sayers, V. (1987). *Due east*. New York: Doubleday.

Schattschneider, E. E. (1960). *The semi-sovereign people*. New York: Holt, Rinehart & Winston.

Schorr, A. L. (1986). *Common decency: Domestic policies after Reagan*. New Haven: Yale University Press.

Schumacher, E. F. (1973). *Small is beautiful: Economics as if people mattered*. New York: Harper & Row.

Schwartz, G. (1989). Confidentiality revisited. *Social Work, 34*, 223–226.

Schwent, A. (1993). River at 47.1': Flood fight continues. *Sun Times (Ste. Genevieve/Perryville, Missouri), 11*(9), 1 & 4.

Schwirian, K. P., & Mesch, G. S. (1993). Embattled neighborhoods: The political ecology of neighborhood change. In R. Hutchinson (Ed.), *Research in Urban Sociology, 3*, (pp. 83–110). Greenwich, CT: JAI Press.

Scott, J. (1989). History in crisis? The others' side of the story. *American Historical Review, 94*, 680–692.

Sears, E. (1989). Skinheads: A new generation of hate mongers. *USA Today, 117* (2528), p. 24–29.

Segal, J. (Ed.). (1973). *The mental health of rural America* (DHEW Publication No. [ADM] 73-9035 or 76-0349). Rockville, MD: National Institute of Mental Health.

Sheppard, M. (1995). Social work, social science and practice wisdom. *British Journal of Social Work, 25*, 265–293.

Sibley, M. Q. (1977). Social welfare and some implication of non-violence. *Journal of Sociology and Social Welfare, 4* (3–4), 611–625.

Silko, L. M. (1983). Private property. In S. J. Ortiz (Ed.), *Earth power coming: Short fiction in Native American literature* (pp. 21–30). Tsaile, AZ: Navajo Community College Press.

Sills, P. (1975). Power and community groups. *Community Development Journal, 10*, 24–28.

Simmel, G. (1950). The secret and the secret society, part four. In K. Wolff (Trans.), *The sociology of Georg Simmel* (pp. 307–379). Glencoe, IL: Free Press.

Simon, B. L. (1990). Rethinking empowerment. *Journal of Progressive Human Services, 1* (1), pp. 27–40.

Simon, S. (1999, January 26). Promise of jobs brings diversity to Iowa farm town. *Arizona Republic* (reprinted from *The Los Angeles Times*), pp. A1, A8.

Slater, P. (1976). *Pursuit of loneliness: American culture at the breaking point*. Boston: Beacon Press.

Smith, P. (1966). *As a city upon a hill: The town in American history.* New York: Knopf.

Soifer, S. (1998). Mobile home park lot "rent control": A successful rural legislative campaign. *Journal of Community Practice, 5* (4), 25–38.

Soleri, P. (Ed.). (1964). *The development by Paolo Soleri of the design for the Cosanti Foundation, AZ. USA.* Raleigh: School of Design, North Carolina State of the University of North Carolina at Raleigh.

Specht, H., & Courtney, M. (1994). *Unfaithful Angels.* New York: Free Press.

Speck, R. V., & Attneave, C. (1971). Social network intervention. In J. Haley (Ed.), *Changing families* (pp. 312–332). New York: Grune & Stratton.

Stekler, P., & Bell, A. (Producers). (1985). *Hands that picked cotton* [Film]. Distributed by PBS.

Stephenson, H. (1999, February 28). When all politics is local: Small towns teach us that people will vote if they believe they can make a difference. *Rutland (Vermont) Herald*, pp. 1, 8.

Stern, K. S. (1996a). *A force upon the plain: The American militia movement and the politics of hate.* New York: Simon & Schuster.

Stern, K. S. (1996b, March 30). A dangerous delay in Montana. *New York Times*, p. 236.

Suttles, G. D. (1972). *The social construction of communities.* Chicago: University of Chicago Press.

Szücs, S. (1995, July). Democratization and the reorganization of the welfare state. *Annals of the American Academy of Political and Social Science, 540,* 105–125.

Tannen, D. (1998). *The argument culture: Moving from debate to dialogue.* New York: Random House.

Tarkington, B. (1900). *The gentleman from Indiana.* New York: Grosset and Dunlap.

Tarasoff v. Board of Regents of the University of California. (1976). 17 Cal.3d 425.

Taylor, J. (1994). Culture and nature: Alternative perceptions of the environment in the context of planned change. In L. Jayasuriya & M. Lee (Eds.), *Social dimensions of development.* Bentley, Western Australia: Paradigm Books.

Teune, H. (1995, July). Local government and democratic political development. *Annals of the American Academy of Political and Social Science, 540,* pp. 11–23.

Thomas, N. (1976). Network intervention in the small town. *Human Services in the Rural Environment, 1,* 19–20.

Toth, S. A. (1990). *Blooming: A small–town childhood.* New York: Ballantine Books.

Trimble, S. (1999, March 21). Land of many contradictions. *Arizona Republic*, pp. T1, T14.

Tuchman, G. (1994). Historical social sciences: Methodologies, methods and meanings. In N. K. Denzin & Y. S. Lincoln (Eds.), *Handbook of qualitative research.* London: Sage.

Turkle, S. (1995). *Life on the screen: Identity in the age of the Internet.* New York: Simon & Schuster.

Van Bienna, D. (1993). When white makes right. *Time, 142* (6), 40–42.

Van Holthoon, F. (1995). Robert Lynd's disenchantment: A study of Robert Lynd's cultural criticism. In H. Bertens and T. D'haen, *The small town in America: A multidisciplinary revisit* (pp. 30–59). Amsterdam: VU University Press.

Van Slambroück, P. (1998, July 24). No ivory tower: Rise of the street–level think tank. *Christian Science Monitor*, p. 1.

Veblen, T. (1994). Absentee ownership and business enterprise in recent times: The case of America & the country town. In *The Collected Works of Thorstein Veblem* (Vol. 9, pp. 142–165). London: Routledge/Thoemmes Press.

Velush, L. (1999, January 8). Tribal computers earn award for installer. *Arizona Daily Sun*, pp. E1–E2.

Veroff, J., Koulka, R.A., & Douvan, E. (1981). *Mental health in America: Patterns of help-seeking from 1957 to 1976*. New York: Basic Books.

Vidich, A. J., & Bensman, J. (1968). *Small town in mass society: Class, power and religion in a rural community*. New York: Anchor Books.

Walker, A. (1982). *Community care: The family, the state and social policy*. Oxford: Basil Blackwell.

Walker, A. (1983). *In search of our mothers' gardens*. San Diego: Harcourt Brace Jovanovich.

Walker, J. (1999, January 17). Modern couple follows old trail. *Arizona Republic*, p. A1.

Ward, J. (1998, November). The natural: Grand Forks' Pat Owens. *American City & County*, pp. 60–66.

Warner, W. L., & Lunt, P. S. (1941). *The social life of a modern community*. New Haven, CT: Yale University Press.

Warner, W. L., & Lunt, P. S. (1942). *The status system of a modern community*. New Haven, CT: Yale University Press.

Warner, L. (1949). *Democracy in Jonesville: A study of inequality*. New York: Harper & Row.

Warner, W. L. (1963). *Yankee city*. New Haven, CT: Yale University Press.

Warren, R. L. (1963). *The community in America*. Chicago: Rand McNally.

Warren, R. L. (1987). *The community in America* (3rd ed.) Chicago: Rand McNally.

Warren, R. L. (Ed.). (1977). *New perspectives on the American community: A book of readings*. Chicago: Rand McNally.

Weber, M. (1920). *Economy and society: An outline of interpretive sociology* [1979 ed.]. Berkeley: University of California Press.

Weil, M. O. (1994). [Editor's introduction to the journal]. *Journal of Community Practice*, 1(1), xxi–xxxiii.

Weinbach, R. W. (1990). *The social worker as manager: Theory and practice*. New York: Longman.

Welch, B. (1986, October 4). Your view of town may depend on your age. *Centre Daily Times*, p. B4.

Wellstone, P. (1978). *How the rural poor got power: Narrative of a grass-roots organizer*. Amherst: University of Massachusetts Press.

Wenger, G. C. (1984). *The supportive network: Coping with old age*. London: Allen & Unwin.

West, D. (1995). *The wedding*. New York: Doubleday.

Wilkinson, K. P. (1991). *The community in rural America*. New York: Greenwood Press.

Williams, J. (1987). *Eyes on the prize: America's civil rights years 1954–1965*. New York: Penguin Books.

Williams, W. M. (1964). Changing functions of the community. *Sociologia Ruralis*, 4, 299–314.

Wilson, W. J. (1973). *Power, racism and privilege: Race relations in theoretical and sociohistorical perspectives*. New York: Free Press.

Wilson, S. J. (1982). Confidentiality. In S. A. Yelaja (Ed.), *Ethical issues in social work* (pp. 338–355). Springfield, IL: Charles C Thomas.

Wolfe, T. (1929). *Look homeward, angel: A story of the buried life*. New York: Modern Library.

Wolfinger, R. E. (1960). Reputation and reality in the study of community power. *American Sociological Review*, 25, 636–644.

Woodward, J. (1965). *Industrial organization: Theory and practice*. London: Oxford University Press.

Wright, K. (1998, September 20). Isolated no longer, teens from rural Nebraska use the Internet to travel the world. And rural developers hope this means they will never leave their homes. *Omaha World-Herald*, p. 1E.

Youmans, R. (1990). Leadership and the rural community's ability to manage change. *Western Wire* (Spring): 5–6.

Yuhui, L. (1996). Neighborhood organization and local social action: A case study. *Journal of Community Practice*, 3 (1), pp. 35–58.

Zablocki, B. (1971). *The joyful community*. Baltimore: Penguin Books.

Index

About the Author

Emilia E. Martinez-Brawley, EdD, ACSW, is Professor of Social Work and Distinguished Community Service Scholar at Arizona State University. She is the former Dean of the School of Social Work at ASU (1992–98). Before coming to ASU, she was professor of social welfare at Penn State. Dr. Martinez-Brawley has also taught at Temple University and La Salle University. She received her MSS at Bryn Mawr College (1970) and her doctorate in curriculum theory from Temple University (1979).

In addition to *Close to Home: Human Services and the Small Community*, Dr. Martinez-Brawley is the author of five other books: *Pioneer Efforts in Rural Social Welfare* (Penn State Press, 1980), *Seven Decades of Rural Social Work* (Praeger, 1981), *Rural Social and Community Work in the U.S. and Britain* (Praeger, 1982), *Perspectives on the Small Community: Humanistic Views for Practitioners* (NASW Press, 1990), and *Transferring Technology in the Personal Social Services* (NASW Press, 1993). Dr. Martinez-Brawley has also written numerous articles on intercultural understanding, ethnic relations, the history of social welfare, science and art in social work research and education, and rural social services. These articles have appeared in *Social Work, The Journal of Education for Social Work, Sociology and Social Welfare, Multicultural Social Work, Arete, Community Development Journal, The British Journal of Social Work, Australian Social Work, Human Services in the Rural Environment, International Social Work*, and *The Peabody Journal of Education*, among others.

Dr. Martinez-Brawley has carried out international research on rural services in Canada, Latin America, Great Britain, the Republic of Ireland, Australia, and Spain. She has been a visiting lecturer at the University of Regina, Saskatchewan, Canada; visiting fellow at the School of Economic and Social Studies of the University of East Anglia in Norwich,

England; a guest faculty member at the University of Western Australia in Perth; a consultant on rural and evaluative issues for the European Centre for Social Welfare Research, an arm of the United Nations in France and Spain; a guest faculty member at the Consejo Superior de Investigaciones Científicas in Madrid, Spain; and a consultant on rural development for projects in Murcia, Navarra, and Catalonia, Spain, and for the Western Australia Department of Community Services. She has delivered lectures in Mexico and Ireland on topics related to social development.

Dr. Martinez-Brawley has been a member of the Commission on Accreditation of the Council on Social Work Education (CSWE) and also serves on the Disciplinary Committee for Fulbright Scholar Awards for the Council for International Exchange of Scholars (CIES). She is a former vice-president of the National Board of the National Association of Social Workers (NASW). Dr. Martinez-Brawley was the recipient of a Hispanic Leadership Fellows Award sponsored by the American Council on Education, the New Jersey Commission on Higher Education, and the Woodrow Wilson Foundation and spent time as an administrative fellow at Penn State and in the Office of the President at California State University, Fresno. She has worked with local governments in Pennsylvania, Catalonia, England, Scotland, and Australia. She has done a number of projects for the Center for Rural Pennsylvania, an arm of the Pennsylvania Legislature, and has been a member of a social service study group working with the Arizona House of Representatives.

Other awards Dr. Martinez-Brawley has received include the Senior Scholar Award from the Australian American Educational Foundation (Fulbright), a Senior Scholar award from the U.S./Israel Bi-National Committee (Fulbright), a research fellowship from the Comite Conjunto Hispano–Norteamericano, the Ida Beam Distinguished Visiting Professor award from the University of Iowa, and the Ruth Hoeflin Family Forum Scholar award at Kansas State University. Her honors include the Women of Color Award from Penn State, an award from Black Families and Children Service in Phoenix, and the Cesar Chavez Award for Service from the Chicano Faculty and Staff Association at ASU.

BOOKS ON COMMUNITY ORGANIZATION FROM NASW PRESS

Close to Home: Human Services and the Small Community, *by Emilia E. Martinez-Brawley.* Peppered with scores of evocative stories drawn from the media and fiction and nonfiction, *Close to Home* delves into theories essential for understanding the complexities of small-town America. Focused on the sociocultural distinctions of these locales, the book explores their way of life, patterns of relationships, and the importance of shared history.

ISBN: 0-87101-312-6. Item #3126. $34.95

Preserving and Strengthening Small Towns and Rural Communities, *Iris B. Carlton-LaNey, Richard L. Edwards, and P. Nelson Reid, Editors.* This volume defines the issues and crises of the surprisingly diverse populations of small towns and rural communities and illustrates the myriad solutions and interventions available to the social worker in these contexts. Contributors analyze the strengths, obstacles, and societal mores found in these communities and present sensitive approaches. This resource offers a much-needed generalist approach to practice in the rural environment, where the dynamics of family and community create a unique opportunity for positive change.

ISBN: 0-87101-310-X. Item #310X. $36.95

Community Building: Renewal, Well-Being, and Shared Responsibility, *Patricia L. Ewalt, Edith M. Freeman, and Dennis L. Poole, Editors. Community Building* is a compilation of NASW Press journal articles organized around ideas of community. This book highlights how community contributes to well-being and renewal.

ISBN: 0-87101-292-8. Item #2928. $29.95

Successful Community Leadership: A Skills Guide for Volunteers and Professionals, *by John E. Tropman.* With this practical how-to manual, you'll learn new techniques and skills to help your community group work cohesively and successfully. Learn how to manage problems of procedure, process, and people.

ISBN: 0-87101-285-5. Item 2855. $25.95

How People Get Power, Revised Edition, *by Si Kahn. How People Get Power* can help organizers and community leaders bring unity and success to those they serve. Kahn describes how an effective organizer enables others to improve their lives by convincing naysayers, persuading policymakers, and using self-determination to create change.

ISBN: 0-87101-236-7. Item #2367. $20.95

Organizing: A Guide for Grassroots Leaders, *by Si Kahn.* A step-by-step guide on how to unite people to effect change. Tells readers how to affect existing power structures, become successful organizers and fundraisers, and bring about social change through grassroots organization and mobilization.

ISBN: 0-87101-197-2. Item #1972. $32.95

(Order form on reverse side)

ORDER FORM

Title	Item #	Price	Total
__ Close to Home	3126	$ 34.95	_____
__ Preserving and Strengthening Small Towns	310X	$ 36.95	_____
__ Community Building	2928	$ 29.95	_____
__ Successful Community Leadership	2855	$ 25.95	_____
__ How People Get Power, Revised Edition	2367	$ 20.95	_____
__ Organizing	1972	$ 32.95	_____
		Subtotal	_____
	+ 10% postage and handling		_____
		Total	_____

❐ I've enclosed my check or money order for $.

❐ Please cha   asterCard

DATE DUE

Credit Card N_____   n Date

Signature ____

＊   ɔrk profession.

Name_____

Address ____

City ____

Country ___

Phone ____

NASW Memb

(Please   to change.)

≡
NASW PRESS   card orders call
P. O. Box 43   1-800-227-3590
Annapolis   a, call 301-317-8688)
USA   o 301-206-7989
                                      .naswpress.org

The Library Store   #47-0106

Visit our Web site at http://www.naswpress.org   MARB200